THE Forbes® BOOK OF GREAT BUSINESS LETTERS

THE Forbes® BOOK OF
GREAT
BUSINESS
LETTERS

MEMOS, MISSIVES, PITCHES, PROPOSALS AND E-MAILS

EDITED BY ERIK BRUUN

Tess Press

Forbes is a registered trademark of Forbes Inc. Its use is pursuant to a license with Forbes Inc.

Published by Tess Press, an imprint of
Black Dog & Leventhal Publishers, Inc.
151 West 19th Street
New York, NY 10011

Cover design by Filip Zawodnik
Interior design by Tony Meisel

ISBN: 1-57912-423-2

h g f e d c b a

Manufactured in the United States of America

CONTENTS

COMPLIMENTS AND COMPLAINTS

NEW IDEAS

RIGHTS

WORK AND BUSINESS ETHICS

PERMISSIONS ACKNOWLEDGMENTS

INDEX

PREFACE

Millions of business letters are written every day. They are the lifeblood of commerce. Good business letters are practical, reasonable and explicit.

"Every paragraph should be so clear, and unambiguous, that the dullest fellow in the world may not be able to mistake it, nor obliged to read it twice in order to understand it," advised the Earl of Chesterfield. "In business, an elegant simplicity, the result of care, not of labour, is required."

But simple doesn't mean easy, and even most well written business letters are not of interest to those not directly involved in the subject of the correspondence. Great business letters speak to issues greater than the particulars at hand. The letters in this collection transcend the confines of their content. They speak to universal themes and reflect historic events that remain relevant to the way we carry ourselves today.

All of the letters in this volume are relevant to business and meet at least two of three additional criteria: eloquence, historic interest, and articulation of a theme. The best letters, such as Benjamin Franklin's advice to a young tradesmen and Bill Gates's correspondence urging Apple Computer to license its Macintosh program, meet all four thresholds.

One of the trickier aspects of the selection process was determining what exactly a business letter is. Money seemed an obvious basis for all business letters. But one's life in business is about much more than rolling up profits. How we decide to spend our professional lives reflects who we are as individuals and how we relate to people. Abraham Lincoln's letters admonishing and encouraging his generals during the Civil War are among the most eloquent examples of personnel management, but they have nothing to do with commerce.

The *Forbes* masthead states, "With all thy getting, get understanding." Each issue of the magazine has a page of quotations under the heading "Thoughts on the Business of Life." For the Forbes family, the purpose of business embraces responsibilities beyond financial self-interest. A well-spent life in business requires consciousness, understanding, and humanity. And so does a great business letter.

ADVICE

BENJAMIN FRANKLIN'S ADVICE TO A YOUNG TRADESMAN, WRITTEN BY AN OLD ONE
"The way to wealth is as plain as the way to market"

A self-made businessman of immense wealth, Benjamin Franklin set the standard for the American business ethic. Preaching the importance of hard work, prudence, and honesty, Franklin equated the values of living well with being successful. He made his money as a printer and newspaper publisher, but he made his reputation as a philosopher, politician, diplomat and scientist. These careers, too, were marked by the principles of his business ethic, as reflected in the following letters in which he dispenses advice still relevant today.

To my Friend A. B.

As you have desired it of me, I write the following Hints, which have been of Service to me, and may, if observed be so to you.

Remember that TIME is Money. He that can earn Ten Shillings a Day by his labour, and goes abroad, or sits idle one half of that Day, tho' he spends but Sixpence during his Diversion or Idleness, ought not to reckon That the only Expence; he has really spent or rather thrown away Five Shillings besides.

Remember that CREDIT is Money. If a Man lets his Money lie in my Hands after it is due, he gives me the Interest, or so much as I can make of it during that Time. This amounts to a considerable Sum where a Man has good and large Credit, and makes good Use of it.

Remember that Money is of a prolific generating Nature. Money can beget Money, and its Offspring can beget more, and so on. Five Shillings turn'd is Six: Turn'd again, 'tis Seven and Three Pence; and so on 'til it becomes an Hundred Pound. The more there is of it, the more it produces every Turning, so that the Profits rise quicker and quicker. He that kills a breeding Sow, destroys all her Offspring to the thousandth Generation. He that murders a Crown, destroys all it might have produc'd, even Scores of Pounds.

Remember that Six Pounds a Year is but a Groat a Day. For this little Sum (which may be daily wasted either in Time or Expence unperceiv'd) a Man of Credit may on his own Security have the constant Possession and Use of an Hundred Pounds. So much in Stock briskly turn'd by an industrious Man, produces great Advantage.

Remember this Saying, That the good paymaster is Lord of another Man's Purse. He that is known to pay punctually and exactly to the Time he promises, may at any Time, and on any Occasion, raise all the Money his Friends can spare. This is sometimes of great Use: Therefore never keep borrow'd Money an Hour beyond the Time you promis'd, lest a Disappointment shuts up your Friends Purse forever.

The most trifling Actions that affect a Man's Credit, are to be regarded. The Sound of your Hammer at Five in the Morning or Nine at Night, heard by a Creditor, makes him easy Six Months longer. But if he sees you at a Billiard Table, or hears your Voice in a Tavern, when you should be at Work, he sends for his Money the next Day. Finer Cloaths than he or his Wife wears, or greater Expence in any particular than he affords himself, shocks his Pride, that have the sharpest Eyes and Ears, as well as the best Memories of any in the World.

Good-natur'd Creditors (and such one would always chuse to deal with if one could) feel Pain when they are oblig'd to ask for Money. Spare 'em that Pain, and they will love you. When you receive a Sum of Money, divide it among 'em in small Sum because you owe a greater. Money, more or less, is always welcome; and your Creditor had rather be at the Trouble of receiving Ten Pounds voluntarily brought him, tho' at ten different Times or Payments, than be oblig'd to go ten Times to demand it before he can receive it in a Lump. It shews, besides, that you are mindful of what you owe; it makes you appear a careful as well as an honest Man; and that still encreases your Credit.

Beware of thinking all your own that you possess, and of living accordingly. 'Tis a mistake that many People who have Credit fall into. To prevent this, keep an exact Account for some Time of both your Expences and your Incomes. If you take the pains at first to mention Particulars, it will have this good Effect; you will discover how wonderfully small trifling Expences mount up to large Sums, and will discern what might have been, and may for the future be saved, without occasioning any great Inconvenience.

In short, the Way to Wealth, if you desire it, is as plain as the Way to Market. It depends chiefly on two Words, INDUSTRY and FRUGALITY; i.e. Waste neither Time nor Money, but make the best Use of both. He that gets all he can honestly, and saves all he gets (necessary Expenses excepted) will certainly become RICH; If that Being who governs the World, to whom all should look for a Blessing on their Honest Endeavours, doth not in his wise Providence otherwise determine.

BENJAMIN FRANKLIN ON WRITING A GOOD LETTER
"Whoever writes a stranger should observe 3 points"

Benjamin Franklin wrote this letter in response to an ambiguous letter from a person who identified himself as Lith offering to help the American colonies in their war for independence.

Passy near Paris, April 6, 1777

Sir,

I have just been honoured with a Letter from you, dated the 26th past, in which you express your self as astonished, and appear to be angry that you have no Answer to a Letter you wrote me of the 11th of December, which you are sure was delivered to me.

In Exculpation of my self, I assure you that I never receiv'd any letter from you of that date. And indeed being then but 4 Days landed at Nantes, I think you could scarce have heard so soon of my being in Europe.

But I receiv'd one from you on the 8th of January, which I own I did not answer. It may displease you if I give you the Reason; but as it may be of use to you in your future Correspondences, I will hazard that for a Gentleman to whom I feel myself oblig'd, as an American, on Account of his Good Will to our Cause.

Whoever writes to a Stranger should observe 3 Points; 1. That what he proposes be practicable. 2. His Propositions should be made in explicit Terms so as to be easily understood. 3. What he desires should be in itself reasonable. Hereby he will give a favourable Impression of his Understanding, and create a Desire of further Acquaintence.

Now it happen'd that you were negligent in *all* these Points: for first you desired to have Means procur'd for you of taking a Voyage to America "*avec Sureté*"; which is not possible, as the Dangers of the Sea subsist always, and at present there is the additional Danger of being taken by the English. Then you desire that this may be "*sans trop grandes Dépenses,*" which is not intelligible enough to be answer'd, because not knowing your Ability of bearing Expences, one cannot judge what may be *trop grandes*. Lastly you desire Letters of Address to the Congress and to General Washington; which it is not reasonable to ask of *one* who knows no more of you than that your Name is Lith, and that you live at Bayreuth.

In your last, you also express yourself in vague Terms when you desire to be inform'd whether you may expect "*d'etre recu d'une maniere convenable*" in our Troops? As it is impossible to know what your Ideas are of the *maniere convenable*, how can one answer this? And then you demand whether I will support you by my Authority in giving you Letters of Recommendation? I doubt not your being a Man of Merit; and knowing it yourself, you may forget that it is not known to every body; but reflect a Moment, Sir, and you will be convinc'd that if I were to practice giving Letters of Recommendation to persons of whose Character I knew no more than I do of yours, my Recommendations would soon be of no Authority at all.

I thank you however for your kind Desire of being Serviceable to my Countrymen: And I wish in return that I could be of Service to you in the Scheme you have form'd of going to America. But Numbers of experience'd Officers here have offer'd to go over and join our Army, and I could give them no Encouragement, because I have no Orders for that purpose, and I know it extremely difficult to place them when they come there. I cannot but think therefore, that it is best for you not to make so long, so expensive, and so hazardous a Voyage, but to take the Advice of your Friends, and stay in Fanconia. I have the honour to be Sir, &c.

Benjamin Franklin

BENJAMIN FRANKLIN TO DR. PRICE
"Sense being preferable to sound"

Residents in a western Massachusetts community decided in the 1780s to name their new town after Benjamin Franklin and to build a steeple in his honor. They asked him to send a bell to complement their meeting-house spire. Franklin, however, refused the request. Saying that sense was preferable over sound, he asked Dr. Price to purchase several books to start a library in Franklin.

Passy, March 18, 1785

My Dear Friend:

My nephew, Mr. Williams, will have the honour of delivering you this line. It is to request from you a list of a few good books to the value of about twenty-five pounds, such as are the most proper to inculcate principles of sound religion and just government. A new town in the State of Massachusetts having done me the honour of naming itself after me, and proposing to build a steeple to their meeting-house if I would give them a bell, I have advised the sparing themselves the expense of a steeple at present, and that they would accept of books instead of a bell, sense being preferable to sound. These are therefore intended as the commencement of a little parochial library for the use of a society of intelligent, respectable farmers such as our country people generally consist of. Besides your own works, I would only mention, on the recommendation of my sister, Stennet's Discourses on Personal Religion, which may be one book of the number, if you know it and approve of it.

With the highest esteem and respect, I am ever, my dear friend, yours most affectionately....

B. Franklin

EARL OF CHESTERFIELD TO HIS SON

"You cannot be too careful, too nice, too scrupulous"

The Earl of Chesterfield, one of the leading noblemen of 18th-century England, wrote hundreds of letters advising his son on many different issues, including matters of business.

London
May 17, 1750

My Dear Friend:

Your apprenticeship is near out, and you are soon to set up for yourself; that approaching moment is a critical one for you, and an anxious one for me. A tradesman who would succeed in his way, must begin by establishing a character of integrity and good manners: without the former, nobody will go to his shop at all; without the latter, nobody will go there twice. This rule does not exclude the fair arts of trade. He may sell his goods at the best price he can, within certain bounds. He may avail himself of the humour, the whims, and the fantastical tastes of his customers; but what he warrants to be good must be really so, what he seriously asserts must be true, or his first fraudulent profits will soon end in a bankruptcy. It is the same in higher life, and in the great business of the world. A man who does not solidly establish, and really deserve, a character of truth, probity, good manners, and good morals, at his first setting out in the world, may impose, and shine like a meteor for a very short time, but will very soon vanish, and be extinguished with contempt. People easily pardon, in young men, the common irregularities of the senses; but they do not forgive the least vice of the heart. The heart never grows better by age; I fear rather worse; always harder. A young liar will be an old one; and a young knave, will only be a greater knave as he grows older. But should a bad young heart, accompanied with a good head (which by the way very seldom is the case) really reform in a more advanced age, from a consciousness of its folly, as well as of its guilt; such a conversion would only be thought prudential and political, but never sincere. But the possession of all the moral virtues, in *actu primo*, as the logicians call it, is not sufficient; you must have them in *actu secundo* too; nay, that is not sufficient neither, you must have the reputation of them also. Your character in the world must be built upon that solid foundation, or it will soon fall, and upon your own head. You cannot, therefore, be too careful, too nice, too scrupulous, in establishing this character at first, upon which your whole depends. Let no conversation, no example, no fashion, no *bon mot*, no silly desire of seeming to be above what most knaves and many fools call prejudices, ever to tempt to avow, excuse, extenuate, or laugh at the least breach of morality;

but show upon all occasions, and take all occasions to show, a detestation and abhorrence of it. There, though young, you ought to be strict; and there only, while young, it becomes you to be strict and severe. But there too, spare the persons, while you lash the crimes. All this relates, as you easily judge, to the vices of the heart, such as lying, fraud, envy, malice, detraction, etc., and I do not extend it to the frailties of youth, flowing from high spirits and warm blood. It would ill become you, at your age, to declaim against them, and sententiously censure a gallantry, an accidental excess of the table, a frolic, an inadvertency; no, keep as free from them yourself as you can: but say nothing against them in others. They certainly mend by time, often by reason; and a man's worldy character is not affected by them, provided it be pure in all other respects.

To come now to a point of much less, but yet of very great consequence at your first setting out. Be extremely upon your guard against vanity, the common failing of inexperienced youth; but particularly against the kind of vanity that dubs a man a coxcomb; a character which, once acquired, is more indelible than that of the priesthood. It is not to be imagined by how many different ways vanity defeats its own purposes. One man decides peremptorily upon every subject, betrays his ignorance upon many, and shows a disgusting presumption upon the rest. Another desires to appear successful among women; he hints at the encouragement he has received from those of the most distinguished rank and beauty, and intimates a particular connection with some one; if it is true, it is ungenerous; if false, it is infamous; but in either case he destroys the reputation he wants to get. Some flatter their vanity by little extraneous objects, which have not the least relation to themselves; such as being descended from, related to, or acquainted with people of distinguished merit, and eminent characters. They talk perpetually of their grandfather such-a-one, their uncle such-a-one, and their intimate friend Mr. Such-a-one, with whom, possibly, they are hardly acquainted. But admitting it all to be as they would have it, what then? Have they the more merit for these accidents? Certainly not. On the contrary, their taking up adventitious, proves their want of intrinsic merit; a rich man never borrows. Take this rule for granted, as a never-failing one—That you must never seem to affect the character in which you have a mind to shine. Modesty is the only sure bait when you angle for praise. The affectation of courage will make even a brave man pass only for a bully; as the affectation of wit will make a man of parts pass for a coxcomb. By this modesty I do not mean timidity and awkward bashfulness. On the contrary, be inwardly firm and steady, know your own value. Whatever real merit you have, other people will discover; and people always magnify their own discoveries, as they lessen those of others.

For God's sake revolve all these things seriously in your thoughts, before you launch out alone into the ocean of Paris. Recollect the observations that you have yourself made upon mankind, compare and connect them with my instructions, and then act systematically and consequentially from them; not *au jour la journée*. Lay your little plan now, which you will hereafter extend and improve by your own observations, and by the advice of those who can never mean to mislead you: I mean Mr. Harte and myself.

Earl of Chesterfield to His Son
"The first thing necessary in writing letters of business"

The Earl of Chesterfield's correspondence included advice on how to write a good business letter. His general instructions on the importance of clarity and grace remain relevant, as do some of his more specific recommendations on grammar and style.

London
December 19, 1751

My Dear Friend:

You are now entered upon a scene of business, where I hope you will one day make a figure. Use does a great deal, but care and attention must be joined by it. The first thing necessary in writing letters of business, is extreme clearness and perspicuity; every paragraph should be so clear, and unambiguous, that the dullest fellow in the world may not be able to mistake it, nor obliged to read it twice in order to understand it. This necessary clearness implies a correctness, without excluding an elegancy of style. Tropes, figures, antitheses, epigrams, etc., would be as misplaced and as impertinent in letters of business, as they are sometimes (if judiciously used) proper and pleasing in familiar letters, upon common and trite subject. In business, an elegant simplicity, the result of care, not of labour, is required. Business must be well, not affectedly dressed; but by no means negligently. Let your first attention be to clearness, and read every paragraph after you have written it, in the critical view of discovering whether it is possible that any one man can mistake the true sense of it: and correct it accordingly.

Our pronouns and relatives often create obscurity or ambiguity; be therefore exceedingly attentive to them, and take care to mark out with precision their particular relations. For example, Mr. Johnson acquainted me, that he had seen Mr. Smith, who had promised him to speak to Mr. Clarke, to return him (Mr. Johnson) those papers, which he (Mr. Smith) had left some time ago with him (Mr. Clarke): it is better to repeat a name, though unnecessarily, ten times, than to have the person mistaken once. *Who*, you know, is singly relative to persons; for one may say, the man *that* robbed or killed such-a-one; but it is much better to say, the man *who* robbed or killed. One never says, the man or the woman *which*. *Which* and *that*, though chiefly relative to things, cannot be always used indifferently as to things; and the *Œn∆nia* must sometimes determine their place. For instance, the letter *which* I received from you, *which* you referred to in your last, *which* came by Lord Albermarle's messenger *which* I showed to such-a-one; I would change it thus—The letter *that* I received from you, *which* you referred to in your last, *that* came by Lord Albermarle's messenger, and *which* I showed to such-a-one.

Business does not exclude (as possibly you wish it did) the usual terms of politeness and good-breeding; but, on the contrary, strictly requires them: such as, *I have the honour to acquaint your Lordship; Permit me to assure you: If I may be allowed to give my opinion*, etc. For the minister abroad, who writes to the minister at home, writes to his superior; possibly to his patron, or at least to one who he desires should be so.

Letters of business will not only admit of, but be better for *certain graces*—but then, they must be scattered with a sparing and skillful hand; they must fit their place exactly. They must decently adorn without encumbering, and modestly shine without letters glaring. But as this is the utmost degree of perfection in letters of business, I would not advise you to attempt those embellishments, till you have first laid your foundation well.

Cardinal d'Ossat's letters are the true letters of business; those of Monsieur d'Avaux are excellent; Sir William Temple's are very pleasing, but, I fear, too affected. Carefully avoid all Greek or Latin quotations; and bring no precedents from the *virtuous Spartans, the polite Athenians, and the brave Romans.* Leave all that to futile pendants. No flourishes, no declamation. But (I repeat it again) there is an elegant simplicity and dignity of style absolutely necessary for good letters of business; attend to that carefully.

Let your periods be harmonious, without seeming to be laboured; and let them not be too long, for that always occasions a degree of obscurity. I should not mention correct orthography, but that you very often fail in that particular, which will bring ridicule upon you; for no man is allowed to spell ill. I wish too that your handwriting were much better; and I cannot conceive why it is not, since every man may certainly write whatever hand he pleases. Neatness in folding up, sealing, and directing your packets, is by no means to be neglected; though I dare say you think it is. But there is something in the exterior, even of a packet, that may please or displease; and consequently worth some attention.

You say that your time is very well employed; and so it is, though as yet only in the outlines, and first *routine* of business. They are previously necessary to be known; they smooth the way for parts and dexterity. Business requires no conjuration nor supernatural talents, as people unacquainted with it are apt to think. Method, diligence, and discretion, will carry a man of good strong common sense, much higher than the finest parts, without them, can do. *Par negotiis, neque supra*, is the true character of a man of business; but then it implies ready attention, and no *absences*, and a flexibility and versatility of attention from one object to another, without being engrossed by any one.

Be upon your guard against the pedantry and affectation of business, which young people are apt to fall into, from the pride of being concerned in it young. They look thoughtful, complain of the weight of business, throw out mysterious hints, and seem big with secrets which they do not know. Do you, on the contrary, never talk of business but to those with whom you are to transact it; and learn to seem *vacuus* and idle, when you have the most business. Of all things, the *volto sciolto*, and the *pensieri stretti*, are necessary. Adieu.

GEORGE WASHINGTON TO HIS NEPHEW BUSHROD WASHINGTON

"As a friend, I give you the following advice"

In addition to being the first President of the United States and commander of the American forces during the American Revolution, George Washington was among the wealthiest men in America. But Washington did not equate wealth with splendor. In this letter to a nephew starting to make his way into the world as a lawyer, Washington preaches the value of simplicity and discipline, even in matters of clothes.

January 15, 1783

Dear Bushrod:

You will be surprized perhaps at receiving a letter from me; but if the end is answered for which it is written, I shall not think my time miss-spent.

Your Father, who seems to entertain a very favorable opinion of your prudence, and I hope you merit it: in one or two of his letters to me, speaks of the difficulty he is under to make you remittances. Whether this arises from the scantiness of his funds, or the extensiveness of your demands, is matter of conjecture, with me. I hope it is not the latter, because common prudence, and every other consideration which ought to have weight in a reflecting mind is opposed to your requiring more than his conveniency and a regard to his other Children will enable him to pay; and because he holds up no idea in his Letter, which would support me in the conclusion. Yet when I take a view of the inexperience of Youth, the temptations in, and vices of Cities; and the distresses to which our Virginia Gentlemen are driven by an accumulation of Taxes and the want of a market; I am almost inclined to ascribe it, in part to both. Therefore, as a friend, I give you the following advice.

Let the object, which carried you to Philadelphia, be always before your Eyes; remember, that it is not the mere study of the Law, but to become eminent in the Profession of it which is to yield honor and profit; the first was your choice, let the second be your ambition, and that dissipation is incompatible with both....

Do not conceive that fine Clothes make fine Men, any more than fine feathers make fine Birds. A plain genteel dress is more admired and obtains more credit than lace and embroidery in the Eyes of the judicious and sensible.

[George Washington]

DR. BENJAMIN RUSH TO WILLIAM CLAYPOOLE
"Never dispute a bill"

Dr. Benjamin Rush was the leading physician in America in the late 1700s. Known for his compassion for the sick and suffering, he also developed a sound understanding of how to balance medicine with business. Here he offers guidance to a younger physician on how one can be both a good businessman and a compassionate doctor.

July 29, 1782

The following short directions to Dr. Claypoole were given as the parting advice of his old friend and master. If properly attended to, they will ensure him business and happiness in North Carolina.

1. Take care of the poor. By becoming faithful over a few, you will become a ruler over many. When you are called to visit a poor patient, imagine you hear a voice sounding in your ears, "Take care of him, and I will repay thee."

2. Go regularly to some place of worship. A physician cannot be a bigot. Worship with Mohamitans rather than stay at home on Sundays.

3. Never resent an affront offered to you by a *sick* man.

4. Avoid intimacies with your patients if possible, and visit them only in sickness.

5. Never *sue* a patient, but after a year's service get a bond from him if possible.

6. Receive as much pay as possible in goods or the produce of the country. Men have not half the attachment to these things that they have to money.

7. Acquire a habit of visiting your patients *regularly* at *one* certain hour.

8. Never dispute a bill. Always make reductions rather than quarrel with an old and profitable patient.

9. Don't insert trifling advice or services in a bill. You can incorporate them with important matters such as a pleurisy or the reduction of a bone.

10. Never make light (to a patient) of any case.

11. Never appear in a hurry in a sickroom, nor talk of indifferent matters till you have examined and prescribed for your patient.

Yours sincerely,
Benjamin Rush

BENJAMIN AND JULIA RUSH TO SON JOHN RUSH
"Be sober and vigilant"

Dr. Benjamin Rush was also one of America's Founding Fathers, playing a role in writing both the Declaration of Independence and the Constitution. Thomas Jefferson, James Madison, John Adams and others sought his advice on matters of business, politics and finance. Shortly before his son set sail to India, Rush and his wife wrote the following letter as guidance on matters of morality, health and finance.

Directions and advice to John Rush from his father and mother composed the evening before he sailed for Calcutta, May 18th, 1796.

We shall divide these directions into four heads, as they relate to *morals, knowledge, health* and *business.*

I. Morals

1. Be punctual in committing your soul and body to the protection of your Creator every morning and evening. Implore at the same time his mercy in the name of his Son, our Lord and Saviour Jesus Christ.

2. Read in your Bible frequently, more especially on Sundays.

3. Avoid swearing and even an irreverent use of your Creator's name. *Flee* youthful lusts.

4. Be courteous and gentle in your behavior to your fellow passengers, and respectful and obedient to the captain of the vessel.

5. Attend public worship regularly every Sunday when you arrive at calcutta.

II. Knowledge

1. Begin by studying Guthrie's *Geography.*

2. Read your other books through carefully, and converse daily upon the subjects of your reading.

3. Keep a diary of every day's studies, conversations, and transactions at sea and on shore. Let it be composed in a fair, legible hand. Insert in it an account of the population, manners, climate, diseases, &c., of the places you visit.

4. Preserve an account of every person's name and disease whom you attend.

III. Health

1. Be temperate in eating, more especially of animal food. Never taste distilled spirits of any kind, and drink fermented liquors very sparingly.

2. Avoid the night air in sickly situations. Let your dress be rather warmer than the weather would

seem to require. Carefully avoid fatigue from all causes both of body and mind.

IV. Business

1. Take no step in laying out your money without the advice and consent of the captain or supercargo.

2. Keep an exact account of all your expenditures. Preserve as vouchers of them all your bills.

3. Take care of all your instruments, books, clothes, &c.

Be sober and vigilant. Remember at all times that while you are seeing the world, the world will see you. Recollect further that you are always under the eye of the Supreme Being. One more consideration shall close this parting testimony of our affection. Whenever you are tempted to do an improper thing, fancy that you see your father and mother kneeling before you and imploring you with tears in their eyes to refrain yielding to the temptation, and assuring you at the same time that your yielding to it will be the means of hurrying them to a premature grave.

Bnjn Rush
Julia Rush

DANIEL WEBSTER TO DANIEL FLETCHER WEBSTER
"It is an honest quackery"

Massachusetts Senator Daniel Webster—a brilliant politician and orator—wrote this consoling letter to his son Fletcher who had been frustrated in his attempts at making a quick fortune as a young man, then 23. Webster advised pursuing a different career more suited to his talents. He also spoke of the practical uses of a liberal education outside of one's expertise.

Washington, January 15, 1836

Dear Fletcher,

I am sorry for your disappointment about the aid-ship; but never mind, I believe you are as well without it; if you think not, I will see more about it, when I get home. I believe the military honors of our family terminated with my father. I once tried to be a captain, and failed, and I canvassed a whole regiment to make your uncle an adjutant, and failed also. We are destined not to be great in the field of battle. We are not the sons of "Bellona's bridegroom"; our battles are forensic; we draw no blood but the blood of our clients.

Your notions of matters and things are quite right, as applicable to your own condition. You must study practical things. You are in a situation of the *haud facile energunts*, and must try all you can to get your head above water. Why should you botanize, when you have not field enough to bear one flower? Why should you geologize who have no right on the earth, except a right to tread on it? This is all very well; I thought so, at your age, and therefore studied nothing but law and politics. I wish you to take the same course; yet still save a little time, have a few *horas subsecivas* in which to cultivate liberal knowledge; it will turn to account, even practically. If, on a given occasion, a man can, gracefully, and without the air of a pedant, show a little more knowledge than the occasion requires, the world will give him credit for eminent attainments. It is an honest quackery. I have practiced it, and sometimes with success…

We find connections and coincidences, helps and succors, where we did not expect to find them. I have never learned anything which I wish to forget; except how badly some people have behaved; and I every day find, on almost every subject, that I wish I had more knowledge than I possess, seeing that I could produce it, if not for use, for effect.

ALFRED KRUPP TO EMPLOYEES
"To raise difficulties is very comfortable"

When he was 14 years old, the German industrialist Alfred Krupp took over his father's small steel mill upon his death. Starting with less than ten workers but an iron-clad belief in the future of crucible steel and an extraordinary work ethic, Krupp built the tiny enterprise into an industrial behemoth despite obstacles of almost every kind. By 1865, the Krupp Works was a major corporation. In this memo to his staff, he offers advice on how to best approach the relatively minor problems that confronted the company at that time.

The Hill, 12.3.1865

Not pressing, only an incidental observation.

If I had not wanted to set to work until all arrangements were complete, I should today be a journeyman. To attain one's end with the smallest means, to work and to earn without losing time, that is the task, and that is what I cannot sufficiently recommend to you gentlemen as the practical thing. To raise difficulties is very comfortable, but to get over difficulties (without making a fuss about them) is what we need—time should be valued more highly.

Reflection and strenuous activity is the one remedy for excuses on the score of "impossibility." It makes the impossible possible—the "impossible" is too readily recognized—as a matter of comfort.

CHARLES WILLIAM ELIOT TO HIS SON
"There is no mystery about successful business intercourse"

As president of Harvard University, Charles William Eliot left a permanent stamp on the American university landscape. He established an undergraduate system that allowed students to select a course of studies from a wide range of choices, and developed graduate programs with a high level of specialization. In this letter to his son, Charles William Eliot, Jr., who was physically frail, Charles, Sr., advises to only work as hard as his health allows and to appreciate his own strengths as a person.

April 20, '86

Dear Charles,

Don't imagine yourself deficient in power of dealing with men. Such dealings as you have thus far had with boys and men you have conducted very suitably. There is no mystery about successful business intercourse with patrons and employees. Nobody can think, and at the same time pay attention to another person, as you seem to expect to do. On the contrary, exclusive attention to the person who is speaking to you is a very important point in business manners. Nothing is so flattering as that. Some audible or visible signs of close attention are of course desirable. Then there is very seldom any objection to the statement, "I should like to think that over"….

I wish that you were tough and strong like me. But you have nevertheless an available measure of strength, and within that measure an unusual capacity of enjoyment…. You get a great deal more pleasure out of your present journeyings than I could ever have. I should not have your feelings of fatigue and weakness, but neither should I have your perception of the beautiful and your enjoyment of it. When you come to professional work, you will have to be moderate in it. Where other men work eight hours a day, you must be content with five. Take all things easily. Never tire yourself out. If you feel the blues coming upon you, get a book and a glass of wine, or go to bed and rest yourself. The morbid mental condition is of physical origin. Take comfort in the thought that you can have a life of moderate labor—the best sort of life. You will have a little money of your own, and need not be in haste to earn a large income. I am strong and can work twelve hours a day. Consequently I do; and if it were not for Mt. Desert, I should hardly have more time for reflection and real living than an operative in a cotton mill….

LOUIS D. BRANDEIS TO WILLIAM HARRISON DUNBAR
"Logic alone cannot make a great lawyer"

Louis D. Brandeis' reputation as a lawyer and jurist lay as much in his understanding of his fellow man as in his knowledge of law. In this letter to William Harrison Dunbar, a young lawyer friend of his, Brandeis encourages him to do more than simply study the law. Success, he wrote, means both grasping law and the context in which it is applied to human affairs.

My Dear Dunbar:

For some time I have intended to lay before you my views in regard to your professional [legal] life—and what it is necessary for you to do in order to attain that degree of success to which your abilities and character clearly entitle you....

Cultivate the society of men—particularly men of affairs. This is essential to your professional success. Pursue that study as heretofore you have devoted yourself to books. Lose no opportunity of becoming acquainted with men of learning, to feel instinctively their inclinations, of familiarizing yourself with their personal and business habits, use your ability in making opportunities to do this. This is for you the indispensable study—as for another the study of law—or good habits of work are the missing desideratum.

The knowledge of men, the ability to handle, to impress them is needed by you—not only in order that clients may appreciate your advice and that you may be able to apply the law to human affairs—but also that you may more accurately and surely determine what the rules of law are, that is, what the courts will adopt. You are prone to legal investigation to be controlled by logic and to underestimate the logic of facts. Knowledge of the decided cases and of the rules of logic cannot alone make a great lawyer....

If you will recall [Sir George] Jessel's opinion you will see what I mean. Knowledge of decisions and powers of logic are mere handmaidens—they are servants not masters. The controlling force is the deep knowledge of human necessities. It was this which made Jessel the great lawyer and the greater judge. The man who does not know intimately human affairs is apt to make of the law a bed of Procrustes. No hermit can be a great lawyer, least of all a commercial lawyer. When from a knowledge of the law, you pass to its application, the need of a full knowledge of men and of their affairs becomes even more apparent.... The great physicians are those who in addition to that knowledge of therapeutics which is opened to all, know not merely the human body but the human mind and emotions, so as to make themselves the proper diagnosis—to know the truth which their patients fail to disclose and who add to this an influence over the patients which is apt to spring from a real understanding of him....

Your law may be perfect, your knowledge of human affairs may be such as to enable you to apply it with wisdom and skill, and yet without individual acquaintance with men, their haunts and habits, the pursuit of the profession becomes difficult, slow and expensive. A lawyer who does not know man is handicapped. It is like practicing in a strange city. Every man that you know makes it to that extent easier to practice, to accomplish what you have in hand. You know him, know how to talk, how to treat him; he knows you and the transaction of business is simplified.

SHERWOOD ANDERSON TO HIS SONS
"First learn something well so that you can always make a living"

The novelist and poet Sherwood Anderson wrote letters to his two sons offering different advice as they contemplated potential careers. The first letter to his son John, who had not decided on a career, urges experience and pragmatism and warns of the uncertainty of depending on the arts for a paycheck. But in the second letter to his other son, Bob, Anderson offers advice on how to improve his chances of success and satisfaction as a writer.

[New Orleans, April 18, 1926]

Dear John:

It's a problem, all right. The best thing, I dare say, is first to learn something well so that you can always make a living. Bob seems to be catching the newspaper business and has had another raise. He is getting a good training by working in a smaller city. As for the scientific fields, any of them require a long schooling and intense application. If you are made for it, nothing could be better. In the long run you will have to come to your own conclusion.

The arts, which probably offers a man more satisfaction, are uncertain. It is difficult to make a living.

If I had my own life to live over, I presume I would still be a writer, but I am sure I would give my first attention to learning how to do things directly with my hands. Nothing brings quite the satisfaction that doing things brings.

Above all avoid taking the advice of men who have no brains and do not know what they are talking about. Most small businessmen say simply, "Look at me." They fancy that if they have accumulated a little money and have got a position in a small circle, they are competent to give advice to anyone.

Next to occupation is the building up of good taste. That is difficult, slow work. Few achieve it. It means all the difference in the world in the end.

I am constantly amazed at how little painters know about painting, writers about writing, merchants about business, manufacturers about manufacturing. Most men just drift.

There is a kind of shrewdness many men have that enables them to get money. It is the shrewdness of the fox after the chicken. A low order of mentality often goes with it.

Above all I would like to see many kinds of men at first hand. That would help you more than anything. Just how it is to be accomplished I do not know. Perhaps a way can be found.

Anyway, I'll see you this summer. We begin to pack for the country this week.

With love,

Dad

[Troutdale, Virginia, August, 1926]

Dear Bob:

I have been thinking of you a good deal lately. I think that with your energy, your quick imagination and your love of life you are bound in the end to go toward one of the arts.

The natural thing would be for you to become, eventually, a prose writer, a story teller.

But here, my dear fellow, you will always be under a handicap. The great difficulty will always be that your father is one. They would always club you with that.

When I am dead, the sons of bitches will begin to heap laurels on me.

You would have to be almost superhuman not, in the end, to hate me.

However, I think there is a way out, and I also think it may be a way that finally may come natural to you.

As you know, I have never touched the stage. Why not begin giving your mind and imagination to that?

It is, of course, a long road, but any road in the arts is long. I think you might begin consciously to let yourself think and feel in that way. You are a natural dramatist with a quick imagination. Let your imagination, at odd moments, begin to play within a confined space, casting people in there, and letting them in imagination play within that confined space.

And then too, Bob, I think that for us, of our tribe, it is almost necessary to have a moral balance.

There is and can be no moral balance like the long difficulty of an art.

If the idea strikes you, begin. Read what all the old and modern dramatists have done. It is entirely possible and rather nice to let your will, in part at least, control your fancy.

A man needs a purpose for real health. It is a suggestion. Think about it.

With love,

Dad

P. T. Barnum to James A. Bailey

"A few words from one who has been more than ordinarily successful"

Written five days before his death, P. T. Barnum offered some final words of advice and affection to his partner James A. Bailey. Bailey ran Barnum & Bailey Circus after Barnum's death, sticking to the principles that Barnum prescribed. More than a century later, the circus is still known as "The Greatest Show on Earth."

Bridgeport, 2 April 1891

My dear Bailey,

Although I would not pain my family by expressing such an opinion openly to them, yet I cannot but feel that my present sickness must necessarily have a fatal termination. If such should be the case, I know you will not consider a few words of advice from me an impertinence, but will heed them and treasure them up as a legacy.

Although all arrangement for the continuance of our show are now completed and I have made further directions for its management in my will, still, a few words from one who has been more than ordinarily successful in the journey of life will not come amiss in the control of your future movements. I fully believe that if you faithfully follow my methods you cannot fail.

It has been my universal plan, as you well know, to make the public aware of what I was about to offer it, to get the best of everything and the most of it, and then to advertise freely and without fear. Never attempt to catch a whale with a minnow.

I am indebted to the press of the United States for almost every dollar which I possess and for every success as an amusement manager which I have ever achieved. The very great popularity which I have attained both at home and abroad I ascribe almost entirely to the liberal and persistent use of the public journals of this country.

But it is of no advantage to advertise unless you intend to honestly fulfill the promises made in this manner. You must—I repeat it, *must*—have always a great and progressive show and also one which is clean, pure, moral, and instructive. Never cater to the baser instincts of humanity, strive as I have always done to elevate the moral tone of amusements, and always remember that the children have ever been our best patrons. I would rather hear the pleased laugh of a child over some feature of my exhibition than receive as I did the flattering compliments of the Prince of Wales. I am prouder of my title "The Children's Friend" than if I were to be called "The King of the World."

I regret exceedingly that my bodily weakness prevents my being present at the exhibition in New York, for I veritably believe that if I could again see the rows of bright-faced children at our matinees and observe their eyes grow round with wonder or hear their hearty laughter, it would do me more good than all the medicine in the world.

I am too weak to write more now, but let me entreat you to never allow the honorable and honestly acquired title of "The Greatest Show on Earth" to be in any way disgraced or lessened in fame. Go on as you have begun and I know you will continue to prosper.

Should this be, as perhaps it may, my last communication to you, I wish to assure you of my unalterable esteem, affection, and trust in you, and to bestow a fatherly blessing upon one who is in every way so worthy to become my successor.

Fraternally yours,

P. T. Barnum

Ed Turner to Ted Turner

"This is my son. He speaks Greek."

Future billionaire businessman Ted Turner announced to his father in 1957 that he was going to major in Greek at Brown University. His father objected violently to the decision, shooting off the following letter railing against the uselessness of a liberal arts education. Ted—who published the letter in the college newspaper anonymously—followed through on his pledge, embracing the impracticalities of learning Greek.

Turner later became one of the most flamboyant businessmen in the country, breaking new ground in television, creating the first "superstation"—a local station broadcast nationwide—and founding CNN, the first 24-hour news network. He also became one of the largest landowners in the United States and among the most generous philanthropists in the world.

My dear son:

I am appalled, even horrified, that you have adopted classics as a major. As a matter of fact, I almost puked on the way home today. I suppose that I am old-fashioned enough to believe that the purpose of education is to enable one to develop a community of interest with his fellow men, to learn to know them, and to learn how to get along with them. In order to do this, of course, he must learn what motivates them, and how to impel them to be pleased with his objectives and desires.

I am a practical man, and for the life of me I cannot possibly understand why you should wish to speak Greek. With whom will you communicate in Greek?…

It isn't really important what I think. It's important what you wish to do with your life. I just wish I could see that the influence of those oddball professors and the ivory towers were developing you into the kind of man we can both be proud of. I am quite sure that we both will be pleased and delighted when I introduce you to some friend of mine and say, "This is my son. He speaks Greek."

I had dinner during the Christmas holidays with an efficiency expert, an economic adviser to the nation of India, on the Board of Regents at Harvard University, who owns some eighty thousand acres of valuable timber land down here, among his other assets. His son and his family were visiting him. He introduced me to his son, then apologetically said, "He is a theoretical mathematician. I don't even know what he is talking about. He lives in a different world." After a little while I got talking to his son, and the only thing he would talk to me about was his work. I didn't know what he was talking about either, so I left early.

If you are going to stay on at Brown, and be a professor of classics, the courses you have adapted will suit you for a lifetime association with [Yale English Literature Professor] Gale Noyes. Perhaps he will even teach you to make jelly. In my opinion, it won't do to help you learn to get along with the real people in this world. I think you are rapidly becoming a jackass and the sooner you get out of that filthy atmosphere, the better it will suit me.

Oh, I know everybody says that a college education is a must. Well, I console myself by saying that everybody said the world was square, except Columbus. You go ahead and go with the world, and I'll go it alone.

I hope I am right. You are in the hands of Philistines, and dammit, I sent you there. I am sorry.
Devotedly,
Dad

DAVID OGILVY TO HIS NEPHEW

"You have a first-class mind. Stretch it."

David Ogilvy, one of the leading advertising executives of the 20th century, had the following advice to offer his nephew, who was pondering the advantages and disadvantages of entering university or launching straight into work.

June 6, 1984

Dear Harry,

You ask me whether you should spend the next three years at a university, or get a job. I will give you three different answers. Take your pick.

Answer A. You are ambitious. Your sights are set on going to the top, in business or government. Today's big corporations cannot be managed by uneducated amateurs. In these high-tech times, they need top bananas who have doctorates in chemistry, physics, engineering, geology, etc.

Even the middle managers are at a disadvantage unless they boast a university degree and an MBA. In the United States, 18 percent of the population has a degree, in Britain, only 7 percent. Eight percent of Americans have graduate degrees, compared with 1 percent of Brits. That more than anything else is why American management outperforms British management.

Same thing in government. When I was your age, we had the best civil service in the world. Today, the French civil servants are better than ours because they are educated for the job in the postgraduate Ecole Nationale d'Administration, while ours go straight from Balliol to Whitehall. The French pros outperform the British amateurs.

Anyway, you are too young to decide what you want to do for the rest of your life. If you spend the next few years at university, you will get to know the world—and yourself—before the time comes to choose your career.

Answer B. Stop frittering away your time in academia. Stop subjecting yourself to the tedium of textbooks and classrooms. Stop cramming for exams before you acquire an incurable hatred for reading.

Escape from the sterile influences of dons, who are nothing more than pickled undergraduates.

The lack of a college degree will only be a slight handicap in your career. In Britain, you can still get to the top without a degree. What industry and government need at the top is not technocrats but leaders. The character traits which make people scholars in their youth are not the traits which make them leaders later in life.

You have put up with education for 12 boring years. Enough is enough.

Answer C. Don't judge the value of higher education in terms of careermanship. Judge it for what it is—a priceless opportunity to furnish your mind and enrich the quality of your life. My father was a failure in business, but he read Horace in the loo until he died, poor but happy.

If you enjoy being a scholar, and like the company of scholars, go to a university. Who knows, you may end your days as a Regius professor. And bear in mind that British universities are still the best in the world—at the undergraduate level. Lucky you. Winning a Nobel Prize is more satisfying than being elected chairman of some large corporation or becoming a Permanent Undersecretary in Whitehall.

You have a first-class mind. Stretch it. If you have the opportunity to go to a university, don't pass it up. You would never forgive yourself.

Tons of love,

David

BEASTS OF BURDEN

WOMEN OF THE THIRD ESTATE TO LOUIS XVI
"We ask to be instructed and given jobs"

Shortly before the outbreak of the French Revolution in 1789, a group of French women presented a letter to Louis XVI asking for the opportunity to work. Craft industries that had traditionally used women were employing men at higher rates of pay than women received.

Sire,

All women of the Third Estate are born poor. Their education is either neglected or misconceived. At the age of fifteen or sixteen, girls can earn five or six sous a day…. They get married, without a dowry, to unfortunate artisans and drag out a gruelling existence producing children whom they are unable to bring up…. If old age overtakes unmarried women, they spend it in tears and as objects of contempt for their nearest relatives. To counter such misfortunes, Sire, we ask that men be excluded from those crafts and practising work that are women's prerogative.

We ask, Sire, to be instructed and given jobs, not that we may usurp men's authority, but so that we might have the means of livelihood.

SUKEY AND ERSEY TO MASTER BEVERLEY TUCKER
"We would rather be sold than go to Texas"

Though most slaves were denied education by their owners, the two slave women who wrote the following letter, to their absentee master in Virginia, were clearly exceptions. Hoping to avoid being moved to Texas, which was then an independent nation, they asked to be sold to local owners in Missouri. The slave owner's response is unknown.

St. Louis, Oct. 24ᵗʰ 1842

Dear Master [Beverley Tucker]—

We, two of your humble Servants have come to the conclusion to write you a few lines upon a subject that has given us much pain, which will be more keenly felt if you will not grant their humble request. We hope and pray that you will not think hard of us in so doing, as we are in much distress, and write the very feelings of our hearts.

About two weeks ago Mr Jones, a neighbour of Mr Bundlett in Texas, called with a letter from Mr Bundlett saying that we must come on with Mr Jones. As we had been there a long time and had become much attached to the place (our Husbands being here) and as we hated the idea of going to Texas, Mr Jones was kind enough to let us remain till March, before which time he expected to hear from you on the subject. Our object in writing dear Master is this: We can't bear to go to Texas with a parcel of strangers—if you were there we should go without saying a word, but to be separated from our husbands forever in this world would make us unhappy for life. We have a great many friends in this place and would rather be sold than go to Texas.

In making this request, dear master, we do not do it through any disrespect (for you have always been kind to us) but merely because we shall be happier here with our friends and Husbands. We don't think there will be the least difficulty in getting ourselves sold, together with our children, the youngest of which is about six weeks old, a fine little Girl. Susan has two Boys, the eldest nearly three years old, and the youngest eight months.

We hope dear Master and Mistress that you will not let us go to Texas, but grant us our humble petition. We are both well, also our children. If you conclude to sell us, please write to any of the following gentlemen, with your terms, with whom you are acquainted. Edward Bates, Andrew Elliott, R.H. Graham or Wm G. Pettus Remember us kindly to Mistress and her children and the Servants & children.

Yours truly, Susan (Sukey) & Ersey

P.T. Barnum to Moses S. Beach
"Ameliorating the condition of women"

Better known for his commercial exploitation of the human condition than his progressive views on employment, P.T. Barnum was a strong advocate for women's rights at work. This letter was written to the treasurer of the Working Women's Protective Union.

American Museum 22 March 1864

Sir:

I take pleasure in sending you fifty dollars for what I regard as the most sensible and effective organization that has yet been formed for ameliorating the condition of women who desire to gain their livelihood by their own honest efforts. It is high time that this class was not only effectually "protected," but also that other avenues were opened for their maintenance. They should learn bookkeeping, telegraphing, money-changing, etc. In France females not onlyact as accountants, clerks in stores, offices, etc., but they also sell the tickets at public places of amusement and engage in hundreds of other branches of light labor that are here filled by men. I could give permanent employ to several females of good character who are judges of money and competent to sell tickets. In fact, I think they have but to fit themselves for many light and pleasant avocations in order to find plenty of chances for employment at such salaries as would enable them to live comfortably and respectably.

Truly yours,

P.T. Barnum

ALFRED KRUPP TO THE MEN OF THE CRUCIBLE-STEEL WORKS
"Mutual loyalty has made the greatness of the Works"

Having built his steel works company from a single foundry as a teenager to a gigantic complex employing thousands of men, Alfred Krupp was infuriated by rumblings of discontent among workers about low wages and working conditions.

In the wake of the extraordinary success of Krupps' artillery during the Franco-Prussian War of 1870, the steel magnate rapidly expanded his company to accommodate a wave of new orders from all over Europe. Fresh hordes of new workmen entered his work force. At the same time, the price of coal and iron ore soared, placing pressure on Krupps' bottom line.

When workers started to consider imposing demands on Krupp for higher wages and explored forming a union, Krupp responded with a strongly worded letter to all his employees, reminding them of his past generosity during difficult times—and warning them of his determination to not let workers run his company.

Essen, 24.6.1872.

To the Men of the Crucible-Steel Works

Forty-five years ago I stood with a few workmen among the original fragments of these Works, inherited from my father. The day-pay for smiths and smelters was then raised from 18 stivers to 7 1/2 silver groschen; the full week's wages amounted to 1 thaler 15 s.gr. For fifteen years I earned just enough to be able to pay the men their wages; for my own work and cares I had nothing more than the consciousness of duty fulfilled. As general conditions changed and the Works began to flourish, I gradually raised the wages, making a rule of always doing this voluntarily, not waiting to be prompted, and this rule shall still remain in force. One useful scheme after another has been started, and many are still pending; to this day every effort has been exerted in the interests of the men, and the new dwellings which have been begun total thousands. When business depression crushed all industry, when orders were lacking, I nevertheless had work continued, and never dismissed a loyal man. There are still many old men in the Works who can testify to this. Ask them what was done for the men in 1848. Who will calculate what is being lost in the present scarcity of coal?

Mutual loyalty has made the greatness of the Works. I know that I deserve your confidence and possess it, and that is why I want to address these remarks to you. Before I have cause to complain of disloyalty and opposition, I warn you of the fate which wandering agitators and their periodicals are striving, under a pretence of benevolence, misusing religious and moral maxims, to bring upon the great working-class. Their harvest will begin when they have irrevocably undermined the existence of your class with false allurements; they seek the general ruin, in order to use their influence to fish in troubled waters.

Enquire about the past of these apostles, about their domestic and moral careers. They find the money paid by the workers for spoken and written scandal is a more convenient and pleasant booty than hard work offers them. The *Essener Blätter*, amongst others is trying by every kind of invention to bring into suspicion the character of the management of my Works, and stated yesterday, for purposes of agitation, that the conference had been forced to grant a considerable increase of wages to one class of furnace worker. To this and similar barefaced lies from malicious enemies I now reply with the following solemn warning. Nothing, and no consequences to follow, will induce me to allow anything to be bullied out of me. The management will continue, with the goodwill which has hitherto been its law, to carry on the works in the spirit of my policy, and on my account, so long as I still regard the men as members of the establishment by reason of their proved loyalty. I can, of course, make over my position any day to others, and, beyond any question, no company of capitalists would be likely to surpass me in goodwill and self-sacrifice. Nobody can well suppose that it is from greed of gain that I subject myself to the pains and labor which are inseparable from the conduct of such a business on my own account. Everyone knows how I have at all times valued the worker and his work, but let everyone rest assured that misconstruction of my motive would be capable of my rooted predilection for them. Let everyone realize that I do not change my mind; that, as always, I promise nothing that I do not perform. I therefore warn you once more against the allurements of a conspiracy against peace and quiet. In all my enterprises, a good and steady workman is afforded the opportunity, after a moderate term of work, to enjoy his pension in his own house—and that on a more favorable scale than anywhere else in the world. I expect and require full confidence; I refuse to comply with any unjustified demands, but shall, as hitherto, anticipate every just claim; I therefore invite all those who will not be content with this to give notice, the sooner the better, in order to anticipate the notice which I shall give, and thus to leave the establishment in a legal manner, and to make room for others, with the assurance that I intend to be and to remain master in my own house, as well as on my own ground.

JAMES CARDINAL GIBBONS TO CARDINAL SIMEONI
"It is the right of the laboring classes to protect themselves"

The most important document in the history of the Catholic Church's relationship with the labor movement was a letter known as "the memorial on the Knights of Labor." It was written a year after the Haymarket Massacre in Chicago. The Archbishop of Baltimore, James Cardinal Gibbons, wrote the letter to Rome stating the Catholic Church's support of the labor movement's peaceful efforts to improve working conditions.

While distancing itself from violent actions of labor groups, the church believed it had to support the unions' overall goals. Membership in the unions was heavily Catholic. Church leaders did not want to lose the support of Catholics. They feared that the Catholic Church might become associated with the rich elite, as it had in Europe.

The decision to endorse labor organizations provided credibility to efforts to improve factory conditions, which by contemporary standards were appalling.

February 20, 1887
TO HIS EMINENCE CARDINAL SIMEONI, PREFECT
OF THE SACRED CONGREGATION OF THE PROPGANDA:

YOUR EMINENCE

In submitting to the Holy See the conclusions which after several months of attentive observation and reflection, seem to me to sum up the truth concerning the association of the Knights of Labor, I feel profoundly convinced of the vast importance of the consequences attaching to this question, which forms but a link in the great chain of the social problems of our day, and especially of our country.

In weighing this question I have been very careful to follow as my constant guide the spirit of the Encyclicals, in which our Holy Father, Leo XIII, has so admirably set forth the dangers of our time and their remedies, as well as the principles by which we are to recognize associations condemned by the Holy See. Such was also the guide of the Third Plenary Council of Baltimore in its teaching concerning the principles to be followed and the dangers to be shunned by the faithful either in the choice or in the establishment of those associations toward which the spirit of our popular institutions so strongly impels them. And considering the dire consequences that might result from a mistake by the thousands and hundreds of thousands, the council wisely ordained that when an association is spread over several dioceses shall condemn it, but shall refer the case to a standing committee of all the archbishops of the United States; and even these are not authorized to condemn unless their sentence be unanimous; and in case they fail to agree unanimously, then only the supreme tribunal of the Holy See can impose a condemnation; all this in order to avoid error and confusion of discipline.

The committee of archbishops held a meeting, in fact, toward the end of last October, especially to consider the association of the Knights of Labor. We were not persuaded to hold this meeting because of any request on the part of our bishops, for none of them had asked for it; and it should also be said that, among all the bishops we know, only two or three desire the condemnation. But the importance of the question in itself, and in the estimation of the Holy See led us to examine it with greatest attention. After our discussion, the results of which have already been communicated to the Sacred Congregation of the Propaganda, only two out of the twelve archbishops voted for condemnation, and their reasons were powerless to convince the others of either the justice or the prudence of such a condemnation.

In the following considerations I wish to state in detail the reasons which determined the vote of the great majority of the committee—reasons whose truth and force seem to me all the more evident today: I shall try at the same time to do justice to the arguments advanced by the opposition.

1. In the first place, in the constitution, laws and official declarations of the Knights of Labor, there can clearly be found assertions and rules which we would not approve; but we have not found in them those elements so clearly pointed out by the Holy See, which places them among condemned associations.

(a) In their form of initiation there is no oath.

(b) The obligation to secrecy by which they keep the knowledge of their business from strangers or enemies, in no wise prevents Catholics from manifesting everything to competent ecclesiastical authority, even outside of confession. This has been positively declared to us by their president.

(c) They make no promise to blind obedience. The object and laws of the association are distinctly declared, and the obligation of obedience does not go beyond these limits.

(d) They not only profess no hostility against religion or the Church, but their declarations are quite to the contrary. The Third Plenary Council commands that we should not condemn an association without giving a hearing to its officers or representatives; "audits ducibus, corypheis vel sociis praecipuis." Now, their president in sending me a copy of their constitution, says that he is a Catholic from the bottom of his heart; that he practices his religion faithfully and receives the sacraments regularly; that he belongs to no Masonic or other society condemned by the Church; that he knows of nothing in the association of the Knights of Labor contrary to the laws of the Church;

that, with filial submission he begs the pastors of the Church to examine all the details of their organization, and, if they find anything worthy of condemnation, they should indicate it, and he promises its correction. Assuredly one does not perceive in all this any hostility to the authority of the Church, but on the contrary last year at Richmond he and several of the officers and members, devout Catholics, made similar declarations concerning their feelings and the action of that convention, the documents of which we are expecting to receive.

(e) Nor do we find in this organization any hostility to the authority and laws of our country. Not only does nothing of the kind appear in their constitution and laws, but the heads of our civil government treat with the greatest respect the cause which they represent. The President of the United States told me personally, a month ago that he was then examining a law for the amelioration of certain social grievances and that he had just had a long conference on the subject with Mr. Powderly, president of the Knights of Labor. The Congress of the United States, following the advice of President Cleveland is busying itself at the present time with the amelioration of the working classes, in whose complaints they acknowledge openly there is a great deal of truth. And our political parties, far from regarding them as enemies of the country, vie with each other in championing the evident rights of the poor workmen, who seek not to resist laws, but only to obtain just legislation by constitutional and legitimate means.

2. These considerations, which show that in this association those elements are not to be found which the Holy See condemns, lead us to study, in the second place, the evils which the associations contend against, and the nature of the conflict.

That there exists among us, as in the other countries of the world, grave and threatening social evils, public injustices, which call for strong resistance and legal remedy, is a fact which no one dares to deny, and the truth of which has been already acknowledged by the Congress and the President of the United States. Without entering into the sad details of these wrongs,—which does not seem necessary here,—it may suffice to mention only that monopolies on the part of both individuals and of corporations, have already called forth not only the complaints of our working classes but also the opposition of our public men and legislators; that the efforts of these monopolists, not always with success, to control legislation to their own profit, cause serious apprehension among the disinterested friends of liberty; that the heartless avarice which, through greed of gain, pitilessly grinds not only the men, but particularly the women and children in various employments, make it clear to all who love humanity and justice that it is not only the right of the laboring classes to protect themselves, but the duty of the whole people to aid them in finding a remedy against the dangers which both civilization and the social order are menaced by avarice, oppression and corruption.

It would be vain to deny either the existence of the evils, the right of legitimate resistance, or the necessity of a remedy. At most doubt might be raised about the legitimacy of the form of the form of resistance and the remedy employed by the Knights of Labor. This then ought to be the next point of our examination.

3. It can hardly be doubted that for the attainment of any public end, association—the organization of all interested persons—is the most efficacious means, a means altogether natural and just. This is so evident, and besides so comfortable to the genius of our country, of our essentially popular social conditions, that it is unnecessary to insist upon it. It is almost the only means to invite public attention, to give force to the most legitimate resistance, to add weight to the most just demands.

Now there already exists an organization which present a thousand attractions and advantages, but which our Catholic workingmen, with filial obedience to the Holy See, refuse to join; this is the Masonic organization, which exists everywhere in our country, and which, as Mr. Powderly has expressly pointed out to us, unites employer and worker in a brotherhood very advantageous for the latter, but which numbers in its ranks hardly a single Catholic. Freely renouncing the advantages which the Church and their consciences forbid, workingmen form associations, having nothing in common with the deadly designs of the enemies of religion and seeking only mutual protection and help, and the legitimate assertion of their rights. But here they also find themselves threatened with condemnation, and so deprived of their only means of defense. Is it surprising that they should be astonished at this and that they ask *Why*?

4. Let us now consider the objections made against this sort of organization.

(a) It is objected that in these organizations Catholics are mixed with Protestants, to the peril of their faith. Naturally, yes, they are mixed with Protestants in the workers' associations, precisely as they are at their work; for in a mixed people like ours, the separation of religious and social affairs is not possible. But to suppose that the faith of our Catholics suffers thereby is not to know the Catholic workers of America who are not like the working men of so many European countries—misguided and perverted children, looking on their Mother the Church as a hostile stepmother—but they are intelligent, well instructed and devoted children ready to give their blood, as they continually give their means (although small and hard-earned) for her support and protection. And in fact it is not in the present case that Catholics are mixed with Protestants, but rather that Protestants are admitted to the advantages of an association, two-thirds of whose members and the principal officers are Catholics; and in a country like ours their exclusion would be simply impossible. . . .

5. Whoever meditates upon the ways in which divine Providence is guiding contemporary history cannot fail to remark how important is the part which the power of the people takes therein at present and must take in the future. We behold, with profound sadness, the efforts of the prince of darkness to make this power dangerous to the social weal by withdrawing the masses of the people from the influence of religion, and impelling them towards the ruinous paths of license and anarchy. Until now our country presents a picture of altogether different character—that of a popular power regulated by love of good order, by respect for religion, by obedience to the authority of the laws, not a democracy of license and violence, but that true democracy which aims at the general prosperity through the means of sound principles and good social order.

In order to preserve so desirable a state of things it is absolutely necessary that religion should continue to hold the affections, and thus rule the conduct of the multitudes. As Cardinal Manning has so well written, "In the future era the Church has no longer to deal with princes and parliaments, but with the masses, with the people. Whether we will or no this is our work; we need a new spirit, a new direction of our life and activity." To lose influence over the people would be to lose the future altogether; and it is by the heart, far more than by the understanding, that we must hold and guide this immense power, so mighty either for good or evil. Among all the glorious titles of the Church which her history has merited for her, there is not one which at present gives her so great influence as that of *Friend of the People*. Assuredly, in our democratic country, it is this title which wins for the Catholic Church not only the enthusiastic devotedness of the millions of her children, but also the respect and admiration of all our citizens, whatever be their religious belief. It is the power of precisely this title which renders persecution almost an impossibility, and which draws toward our holy Church the great heart of the American people. . . .

Therefore, with complete confidence, I leave the case to the wisdom and prudence of your Eminence and the Holy See.

Rome, February 20, 1887.
J. Cardinal Gibbons,
Archbishop of Baltimore

Eugene V. Debs to Frank X. Holl
"Organize thoroughly. Stand up and be men."

One of the most successful labor leaders in American history, Eugene V. Debs came to national prominence in the early 1890s as the head of the American Railway Union. Debs and several other activists organized the A.R.U. after being disillusioned by the discord and selfishness among existing railroad unions.

Debs forged an effective and united front among labor workers against the railroad companies. His first major test came in the spring of 1894 when the Great Northern Railroad president, James J. Hill, tried to squash the fledgling A.R.U. As the following letter shows, Debs responded to the threat with vigor and determination, and the A.R.U. mounted a successful eighteen-day strike.

One year later, the victory emboldened the A.R.U. to trigger the great Pullman strike, one of the most effective labor actions in American history. In support of other striking workers at the Pullman Palace Car Company, the A.R.U. approved a boycott of trains handling Pullman cars. Train service—then the lifeblood of American commerce—came to a screeching halt in 27 states and territories in the western United States.

[April] 16, 1894

Terra Haute, Indiana

Confidential

Dear Sir and Brother:

I am just advised of a carefully devised secret scheme to break up the A.R.U. on the great Northern System preliminary to sweeping reductions in wages in every department. Some of our best men have been discharged at various points for no other reason than that they were active A.R.U. men. The scheme is to discharge our local leaders at various points and thus demoralize and stampede the Order, reducing the numbers to a headless, disorganized mob, a condition under which it will be unable to resist the sweeping reductions of wages that are to be made. Some reductions have already been made. Other and greater ones are to follow.

There is but one hope. Everything depends upon immediate action. Organize solidly at every point. Get every good man into your Union at once. There must not be a moment's delay. Men have been indiscriminately discharged. Wages have been reduced and unless prompt measures are taken the men on the Great Northern will be reduced to a horde of slaves. The issue will be pressed by the

Company. We must prepare to meet it. The reinstatement of the men discharged without cause will be demanded. The A.R.U. will stand by them with all its resources. Not only this, but if the case demands it I propose to go over the Great Northern in person; hold popular mass meetings at every point; appeal to the whole people to stand by us in this unholy massacre of our rights. Get together promptly. Organize thoroughly. Stand up and be men. You may rest assured that you will not want for the support of courageous, manly men. Let me hear from you at once.

Yours fraternally,
Eugene V. Debs

GEORGE F. BAER TO WILLIAM F. CLARK
"The rights and interests of the laboring man will be protected"

The early 1900s were marked by bitter, violent strikes, particularly in the anthracite coal mines, where working conditions were very difficult and pay low. In July 1902 a photographer from Wilkes-Barre, Pennsylvania, wrote the president of the Reading Railroad, George F. Baer, urging him to intervene and settle the strike, writing that God would "send the Holy Spirit to reason in your heart." Baer wrote the following response, which became known as the "divine right" letter.

17th July 1902

My dear Mr. Clark:

I have your letter of the 16th inst. I do not know who you are. I see that you are a religious man; but you are evidently biased in favor of the right of the workingman to control a business in which he has no other interest than to secure fair wages for the work he does.

I beg of you not to be discouraged. The rights and interests of the laboring man will be protected and cared for—not by the labor agitators, but by the Christian men of property to whom God has given control of the property rights of the country, and upon the successful management of which so much depends. Do not be discouraged. Pray earnestly that right may triumph, always remembering that the Lord God Omnipotent still reigns, and that His reign is one of law and order, and not of violence and crime.

A Reader to *Jewish Daily Forward* Editor
"We could see the tears running down his cheeks"

The Jewish Daily Forward newspaper served the large Jewish immigrant population in New York City's Lower East Side at the turn of the 19ᵗʰ century. Like many recent arrivals to the United States, immigrant Jewish workers often worked at the whim of their employers, as the letter below shows. The newspaper's sympathetic response reflected the pro-labor position of the readership.

[1908]

Esteemed Editor,

We were sitting in the shop and working when the boss came over to one of us and said, "You ruined the work: you'll have to pay for it." The worker answered that it wasn't his fault, that he had given out the work in perfect condition. "You're trying to tell me!" The boss got mad and began to shout. "I pay you wages and you answer back, you dog! I should have thrown you out of my shop long ago."

The worker trembled, his face got whiter. When the boss noticed how his face paled, he gestured, spat and walked away. The worker said no more. Tired, and overcome with shame, he turned back to his work and later exclaimed, "For six years I've been working here like a slave, and he tells me 'You dog, I'll throw you out!' I wanted to pick up an iron and smash his head in, but I saw before me my wife and five children who want to eat!"

Obviously, the offended man felt he had done wrong in not standing up for his honor as a worker and human being. In the shop, the machines hummed, the irons thumped, and we could see the tears running down his cheeks.

Did this unfortunate man act correctly in remaining silent under the insults of the boss? Is the fact that he has a wife and children the reason for his slavery and refusal to defend himself? I hope you will answer my questions in the "Bintel Brief."

Respectfully,

A.P.

Answer:

The worker cannot help himself alone. There is no limit to what must be done for a piece of bread. One must bite his lips till they bleed, and keep silent when he is alone. But he must not remain alone. He must not remain silent. He must unite with his fellow workers and fight. To defend their honor as men, the workers must be well organized.

CÉSAR CHÁVEZ TO E.L. BARR, JR.

"We are not beasts of burden"

César Chávez grew up as a itinerent farm worker and in 1962 founded the Farm Workers Association in California to represent the rights of migrant workers. Using hunger strikes, protest marches and boycotts, he brought national attention to the plight of migrant workers. The FWA sought to raise wages, improve working conditions and stop unhealthy practices like spraying pesticides while workers were picking fruit.

Chávez's most notable action was a nationwide boycott of grapes. He wrote the following letter to the president of the California Grape and Tree Fruit League in response to accusations of having used violent tactics. Chávez's success helped stimulate improvements in the way businesses treated migrant workers, demonstrated how the use of consumer boycotts could impact business policies and helped empower the rapidly growing Hispanic community in the United States, encouraging them to take an active role in the ways business is conducted.

Good Friday 1969
E.L. Barr, Jr. President
California Grape and Tree Fruit League
717 Market St.
San Francisco, California

Dear Mr. Barr,

I am sad to hear about your accusation in the press that our union movement and table grape boycott have been successful because we have used violence and terror tactics. If what you say is true, I have been a failure and should withdraw from the struggle; but you are left with the awesome moral responsibility, before god and Man, to come forward with whatever information you have so that corrective action can begin at once. If for any reason you fail to come forth to substantiate your charges, then you must be held responsible for committing violence against us, albeit of the tongue. I am convinced that you as a human being did not mean what you said but rather acted hastily under pressure from the public relations firm that has been hired to try to counteract the tremendous moral force of our movement. How many times we ourselves have felt the need to lash out in anger and bitterness.

Today on Good Friday, 1969, we remember the life and the sacrifice of Martin Luther King, Jr., who gave himself totally to the nonviolent struggle for peace and justice. In his Letter From a Birmingham Jail Dr. King describes better than I could our hopes for the strike and boycott: "Injustice must be exposed, with all the tensions its exposure creates, to the light of human conscience and the air of national opinion before it can be cured." For our part I admit that we have seized upon every tactic and strategy consistent with the morality of our cause to expose that injustice and thus to heighten the sensitivity of the American conscience so that farmworkers will have, without bloodshed, their own union and the dignity of bargaining with their agribusiness employers. By lying about the nature of our movement, Mr. Barr, you are working against nonviolent social change. Unwittingly perhaps, you may unleash the other force upon which our union by discipline and deed, censure and education has sought to avoid, that panacean shortcut: that senseless violence which honors no color, class, or neighborhood.

You must understand—I must make you understand—that our membership and the hopes and aspirations of the hundreds and thousands of the poor and dispossessed that have been raised on our account are, above all, human beings, no better and no worse than any other cross-section of human society; we are not saints because we are poor, but by the same measure neither are we immoral. We are men and women who have suffered and endured much, and not only because of our abject poverty but because we have been kept poor. The colors of our skins, the languages of our cultural and native origins, the lack of our formal education, the exclusion from the democratic process, the numbers of our men slain in recent wars—through all these burdens generation after generation have sought to demoralize us, to break our human spirit. But God knows that we are not beasts of burden, agricultural implements or rented slaves; we are men. And mark this well Mr. Barr, we are men locked in a death struggle against man's inhumanity to man in the industry that you represent. And this struggle itself gives meaning to our life and ennobles our dying.

As your industry has experienced, our strikers here in Delano and those who represent us throughout the world are well trained for this struggle. They have been under the gun, they have been kicked and beaten and herded by dogs, they have been cursed and ridiculed, they have been stripped and chained and jailed, they have been sprayed with the poisons used in the vineyards; but they have been taught not to lie down and die nor flee in shame, but to resist with every ounce of human endurance and spirit. To resist not with retaliation in kind but to overcome with love and compassion, with ingenuity and creativity, with hard work and longer hours, with stamina and patient tenacity, with truth and public appeal, with friends and allies, with mobility and discipline, with politics and law, and with prayer and fasting. They were not trained in a month or even a year; after all, this new harvest season will mark our fourth full year of strike and even now we continue to plan and prepare for the years to come. Time accomplishes for the poor what money does for the rich.

This is not to pretend that we have everywhere been successful enough or that we have not made mistakes. And while we do not belittle or underestimate our adversaries—for they are the rich and the powerful and they possess the land—we are not afraid nor do we cringe from confrontation. We welcome it! We have planned for it. We know that our cause is just, that history is a story of social revolution, and that the poor shall inherit the land.

Once again, I appeal to you as the representative of your industry and as a man. I ask you to recognize and bargain with our union before the economic pressure of the boycott and strike takes an irrevocable toil; but if not, I ask you to at least sit down with us to discuss the safeguards necessary to keep our historic struggle free of violence. I make this appeal because as one of the leaders of our nonviolent movement, I know and accept my responsibility for preventing, if possible, the destruction of human life and property. For these reasons, and knowing Gandhi's admonition that fasting is the last resort in place of the sword, during a most critical time in our movement last February 1968 I undertook a 25-day fast. I repeat to you the principle enunciated to the membership at the start of the fast: if to build our union required the deliberate taking of life, either the life of a grower or his child, or the life of a farmworker or his child, then I choose not to see the union built.

Mr. Barr, let me be painfully honest with you. You must understand these things. We advocate militant nonviolence as our means for social revolution and to achieve justice for our people, but we are not blind or deaf to the desperate and moody winds of human frustration, impatience and rage that blow among us. Gandhi himself admitted that if his only choice were cowardice or violence, he would choose violence. Men are not angels, and time and tide wait for no man. Precisely because of these powerful human emotions, we have tried to involve masses of people in their own struggle. Participation and self-determination remain the best experience of freedom, and free men instinctively prefer democratic change and even protect the rights guaranteed to seek it. Only the enslaved in despair have need of violent overthrow.

This letter does not express all that is in my heart, Mr. Barr. But if it says nothing else it says that we do not hate you or rejoice to see your industry destroyed; we hate the agribusiness system that seeks to keep us enslaved and we shall overcome and change it not by retaliation or bloodshed but by a determined nonviolent struggle carried on by those masses of farm workers who intend to be free and human.

Sincerely yours,

César E. Chávez

United Farm Workers Organizing Committee

A.F.L.-C.I.O.

(Letters of a Nation, pp.229-232)

CURT FLOOD TO BOWIE KUHN
"I do not feel that I am a piece of property"

A star outfielder of the St. Louis Cardinals baseball team, Curt Flood was traded to the Philadelphia Phillies in 1969. He refused to go. Flood wrote a letter to baseball commissioner Bowie Kuhn objecting to his being forced to work for another employer against his will. Flood brought his case to the Supreme Court, which voted five to three against him. Nevertheless, the case opened the way for free agency in baseball.

(December 24, 1969)

Dear Mr. Kuhn,

After 12 years in the major leagues, I do not feel that I am a piece of property to be bought and sold irrespective of my wishes. I believe that any system that produces that result violates my basic rights as a citizen and is inconsistent with the laws of the United States and the several states.

It is my desire to play baseball in 1970 and I am capable of playing. I have received a contract from the Philadelphia club, but I believe I have the right to consider offers from other clubs before making any decisions. I, therefore, request that you make known to all the major league clubs my feelings in this matter, and advise them of my availability for the 1970 season.

Curt Flood

BUSINESS AND GOVERNMENT

EDWARD I TO THE SHERIFF OF NORTHAMPTONSHIRE, SUMMONING BURGHERS FOR THE "MODEL" PARLIAMENT

"The Kings Commissioners . . . were lately at Norton within the same county, for the suppressing of the Abby there."

In 1295, King Edward I formally invited the mercantile interests of England to join Parliament for the first time. It marked the start of a formal relationship between commercial interests of England, who were not nobles, and the ruling government. The Parliament of 1295 became known as the "Model" Parliament because later gatherings used the same format.

Since we intend to have a consultation and meeting with the earls, barons, and other principal men of our kingdom with regard to providing remedies against the dangers which are in these days threatening the same kingdom, and on that account have commanded them to be with us on the Lord's day next after the feast of St. Martin, in the approaching winter, at Westminster, to consider, ordain, and do as may be necessary for the avoidance of those dangers, we strictly require you to cause two knights from the aforesaid county, two citizens from each city in the same county, and two burgesses from each borough, of those who are especially discreet and capable of laboring, to be elected without delay, and to cause them to come to us at the aforesaid time and place.

Moreover, the said knights are to have full and sufficient power for themselves and for the community of the aforesaid county, and the said citizens and burgesses for themselves, and the communities of the aforesaid cities and boroughs separately, then and there, for doing what shall then be ordained according to the common council in the premises; so that the aforesaid business shall not remain unfinished in any way for defect of this power. And you shall have there the names of the knights, citizens, and burgesses, together with this writ.

Witness the king, at Canterbury, on the 3d of October.

SIRE PIERS DUTTON TO SIR THOMAS AUDELEY, AND GEORGE, EARL OF SHREWSBURY, TO JOHN SCUDAMORE

"The said commissioners were in fear of their lives"

The relationship between the government and financial interests in Western Europe has often been a tenuous one. In the 16th century, Henry VIII seized the property of the Catholic Church in England, by far the island-nation's wealthiest institution. As the letters below reflect, there was little difference between brute force and negotiation over the rights of property.

The first letter from Sir Piers Dutton to Sir Thomas Audeley describes the taking of a monastery. The following correspondence is a request from the Earl of Shrewsbury for a portion of the church lands.

Please it your good Lordship to be advised [that] Mr. Combes and Mr. Bolles, the Kings Commissioners with the County of Chester, were lately at Norton within the same county, for the suppressing of the Abby there. And when they had packed up such jewels and stuff as they had there and thought the next day to depart from there, the Abbot gathered a great company together to the number of two or three hundred persons, so that the said Commissioners were in fear of their lives, and were glad to take [to] a tower there, and thereupon sent a letter unto me, informing me what danger they were in, and desired me to come to assist them or else they were never like to come from there. Which letter came to me about nine of the clock in the night upon Sunday last, and about two of the clock in the same night I came to that place with such of my tenants as I had near about me. . . . I used some bold tactics and came suddenly upon them, so that the company that was there fled. . . . And it was thought [that] if the matter had not been quickly handled it would have grown . . . to what danger God only knows. . . . I took the Abbot and three of his Canons and brought them to the King Castle of Halton, and there committed them to confinement to the Constable to be kept as the Kings Rebellious . . .; and William Parker, the Kings servant who was appointed to be the Kings farmer there was restored to his possession. Wherefore it may please your good Lordship that the King may have knowledge [of this action of mine], and that his pleasure may be further known, which I shall always be ready and glad to do. . . .

Welbiloved friende . . . I understand that for the especyall truste and confydence that the Kyngs Highness has in you he has appoynted you to be one of his Survayors of diverse Abbies within the Countye of Hereforde and others appoynted to be subpressed. Trouth it is [that] in the poore house of Wormseley, within the said Countye of Hereforde, which is of my foundation, many of my ancestors do lye. . . . So that if I myght by any pursute [pleading] to be made upon the Kyngs Grace for the same, I would be very sorye it should be surpressed. And therefore I desyre and heartily pray you to use your lawful favor, and to be good therein, at this my desyre, so that by your good helpe and meanes I may the soner atteyn that the same may stande and contynewe. And I shalbe glad to do unto you pleasure at all tymes, as knowth our Lord who have you in his governance.

Yor ffelow

G. Shrewsbury

To my hertly biloved fellow,

JohnSkydmore, boon of the gentylmen usshers

Of the Kyngs most honerable Chamber.

JEAN BAPTISTE COLBERT TO LOUIS XIV
"To reestablish domestic and foreign commerce"

King Louis XIV of France oversaw one of the earlier and more concerted efforts to encourage economic activity in his country. By the 1600s, capitalism had progressed to the point where national rulers saw the benefits of a free market. Many of those rulers began taking steps to encourage it.

This 1664 letter from Jean Baptiste Colbert, Louis XIV's controller-general of finance, outlines some of the basic tenets of France's economic policy. The basic outline is remarkably similar to modern economic development programs: improve transportation infrastructure, provide government incentives for investment, enforce consistent laws to regulate commerce fairly, and promote an active foreign trade policy.

Having considered how useful it would be to this realm to reestablish domestic and foreign commerce . . . we have decided to hold, with this end in mind, every two weeks in our presence a special commerce council, in which the merchants' interests and the means of arriving at this reestablishment will be examined and resolved, as well as everything concerning manufactures. We also inform you that we are setting aside . . . a million *livres* per year for the reestablishment of manufactures and the increase of navigation, not counting more considerable sums that we are raising to furnish the companies of the East and West Indies;

That we are constantly working to abolish all tolls levied on navigable rivers;

That more than a million *livres* has already been spent to repair public roads, on which we will continue to work;

That we will aid with funds from the royal treasury all those who wish to undertake the reestablishment of old manufactures or who propose new ones;

That we order all our ambassadors or residents at the courts of the princes our allies, to make, in our name, all the proper efforts to have justice rendered on all complaints of merchants, and to assure for them an entire freedom of commerce;

That we will have lodged comfortably, at our court, each and every merchant who has business here, for the entire time that they are obliged to stay there, having ordered the grand marshal of our palace to indicate a proper place for that purpose, which will be called the House of Commerce. . . .

That all merchants and traders by sea who buy ships or build new ones for trade or commerce will receive subsidies from us to help them in these purchases or the construction of these vessels;

And all those who undertake long voyages will receive from us, if they bring back certification in the form we have prescribed, subsidies for each ton of merchandise that they carry or bring back from these voyages.

In this letter, we have wanted to inform you of all these things, and as soon as you have received it, you are to assemble all the merchants and traders of your town of Marseilles and explain particularly well our intentions in all the matters mentioned above, so that, being thus informed of the favorable treatment we wish to give them, they may be more eager to apply themselves to commerce. Have them understand that for everything that concerns the welfare and advantage of the same, they are to address themselves to Sieur Colbert. . . .

ANTHONY HENLEY TO CONSTITUENTS
"You know that I bought you"

The blending of government and economic interests often created tensions and opportunities for abuse between politicians and businesspeople. Anthony Henley served as a Member of the British Parliament for Southampton from 1727 to 1734. At the end of his tenure, Henley married a 15-year-old heiress, Lady Betty Berkeley, and left his seat. Just before departing, however, Henley composed this choice letter to some of his constituents responding to their complaints about an Excise Bill before Parliament, reflecting the sometimes conflicted relationship.

Gentlemen,

I received yours and am surprised by your insolence in troubling me about the Excise. You know, what I very well know, that I bought you. And I know, what perhaps you think I don't know, you are now selling yourselves to Somebody Else; and I know, what you do not know, that I am buying another borough. May God's curse light upon you all: may your houses be as open and common to all Excise Officers as your wifes and daughter were to me, when I stood for your scoundrel corporation.

Yours, etc.,
Anthony Henley

Earl of Chesterfield, on Buying a Seat in Parliament

"[I] offered five-and-twenty hundred pounds for a secure seat in Parliament"

As government played an increasingly important role in business and trade, the value of influencing government policy grew. By the 1700s, it was important enough that British businessmen often paid their way to secure seats in Parliament. The letter below from the Earl of Chesterfield reflects his consternation at the increasing price of literally buying a position in government.

Bath, December 19, 1767

My Dear Friend,

. . . In one of our conversations here, this time twelvemonth; I desired him to secure you a seat in the new parliament; he assured me he would; and I am convinced, very sincerely; he said even that he would make it his own affair; and desired I would give myself no more trouble about it. Since that, I have heard no more of it; which made me look out for some venal borough; and I spoke to a borough-jobber, and offered five-and-twenty hundred pounds for a secure seat in Parliament; but he laughed at my offer, and said, that there was no such thing as a borough to be had now; for the that the rich East and West Indians had secured them all, at the rate of three thousand pounds at least; but many at four thousand; and two or three, that he knew of, at five thousand. This, I confess, has vexed me a good deal; and made me the more impatient to know whether Lord Chatham had done anything in it; which I shall know when I go to town, as I propose to do in about a fortnight; and, as soon as I know of it, you shall. To tell you truly what I think –I doubt, from all these nervous disorders, that Lord Chatham is hors de combat, as a Minister, but do not even hint this to anybody. God bless you!

Chesterfield

1807

I shall procure myself a seat in the new Parliament, unless I find that it will cost so large a sum, as, in the state of my family, it would be very imprudent for me to devote to such an object, which I find is very likely to be the case. Tierney, who manages this business for the friends of the late administration, assures me that he can hear of no seats to be disposed of. After a Parliament which has lived little more than four months, one would naturally suppose, that those seats which are regularly sold by the proprietors of them would be very cheap; they are, however, in fact, sold now at a higher price than was ever given for them before. Tierney tells me that he has offered *£10,000* for the two seats of Westbury, the property of the late Lord Abingdon, and which are to be made the most of by trustees for creditors, and has met with a refusal. . . .

This buying of seats is detestable; and yet it is almost the only way in which one in my situation, who is resolved to be an independent man, can get into Parliament. To come in by a popular election, in the present state of the representation, is quite impossible; to be placed there by some great lord, and to vote as he shall direct, is to be in a state of complete dependence; and nothing hardly remains but to owe a seat to the sacrifice of a part of one's fortune. It is true that many men who buy seats, do it as a matter of pecuniary speculation, as a profitable way of employing their money: they carry on a political trade; they buy their seats, and sell their votes. For myself, I can truly say that, by giving money for a seat, I shall make a sacrifice of my private property, merely that I may be enabled to serve the public. I know what danger there is of men's disguising from themselves the real motives of their actions; but it really does appear to me that it is from this motive alone I act.

JOE KENNEDY TO JOHN F. KENNEDY
"Don't buy a single vote more than necessary"

The sometimes insidious relationship between money and politics continues to this day. While campaigning for the presidency in 1960, John F. Kennedy poked fun at the role of money in elections. During a speech a few weeks before the election, he pulled out the following telegram he had received from his wealthy father, Joe Kennedy. It drew a big laugh from the crowd. Kennedy won the election in a cliff-hanger.

October 19, 1960
John F. Kennedy
3307 N Street W
Washington DC

Dear Jack:

Don't buy a single vote more than necessary. I'll be damned if I'm going to pay for a landslide.
Joe Kennedy

LONDON MERCHANTS TO BRITISH PARLIAMENT
"A great stagnation of the commerce"

The American Revolution was not just about democratic ideals, it was also about commerce. Americans objected to infringements on trade and business taxes imposed by the British Parliament. As the dispute between the American colonies and the English government approached the boiling point, trade between the Crown and the colonies all but collapsed, and London merchants saw commercial activity with their American counterparts drop 90 percent. Hoping to restore trade with America, London merchants wrote the British Parliament urging reconciliation.

January 23, 1775

Mr. Alderman Hayley said he had a petition from the merchants of the city of London concerned in the commerce to North America, to that honourable House, and desired leave to present the same, which being given, it was brought up and read, setting forth:

"That the petitioners are all essentially interested in the trade to North America, either as exporters and importers, or as venders of British and foreign goods for exportation to that country; and that the petitioners have exported, or sold for exportation, to the British colonies in North America, very large quantities of the manufacture of Great Britain and Ireland, and in particular the staple articles of woollen, iron, and linen, also those of cotton, silk, leather, pewter, tin, copper, and brass, with almost every British manufacture; . . . and that the petitioners have likewise exported, or sold for exportation, great quantities of the various species of goods imported into this kingdom from the East-Indies, part of which receive additional manufacture in Great Britain; and that the petitioners receive returns from North America to this kingdom directly, viz. pig and bar iron, timber, staves, naval stores, tobacco, rice, indigo, deer, and other skins, beaver and furs, train oil, whalebone, bees wax, pot and pearl ashes, drugs and dyeing woods, with some bullion, and also wheat flour, Indian corn and salted provisions, when, on account of scarcity in Great Britain, those articles are permitted to be imported; . . . and that the petitioners have great reason to believe, from the best informations they can obtain, that on the balance of this extensive commerce, there is now due from the colonies in North America, to the said city only, 2,000,000 l. sterling, and upwards; and that, by the direct commerce with the colonies, and the circuitous trade thereon depending, some thousands of ships and vessels are employed, and many thousands of seamen are bred and maintained, thereby increasing the naval strength and power of Great Britain; and that, in the year 1765, there was a great stagnation of the commerce between Great Britain and her colonies, in consequence of an Act for granting and applying certain stamp duties, and other duties, in the British colonies and plantations in America, by which the merchants trading to North America, and the artificers employed in the various manufactures consumed in those countries, were subjected to many hardships; and that, in the following year, the said Act was repealed, under an express declaration of the legislature, that the continuance of the said Act would be attended with many inconveniences, and might be productive of consequences greatly detrimental to the commercial interests of these kingdoms; upon which repeal, the trade to the British colonies immediately resumed its former flourishing state; and that in the year 1767, an Act passed for granting certain duties, to be paid in America, on tea, glass, red and white lead, painters' colours, paper, paste-board, mill-board, and scale-board, when the commerce with the colonies was again interrupted; and that in the year 1770, such parts of the said Act as imposed duties on glass, red and white lead, painters' colours, paper, paste-board, mill-board, and scale-board, were repealed, when the trade to America soon revived, except in the article of tea, on which a duty was continued, to be demanded on its importation into America, whereby that branch of our commerce was nearly lost; and that, in the year 1773, an Act passed, to allow a drawback of the duties of customs on the exportation of tea to his Majesty's colonies or plantations in America, and to empower the commissioners of the Treasury to grant licenses to the East India Company, to export tea, duty free; and by the operation of those and other laws, the minds of his Majesty's subjects in the British colonies have been greatly disquieted, a total stop is now put to the export trade with the greatest and most important part of North America, the public revenue is threatened with a large and fatal diminution, the petitioners with grievous distress, and thousands of industrious artificers and manufacturers with utter ruin; under these alarming circumstances, the petitioners receive no small comfort, from a persuasion that the representatives of the people, newly delegated to the most important of all trusts, will take the whole of these weighty matters into their most serious consideration; and therefore praying the House, that they will enter into a full and immediate examination of that system of commercial policy, which was formerly adopted, and uniformly maintained, to the happiness and advantage of both countries, and will apply such healing remedies as can alone restore and establish the commerce between Great Britain and her colonies on a permanent foundation; and that the petitioners may be heard by themselves, or agents, in support of the said petition."

EDWARD CARRINGTON TO ALEXANDER HAMILTON
"No Country under the sun, is capable of producing more than Virginia"

Treasury Secretary Alexander Hamilton, the first man to hold this position in America, took it upon himself to develop a comprehensive report aimed at creating a government policy to stimulate manufacturing. The U.S. economy in the 1790s relied almost entirely on agriculture, so Hamilton searched far and wide, gathering data and conducting surveys throughout the United States on the current condition of manufacturing in order to bolster his case.

Edward Carrington, a personal friend of George Washington's and the supervisor of revenue for Virginia, supplied the following letter to Hamilton about the status of manufacturing in Virginia. Virginia's heavy reliance on the labor-intensive tobacco farming, he wrote, prevented the development of a significant manufacturing sector. At the time, Virginia was the largest and wealthiest state in the fledgling nation, though it would lose this lead within thirty years as northern states embraced manufacturing and flourished.

Hamilton's Report on Manufactures, *delivered to Congress two months after this letter, urged government policies such as protective tariffs, transportation improvements, promoting immigration, encouraging invention, and regulation of goods produced to encourage manufacturing in the United States. The document helped shape the country's economic policy for more than a century.*

Richmond October 4th 1791

The enclosed papers contain parts of the information which I expect to furnish upon the subject of Manufactures in Virginia, and are transmitted agreeably to your request. These papers have come from the two lower Surveys of the district; the information they contain as to the particular neighbourhoods from which they are drawn, may be applied, with property to the whole of those Surveys: indeed, so equally do the people of Virginia go into Manufactures within themselves, that the application might be made to the whole Country, with only a few allowances, from a consideration of their respective staples, which I will in some degree enable you to make, upon the following principles. In regard to staples, Virginia is contemplated under three divisions, the Lower, the Middle, & the Upper: the first is comprehended between the Sea and the falls of our great rivers; the Second, between these falls and the blue ridge of Mountains—the latter takes all the Country beyond the Mountains.

The staples of the first are Indian corn principally, small crops of indifferent Tobacco, small crops of wheat, &, in some parts, lumber.

The Middle Country produces our great exports of Tobacco & wheat.

The Upper country produces Hemp, Flax & wheat principally, and small indifferent crops of Tobacco.

I have observed that the people of the whole Country, are in habits of Domestic Manufactures pretty equally, except that some allowances must be made on Account of field labour upon their respective staples, these are as follows; the staples of the lower country require moderate labour, and that at particular seasons of the year. The consequence is, that they have much leisure and can apply their hands to Manufacturing so far as to supply, not only the cloathing of the Whites, but of the Blacks also.

The great staple, Tobacco, in the Middle Country requires much labor when growing, and, what with fitting it for market and preparing the land for succeeding Crops, leaves but little time for the same hands to Manufacture: the consequence is, that the latter business is carried on only by the white females in poor families, and, in wealthy families, under the Eye of the Mistress, by female slaves drawn out of the Estates for that purpose, aided by the superfluous time of a superabundance of house-servants; the consequence is, that less is manufactured here than in the lower Country, Yet the difference is, I believe, no greater than as to the cloathing of the field slaves, for which purpose Kendal Cotton, oznabrigs, & hempen rolls are purchased, but the owner of every plantations tans the hides of the Cattle which are killed or casually die, and, by that means, supplies the slaves in shoes for winter.

The staples of the upper Country require somewhat more field labour than those of the lower, and much less than those of the Middle, & having however but few slaves, and being distant from foreign intercourse, the people depend principally upon home Manufactures, and, at least, equal the lower Country in them.

As to raw materials, no Country under the sun, is capable of producing more than Virginia.—the lower country produces fine Cotton & Wool, and, both might be encreased even to satisfy great foreign demands—in many parts good flax is also made. The Middle Country produces fine Cotton, but the most valuable staples of Wheat and Tobacco, confine the production to the demands of the private Manufactures of the Country itself—it is also well adapted to Hemp & Flax: of the first, some is produced for market; of the latter, every family makes for its own use: to some extent Wool is also produced.

The Upper Country supplies our Markets with great quantities of hemp, said to be equal to any in the World, flax is also here produced in high perfection, and in great quantities, the people using it for purposes to which, Cotton is applied below: for supplying the Article of Wool this part of Virginia is so favorable that large droves of sheep go from it, to the lower Town Markets.

The mountainous parts of Virginia, abound in Iron Ore, from which most of the Iron, and some of the steel, used in the state, are supplied, and the productions of both might be so increased as to make great exports. We have also a valuable lead mine, in the Southwestern part of the Upper Country, from which new Manufactures are daily coming into practice, such as sheet lead for roofing, shot &c.—there is a shot factory in Richmond, well established by the present worker of this Mine, and the same hand has furnished the lead for covering the roof our Capitol, or State House. This mine was, during the War, worked under the public direction of this state, and supplied all the lead used in the Southern service: supplies of it also went to the Main Army, but whether for the whole service, I will not undertake to say.

As to regular Trades we have but few, they are, however, encreasing daily—in the upper Country, there are several fulling mills, from which good Cloth is seen. I will endeavour to obtain samples.

I have now endeavored to give you, in addition to the enclosed papers, such information as will furnish a general idea of the Manufactures throughout the Commonwealth, and having been tolerably attentive to these circumstances, for several Years, as I have passed through the various parts of the Country, am persuaded you may rely upon it, as well founded. I have been led to do it, from a consideration, that the approach of the session, requires an early communication, and from the information expected from the upper Inspectors, having not arrived: When I receive the reports, they shall be forwarded immediately.

I beg you to be assured, that this business has been attended with no material trouble or inconvenience, and that it has given pleasure to both myself & the Inspectors that you requested and our assistance in obtaining the desired information.

I have the Honor to be
With great respect
Sir
Your Most Obt. St.
Ed Carrington
Supervisor D: Virg

LETTERS TO TREASURY SECRETARY ALBERT GALLATIN, ON ABOLISHING THE U.S. MINT
"If the coinage of copper is continued"

Concerned about the high cost of striking coins, the federal government considered shutting down the U.S. Mint in the early 1800s. The following three letters to Secretary of the Treasury Albert Gallatin reflect some of the business and financial issues involved in the decision.

Mint of the United States, Philadelphia

February 27, 1802

Sir:

In answer to your letter which I had the honor of receiving by this day's post, I must inform you, that, having met with great difficulties the two last years, in obtaining a full supply of copper, from various causes attending the means of payment, I wrote to Mr. Boueton, early in the Fall, promising to make remittances, during the winter, for the next shipment. There will be due him on such shipment, about twelve or fifteen thousand dollars, which I am striving to provide for, by finishing the cents as fast as possible.

This contract is obligatory on us, and must be paid for; but I shall be able to prevent any further shipment, at any time before the first of May, by which, I hope, we shall know the mind of the Legislature on the subject of the mint.

We have near twenty tons of planchettes on hand, and which will keep us employed during the winter, but the expected shipment will remain for the summer's work, if the coinage of copper is continued.

I shall, therefore, expect your warrant, as requested, and shall push finishing the planchettes on hand, as fast as possible, to make good the residue of the payment.

As to importing the cents complete from Europe, it can certainly be done for a trifling sum above the price of the planchettes, say about £20 sterling per ton, did the policy of the Government admit of it. Of this, I would not venture to determine, the Legislature, alone, being competent to that purpose. I once stated it to a committee of both Houses, but they determined that it would be dangerous to measure, and would not hearken to it.

An importation of cents, complete, would not diminish the security of having good copper, but it would hazard the running of a flood of cents, lighter than allowed by law, into the United States, and the difficulty of venting the evil would be very great. It would be a greater security to Government to have the coinage of copper executed here by contract, which might be done without expense to the Union, provided Government would take the cents.

I have the honor to be, with great respect, sir, your obedient humble servant,

Elias Boudinot

Director

The Hon. the Secretary of Treasury, Washington.

Mint, Philadelphia

March 4th, 1802

Sir: The probability of the abolition of the mint establishment, induces me, thus early, to state to you, that, if the Legislature should not be disposed altogether to abandon the copper coinage, or might be willing, after repealing the laws establishing the mint, to allow of a copper coinage, provided it may be done without any expense to the public, I would solicit your interests and influence to promote a proposition of that kind, which I do not presume on, only so far as you may deem it consist with the public good; in connexion with which, I flatter myself you will not be wanting, independent of any other claim I may have, or pretension to public patronage.

However, I need not omit informing you, that, on the first establishment of the mint, I relinquished a profession, at least equally productive and beneficial as that of the engraver's place in the mint, which I have filled, and I believe without reproach, ever since; by the loss of which, I shall be left without resource, being so long out of the practice of my former profession, that I feel an incapacity to prosecute it with any more effect. I, therefore, submit the following proposition for your consideration, to the consideration of Congress, or to the Department where it may properly belong:

That I may be vested with the exclusive privilege, according to law, of coining cents of the United States, as well from abroad as within the realm, under such restrictions and provisions, either with respect to time or quantity, as Congress, in their wisdom, may deem proper; that the cents shall be of the present weight and quality, and that they shall be coined free of all expense to Government, excepting that of receiving them when coined, and paying the nominal amount.

Should the above propositions meet with your approbation or otherwise, I should still be happy to know your determination to forward them or not; if the former, I would beg to know the most proper mode of introducing it to Congress, whether by petition, and how conceived, or otherwise.

I am sir, with the highest respect, your most obedient servant,

Robert Scot

Albert Gallatin, Esq.

Secretary of the Treasury

City of Washington.

Mint of the United States, Philadelphia, March 22, 1802.

Sir:

I am honored with your letter of the 10th instant, and hasten to give you the best answer that I can, with regard to the real and personal estate of the mint establishment, etc. this consists of—

Two lots on Seventh street, between Market and Arch streets, 20 feet each on Seventh street, and extending back about 100 feet, with a dwelling house on the north lot, and a shell of a house on the south lot, which last lot widens on the rear to about 60 feet, on which the stable stands. These lots pay a ground rent of $27.50 per annum.

A lot on Sugar alley, at the rear of the above, 20 feet front on the alley, and about 100 feet deep.

A frame building, improved for a large furnace, in the commons at the north end of Sixth street, of little value, the ground being merely loaned to us.

As to personal estate, this consists wholly of the copper planchettes on hand, amounting to about 22 tons.

Three horses, good for little but for the use of the mint. The machinery of the mint, of no value but for the use of the mint.

Five striking presses.

One milling machine.

Five pair of rollers, great and small.

One drawing machine.

Three pair of smith's bellows.

A set of blacksmith's tools.

A large number of hubs and dies, on hand, of different denominations.

Carpenter's tools.

Seven stoves.

One turning lathe.

Six scale beams, scales, and weights.

Two sets assay scales, and sundry adjusting scales.

Furniture in the clerk's rooms.

Various implements used in the several departments.

About 2,000 bushels of charcoals.

Engraver's tools, pots, bottles, etc.; an old horse, cart, and gears.

About 2,000 fire brick; a considerable quantity of old iron.

It is impossible to ascertain the value of these articles, as most of them are of but little consequence, except for the use of the mint, or to persons who may intend to put them to the like uses; and if sold at public sale, probably will not bring half their real value. The machinery of the mint may last a year longer, with small repair. The horses may, also, last another year, but must then, at farthest, be replaced by others.

If it should be thought best to continue the mint, the establishment should be rendered permanent, and the machinery should be moved by steam instead of horses, which would, in some measure, reduce the annual expenses of labor, as almost the whole of it could be carried on with the same original force. Our lots are much too small, by which we are greatly cramped as to room. They are now very valuable, being in the heart of the city; their price would purchase a very advantageous lot in a less public place, and buildings might be now planned, so as to reduce the expenses of a mint. But I am perfectly satisfied, that no modification of the mint could be contrived to lessen them below seventeen or eighteen thousand dollars per annum; though if a larger quantity of bullion could, by any means, be provided, a greater quantity of coin could be annually made with the same expense, although I am, individually, of opinion, that its present issue, of about five hundred thousand dollars annually, in addition to the current coin of the Union, is sufficient for the present welfare of the United States.

It is the absolute necessity of strict and regular checks, throughout the whole establishment, that makes the expense of the mint so great, and this cannot be dispensed with, under any modification that can be proposed. I verily believe, that, under no given circumstance, can the necessary coin of the United States be produced with safety to the Government, at a much less expense than it is at present; and I believe, that, in the consideration of the subject, it would not be safe to estimate the expense, at any rate, much under twenty thousand dollars.

In the above estimate of expenses, it should be remembered that the copper cents may produce a profit of five thousand dollars per annum, that ought to be credited against the expenditures of the mint in future, which reduces the amount considerably.

I have the honor to be, very respectfully, sir, your obedient humble servant,

Elias Boudinot
Director
The Hon. the Secretary of the Treasury, Washington.

W. HARRISON TO THADDEUS STEVENS
"The Bankrupt law is a relief"

Responding to the financial trauma that the Civil War caused to the South, Congress passed a bill in 1867 creating the first uniform bankruptcy law. Through it, government could play the role of disinterested arbitrator and establish national rules for resolving severe financial stress. The law allowed anyone living in the United States owing more than $300 to file for bankruptcy, provided he or she was willing "to surrender all his estates and effects for the benefit of his creditors." A uniform bankruptcy law is now considered one of the fundamental planks of a functioning free-market economy.

This letter from a debtor in North Carolina to Congressman Thaddeus Stevens describes the plight of Southerners who had borrowed money before and during the Civil War and articulates his wishes that the government go even further to help the South. The economic impact of the war there was devastating. Cities and plantations were laid waste by invading Union armies and a four-year blockade virtually shut down the Southern economy. In addition, slaves had constituted much of the South's wealth prior to the war. When they were freed, their owners' net worth plunged even further.

Stevens was a leading Republican congressman who vigorously advocated tough Reconstruction policies to punish the South. He opposed the bankruptcy law.

Battleboro N.C. 13 March [1867]

Honr. Thad. Stevens

Dear Sir,

As you seem to be a friend to all honest men, and a supporter of humanity, I would like to call your attention to a subject of very great concern to the people of the South. There is here a vast amount of individual indebtedness created and in existence previous to Lee's surrender. The means left with which to liquidate this indebtedness bears but a small proportion to the amount available at the time of their creation. Creditors are clamorous for the last dollar and last pound of flesh; Debtors think it is not just to make an insurance company of them, against unexpected and great national calamities— That many of these debts are due for confederate notes, for corn at $100 pr bl, for Bank bills &c &c, and that justice demands that these claims together with those existing before the war should be reduced to a paralel with the means left in the country. Generally they think about one half of these amounts existing before the war should be paid—and nothing for claims created during the war.

It is unnecessary to extend remarks on the subject—as you will comprehend the whole matter at once when you devote to it a consideration. Reasonable relief from any action of Congress would be hailed as a 'god send' by a majority of our people. The Bankrupt law is a relief to some extent— But this requires a full surrender of all to pay debts which debtors think should be scaled to a minimum below what they call for. This letter is a private one and the writer would be obliged if you have the time for your private views on the subject; If upon reflection you think the subject worthy of congressional action. It will be for you to inaugurate a measure calculated to secure an invaluable blessing to our people— and their lasting gratitude. The suits in our courts are more numerous than ever before. The costs alone are likely to amount to a sum greater than all our taxes combined. The lawyers and creditors like ravenous wolves—pressing poor debtors to the wall—declaring that it is unconstitutional to do anything for their relief— Hoping to hear soon from you I am Sir very respectfully

W. Harrison

P.S. would like to get your assistance in establishing a Post Office at this place—to be called Valleycot—we have a hundred petitioners.

K. TAKAHIRA TO ELIHU ROOT
"Equal opportunity for commerce and industry in China"

Ambassador Takahira of Japan and Secretary of State Elihu Root of the United States exchanged a series of letters in the early 1900s setting parameters for their countries' commercial interests in China and the Pacific Ocean. Over the next 40 years, the gradual breakdown of the agreement, which was set forth in the letter below, led to serious economic disputes climaxing with the Japanese surprise attack on the American fleet at Pearl Harbor in 1941.

The Japanese Ambassador to the Secretary of State

Imperial Japanese Embassy

Washington, November 30, 1908

Sir:

The exchange of views between us, which has taken place at the several interviews which I have recently had the honor of holding with you, has shown that Japan and the United States holding important outlying insular possessions in the region of the Pacific Ocean, the Governments of the two countries are animated by a common aim, policy, and intention in that region.

Believing that a frank avowal of that aim, policy, and intention would not only tend to strengthen the relations of friendship and good neighborhood, which have immemorially existed between Japan and the United States, but would materially contribute to the preservation of the general peace, the Imperial Government have authorized me to present to you an outline of their understanding of that common aim, policy and intention.

1. It is the wish of the two Governments to encourage the free and peaceful development of their commerce on the Pacific Ocean.

2. The policy of both Governments, uninfluenced by any aggressive tendencies, is directed to the maintenance of the existing status quo in the region above mentioned and to the defense of the principle of equal opportunity for commerce and industry in China.

3. They are accordingly firmly resolved reciprocally to respect the territorial possessions belonging to each other in said region.

4. They are also determined to preserve the common interest of all powers in China by supporting by all pacific means at their disposal the independence and integrity of China and the principle of equal opportunity for commerce and industry of all nations in that Empire.

5. Should any event occur threatening the status quo as above described or the principle of equal opportunity as above defined, it remains for the two Governments to communicate with each other in order to arrive at an understanding as to what measures they may consider it useful to take.

If the foregoing outline accords with the view of the Government of the United States, I shall be gratified to receive your confirmation.

I take this opportunity to renew to your excellency the assurance of my highest consideration.

K. Takahira

HUEY P. LONG TO CHARLES STAIR
"I want every damned man who wants a telephone to have a telephone"

Railing against business interests has a long history in American politics. Criticizing utilities for profiteering and demanding that businesses distribute their products more widely at lower prices are staples of populist tradition. Louisiana politician Huey P. Long may have set the standard for populist flamboyance and using the power of government to browbeat businesses into submission. He wrote this letter to a local telephone company shortly before being elected governor.

August 28, 1924
Mr. Chas. A. Stair, La. Mgr.,
Cumberland Telephone & Telegraph Co.,
New Orleans, La.

Dear Sir:

It doesn't make a bit of difference with me how many telephones you promised. What I am interested in is one thing only:

I want every damned man who wants a telephone to have a telephone, and I want you to get your affairs in shape that you can give every human being a phone who wants one. No other kind of program is worth anything to me or this state. I am covered up, knee deep, with people in this town and the surrounding territory trying to get telephones and can't get them. We are in just as bad shape as ever, so far as I am concerned. I have been pretty patient with this thing, but my patience has reached the absolute extreme limit. I am damned disgusted with the way it has been running and don't intend to continue to condone it.

Now, this means exactly the words and terms stated here.

Sincerely yours,
Huey P. Long

JOHN MAYNARD KEYNES TO FRANKLIN D. ROOSEVELT

"The object of recovery is to increase the national output"

Renowned British economist John Maynard Keynes engaged in a correspondence with President Franklin D. Roosevelt on ways to use the full might of the federal government to pull the United States out of the depths of the Great Depression.

Economic orthodoxy at the time frowned upon governments spending deep budget deficits on borrowed money for purposes other than war. Keynes, however, saw government fiscal policy as a vehicle for priming a nation's economic pump. During depressions, Keynes argued, it made sense for a government to borrow money to stimulate the economy.

Roosevelt's New Deal policies reflected much of Keynes's economic theories. Starting with Roosevelt's election in 1932, the two men exchanged letters and met once to explore the practicalities of applying economic theory to the realities of a severely depressed economy.

The first letter below was written as an "open letter" to Roosevelt, and was published in newspapers shortly before a meeting between the two men. The subsequent letters were written several years later, after Roosevelt relaxed some of his aggressive economic programs as the economy started to improve. Economic activity, however, plunged again when Roosevelt tightened his fiscal policies.

December 30, 1933

An Open Letter to President Roosevelt

You have made yourself the trustee for those in every country who seek to mend the evils of our condition by reasoned experiment within the framework of the existing social system.

You are engaged on a double task, recovery and reform. For the first, speed and quick results are essential. The second may be urgent, too; but haste will be injurious.

The object of recovery is to increase the national output.

Broadly speaking, an increase of output cannot occur unless by the operation of one or other of three factors. Individuals must be induced to spend more out of their existing incomes, or the business world must be induced, either by increased confidence in the prospects or by a lower rate of interest, to create additional current incomes in the hands of their employees, which is what happens when either the working or the fixed capital of the country is being increased; or public authority must be called in aid to create additional current incomes through the expenditure of borrowed or printed money.

In bad times the first factor cannot be expected to work on a sufficient scale. The second factor will only come in as the second wave of attack on the slump, after the tide has been turned by the expenditures of public authority. It is, therefore, only from the third factor that we can expect the initial major impulse.

Now there are indications that two technical fallacies may have affected the policy of your administration. The first relates to the part played in recovery by rising prices. Rising prices are to be welcomed because they are usually a symptom of rising output and employment. When more purchasing power is spent, one expects rising output at rising prices. Since there cannot be rising output without rising prices, it is essential to insure that the recovery shall not be held back by the insufficiency of the supply of money to support the increased monetary turnover.

But there is much less to be said in favor of rising prices if they are brought about at the expense of rising output. Thus rising prices caused by deliberately increasing prime costs or by restricting output have a vastly inferior value to rising prices, which are the natural result of an increase in the nation's purchasing power.

I do not mean to impugn the social justice and social expediency of the redistribution of incomes aimed at by the NRA [National Recovery Act] and by the various schemes for agricultural restriction. But too much emphasis on the remedial value of a higher price-level as an object in itself may lead to serious misapprehension of the part prices can play in the techniques of recovery.

Thus, as the prime mover in the first stage of the technique of recovery, I lay overwhelming emphasis on the increase of national purchasing power resulting from governmental expenditure which is financed by loans, and is not merely a transfer through taxation, from existing incomes.

In the past, orthodox finance has regarded a war as the only legitimate excuse for creating employment by government expenditure. You, Mr. President, having cast off such fetters, are free to engage in the interests of peace and prosperity, the technique which hitherto has only been allowed to serve the purposes of war and destruction.

The setback American recovery experienced this past Autumn was the predictable consequence of the failure of your administration to organize any material increase in new loan expenditure during your first six months of office.

The other set of fallacies, of which I fear the influence, arises out of a crude economic doctrine commonly known as the quantity theory of money. Rising output and rising incomes will suffer a setback sooner or later if the quantity of money is rigidly fixed. Some people seem to infer from this that output and income can be raised by increasing the quantity of money. But that is like trying to get fat by buying a larger belt. It is a most misleading thing to stress the quantity of money, which is only a limiting factor, rather than the volume of expenditure, which is the operative factor.

It is even more foolish an application of the same ideas to believe that there is a mathematical relation between the price of gold and the prices of other things.

These criticisms do not mean that I have weakened in my advocacy of a managed currency. But the recent gyrations of the dollar have looked to me more like a gold standard on the booze than the ideal managed currency of my dreams.

If you were to ask me what I would suggest in concrete terms for the immediate future, I would reply thus:

You can announce that you will control the dollar exchange by buying and selling gold and foreign currencies at a definite figure so as to avoid wide or meaningless fluctuations, with a right to shift the parities at any time, but with a declared intention only so to do either to correct a serious want of balance in America's international receipts and payments or to meet a shift in your domestic price level relative to price levels abroad.

In the field of domestic policy, I put in the forefront a large volume of loan expenditures under government auspices.

I put in the second place the maintenance of cheap and abundant credit, in particular the reduction of the long-term rate of interest.

With these adaptations or enlargements of your existing policies, I should expect a successful outcome with great confidence. How much that would mean, not only to the national prosperity of the United States and the whole world, but in comfort to men's minds through a restoration of their faith in the wisdom and the power of government!

To Franklin Delano Roosevelt, 1 February 1938

Private and Personal

Dear Mr President,

You received me so kindly when I visited you some three years ago that I make bold to send you some bird's eye impressions which I have formed as to the business position in the United States. You will appreciate that I write from a distance, that I have not re-visited the United States since you saw me, and that I have access to a few more sources of information than those publicly available. But sometimes in some respects there may be advantages to these limitations! At any rate, those things which I see, I see very clearly.

1. I should agree that the present recession is partly due to an "error of optimism" which led to an overestimation of future demand, when orders were being placed in the first half of this year. If this were all, there would not be too much to worry about. It would only need time to effect a readjustment;—though, even so, the recovery would only be up to the point required to take care of the revised estimate of current demand, which might fall appreciably short of the prosperity reached last spring.

2. But I am quite sure that this is not all. There is a much more troublesome underlying influence. The recovery was mainly due to the following factors:—

(i)   the solution of the credit and insolvency problems, and the establishment of easy short-term money;

(ii) the creation of an adequate system of relief for the unemployed;

(iii) public works and other investments aided by Government funds or guarantees;

(iv) investment in the instrumental goods required to supply the increased demand for consumption goods;

(v)   the momentum of the recovery thus initiated.

Now of these (i) was a prior condition of recovery, since it is no use creating a demand for credit, if there is no supply. But an increased supply will not by itself generate an adequate demand. The influence of (ii) evaporates as employment improves, so that there is a dead point beyond which this factor cannot carry the economic system. Recourse to (iii) has been greatly curtailed in the past year. (iv) and (v) are functions of the forward movement and cease—indeed (v) is reversed—as soon as the position fails to improve further. The benefit from the momentum of the recovery as such is at the same time the most important and the most dangerous factor in the upward movement. It requires for its continuance, not merely the maintenance of recovery, but always *further* recovery. This it always flatters the early stages and steps from under just when support is most needed. It was largely, I think, a failure to allow for this which caused the "error of optimism" last year.

Unless, therefore, the above factors were supplemented by others in due course, the present slump could have been predicted with absolute certainty. It is true that the existing policies will prevent the slump from proceeding to such a disastrous degree as last time. But they will not by themselves—at any rate, not without a large-scale recourse to (iii)—maintain prosperity at a reasonable level.

3. Now one had hoped that the needed supplementary factors would be organised in time. It was obvious what these were—namely increased investment in durable goods such as housing, public utilities and transport. One was optimistic about this because in the United States at the present time the opportunities, indeed the necessity, for such developments were unexampled. Can your Administration escape criticism for the failure of these factors to mature?

Take housing. When I was with you three and a half years ago the necessity for effective new measures was evident. I remember vividly my conversations with Riefler at that time. But what happened? Next to nothing. The handling of the housing problem has been really wicked. I hope that the new measures recently taken will be more successful. I have not the knowledge to say. But they will take time, and I would urge the great importance of expediting and yet further aiding them. Housing is by far the best aid to recovery because of the large and continuing scale of potential demand; and because the sources of its finance are largely independent of the stock exchanges. I should advise putting most of your eggs in this basket, *caring* about this more than about anything, and making absolutely sure that they are being hatched without delay. In this country we partly depended for many years on direct subsidies. There are few more proper objects for such than working-class houses. If a direct subsidy is required to get a move on (we gave our subsidies *through* the local authorities), it should be given without delay or hesitation.

Next utilities. There seems to be a deadlock. Neither your policy nor anyone else's is able to take effect. I think that the litigation by the utilities is senseless and ill-advised. But a great deal of what is alleged against the wickedness of holding companies as such is surely wide of the mark. It does not draw the right line of division between what should be kept and what discarded. It arises too much out of what is dead and gone. The real criminals have cleared out long ago. I should doubt if the controls existing today are of much *personal* value to anyone. No one has suggested a procedure by which the eggs can be unscrambled. Why not tackle the problem by insisting that the *voting power* should belong to the real owners of the equity, and leave the existing *organisations* undisturbed, so long as the voting power is so rearranged (e.g. by bringing in preferred stockholders) that it cannot be controlled by the holders of a minority of the equity?

Is it not for you to decide either to make real peace or to be much more drastic the other way? Personally, I think there is a great deal to be said for the ownership of all the utilities by publicly owned boards. But if public opinion is not yet ripe for this, what is the object of chasing the utilities round the lot every other week? If I was in your place, I should buy out the utilities at fair prices in every district where the situation was ripe for doing so, and announce that the ultimate ideal was to make this policy nation-wide. But elsewhere I would make peace on liberal terms, guaranteeing fair earnings on new investments and a fair basis of valuation in the event of the public taking them over hereafter. The process of evolution will take at least a generation. Meanwhile a policy of competing plants with losses all round is a ramshackle notion.

Finally the railroads. The position there seems to be exactly what it was three years ago. They remain, as they were then, potential sources of substantial demand for new capital expenditure. Whether hereafter they are publicly owned or remain in private hands, it is a matter of national importance that they should be made solvent. Nationalise them if the time is ripe. If not, take pity on the overwhelming problems of the present managements. And here too let the dead bury their dead. (To an Englishman, you Americans, like the Irish, are so terribly historically minded!)

I am afraid I am going beyond my province. But the upshot is this. A convincing policy, whatever its details may be, for promoting large-scale investment under the above heads is an urgent necessity. Those things take time. Far too much precious time has passed.

4. I must not encumber this letter with technical suggestions for reviving the capital market. This is important. But not so important as the revival of the sources of demand. If demand and confidence reappear, the problems of the capital market will not seem so difficult as they do today. Moreover it is a highly technical problem.

5. Businessmen have a different set of delusions from politicians; and need, therefore, different handling. They are, however, much milder than politicians, at the same time allured and terrified by the glare of publicity, easily persuaded to be "patriots", perplexed, bemused, indeed terrified, yet only too anxious to take a cheerful view, vain perhaps but very unsure of themselves, pathetically responsive to a kind word. You could do anything you liked with them, if you would treat them (even the big ones), not as wolves and tigers, but as domestic animals by nature, even though they are have been badly brought up and not trained as you would wish. It is a mistake to think that they are more *immoral* than politicians. If you work them into the surly, obstinate, terrified mood, of which domestic animals, wrongly handled, are so capable, the nation's burdens will not get carried to market; and in the end

public opinion will veer their way. Perhaps you will rejoin that I have got quite a wrong idea of what all the back-chat amounts to. Nevertheless I record accurately how it strikes observers here.

6. Forgive the candour of these remarks. They come from an enthusiastic well-wisher of you and your policies. I accept the view that durable investment must come increasingly under state direction. I sympathise with Mr Wallace's agricultural policies. I believe that the [Securities and Exchange Commission] is doing splendid work. I regard the growth of collective bargaining as essential. I approve minimum wage and hours regulation. I was altogether on your side the other day, when you deprecated a policy of general wage reductions as useless in present circumstances. But I am terrified lest progressive causes in all the democratic countries should suffer injury, because you have taken too lightly the risk to their prestige which would result from a failure measured in terms of immediate prosperity. There *need* be no failure. But the maintenance of prosperity in the modern world is extremely *difficult*, and it is so easy to lose precious time.

I am, Mr President
Yours with great respect and faithfulness,
J. M. Keynes

From Franklin Delano Roosevelt, 3 March 1938

Personal and Private

Dear Mr Keynes,

I am in receipt of your letter of February first, which I enjoyed reading. It was very pleasant and encouraging to know that you are in agreement with so much of the Administration's economic program. This confirmation coming from so eminent an economist is indeed welcome.

Your analysis of the present business situation is very interesting. The emphasis you put upon the need for stimulating housing construction is well placed, and I hope that our efforts will be successful in removing the barriers to the revival of this industry.

The course of democracy and world peace is of deep concern to me. Domestic prosperity, you will agree, is one of the most effective contributions the United States can make to their maintenance. You will likewise appreciate, I am sure, that prosperity in the United States will be more potent in attaining the ends we are all interested in if other democracies strive persistently for similar objectives.

I remember your previous visit very well and I hope we may have the opportunity to meet again.

Very sincerely yours,
Franklin D. Roosevelt

To Franklin Delano Roosevelt, 25 March 1938

Dear Mr President,

It is very good of you to have written in acknowledgement of my letter. I do not mean to give you the trouble of doing so again by sending another brief comment. But further experience since I wrote does seem to show that you are treading a very dangerous middle path. You must either give more encouragement to business or take over more of their functions yourself. If public opinion is not ready for the latter, then it is necessary to wait until public opinion is educated. Your present policies seem to presume that you possess more power than you actually have.

Today, however, our thoughts are occupied with other things than economic prosperity. I venture to enclose an article which I have published today ["A Positive Peace Programme"]. At any rate the poem which serves as its motto is very good. The tragedy is that the right-minded show no indication of supporting one another. You will be reluctant to support us; we are reluctant to support France; France is reluctant to support Spain. At long last we shall get together. But how much harm will have been done by then?

Yours very sincerely,

J. M. Keynes

DAVID SARNOFF TO FRANKLIN D. ROOSEVELT
"Encourage industry to stimulate employment"

In addition to using government action as a means of direct stimulus to the economy, several leading figures urged Roosevelt to develop tax and business incentives for companies to invest and hire more workers. David Sarnoff, founder of the Radio Corporation of America, made this proposal in person and through the mail. He also called for the government to bolster its efforts in gathering basic statistical information in order to better gauge the condition of the economy. Prior to Roosevelt, there were no reliable statistics for measuring such basics as the national unemployment rate.

June 12, 1936

President Franklin D. Roosevelt:

During my recent visit to your office in Washington, I took the liberty of making several suggestions to you orally and you were good enough to ask me to set them forth to you in a letter. I am sending this communication to you so that it may reach you about the time of your return from your present trip.

The suggestions I respectfully submit for your consideration are as follows:

There appears to be a great deal of controversy as to the actual number of people in our country now unemployed. Various estimates of the number have been made by different agencies, and some of them differ substantially from others. None of these estimates contain definite information as to the exact number of unemployed in the different states and cities, the nature of the work in which those now out of employment were previously engaged, their age, sex, and citizenship, and whether or not they are employable at this time. Already one hears talk in various parts of the country of the shortage of skilled labor and, indeed, of unskilled labor.

Since the subject of unemployment is doubtless one of the major problems, if not the major problem, of the country facing all of us and since a great part of legislation, both enacted and likely to be enacted, must necessarily take this problem of unemployment into account, I firmly believe it would be helpful to those in and out of government to have before them the precise facts of the situation.

With the foregoing in mind, it occurs to me to suggest that there be designated an existing governmental agency in each local community—for example, the local post office or the machinery of the draft—to which all those now on relief or unemployed be requested to come and fill out a questionnaire which would give the answers to the questions above indicated and such other information as might be desired by the government. The Department of Labor could doubtless prepare a simple form of questionnaire calling for all the information on the subject which might be desired.

In order to facilitate such a program of inquiry, the broadcasting stations of the country, and in particular the networks, might be asked to make a suitable announcement over the air each day or evening for a consecutive period of thirty days, encouraging those concerned to cooperate with the government by promptly filling out the questionnaire at the place designated in their respective locality. The President of the United States might launch this appeal officially, and this would doubtless stimulate early response. . . .

The completed questionnaires should be mailed by the local agencies to a central office in Washington designated for this purpose. At such place, the questionnaires could be tabulated and the essential information summarized for ready reference. If the proposed idea proved workable, the central office in Washington could devise plans for keeping this information up to date, in order that a revised statement of the facts and figures could be made available monthly. In this way, there would be before you and the country current facts on this vital subject of unemployment.

My second suggestion is that either in the tax bill now under consideration or in a separate bill there be included a provision giving employers of labor abatement of income taxes in direct ratio to their increased employment of labor for a stated period—perhaps two years. The effects of this provision might apply to such increases in employment as are made from the date of the passage of the bill. The object of this suggestion is to encourage industry to increase employment speedily. The Treasury Department experts could doubtless devise a suitable formula dealing more specifically than I am in this letter with the ratio of tax abatement to increased employment.

To the extent that this idea would prove effective in operation, the government would be relieved from payments now made to those on relief who might be absorbed by industry. Increased employment means increased consumption, which, in turn, means increased business and profits and therefore increased tax returns to the government. Thus what the government might yield on the one hand it should more than regain on the other. Again, should the idea not result in increased employment by industry, then of course there would be no abatement in taxes and thus no decrease in tax revenue to the government.

The creation and development of new industries were never more vitally necessary than now. These mean added work, increased employment, new national wealth, and wider opportunities for those in our country. New enterprises necessarily involve greater risks for capital than established businesses do. Those who have capital to invest are often more reluctant to risk that capital in times of depression than they are in periods of prosperity. This reluctance and this doubt on the part of owners of idle capital are cumulative in their adverse effects. When to these effects there is added the obligation to pay a high income tax on profits which might be derived from venturing into the unknown, the tendency is to avoid risking the definite principal for indefinite profits. This vicious circle results in idle money, and its unemployment is also devastating in its effects upon society.

In view of the above, my third suggestion for your consideration is that in order to put idle money to work, especially in new enterprises, the tax bill now under discussion, or a new tax bill, incorporate a provision relieving corporations or individuals who invest their funds in the creation and development of new enterprises from a large measure of taxes on profits earned on their investments in such enterprises during a reasonable period of time, at least such time as may be necessary to enable the investor to determine the stability of the enterprise or to obtain a reasonable portion of his principal. Such a provision would encourage idle capital to seek investment in new enterprises and would also serve the purpose of retaining in such new enterprises the capital needed for their rapid development.

I recognize the need of defining "new enterprises" specifically if this suggestion should prove of interest. I have not attempted to do so in this letter because such definition can best be devised by the experts in the various government departments who are in contact with the many industries of this country.

David Sarnoff

COLONEL GEORG THOMAS TO ADOLF HITLER
"The Führer should assume economic leadership"

Taking a strikingly different approach from what the architects of a free market proposed, the German military during the Great Depression of the 1930s urged direct government control of the economy. Dictatorial economic power was envisioned as a preliminary step toward developing a wartime economy.

The plea came in the wake of more than a decade of economic weakness and occasional financial chaos. The military, industry and the Nazi Party was fed up with meddlesome politicians, fiscal policies aimed at spurring consumption, and a plunging balance of payments.

Colonel Georg Thomas, head of the military's Defense Economy and Weapons Bureau, urged Adolf Hitler in 1934—five years before the start of World War II—to seize the reins of power over the German economy. Less than two weeks later, a law was passed giving the Minister of Economics virtually unlimited fiscal power.

Although the German economic policy represented a full-throttled application of Keynes's advocacy of the government borrowing money to stimulate the economy, Keynes did not support spending that money on the military and strongly opposed Hitler's use of authoritarian power to implement economic policies.

20 June 1934

The Reich Defense Ministry has for years been pointing out the necessity of preparing the economy for the event of war. It has demanded stockpiling, revealed the dangers of the loss of foreign exchange and the collapse of exports for the defense of the country and has especially requested the regulation of the peacetime economy in accordance with the needs of war. Only the present Reich Government has decided to fulfill these demands, but unfortunately economic developments threaten to nullify these efforts which have hardly begun.

The information from industry and the reports from the supervisory offices for raw materials show clearly that the raw materials situation is becoming daily more acute. Not only does this endanger the government's work program, but also the basis for an operational commitment of the Wehrmacht is becoming more and more remote and everywhere the questions is being asked, What is the point of a larger army if it lacks supplies, its lifeblood? The raw materials situation is taken far more seriously by the business community than by the Reich Economics Ministry, and since everybody is clear about the fact that we are in the middle of an economic war, it is incomprehensible that decisions are not taken to overcome the danger which threatens. For months we have noticed the drain of foreign exchange followed by the melting away of stocks of raw materials, but so far there has been no firm intervention to remove the danger, with a few exceptions which have proved insufficient. What has happened to all the lessons we have learned from the Great War in the economic field? Because of struggles between capitalist interest groups, the wishes of Party officers, and the misguided interventions and opinions of individuals, no decisions are taken. . . .

The economic crisis, which is imminent because of the raw materials and foreign exchange situation, is recognized in all informed quarters; the will of the Führer to overcome it is irreversible. Why is the nation not urged to undergo self-denial and restrictions in order to overcome this economic crisis? The measures of individual leaders of the Labor Front run directly counter to these requirements. In this situation employees should not be lectured about the necessity for a higher standard of living, which leads everywhere to the desire for wage increases. The Labor Front imposes financial demands on employers, which small and medium-sized industry cannot endure in the long run and which are not intelligible so long as the Labor Front spends large amounts on buying luxurious houses and similar extravagances. Actions of this kind weaken the financial power of industry and what must be particularly avoided, weaken confidence in the leadership.

These impressions of economic life today keep reappearing and can now no longer be wished away with hopeful optimism. They are supported by the news about the harvest situation which may well give cause for further disquiet about the economy. It must be clear that in overcoming the crisis we have to fight for time, that the economy will not survive the coming struggle if this conflict between the various authorities and the present indecisiveness of the economic leadership continues.

The whole situation calls for a resolute and unified economic leadership which can direct the work of the Ministries of Economics, Agriculture, Labor, and Finance, the Reichsbank and all offices of the Labor Front by dictatorial methods. If one returns to question [on the effect of the economy on the Army in the event of war] posed at the beginning, one must come to the unequivocal conclusion that, with regard to the situation of the German economy described above, the economic crisis represents a serious threat to the defense of the country and that in these circumstances the economy is not in a position to meet the supply requirements of the Wehrmacht in its enlarged form.

As the Ministry responsible for the security of the Reich, the Reich Defense Ministry must now demand sweeping measures. . . .

I wish to make the following proposals to deal with the situation.

1. The Führer should assume economic leadership. A permanent official should be appointed as

his subordinate with the title of Economics Deputy of the Führer, together with an adviser on industry, agriculture, commerce and banking respectively, and also one liaison officer from the Reich Defense Ministry.

The Economics Deputy must be an exceptionally able man, enjoying the confidence of the widest and most authoritative circle and possessing the utmost resources of energy and authority. He must have the power to issue decrees of decisive importance and have the means to carry them through ruthlessly in the face of all authorities and party offices.

2. The Reich Ministries of Economics, Agriculture, Labor and Finance, the Reichbank, the leaders of industry and the Labor Front shall be subordinate to him.

All Party and other offices should be prohibited from carrying out any economic measures which do not come from the Economics Deputy and have not been approved by him.

3. The branches of the economy which are important for war and are still unattached should be integrated in a planned economy.

For this purpose the following are necessary:

The creation of trade monopoly offices for all raw materials which are important for war.

The detailed regulation of the import, export and supplies of all materials pertaining to war.

An immediate start with this process of mobilization and a clear lead from the Government in building up the country's sources of raw materials.

The establishment of a central office for all foreign trade.

The nation should be thoroughly informed about the serious state of the economy, and determined measures should be taken to train the people in thrift and moderation.

Measures should be taken to overcome this year's bad harvest.

TAXPAYERS TO THE INTERNAL REVENUE SERVICE
"I see the abuses of the expense account deductions"

Business and pleasure sometimes mix in inappropriate ways. Tax deductions for business expenses can become a touchy issue, especially before tax reforms in 1986 ended loose standards for entertainment expenses. The three letters below written by anonymous taxpayers in the 1960s explore some of the issues involved in the potentially volatile mix of business, entertainment and tax deductions.

Dear Sir:

I am 100% for the crack down on expense accounts. I work for a large motel corporation as a desk clerk, and at times as a dining room hostess. I see the abuses of the expense account deductions. Why should the stockholders, in the case of the corporation man, underwrite his weekend pleasure trips for himself and his inlaws; or in the case of an individual owner business man, why should I and my fellow workers underwrite him by paying additional taxes?

The corporation for whom I work maintains a yacht. I fail to see how this boat would entice the highway traveler to stop at this corporation's motel. Yet the entire expense of the boat probably is taken as a business expense deduction.

If all businesses secured their business on the merits of its products and/or its services, then they could price their wares cheaper and consumers would have more money to spend.

I hope your department does not relent and retreat.

Dear Sir:

Having access only to the TV and press releases emanating from the recent hearings you held on expense deductions, I can't be sure that the point I want to call to your attention wasn't brought up. However, I feel sure that had it been, the press would have exploited it.

I am a housewife in my fifties. I spent twenty years in the business world from positions of secretary to executive. For the past sixteen years I have been married to a business executive. I think I see the whole picture from a good perspective.

Thirty years ago, the executive who took his wife on a business trip or convention was considered a square or henpecked. In recent years the man in business is a whole man and he and his company give consideration to his wife and family. The more mature, stable business man prefers to take his wife on trips occasionally—it makes her life richer, and therefore his, and it's a welcome change of pace for both. This is a far cry from the times I remember when the visiting fireman always arrived in the city alone and the host company felt obliged to include in the entertainment escorts from the secretarial pool or a call house. Nearly always either the host or the guest had no taste for the proceedings, but it was the "thing that was done." The result was not good for the family life either. And I know the deductible tabs for that kind of entertainment ran a lot higher than when the visitor arrives with his wife, her travel expense not withstanding.

From what I read, corporations take more than a passing interest in the wife of a prospective executive, and it seems of importance to them to find the marital status happy and adjusted. This interest of the company is mature thinking because an executive's work must extend into is personal life in many ways.

One threat to marriage has always been that the man outgrows his wife because of his travels and experiences that she can't share. The thing that brings that about is that the man gets on an expense account what he can't afford personally or for his wife. In recent years mature men have recognized this, and as heads of companies have made it possible for wives to share a bit now and then in the stratosphere in which their husbands are at home. As a result, there is better understanding in families and family life in the United States is more stable. Of course, I don't attribute this entirely to the fact that wives are sometimes included in expense accounts. Rather it is the result of an evolving maturity and the corporations' attitude is one facet of it.

I would hate to see Uncle Sam responsible for turning the tide of this evolving maturity. It would be a shame to be headed back in that other direction where the call girl flourished.

Dear Sir:

We tightened up on reporting expenses a couple of months ago to get our people used to it before the new rules go into effect but if you go through with it … it will be a major sized headache for us.

Our people go to a convention and get half boiled right away. (This is the condition which makes salesmen most effective.) The reports they turn in look like second grade arithmetic and they have forgotten most of the expenses. Their reports do not jibe with the money they have actually spent and we know darned well that none of these people are thieves.

The Internal Revenue Bureau Examiners have always agreed that the amount we spend on entertainment is reasonable and fair considering our volume. If we crack down on our Representatives we are bound to lose business. Our hotel suite would look like Coney Island in January if we didn't serve liquor and if we do our own boys will drink it. If we fail to put our products over at conventions we will not be paying ANY taxes.

A better system would be to allow businesses like ours a certain percentage of sales for entertainment right off the top. Make it a reasonable figure on the conservative side and then if more is needed the department could grant it providing the need could be proved. Each type of business could be granted a certain percent for entertainment. That would save your department a lot of criticism for making arbitrary decision which are unfavorable to taxpayers.

JOHN KENNETH GALBRAITH TO JOHN F. KENNEDY
"The pressure that is mounting on taxes"

The liberal economist John Kenneth Galbraith was an unabashed opponent of tax cuts when serving as an economic adviser to President John F. Kennedy in the early 1960s. Saying the government could use the tax revenues to address many complex problems, he urged Kennedy in the following letter not to give in to the intense pressure to reduce taxes in the face of a possible economic downturn. Kennedy, however, soon proposed a general tax reduction that was enacted the following year.

New Delhi

July 10, 1962

CONFIDENTIAL

Dear Mr. President:

I read with a good deal of concern about the pressure that is mounting on taxes. I also sense that your instinct is to resist and I hope you continue to do so. I submit the following thoughts:

1) A very large part of American conservative and business opinion is simply against taxes regardless. It will thus argue with great enthusiasm for tax reduction, quite apart from the consequences fiscal and otherwise about which they couldn't care less. Of course, after the taxes are reduced, these people will not hesitate to attack you for an unbalanced budget. Some of them may be sophisticated enough to hope the new lower tax revenues will set a new lower ceiling on spending. The rest welcome the liberal initiative as assistance from an unexpected quarter.

2) The momentary alliance with my friends is more apparent than real. The people who are simply anti-tax will want an across-the-board and upper brackets reduction including, though less urgently, the corporation tax. The liberals and unions will want relief in the withholding brackets and here, of course, it would have its effect on spending. (The effect of upper bracket and corporation tax on business outlays and spending will be slight or negligible.) So a proposal to reduce taxes, while it looks simple and fast, will produce a nasty Congressional brawl with a disagreeable aftermath. What will satisfy the liberals will outrage the rich and vice-versa.

3) From this distance I don't see that the condition of the economy is all that bad. Personal income seems to be holding up very well. The investment plans seem not to have been seriously revised. The stock market is steadier for the moment at a safer level. Unemployment is, to be sure, substantial. But without excusing it, it remains that we have been living with something like this volume of unemployment for a long while. Once we would have thought it creditably low.

4) Most of what I read on the politics of the situation makes no sense at all. While you are aware of my reluctance to lecture you on this curious subject, perhaps I could make three points: a) No tax cut has the slightest chance of having the slightest effect on the economy by November. b) The unemployed are (to their misfortune) a small minority and few can be so silly as to suppose they will do better under the Republicans. c) The unemployed stiff may have become extremely well educated in recent months but I still can't imagine him applauding the Kennedy Administration for helping him by reducing the taxes of the guy who has a job or the fellow he would be working for if he had a job.

5) I needn't remind you (but nevertheless I always deem it wise) that the glories of the Kennedy Era will be written not in the rate of economic growth or even in the level of unemployment. Nor, I venture, is this where its political rewards lie. Its glory and reward will be from the way it tackles the infinity of problems that beset a growing population and an increasingly complex society in an increasingly competitive world. To do this well costs the money that the tax reducers would deny.

If the economic outlook for next year is not good, this means that economists and planners should now get down to work on how men can be employed if jobs are needed. Then when next year comes there will be no reason to say that spending for the things that society so desperately needs is too time-consuming a remedy.

With this, I turn my thoughts back to the local scene.

Yours faithfully,
John Kenneth Galbraith

J. B. LEE, JR., TO CONGRESSMAN ED FOREMAN

"I am going into the not-raising hogs business next year"

Some government policies designed to help overall economic conditions often appear to make no sense at all when viewed from a different perspective. A prime example was the federal policy of paying farmers not to grow crops or raise livestock.

This policy was introduced as part of Roosevelt's New Deal to reduce the oversupply of farm products, which had been causing prices to plummet. A vicious cycle had been developing in which farmers kept growing more and more goods to make up for their lost income. The effect, however, was lower and lower prices. To break the cycle, the government decided to pay farmers to stop growing goods. Supply tightened, prices rose, and farming became a profitable venture again.

But as this letter from a Texan farmer to his congressman reflects, federal farm subsidies made mincemeat of common sense, at least from his view as a hardworking hog farmer.

March 20, 1963

The Honorable Ed Foreman

House of Representatives

Congressional District #16

Washington 25, D. C.

Dear Sir:

My friend over in Terebone Parish received a $1,000 check from the government this year for not raising hogs. So I am going into the not-raising hogs business next year.

What I want to know is, in your opinion, what is the best kind of farm not to raise hogs on and the best kind of hogs not to raise? I would prefer not to raise Razorbacks, but if that is not a good breed not to raise, I will just as gladly not raise any Berkshires or Durocs.

The hardest work in this business is going to be in keeping an inventory of how many hogs I haven't raised.

My friend is very joyful about the future of his business. He has been raising hogs for more than 20 years and the best he ever made was $400, until this year, when he got $1,000 for not raising hogs.

If I can get $1,000 for not raising 50 hogs, then will I get $2,000 for not raising 100 hogs? I plan to operate on a small scale at first, holding myself down to 4,000 hogs which means I will have $80,000 coming from the government.

Now, another thing: these hogs I will not raise will not eat 100,000 bushels of corn. I understand that you also pay farmers for not raising corn. So will you pay me anything for not raising 100,000 bushels of corn not to feed the hogs I am not raising?

I want to get started as soon as possible as this seems to be a good time of year for not raising hogs.

One thing more, can I raise 10 or 12 hogs on the side while I am in the not-raising-hog-business just enough to get a few sides of bacon to eat?

Very truly yours,
J. B. Lee, Jr.
Potential Hog Raiser

John Wayne to President Lyndon B. Johnson

"We want to tell the story of our fighting men in Vietnam"

Mixing politics and business, legendary actor John Wayne produced The Green Berets *in 1966 as a patriotic film to support U.S. involvement in the war in Vietnam. In this letter to President Lyndon B. Johnson, he describes his goal and asks for the government's assistance. Johnson's aide, Jack Valenti, subsequently wrote a memo endorsing the idea, noting that a commercial film can achieve the goals of the government without having "to be factual." Wayne received the cooperation of the Defense Department in making the film.*

December 28, 1965

The President

The White House

Washington, D.C.

Dear Mr. President:

When I was a little boy my father always told me that if you want to get anything done see the top man—so I am addressing this letter to you.

We are fighting a war in Vietnam. Though I personally support the Administration's policy there, I know it is not a popular war, and I think it is extremely important that not only the people of the United States but those all over the world should know why it is necessary for us to be there.

The most effective way to accomplish this is through the motion picture medium. Some day soon a motion picture *will* be made about Vietnam. Let's make sure it is the kind of picture that will help our cause throughout the world. I believe my organization can do just that and still accomplish our purpose for being in existence—making money. We want to tell the story of our fighting men in Vietnam with reason, emotion, characterization and action. We want to do it in a manner that will inspire a patriotic attitude on the part of fellow-Americans—a feeling which we have always had in this country in the past during times of stress and trouble. I feel my organization can make a vehicle which will accomplish this. We want to do it through the use of the point of view of our Special Forces. In order to properly put it on the screen we are going to need the help and cooperation of the Defense Department.

My record in this field is a worthy one. Thirty-seven years a star, I must have some small spot in more than a few million people's lives. You cannot stay up there that long without having identification with a great number of people. It has been my good fortune to be associated with some motion pictures which portrayed the integrity and dignity of our military, and imbued our people with pride. In films such as "The Longest Day", "The Sands Of Iwo Jima", and "The Fighting Seabees" we worked closely with the branches of the military involved, and the pictures turned out to be something of which everyone could be proud.

Perhaps you remember the scene from the film "The Alamo", when one of Davy Crockett's Tennesseans said: "What are we doing here in Texas fighting—it ain't our ox that's getting gored." Crockett replied "Talkin' about whose ox gets gored, figure this: a fella gets in the habit of gorin' oxes, it whets his appetite. May gore yours next. Unquote. And we don't want people like Kosygin, Mao Tse-Tung, or the like, "gorin' our oxes".

Perhaps it is presumptuous on my part to write direct to your Office for guidance, but I feel this picture can be extremely helpful to the Administration. Your assistance in getting us Defense Department cooperation will certainly expedite our project, as we are anxious to move ahead on it immediately. Therefore, we would appreciate hearing from your Office concerning your reactions.

Best wishes for the coming year.

Respectfully yours,
John Wayne

January 6, 1966

Mr. President:

You asked Bill Moyers to look into the proposal made by John Wayne—who wants to make a picture about Vietnam, focusing on Special Forces.

Bill is investigating this now.

Meanwhile, I think Wayne ought to get an acknowledgement of his letter to you promptly and courteously.

Do you want such a letter prepared—which would be signed by someone on your staff. (I attach a sample letter)

My own judgment is that Wayne's politics are wrong, but insofar as Vietnam is concerned, his views are right. If he made the picture he would be saying the things we want said.

Moreover, a commercial film about Vietnam, with popular stars in it, would probably have a more beneficial effect, and seen by more people than any film the government could make, or any documentary other people would make. The principal defect of a documentary is that we have no film of the Viet Cong and no depiction of their atrocities. Documentaries have to be factual.

In a commercial film, however, there is no restriction on actual film. The film makers can portray the Viet Cong as they really are.

So I recommend we give Wayne permission to make the film—and also give MGM (our friends politically) who also want to make a similar film. The quicker the better. It will take about six months, minimum, to turn out a quality film.

Jack Valenti

LEE IACOCCA TO
NATIONAL ASSOCIATION OF MANUFACTURERS
"The free market system which 'allows for both failure and success'"

Lee Iacocca, former Ford Motors president, came to Chrysler Corporation in the 1970s to turn the ailing motor company around with an annual salary of one dollar. The straight-shooting executive, who had introduced the Mustang a decade earlier, embarked on a series of cost-cutting measures, product overhauls, and financing strategies to rescue Chrysler. The most controversial step was seeking and receiving a loan backed by the federal government.

Many other business leaders attacked the deal, saying it represented an assault on the proven success of a survival-of-the-fittest free marketplace. On November 13, 1979, the National Association of Manufacturers issued a press release blasting the government's action. "At a time when government, business, and the public are becoming more and more aware of the costs and inefficiencies of government intervention in the economy, it would be highly inappropriate to recommend a course of even deeper involvement," the press release stated. "Now is the time to reaffirm the principle of 'no federal bailouts.'"

Infuriated by the assault from fellow business executives, Iacocca fired back the following letter explaining the rationale for the action, noting that government and business had intermingled many times before in ways that have been both good and bad for business.

Gentlemen:

I was deeply disturbed to learn that on the same day I testified in Washington on behalf of Chrysler Corporation's request for loan guarantees, the Business Roundtable, of which Chrysler is a member, issued a press release against "federal bailouts."

I have several observations to make.

First—the basic charter of the Roundtable is to contain inflation. Its goals have since been extended to a discussion of other economic issues of national importance. These discussions have traditionally taken place in an open and free atmosphere in which all points of view are considered. The fact that we did not have an opportunity to present the facts of the Chrysler case to the members of the Policy Committee runs directly counter to that tradition.

Second—it is ironic that the Roundtable took no similar position on federal loan guarantees to steel companies, to shipbuilders, to airlines, to farmers, and to the housing industry. Nor did it protest the establishment of "trigger prices" on foreign steel, or the provisions of federal assistance to American Motors.

Third—the Roundtable statement invokes the principles of the free market system which "allows for both failure and success." It totally ignores the fact that government regulatory intrusion into the system has contributed greatly to Chrysler's problem. It is in fact entirely consistent with the workings of the free market system for the government to offset some of the adverse effects of federal regulation. Federal loan guarantees to steel companies were made precisely for that reason.

Fourth—the Roundtable statement is wrong in its declaration that reorganization under the new bankruptcy statute is practical. Our need is not to scale down debt, but to raise huge amounts of new capital. It would be impossible for us to raise the necessary amounts of capital during a bankruptcy proceeding. We have consulted with one of the nation's leading experts on bankruptcy, Mr. J. Ronald Trost, of Shutan and Trost, whose analysis of the new law led him to testify that bankruptcy is not practical for Chrysler and would lead quickly to liquidation.

Your own Roundtable staff has indicated that no bankruptcy experts were consulted during the preparation of your statement. If they had been, I feel sure the statements would have been considerably less confident on the subject of the virtues of bankruptcy.

Fifth—it is most unfortunate that the Roundtable has chosen to engage in sloganeering in this campaign. To proclaim a policy of "no federal bailouts" in a press release is to reduce the discussion to its lowest level. The hundreds of thousands of workers across the country who depend on Chrysler for employment deserve far better in the debate over their future.

Finally, I believe my acceptance of your current invitation to become a member of the Roundtable would be a source of embarrassment to the other members. I had looked forward to joining a business forum that openly discusses vital economic and social issues in an atmosphere of mutual trust and respect. The Roundtable's press release indicates that such an opportunity does not exist in the Policy Committee. Therefore, please accept my sincere regrets and the resignation of Chrysler Corporation from Business Roundtable membership.

THE COMPETITIVE EDGE

DUTCH WEST INDIA COMPANY TO DUTCH GOVERNMENT
"The Company, will once more, in good faith, plead ignorance"

Before free market economies took hold in Europe and America, business competition was often more a function of force than efficiency. This was particularly the case in the scramble for colonies, as evidenced in the correspondence below.

European sovereigns of the time often created trading companies to oversee the settlement of foreign colonies and establish trading posts. One of the most important was the Dutch West India Company, which settled New Netherlands along the eastern coast of America, with the main trading settlement at New Amsterdam—now New York City. Although the Dutch business class was among the most advanced in the world at the time, the company's New World colony fell victim to the might of the British navy in 1664.

The last Dutch governor of New Netherlands, Peter Stuyvesant, tried to assign blame for the loss to lack of support from the Dutch West India Company and Dutch military. The company responded with the letter below.

To the Honorable Mighty Lords, their High Mightinesses' Deputies for the Affairs of the West India Company

… First taking up the Want of provisions: The Company will once more, in good faith, plead ignorance of there having been an insufficient supply of provisions, since it cannot imagine that, in a country so productive as New Netherland, any scarcity should exist in a year of such abundance as that of 1664….

… Further, that there is not the least foundation for what he sets forth both generally and particularly in his Defence, viz.: that he had not timely notice of the designs which the English, and especially the aforesaid frigates might have had against New Netherland, and that the Company had, on the contrary, as he gives out, informed him, from this place, that the English had no intention to use violence against New Netherland. For, it is true and certain that, in order that he might victual the place and fort of new Amsterdam and keep it victualed, the aforesaid Stuyvesant was warned time enough from and from New England, of the apparent difficulties between this State and the English, and, more particularly, of the equipment and approach of the aforesaid frigates;…

Secondly. Herewith falls the excuse he makes, that the farmers were constrained by the English not to convey any grain into the fort, and that the said English had everywhere cut off the communication, so that grain could not be conveyed across the river; for, having been warned in time, they ought not to have waited the arrival of the frigates … to provide themselves with grain….

Want of ammunition being represented as the second fundamental cause of the surrender of the aforesaid fort, city and province of New Netherland, the abovenamed Company will also, in good faith, plead ignorance of that want; yea, will, on the contrary, assert that it is informed for certain that, if there had not been a sufficient supply in store, a very considerable quantity of gunpowder would be found among the Burgers, and particularly at Fort Orange and the Colonie Renslaers Wyck among the traders;…

… The third point of his defence—the Unwillingness of the Burghers to defend the city—since all the world sufficiently knows what zeal they had exhibited to protect their property; working with all their might at the defence of the place, until the want of provisions and ammunition was instilled into their minds by the government, and the enemy's strength represented to be much greater that it was in fact, and, moreover, security for their private property had been given by the English, in case of surrender; and finally, until the two frigates passed the fort unobstructed, when their courage began to fail and the idea of surrender gained ground, on perceiving the intention of the government after it had permitted the aforesaid frigates to pass freely the fort unimpeded; although, under all circumstances, it is sufficiently shown in the Observations aforesaid, that the unwillingness of the Burghers to fight, cannot be any excuse for him, inasmuch as it was his duty to defend the fort….

The fourth point was: that they had no hope of relief. This is spread out so broad, as if, for this reason alone, the place ought not to be defended. On this point the Company will merely persist in what is stated in its Observations, and accordingly submit, that it could not know what the aforesaid Director also might say if no relief should arrive. In all cases, he was not at liberty to surrender such a place without striking a blow, especially so long as it was not really attacked; for, as regards relief, they did not know what help would arrive from Fatherland, because the Company's last letters had assured them of immediate assistance or a settlement of the Boundary. Consequently, the one or the other being to happen, he ought not to have adopted so rash a resolution….

CORNELIUS VANDERBILT TO HIS FORMER PARTNERS
"I'll ruin you"

One of the most successful businessmen in American history, Cornelius Vanderbilt started his career with a $100 loan from his parents that he used to buy a small transport for carrying passengers and freight on the Hudson River in the early 1800s. He was a relentless worker and extremely savvy, and constantly upgraded his ships to keep up with the latest technologies of the era.

By the 1840s, Vanderbilt had become a millionaire. When gold was discovered in California in 1848, Vanderbilt established a route through Nicaragua using steamships and stagecoaches that shortened the trip around South America. When he went on the first vacation in his life, his agents double-crossed him and took over the route. Vanderbilt wrote this letter, one of the most famous in the history of American business.

True to his word, Vanderbilt set up a competing route through Panama and slashed prices, driving his former associates out of business.

Gentlemen:

You have undertaken to cheat me. I won't sue you, for the law is too slow. I'll ruin you.

Yours truly,
Cornelius Vanderbilt

GEORGE MAY TO JOSEPH CURTISS
"We are too late"

Sometimes the wisest business decisions are for investments not made. The following letter was written by the agent of a coin manufacturer who arrived in California in 1849 in the middle of the gold rush. He had planned on setting up shop in the thriving community and making money—literally. His hopes were dashed, however, when he and his companion discovered they were too late, too small, and too unconnected to start a successful coinage firm. The competition was too fierce.

20 November 1849

You will have rec'd my last informing you of my arrival before this reaches. I regret to say that the prospect of doing anything at our contemplated [plan] is forbidding, that both Randall and myself judge it not best to make a trial at it. First we are too late—the time for commencing the coining business is past. There are already four establishments of this kind in California now, only two of which are doing a profitable business. One is Moffitt & co., the other the Miners Bank, both of them (particularly the latter) with large capital. Had we arrived at the time contemplated we might perhaps have succeeded, but it is certainly too late now.

There are some dozen small concerns which left the States for this business that have abandoned it altogether. All the large merchantile and other business houses from motives of interest use their influence against it. It is more for their interest to buy the dust and send to the States than give circulation to coin made here. Unless therefore it be done by a league with some of these large establishments (which we cannot make) it is difficult to get much circulation for such coin. The agent of an organization for this business with a capital of some $20,000 has recently arrived from New England. He is [a] personal and intimate friend of mine and tells me it is quite doubtful if they attempt it all. Moffit & Co. and the Miners Bank have considerable in circulation. The former has obtained his circulation principally through the gamblers, who circulate more money here than any other class of men. The latter is a heavy concern owning a large amt of real estate and which redeems its coin with government coin when called upon to do so.

LETTERS TO JOHN D. ROCKEFELLER ON CUT-THROAT TACTICS

"Our public character is not one to be envied"

John D. Rockefeller is considered perhaps the toughest, most cut-throat businessperson in history. Starting with a small Cleveland refinery during the 1860s oil boom in western Pennsylvania, Rockefeller consolidated almost the entire oil industry under the control of his company, Standard Oil, during the following quarter century.

Although Rockefeller was convinced his actions were necessary for the health of the oil industry, his ruthless tactics were legendary. In the first letter below, a Standard operative writes to Rockefeller explaining how Standard stopped a small competitor, Lewis Emery, Jr., from linking up his pipeline with the railroad. Using Standard's massive capacity to provide railroads with the oil-freight business, Standard could effectively force the railroads not to service Standard's competitors, or risk losing Standard's business.

The second letter is from the owner of a small oil concern who has cursed Standard Oil in the past, but is now looking to sell out to Rockefeller and enjoy the benefits of becoming a Standard shareholder. The third letter, from William G. Warden, a Standard Oil executive, illustrates the toll Rockefeller's tactics took on Standard Oil's reputation. Warden proposes to develop a profit-sharing plan that would benefit oil producers. Despite Warden's plea to dampen his ruthlessness, Rockefeller's response was a muted "be assured [your letter's] contents will not escape me"—and no let-up in his tactics.

John D. Archbold to John D. Rockefeller

July 11, 1892

We have had further interviews with the Ontario & Western people, and feel that we have made some progress toward a possible understanding with them. It is now entirely sure that there has been no definite engagement entered into by them with the Emery party, and we think they are now convinced that the rates they had been talking about with the Emery party are absurdly low, and that business on any such basis would be undesirable and unprofitable. We have made them a proposition of business covering a period of five years, and expect an answer from them this week. Our proposition is that we put over their lines 400,000 barrels of oil yearly, or, in default of any part of the amount, pay a penalty of 10 per cent of the existing rates. We think it a very liberal proposition to them.

John D. Archbold

June 10, 1888

I am a poor devil of a pyker on the oil market and have been in the business for eight years. During all this time I have been cursing the Standard Oil Company with the rest of the boys—curses loud and deep. But with all the anathemas hurled at it the S.O.C. is still in existence and continues to pile up enormous wealth. Now as the market is completely dead and my occupation gone, I have come to the conclusion that it would be wisdom to stop cursing the Standard and strike it for a good fat position.

P. O. Laughner

May 24, 1887

We have met with a success unparalleled in commercial history, our name is known all over the world, and our public character is not one to be envied. We are quoted as representative of all that is evil, hard hearted, oppressive, cruel (we think unjustly), but men look askance at us, we are pointed at with contempt, and while some good men flatter us, it's only for our money and we scorn them for it and it leads to a further hardness of heart. This is not pleasant to write, for I had longed for an honored position in commercial life. None of us would choose such a reputation; we all desire a place in the good will, honor & affection of honorable men....

Don't put this down or throw it to one side, think over it, talk with Mrs. Rockefeller about it—She is the salt of the earth. How happy she would be to see a change in public opinion & see her husband honored & blessed. May he who's wisdom alone can put it on our hearts to love our fellow men, guide and direct you at this time.... The whole world will rejoice to see such an effort made for the people, the working people.

William G. Warden

P. T. BARNUM TO JAMES A. BAILEY

"A complete monopoly which nobody would ever dare to assail"

Legendary circus owner P. T. Barnum described in this letter to his partner James Bailey the future of American circuses and outlined how their company could dominate the industry. Two years after writing the letter and shortly after the death of competitor Adam Forepaugh, Barnum & Bailey acquired Forepaugh's circus. By the 1920s, the Ringling brothers had succeeded Barnum & Bailey as operators of their combined shows, and established a virtual monopoly with the purchase of the American Circus Corporation, an alliance of five small circuses. Today, the combined Ringling Bros. and Barnum & Bailey Circus has two complete traveling shows that dominate the circus industry in the United States.

Private

Paul Smith's, N.Y., 27 August 1888

Dear Bailey,

You notice Park & Tilford have numerous stores. One only advertises the other—all succeed because all are equally good. Caswell and Massey, the good druggists, do the same thing with the same success. I continually feel that somehow we ought to have 2 shows, one east & the other west, & this can only be done successfully by absorbing Forepaugh's show. He is really getting more public recognition and making more and more money each year, and there is a constant danger that Cole & Hutchinson may join him & thus strengthen his name and compel us to keep up a too expensive show. Forepaugh's wife is young and wants him to stop traveling personally. He dare not trust it to his son, but he would like to stop traveling and join us in a stock co. of 2 millions, he retaining stock enough to keep young Forepaugh teaching animals & traveling under our management.

Now perhaps if we give Forepaugh to understand that we intend to start 2 shows, he may be induced to put his son, his name, & his show property into a stock company with ours, he taking one quarter and we 3 quarters of the whole stock. A still better way, perhaps, would be for it to go to the public that Forepaugh has retired from business, that the Barnum & Bailey have bought him out and absorbed it, and will make a new show equal to the other & thus run 2 shows. Under such an announcement we give Forepaugh 1/2 of the stock or such share as we may agree on & take from him & his son a private obligation & bond that they will never again let their names be used, that they will not sell out their stock & that Adam Jr. shall devote himself to the interests of the co., that we shall manage the whole & that the Forepaughs may have an accountant travel with the show to look after their interests, that old Adam shall privately advise, consult, aid in buying horses or in any manner that might benefit the co., but shall not travel with it.

Some sort of plan of this kind would fortify us against all opposition, give us a full sweep of the country and the world, enable us to hire attractions cheaper, make it unnecessary to have quite so big shows, and get our printing and all other work done cheaper, pay less salaries to advance agents, &c. &c.—because we should have a complete monopoly which nobody would ever dare to assail. Then the new company could gradually establish museums and do everything else to give it strength & profit for generations. If you privately and seriously think this matter over, I am sure you will see some such plan to remove all opposition will pay best in the long run.

I don't like Forepaugh any better than you do, but he is a stubborn old chap with considerable horse sense, and his show is a continual annoyance and injury to us—and also a menace, for in his anxiety to stop traveling personally he is almost sure to get showmen of capital to buy a share of his show cheap and relieve him of the trouble of managing it. His son, Adam Jrs., of course has his faults, but if he is managed by us he can be useful as a trainer of animals & a performer. Old Adam is determined to keep his son in the business, so if we can keep his claws cut and have him interested in making the show attractive & successful, we thus "chain" the young tiger. You & I or my estate would always hold majority of stock and would have an agreement & bond signed that we should never be voted on, either by its owners nor by you nor me. Other parties desirable might become small owners of stock occasionally so as to keep good coming men in training, but your estate & mine, which now own the whole, must always retain the controlling power. Let us get Forepaugh out of our path someway & we sweep the board for all time.

P. T. B.

P.D. ARMOUR TO SONS OGDEN AND PHIL ARMOUR
"Pay a little attention to supporting and helping the House"

Philip D. Armour founded a meat-packing business in Chicago in 1867, and thirty years later, it was one of the largest processors of pork in the world. The company was very profitable, but Armour's slaughterhouses were infamous, and provided Upton Sinclair with the model for the slaughterhouses in his novel, The Jungle, *which depicted the horrible working conditions in Chicago.*

In this letter to his two sons, who would inherit the company upon his death six years later, Armour writes about the importance of instilling a company-wide ethic of company marketing and promotion.

April 1, 1895

My dear Ogden and Phil:

Mr. Earling, superintendent of the C. M. & St. P. Railway, rode home with me from Carey's funeral yesterday, and in the course of conversation related a little incident to illustrate why railroads don't succeed better. It struck me very forcibly, and I think the meat of it will apply to the packing business.

He said that while he was in Minneapolis last week he stepped into a little cigar store near the depot and bought a couple of cigars. As he was lighting one he asked the man whether he was doing a good business. He said, yes; he had all the Milwaukee & St. Paul Railroad trade, and that was a very large volume indeed; in fact, it was practically all the business he had.

Then Earling asked him where he bought his cigars, and he replied, "In New York."

He then asked him how he shipped them, and he answered, "Via the Burlington Road."

"You get all your patronage from the St. Paul, and yet you give all your patronage to the Burlington, a road that you have never had a bit of trade from."

"Oh, well," said the cigar man, "I never thought anything about that. *I have never been asked by any of the St. Paul people to ship them via their road.*"

Mr. Earling said that fundamental principle was the same all through the railroad business—the men about the road did simply what they were told to do and what they thought was their duty, but they were not inventive in their heads nor tried to help the railroad. They never looked so far ahead as to see that by boosting the railroad for which they worked they also helped themselves.

Of all the great number of employees who supported that tobacco store, not one had ever asked the cigar man to send his business over the St. Paul Railroad. Of course, they were not the commercial men, exactly, of the road, but they thought nothing concerned them except their special duties and whatever was doled out to them.

Consequently, that was why railroads in a great measure fell short of giving the results to the stockholders that they might give, and naturally, that meant they did not pay the men what they might pay them.

Now, I think this holds good all through Armour & Company to a great extent.

If every man about Armour & Company would pay a little attention to supporting and helping the House, it would go a very long way toward the success of the House: and no one connected with Armour & Company could go out of his way and show that he took an interest in their success but what the House would soon find it out.

It would be a very simple matter for any of our boys, on going to a store, if they didn't see our goods, to ask why, and if they could not find out, it would be easy enough to report it to the commercial part of the house.

Sincerely yours,
Philip D. Armour

ANGLO-PERSIAN OIL COMPANY COMPETES FOR OIL IN PERSIAN GULF

"Whether there are oil deposits of any value in Koweit is entirely problematic"

Before the Persian Gulf served as the world's main source of oil, oil companies vied for the rights to the oil without knowing exactly what they would find. As late as the 1930s many experts considered discovering oil in Kuwait a "very long shot." But, then again, nobody wanted to risk missing out on a potential fortune. Front and center in the competition was the Anglo-Persian Oil Company. It worked hand-in-hand with the British government, which had recently converted its naval fleet from coal- to oil-burning ships.

This letter from an Anglo-Persian Oil Company official to a British officer in Kuwait reflects the uncertainty regarding oil in the Arabian deserts, as well as the intense rivalry between interests over control of oil. The British secured the concession rights to Kuwaiti oil more than 20 years later. As it turned out, Kuwait sits atop one of the world's largest supplies of oil.

Lt.-Col. P. Z. Cox, C.S.I., C.I.E.

Bushire

My dear Cox,

It has come to my knowledge that Mr. Reynolds—our ex-employee—is endeavoring to induce the Shell Co., which is now only a small share-holding Company in the Royal Dutch Co., to secure a Concession in Koweit.

I do not know what reason Reynolds has for assuming that there are any oil deposits of value in Koweit but if in the course of his duties for the Company he discovered any oil indications there he should have brought them to our notice, and have recommended our applying for a Concession, because he was well aware that it would be very prejudicial to our interests to have a powerful foreign rival close on our heels in the Persian Gulf.

However that may be, it would, of course, not at all suit our book to allow the Shell Co. to get an Oil Concession at this place, nor would it, I think, any more suit the policy of the British Government, because the Shell and Royal Dutch Companies are closely associated with the Deutsche Bank, and it is quite probable that they, knowing that they would receive the cold shoulder from our Government, would, if they desired to obtain a Concession at this place, endeavour to obtain it from Turkey through the Deutsche Bank or some other German channel.

I should therefore be much obliged if you could lend us your help in this matter, and let me know whether you think a valid Concession for working Oil in Koweit is obtainable from the Sultan without reference to the Turkish Government. If so, I should like you to put forward an application on behalf of the Anglo-Persian Oil Co. for a Prospecting License, the draft terms of which I will send to you later on if you think there is any chance of a Concession being obtainable.

The question of whether or not there are oil deposits of any value in Koweit is, of course, entirely problematic, and consequently we should only in the first place be prepared to take out a Prospecting License, which in view of the difficulties of prospecting in this place should be for a fairly long period, say ⅔ years.

Yours sincerely,
C. Greenway

ALFRED P. SLOAN, JR., TO GENERAL MOTORS EXECUTIVES
"A great deal could be gained by cooperation between our various operations"

When Alfred P. Sloan, Jr., joined General Motors in 1918, it was a sprawling, loosely organized company that would soon skirt with financial disaster. Within a few years of his arrival at the company, Sloan became president and forged a new type of corporate organization that sought to balance centralized policy control and decentralized operational responsibility. Sloan's success helped spur GM to become the world's largest manufacturer.

Sloan describes a major step in this process in a memo distributed to GM executives in September 1922. In it, he proposes to expand the centralized marketing and purchasing systems to include engineering and technical challenges that all of the GM divisions faced.

I have felt for a long time past that if a proper plan could be developed that would have the support of all those interested that a great deal could be gained for the Corporation by co-operation of an engineering nature between our various Operations, particularly our Car Divisions, dealing as they do in so many problems having the same general characteristics. Activities of this type have already been started in the way of purchasing and have been very helpful and I am confident that as time goes on will be justified in a great many different ways beside[s] resulting in very material profit to the Corporation. The activities of our Institutional Advertising Committee have been constructive and Mr. du Pont remarked to me the other day after one of those meetings that even if it was assumed that the value of the advertising was negligible the other benefits accruing to the Corporation by the development of a General Motors atmosphere and the working together spirit of all members of the Committee representing the various phases of the Corporation's activities ... the cost was well justified. I am quite confident that we all agree as to these principles and assuming that is the case and there is no reason why the same principle does not apply to engineering, it appears to me to be well worth a serious attempt to put the principle into practical operation. I am thoroughly convinced that it can be made a wonderful success. I believe, therefore, that we should at this time establish what might be termed a General Technical Committee which Committee would have certain powers and functions which should be broadly defined at the start and amplified in various ways as the progress of the work seems to justify.

Before attempting to outline even the general principles upon which I believe a start could be made, I think it should be very clearly set forth and distinctly understood by all that the functions of this Committee would not in any event be to deal with the specific engineering activities of any particular Operation. According to General Motors plan of organization, to which I believe we all heartily subscribe, the activities of any specific Operation are under the absolute control of the General Manager of that Division, subject only to very broad contact with the general officers of the Corporation. I certainly do not want to suggest a departure even to the slightest degree from what I believe to be so thoroughly sound a type of organization. On the contrary I do believe and have believed for a long time that one of the great problems that faces the General Motors Corporation was to add to its present plan of organization some method by which the advantages of the Corporation as a whole could be capitalized to the further benefit of the stockholders. I feel that a proper balance can and must necessarily be established in the course of time between the activities of any particular Operation and that of all our Operations together and as I see the picture at the moment no better way or even as good a way has yet been advanced as to ask those members of each organization who have the same functional relationship to get together and decide for themselves what should be done where coordination is necessary, giving such a group the power to deal with the problem where it is felt that the power can be constructively applied. I believe that such a a plan properly developed gives the necessary balance between each Operation and the Corporation itself and will result in all the advantages of co-ordinated action where such action is of benefit in a broader way without in any sense limiting the initiative of independence of action of any component part of the group.

Assuming that this is correct in principle, I might set forth specifically what the functions in the case of the General Technical Committee would be, although this discussion would, I think, apply equally well to other Committees dealing with all functions common to all manufacturing enterprises.

1. The Committee would deal in problems which would be of interest to all Divisions and would in dealing with such matters largely formulate the general engineering principles of the Corporation.

2. The Committee would assume the functions of the already constituted Patent Committee which would be discontinued and in assuming these functions would have the authority to deal with patent matters, already vested in the Patent Committee.

3. The Committee would not, as to principle, deal with the specific problems of any individual Operation. Each function of that Operation would be under the absolute control of the General Manager of that Division.

It is to be noted that the functioning of the Patent Section, Advisory Staff, differs materially from that of any other staff activity and is in a sense an exception to General Motors plan of organization in the fact that all patent problems come directly under the control of the Director of the Patent Section.

In other words, all patent work is centralized. The patent procedure provides, however, for an Inventions Committee and for co-operation with the Director of the Patent Section and the dividing under certain conditions of responsibility in patent matters. In view of the fact that the personnel of the Inventions Committee must necessarily largely parallel that of the General Technical Committee it is thought advisable to consolidate the two for the sake of simplification.

There is also to be considered the functions of the General Motors Research Corporation at Dayton. I feel that up to the present time the Corporation has failed to capitalize what might be capitalized with a proper system of administration, the advantages that should flow from an organization such as we have at Dayton. In making this statement I feel that there are a number of contributing causes, the most important being a lack of proper administrative policy or, I might say, a lack of getting together which it is hoped that this program will provide not only, as just stated, for better co-ordination with the Research Corporation but better co-ordination also among the Operating Divisions themselves. I believe that we would all agree that many of our research and engineering problems in Dayton can only be capitalized through the acceptance and commercializing of same by the Operating Divisions. I fully believe that a more intimate contact with what the Research Corporation is trying to do will be all that is necessary to effect the desired result and strengthen the whole engineering side of the entire Corporation.

It is my idea that the General Technical Committee should be independent in character and in addition to developing through its Secretary, as hereafter described, a program for its meetings, which it is believed would be helpful and beneficial to all the members of the Committee, would conduct studies and investigations of such a character and scope as its judgment would dictate as desirable and for that purpose would use the facilities of the Research Corporation or of any Operating Division or of any outside source that in its judgment would lead to the most beneficial result. Projects of this character would be presented to the Committee by any member of the Committee itself, by the Research Corporation or by any member of the General Motors Corporation through the Corporation's Secretary. Beginning January 1, 1924 the cost of operating the General Motors Corporation will be under the control of a budget system and funds will be provided in that budget to cover this purpose.

I have presented the above ideas at an Operations Committee meeting of which all the General Managers of the Car Divisions primarily interested in this matter and the Group Vice presidents are members and they all seemed to think that the step was a constructive one and would have the support of all.

In order, therefore, that all the above may be crystallized in a few principal points which will be sufficient to form a starting point, I propose the following:

That co-operation shall be established between the Car divisions and the Engineering Departments within the Corporation, including the engineering and research activities of the General Motors Research Corporation and that co-operation shall take the form of a Committee to be established to be termed the General Technical Committee.

The Committee will consist as to principle, of the Chief Engineers of each Car Division and certain additional members....

Alfred P. Sloan, Jr.

WILLIAM RANDOLPH HEARST TO HIS EDITORS
"Success depends upon a complete victory"

William Randolph Hearst built the first great publishing empire, starting with a single newspaper and eventually controlling 28 major newspapers and eighteen magazines. Appealing to the mass market, he charged a penny for his newspapers and pioneered many techniques of tabloid journalism, including oversized headlines, sensational photographs and stories that often tested the standards for accuracy.

Hearst outlined some of his basic principles on how to publish a newspaper in this 1933 letter to his editors and publishers.

Have a good exclusive new feature as often as possible.

PAY LIBERALLY for big exclusive stuff and encourage tipsters. Get reporters with acquaintance.

When a big story must get in all the papers, try to have notably the best account in your paper.

Try to get scoops in pictures. They are frequently almost as important as news. I don't mean pictures of chorus girls, but pictures of important events.

Make the paper thorough. Print all the news. Get all the news into your office and see that it gets into the paper. Condense it if necessary. Frequently it is better when intelligently condensed BUT GET IT IN.

Get your best news on your first page and get as much as possible on that page.

Don't use up your whole first page with a few long stories, but try to get a large number of interesting items in addition to your picture page and your two or three top head stories.

Of course, if your feature is big enough it must get display regardless of everything, but mere display does not make a feature. When you have two features it is frequently better to put one on the first page rather than make it run longer inside. Make your departments complete and reliable so that the reader will know that he can find a thing in your paper and that he can find it right.

Make a paper for the NICEST KIND OF PEOPLE—for the great middle class. Don't print a lot of dull stuff that they are supposed to like and don't.

Omit things that will offend nice people. Avoid coarseness and slang and a low tone. The most sensational news can be told if it is written properly.

Make the paper helpful and kindly. Don't scold and forever complain and attack in your news columns. Leave that to the editorial page.

Be fair and impartial. Don't make a paper for Democrats or Republicans, or Independent Leaguers. Make a paper for all the people and give unbiased news of ALL CREEDS AND PARTIES. Try to do this in such a conspicuous manner that it will be noticed and commented upon.

PLEASE BE ACCURATE. Compare statements in our paper with those in other papers, and find out which are correct. Discharge reporters and copy readers who are persistently inaccurate.

Don't allow exaggeration. It is a cheap and ineffective substitute for real interest. Reward reporters who can make THE TRUTH interesting, and weed out those who cannot.

Make your headlines clear and concise statements of interesting facts. The headlines of a newspaper should answer the question "WHAT IS THE NEWS?" Don't allow copy readers to write headlines that are too smart to be intelligible.

Don't allow long introduction to stories, or involved sentences. Don't repeat unnecessarily. Don't serve up the story in the headlines and then in the introduction and then in the box. Plunge immediately into the interesting part of the story.

Run pretty pictures and interesting layouts, but don't run pictures just to "illuminate the text." If a picture occupies a column of space it should be as interesting as a column of type. Pictures of pretty women and babies are interesting. Photographs of interesting events with explanatory diagrams are valuable. They tell more than the text can, and when carefully and accurately drawn people will study them…. Make every picture worth its space.

Please sum up your paper every day and find wherein it is distinctly better than the other papers. If it isn't distinctly better you have missed that day. Lay out plans to make it distinctly better the next day.

If you cannot show conclusively your own paper's superiority, you may be sure the public will never discover it.

A succession of superior papers will surely tell.

When you beat your rivals one day try harder to beat them the next, for success depends upon a complete victory.

Thomas J. Watson, Jr., to IBM Research Department
"I fail to understand why we have lost our industry leadership position"

IBM dominated the computer industry in the 1950s and 1960s. But in 1961, CEO Thomas J. Watson, Jr., all but shut down the supercomputer research department at IBM because of cost overruns and delays. Two years later, IBM paid the price of Watson's mistake, when Control Data announced the invention of a new machine, the 6600, that delivered three times the power of IBM's largest computer for less money.

Furious, Watson fired off the following memo to his research department. The letter, which became known as the "janitor memorandum," was later used by the government in an antitrust case against IBM for its subsequent actions to corner the supercomputer market. In his autobiography many years later, Watson acknowledged that the lapse in IBM's leadership was his own fault.

August 28, 1963

Last week Control Data had a press conference during which they officially announced their 6600 system. I understand that in the laboratory developing this system there are only 34 people, including the janitor. Of these, 14 are engineers and 4 are programmers, and only one person has a Ph.D., a relatively junior programmer.

Contrasting this modest effort with our own vast development activities, I fail to understand why we have lost our industry leadership position by letting someone else offer the world's most powerful computer.

RAY KROC TO MCDONALD'S OPERATORS
"I urge all good McDonald's men to rally"

There are now nearly thirty thousand McDonald's restaurants worldwide, with nearly two thousand new ones opening each year. The chain hires about one million people each year, more than any other business or organization in the country, and has employed about one out of every eight American workers. McDonald's is the world's largest owner of retail property and the country's largest purchaser of potatoes, beef and pork.

Spending more money on advertising than any other company, McDonald's is the world's most famous brand. Santa Claus is the only fictional character with a higher rate of recognition among American children than Ronald McDonald. The restaurant's famous Golden Arches are more widely recognized than the Christian cross.

But it was not always so. Ray Kroc launched the McDonald's fast-food chain in 1955, using a restaurant owned by Maurice and Richard McDonald as his model. The concept of drive-in restaurants with fast delivery of hamburgers, milk shakes and French fries caught on. In 1970, McDonald's operated about one thousand restaurants.

Bracing his workers for "the biggest month ever" in the company's history, Kroc wrote the following letter urging the company to continue emphasizing the qualities of cleanliness, integrity and dedication to which he attributed the company's success.

April 6, 1970

MEMO TO: All McDonald's Operators

FROM: Ray A. Kroc

May, 1970, will be the biggest month ever experienced in McDonald's history—if you are ready.

This May we have five Fridays, five Saturdays, and five Sundays—plus whatever benefit may be derived from Memorial Day, May 30, being on Saturday.

May is our first month of Daylight Savings Time, with its effect on our supper-hour business. With 15 days of May, virtually half of the month—falling on Fridays, Saturdays, and Sundays, you can see we have a great opportunity to break all records. Another important item, for those stores near college campuses, is that this is the last full month of the regular college season.

In addition, May is really the first month of nice spring weather. There is optimism in the air, and everybody looks ahead to a wonderful summer. We want to make sure that they find happiness and satisfaction at McDonald's.

Let's plan to be all spruced up by the 24th of April when Daylight Savings Time is ready to start, so we can ignite the May Day spirit. Have your patios ready and inviting, new uniforms for the crew—both men and women. Your landscaping should be in, up to date, and ready to bloom.

I urge all good McDonald's men to rally to the most exciting month in our history. Let's have everything ready for the big summer volume, but let's keep quality and cleanliness before the dollars. If we do this, we will leave the competition, far, far behind.

Sincerity, dedication, and integrity are the only things that will win—win and conquer all.

Ray A. Kroc

DAVID OGILVY TO OGILVY & MATHER BOARD OF DIRECTORS
"Character is the most important thing of all"

Advertising executive David Ogilvy soared to the top of his field because of his creativity and management skills. In a memo to his board of directors, however, Ogilvy said the determining factor for a successful company was strength of character.

December 8, 1971

Gentlemen—With Brains

In *Principles of Management* I said, "One of the most priceless assets Ogilvy & Mather can have is the *respect* of our clients and the whole business community."

With every passing year, I am increasingly impressed with the truth of this.

It is not enough for an agency to be respected for its professional competence. Indeed, there isn't much to choose between the competence of the big agencies.

What so often makes the difference is the character of the men and women who represent the agency at the top level, with clients and the business community.

If they are respected as admirable people, the agency gets business—whether from present clients or prospective ones. (I am coming to think that it also counts with the investment community.)

…John Loudon recently said to me, "In choosing men to head countries for Shell, I have always thought that *character* is the most important thing of all."

Ogilvy & Mather must have "gentlemen with brains"—not only in London and New York, but in *all* our countries.

To compromise with this principle sometimes looks expedient, short term. But it can never do Ogilvy & Mather any permanent good.

D.O.

P.S. by "gentlemen" I do not, of course, mean Old Etonians and all that.

ROGER ENRICO TO PEPSI PERSONNEL
"After 87 years of going eyeball to eyeball, the other guy just blinked"

When the Coca-Cola Company announced it would be unveiling a new brand of its famous soda, Pepsi-Cola President Roger Enrico both celebrated the move as a great sign of success for Pepsi and a marketing opportunity. He wrote the following letter to bottlers and employees congratulating them on Pepsi's victory and gave every employee a day off as a reward.

The letter was also used as a full-page ad in newspapers across the country. Pepsi officials leaped on Coca-Cola's switch as a testament to Pepsi's popularity and superiority over Coke, contacting more than 200 reporters to plant leading and awkward questions for Coca-Cola officials at the formal introduction of New Coke.

(April 21, 1985)

To all Pepsi Bottlers and

Pepsi-Cola Company personnel:

It gives me great pleasure to offer each of you my heartiest congratulations.

After 87 years of going eyeball to eyeball, the other guy just blinked.

Coca-Cola is withdrawing their product from the marketplace, and is reformulating brand Coke to be "more like Pepsi." Too bad Ripley's not around … he could have had a field day with this one.

There is no question the long-term market success of Pepsi has forced this move.

Everyone knows when something is right it doesn't need changing.

Maybe they finally realized what most of us have known for years … Pepsi tastes better than Coke.

Well, people in trouble tend to do desperate things … and we'll have to keep our eye on them.

But for now, I say victory is sweet, and we have earned a celebration. We're going to declare a holiday on Friday.

Enjoy!

Best Regards,

Roger Enrico

President, Chief Executive Officer

Pepsi-Cola USA

RICHARD BRANSON AND LORD KING CORRESPONDENCE
"I run my airline, Richard Branson runs his"

In 1990, Virgin Airlines, the company founded and run by the colorful Richard Branson, applied for and received permission to schedule flights from London to Tokyo. Until then, the route had belonged exclusively to British Airways. Shocked by the assignment of the route to the upstart Virgin Airlines, British Airways engaged in an aggressive campaign against Virgin.

Branson wrote the head of British Airways, Lord King, objecting to accusations by British Airways that Virgin Airlines was financially weak and raising questions about Branson that he believed were personal in nature. King fired back a two-sentence reply that was not even addressed directly to Branson. The exchange marked the opening salvos of a bitter two-year feud between the two companies, marked by highly publicized accusations and counter-accusations of dirty tricks.

About half way through the feud, Branson attempted to contact directors of British Airways to intervene in the dispute, an excerpt of which is below, reminding them of a similar case several years earlier with Laker Airways that ended badly for British Airways.

The feud ended in court with British Airways agreeing to pay Branson £500,000 for personal libel—the highest uncontested libel payment ever made in British legal history—and to pay Virgin Atlantic £110,000 for corporate libel. Branson shared his settlement with Virgin Atlantic employees.

31 January 1991

[Lord King]

I am writing to put on record to you that I resent the level of personal abuse your people at British Ariways have recently resorted to. As Chairman of a small independent airline I have behaved no differently than you would have done in my place. I have argued our case with the CAA [Civil Aviation Authority] over Tokyo slots. They have decided in our favour. That decision is now under review. We have argued our case for access to Heathrow [Airport]. The CAA have decided in our favour and we are waiting on the Secretary of State's final decision.

In none of these issues have we behaved improperly. We have sought remedies through the CAA, the Department of Transport, the EEC and the High Court when appropriate. We have not at any stage made offensive personal remarks about you or Sir Colin Marshall. I would expect the same courtesy from your company.

Richard Branson

5 February 1991

I run my airline, Richard Branson runs his. Best of luck to him.

Lord King

11 December 1991

… I have found it hard to believe that a major public company like BA [British Airways] could be behind the sort of conduct identified in this letter whose primary purpose can only be the discrediting of a competitor and the damaging of its business. I am writing to you because I doubt whether you would want a company of which you are a director to conduct itself in such a way and in the hope that the directors of BA would wish to be absolutely and unequivocally disassociated from any such activities because they would agree that it was not the proper way to run a business.

I would like you to investigate the matters raised in this letter, provide detailed responses and give me your assurance that you will ensure that the conduct revealed to you on investigation or any similar conduct is stopped and never again repeated.

I would have thought that British Airways' experience of trying to eliminate the competitive threat posed by Laker Airways was sufficient deterrent against trying to do the same to others. I am sure you remember the impact upon BA of its actions towards Laker Airways. BA's privatisation plans were disrupted, the directors in the United States were threatened with criminal prosecution, there was a huge waste of management time, BA attracted considerable adverse publicity, millions of dollars were spent in legal expenses and BA made the biggest single contribution to the massive legal settlement fund.

Herb Kelleher to Southwest Airlines Employees
"The war begins with United Shuttle"

Quoting Winston Churchill, Southwest Airlines CEO Herb Kelleher wrote a memo to employees urging them to meet the challenge of directly competing with United Airlines, the world's largest airline. He titled the letter "Commencement of Hostilities." The letter rallied the company, with some employees even wearing combat fatigues to work.

Since the collapse of Russia's Aeroflot, United Airlines has become the largest airline in the world, approximately seven times the size of Southwest, in terms of gross revenues per year.

The world's largest airline has recently announced that it will launch its initial direct assault against Southwest, in the western part of our route system.

This initial attack will utilize roughly 25 of the 125 737s that United can devote to its "United Shuttle" operation, signifying that an additional 100 airplanes are in reserve to be hurled against us, at a later date.

United has, on hand, over $1,000,000,000 in cash; can cross-subsidize its efforts against Southwest with revenues derived from its worldwide service; and has substantially reduced its costs by recently obtaining substantial wage and benefit reductions from most of its employees.

In addition to our stock price, our wages, our benefits, our job security, our expansion opportunities, and foremost, our pride of accomplishment as a our nation's best airline are all on the line, as the war begins with United Shuttle on October 1, 1994, when it first takes to the air.

At its beginning, Southwest routed Braniff, Trans Texas, and Continental, with three airplanes. And Southwest can thwart United's actions against us with our 200 airplanes. The crucial elements are the martial vigor, the dedication, the energy, the unity, and the devotion to warm, hospitable, caring and loving Customer Service of all of our people.

Southwest's essential difference is not machines and "things." Our essential difference is minds, hearts, spirits and souls. Winston Churchill stated: "Success is never final." Indeed, "success" must be earned over and over again, or it disappears. I am betting on your minds, your hearts, your souls, and your spirits to continue our success. Let's win this one and make aviation history—again!

JACK WELCH TO SHAREHOLDERS, CUSTOMERS AND EMPLOYEES
"Driving to get the soul of a small company into this sometimes muscle-bound, big-company body"

As CEO of General Electric, Jack Welch guided the company to unprecedented success in the 1980s and 1990s by placing an emphasis on shareholder value. He earned widespread recognition for his management of the company by setting high standards, maintaining accountability, and taking a highly disciplined approach whereby GE only did business if it could be one of the top two companies in the industry.

GE shareholders benefited enormously during Welch's tenure, and stocks soared in value at an annual rate of 23.5 percent. Welch's 1999 letter to GE shareholders describes the results of his highly competitive management style, as well as some of the principles behind his approach to running GE.

To Our Share Owners, Customers and Employees

The final year of the century was our finest, as 340,000 GE people around the globe posted the strongest results in the Company's 122-year history.

Revenues rose 11% to $112 billion, a record.

Earnings increased 15% to $10.7 billion, the first time GE has broken the $10 billion mark in earnings from operations.

Earnings per share were up 15%.

Free cash flow was a strong $11.8 billion, up 17%.

Our ongoing operating margin rate grew to 17.8%, a gain of more than a full point from '98 and the third straight year of more than a full point improvement. Working capital turns hit an all-time high of 11.5—an improvement of 2.3 turns. The 80% improvement in this key performance measure over the past three years has added $4 billion to our cash flow. GE made 134 acquisitions in 1999, worth almost $17 billion. This marks the Company's third year in a row with over 100 acquisitions, totaling over $51 billion.

GE was named, for the second consecutive year, Fortune magazine's "Most Admired Company in America." Also for the second straight year, we were named "The World's Most Respected Company" by the Financial Times. A Business Week survey named the GE Board of Directors "Best Board," and Time magazine described GE as "The Company of the Century." We repurchased $1.9 billion in GE stock in 1999, raised the dividend 17% for the second consecutive year, and proposed a 3-for-1 stock split, the fifth split in 17 years, which will take effect after share owner approval in April 2000.

Our share owners—including our active and retired employees who have $24 billion of GE stock in their savings plans—were rewarded for this performance. The total return on a share of GE stock in 1999 was 54%. This followed returns of 41% in 1998, 51% in 1997, 40% in 1996 and 45% in 1995.

Understanding GE

In this report, for the first time, the CEOs of the top 20 GE businesses will describe the highlights and, in a few cases, the shortfalls of the year, and their plans for the future. Fourteen of these 20 businesses produced double-digit earnings increases in 1999: five grew more than 40%; four between 25-40%; five between 15-25%; three were about flat; three were down.

We never get it all "right" in any year, and probably never will, but it is the scale and leading market positions of these businesses, and the quality of the teams that run them, that allow us to have one great year after another. 1999 was an outstanding year—our best ever—but the past five have been great as well, as have the past 20. For that matter, it's been a great century. Edison would be pleased.

We believe annual reports are as much about where we can go as where we have been; and our message to you this year should enable you to look forward to the brightest of futures for GE in its third century of operation.

Much has been said of the difficulty of "understanding" GE because of the enormous diversity of its products and services and the breadth of its global operations. But it's actually easy to understand this Company, and to feel confident about its future growth, if you look at its array of world-class businesses and grasp the two fundamental forces that drive GE—its social architecture and its operating system.

The Social Architecture

GE's current social architecture began to form in the early '80s when we became convinced that the only way a company like ours could move quickly and successfully through times of radical change was to use every mind in the Company and to involve everyone in the game—to leave no one, and no good idea, out. To achieve this radical cultural transformation, we developed something we called "Work-Out," which is based on the simple premise that those closest to the work know it best. Over the years there have been literally hundreds of thousands of Work-Out "town meetings," where the views and ideas of every employee, from every function, in every business, were solicited and turned into action—usually on the spot. People saw the value we attached to their intellect and their ideas—and as a result, their ideas began to flow in torrents.

The second facet of the social architecture involved the cultivation of what we call "boundaryless" behavior by the removal of every organizational and functional obstacle to the free and unimpeded flow of ideas—inside the Company across every operation, and outside the Company from the best thinking in world business. We measured this boundaryless behavior in our leadership—and rewarded or removed people based on it. We anonymously survey thousands of employees every year to measure our progress and see if our rhetoric matches their reality. When it does not, we take action.

The combination of involving everyone in the game and of responding to this flow of ideas and information turned GE into what we are today—a learning company. By becoming a learning company, we have taken market and geographic diversity, the traditional handicap of multi-business companies, and turned them into a decisive advantage—unlimited access to the most enormous supply of best ideas, information and intellectual capital the business world has to offer.

Our social architecture—our values—is the software that drives what we call the operating system of GE.

The GE Operating System

The operating system of GE was devised to channel and focus this torrent of ideas and information and put it to use through the medium of Company-wide "initiatives," as well as to track, measure and expand these initiatives as they take hold and flourish.

This operating system is based on an informal but intense, regular schedule of reviews designed to create momentum for the initiative. It progresses with a drumbeat regularity throughout our business year—year after year.

A typical initiative—Product Services, say, or Six Sigma Quality—is launched with passionate intensity at the meeting of our 600 global leaders in January. A commitment to the initiative is made. Every subsequent event in the Company is developed around implementing and expanding the initiative: resources are allocated; high visibility jobs are created; intense communications start throughout the businesses; and work begins.

Each quarter throughout the year, the leaders of our businesses meet to share what each of them has done to drive the initiative. At these meetings, leaders ranging from the Reinsurance CEO, to the NBC executive, to the head of the Industrial Systems business describe how they are implementing the particular initiative in their own operations. The incredible amount of learning that comes from this shared experience expands the initiative and energizes their efforts.

Every Company activity and every Company event during the year add energy and momentum to the initiative. In these same quarterly meetings, for example, every Business Management Course class at our Management Development Institute—50 to 60 of our highest potential leaders—reports back on its three-week experience in the field on the best practices they found from other companies around the world—and they are brutally honest on how we stack up vis-à-vis the best they saw. This candid feedback really picks up the pace.

The same is true for Human Resources reviews. In April and May, the Corporate Executive Office and Human Resources leaders go into the field for full-day personnel reviews at each location, where the people leading and practicing the initiatives present their progress, and a clear assessment is made of the capabilities and the level of intensity of the people involved in the initiative. We want only the best, the brightest and the most committed to be in these leadership roles, and the focus on talent is relentless.

By October, role models—heroes—have emerged in all the businesses, and they are selected to present to the 150 Corporate Officers at their annual meeting. This meeting serves as a platform where each business can measure its progress against that of the best of its peers.

This takes us full circle to January, when the 600 global leaders of our Company meet and focus, once again, on the initiatives. The initiative from the prior January usually occupies the entire first day, and the role models present their stories and share their learning. On Day 2, new ideas around other ongoing initiatives—some several years old—are shared. This year, for example, the first full day was on e-Business. Day 2 covered new thinking in Globalization, Six Sigma and Product Services.

This operating system propels what has become a "learning engine" and embeds these initiatives in the DNA of the Company.

Crucial to the success of this social architecture and operating system is their synchronization with our reward and incentive system. How well people capitalize on these initiatives, how open they are to change, determines the level of their reward. Making the numbers at GE gets you into the game. Living the values and leveraging the operating system is the road to promotions and greater personal rewards.

Globalization

The oldest current initiative in GE, driven by the GE operating system for about 15 years, is, like Work-Out, becoming so pervasive and ingrained in the Company that it's less an "initiative" now and more a reflex. Globalization began with a GE that derived more than 80% of revenues from the U.S. and has taken us to where we are today, with 41% of revenues from outside the U.S. and moving toward a majority sometime in this decade.

Globalization evolved from a drive to export, to the establishment of global plants for local consumption, and then to global sourcing of products and services. Today, we are moving into its final stages—drawing upon intellectual capital from all over the world —from metallurgists in Prague, to software engineers in Asia, to product designers in Budapest, Monterrey, Tokyo, Paris and other places around the globe. Our insatiable appetite for more advanced technology is being fed, not by a new wing on our world-class Corporate R&D Center in Schenectady, New York, but by a soon-to-open greenfield laboratory in the suburbs of Bangalore, India.

There has been an enormous amount of comment recently on the subject of globalization. Let us assure you that GE brings only world-class business and work practices and careful, compliant and proactive environmental processes to every one of our global operations. We understand that to be a truly great global company, we must be a great local citizen.

Today, American GE business leaders located outside the United States have become fewer and fewer as local leaders, trained in GE operating methods and steeped in our values but with their own unmatchable customer intimacy and market savvy, are replacing them. Our objective is to be the "global employer of choice," and we are striving to create the exciting career opportunities for local leaders all over the world that will make this objective a reality. This initiative has taken us to within reach of one of our biggest and longest-running dreams—a truly global GE.

Product Services

The precursor to our Product Services initiative was a GE where new product development was primarily "where the action was" for our huge corps of engineers and scientists. The best and brightest of these wanted to work on the highest-thrust jet engine, the fastest medical scan or the leading-edge electrical turbine design. Product services consisted of less-exciting maintenance of our high-value machines—turbines, engines, medical devices and the like.

As recently as 1995, when this initiative was launched, GE derived $8 billion a year in revenues from product services. In 2000, this number will be $17 billion.

The premise for the Product Services initiative was the collective realization that while GE cannot win, and shouldn't play, in the "wrench-turning" game, it could find enormous growth in the high-technology, customer-productivity game—where there are few, if any, who can do the things we can do for that customer.

The human resources focus in the operating system made services the new "place to be" for the best and brightest. Big, exciting, high-technology jobs in services were created. And the GE values system—increasingly tied to customer focus—reinforced the shift.

But the most important key to the long-range success of our services initiative is the understanding that leading-edge technology can only be derived from creating great products. By driving this leading-edge technology back into the installed base of older equipment, we can increase our customers' productivity and, in turn, make them more competitive—with significantly lower investment on their part. We want being a product services customer of GE to be analogous to bringing your car in for a 50,000-mile check and driving out with 100 more horsepower, better gas mileage and lower emissions.

For example, the technology in the world's most advanced, highest-thrust jet engine—the GE90—is now being migrated into yesterday's installed base, refreshing 20-year-old customer engines, improving their thrust, fuel efficiency and time on-wing.

"H" gas turbine technology, the world's most advanced, is now improving the efficiency and heat rate of customers' 20- and 30-year-old power plants. Twenty-first century AC locomotive technology is making 1980s' locomotives more reliable; and 1990s' CT machines are producing better scans because of infusions of technology from Six Sigma-designed twenty-first century platforms.

We understand that to be a great services company, we must be a great leading-edge product technology company—they go hand in hand. Using tomorrow's technology to upgrade yesterday's hardware will make our customers more successful and create for GE a rapidly expanding services business for decades to come.

Six Sigma Quality

The Six Sigma initiative is in its fifth year—its fifth trip through the operating system. From a standing start in 1996, with no financial benefit to the Company, it has flourished to the point where it produced more than $2 billion in benefits in 1999, with much more to come this decade.

In the initial stages of Six Sigma, our effort consisted of training more than 100,000 people in its science and methodology and focusing thousands of "projects" on improving efficiency and reducing variance in our internal operations—from industrial factories to financial services back rooms. From there, our operating system steered the initiative into design engineering to prepare future generations of "Design for Six Sigma" products—and drove it rapidly across the customer-interactive processes of the financial services businesses. Medical Systems used it to open up a commanding technology lead in several diagnostic platforms and has achieved dramatic sales increases and customer satisfaction improvements. Every GE product business and financial service activity is using Six Sigma in its product design and fulfillment processes.

Today, Six Sigma is focused squarely where it must be—on helping our customers win. A growing proportion of Six Sigma projects now under way are done on customer processes, many on customer premises.

The objective is not to deliver flawless products and services that we think the customer wants when we promise them—but rather what customers really want when they want them.

One thing that the truly great companies of the world have in common, regardless of the diversity of their industries, is a total business focus on servicing customers. With Six Sigma as the enabler, we intend to meet that standard.

E-Business

E-Business, which entered the operating system at the January Managers Meeting little more than a year ago, is already so big and transformational that it has almost outgrown the bounds of the word "initiative." While we are already generating billions in Web-based revenues, the contribution of e-Business to GE has been so much more. It is changing this Company to its core.

For 20 years, we've been driving to get the soul of a small company into this sometimes muscle-bound, big-company body. We described the contribution of Work-Out, and there was more. We delayered in the '80s, eliminating many of the filters and gatekeepers. We got faster by reducing corporate staff. We launched venture units, in imitation of start-ups. We made close to 30,000 people stock optionees in a Company that used to have under 500. And we ridiculed and removed bureaucrats until they became as rare around GE as whooping cranes.

Every year we got better, faster, hungrier and more customer-focused—until the day this elixir, this tonic, this e-Business came along and changed the DNA of GE forever by energizing and revitalizing every corner of this Company.

The first effect of e-Business was to further energize and refresh our other three initiatives. For one, it enabled us to put to customer advantage the enormous databases we had compiled on customer processes as part of Six Sigma projects.

What we are rapidly moving toward is the day when "Dr. Jones," in radiology, can go to her home page in the morning and find a comparison of the number, and clarity, of scans her CT machines performed in the last day, or week, to more than 10,000 other machines across the world. She will then be able to click and order software solutions that will bring her performance up to world-class levels.

And the performance of her machines might have been improved, online, the previous night, by a GE engineer in Milwaukee, Tokyo, Paris or Bangalore.

The day is almost here when the chief engineer at the local utility may check the heat rate and fuel burn of his turbines—before he has coffee in the morning—to learn how he stacks up with 100 other utilities. Again, with a click to a home page, he can look at what GE services can provide to increase his competitiveness. Here, a number of GE's service packages are offered that will take him quickly to world-class levels.

The efficient harvesting of intellectual capital, which is the state-of-the-art of the globalization initiative, is impossible without the Internet, and GE products are today being designed collaboratively online around the globe 24 hours a day—as our Industrial Systems business does with its "Web City." But the transformation e-Business is bringing about at GE is more pervasive than even this growing magic.

When you think about this e-Business revolution that is transforming the world, an obvious question comes to mind: Why wasn't the e-revolution launched by big, highly resourced, high-technology companies rather than the small start-ups that led it? The answer may lie, as perhaps is true in GE's case, in the mystery associated with the Internet—the perception that creating and operating Web sites was Nobel Prize work—the realm of the young and wild-eyed. In our case, we once again used a best practice from one of our businesses to overcome this discomfort. We took the top 1,000 managers in the Company and asked them to become "mentees" of 1,000 "with it", very bright e-Business mentors — many brand new to GE — and to work with them three to four hours a week, traveling the Web, evaluating competitor sites, and learning to organize their computers, and their minds, for work on the Internet. It was this mentor-mentee interaction—which in some cases resembled that of "Stuart" and his boss in the Ameritrade commercial—that helped overcome the only real hurdle some of us had—fear of the unknown. Having overcome that fear, and experienced the transformational effects of e-Business, we find that digitizing a company and developing e-Business models is a lot easier—not harder—than we had ever imagined.

Start-ups have energized the business landscape, supported by a strong venture capital environment and healthy IPO market; however, much of their resources must go to establish brand, develop real content and achieve fulfillment capability. We already have that! We already have the hard stuff—over 100 years of a well-recognized brand, leading-edge technology in both product and financial services, and a Six Sigma-based fulfillment capability. The opportunities e-Business creates for large companies like GE are unlimited.

But digitizing a company does more than just create unlimited business opportunities; it puts a small company soul into that big company body and gives it the transparency, excitement and buzz of a start-up. It is truly the elixir for GE and others who relish excitement and change.

E-Business is the final nail in the coffin for bureaucracy at GE. The utter transparency it brings about is a perfect fit for our boundaryless culture and means everyone in the organization has total access to everything worth knowing.

The speed that is the essence of "e" has accelerated the metabolism of the Company, with people laughing out loud at presentations of business plans for "the third quarter of next year" and other tortoise-like projections of action. Time in GE today is measured in days and weeks.

The accelerating pace of our success in this initiative is leading to a lot of spontaneous celebrating—something big companies, including GE, have always had trouble doing as well as small companies. It generates more fun across a business than anything we've ever seen. The informality, joy of work and endless celebration that comes with "e" life is something on which we are thriving. E-Business was made for GE, and the "E" in GE now has a whole new meaning. We get it—we all get it.

We begin this century with a GE totally focused on the customer, utterly energized and rejuvenated by e-Business, and driven by the relentless beat of a unique operating system and social architecture. This Company is poised to move forward to levels of performance, growth and excitement undreamed of in the past.

We thank you all for your support in helping make this future so bright.

John F. Welch, Jr.

TOM PAQUIN TO NETSCAPE ENGINEERS
"We do whatever it takes"

A tiny start-up company, Netscape took the computer world by storm in the 1990s by developing a web browser that challenged Microsoft's supremacy in computer programming. Led by 23-year-old computer programmer Mark Andreesen and the maverick visionary Jim Clark, Netscape engineers worked frantically to finish their browser program in time for an initial public offering of the company.

In an internal e-mail, manager Tom Paquin urged Netscape's computer engineers to re-dedicate themselves to finishing the program under a very tight deadline.

To: engdept

From: paquin@mcom.com

Subject: Welcome to the Silicon Valley

Ok, we have decided we need to ship a product in October. This is great—it's what this "valley" is all about. If you can't tell, I'm kinda pumped by this, or, as [Chris Houck] would say, I'm all over it.

Here's the deal. We need to do a 3-platform NCSA-function-only release in October. The business case is pretty overwhelming; we can talk details tomorrow. We'll have to completely refocus our plans on this…. We do whatever it takes. And feel damn great about it when we pull it off.

I'll be grabbing people Friday to collect some data and responses. You can bet our Friday meeting will be about this. One thing's for sure: Busting our asses won't be enough for this; we must also focus.

Think roughly NCSA function done mid-August, everything done, including GUI [graphical user interface] end August, debugging & whatever else we need to do through September. Ship to customers for evaluation Sep 30. Release 10/14. I have some wacky ideas about testing starting mid-late August through end Sept. We can talk about this.

Start thinking How many boxes of Nodoz should we buy?

Tom

COMPLIMENTS AND COMPLAINTS

COMPLIMENTS

MARK TWAIN TO NEW YORK WESTERN UNION PRESIDENT
"A compliment ought always to precede a complaint"

To stay in operation, most businesses aim to please their customers. But this is not always possible. Customers often let companies know what they are doing right and what they are doing wrong. Some of history's most famous and infamous men and women have written businesses to critique their services.

The writer Mark Twain, whose real name was Samuel Clemens, often exercised his pen and wit on missives to major companies. Here he writes a letter in 1902 to the president of Western Union. Before launching into his complaint about the local telegraph services, Twain complimented the company for accomplishments that impressed him.

"The Pines"
York Harbor, Maine

Dear Sir,— I desire to make a complaint, and I bring it to you, the head of the company, because by experience I know better than to carry it to a subordinate.

I have been here a month and a half, and by testimony of friends, reinforced by personal experience I now feel qualified to claim as an established fact that the telegraphic service here is the worst in the world except that in Boston.

These services are actually slower than was the New York and Hartford service in the days when I last complained to you—which was fifteen or eighteen years ago, when telegraphic times and train time between the mentioned points was exactly the same, to-wit, three hours and a half.

Six days ago—it was that raw day which provoked so much comment—my daughter was on her way up from New York, and at noon she telegraphed me from New Haven asking that I meet her with a cloak at Portsmouth. Her telegram reached me four hours and a quarter later—just 15 minutes too late for me to catch my train and meet her.

I judge that the telegram traveled about 200 miles. It is the best telegraphic work I have seen since I have been here, and I am mentioning it in this place not as a complaint but as a compliment. I think a compliment ought always to precede a complaint, where one is possible, because it softens resentment and insures for the complaint a courteous and gentle reception.

Still, there is a detail or two connected with this matter which ought perhaps to be mentioned. And now, having smoothed the way with the compliment, I will venture them. The head corpse in the York Harbor office sent me that telegram altho (1) he knew it would reach me too late to be of any value; (2) also, that he was going to send it to me by his boy; (3) that the boy would not take the trolley and come the 2 miles in 12 minutes, but would walk; (4) that he would be two hours and a quarter on the road; (5) and that he would collect 25 cents for transportation, for a telegram which the h. c. knew to be worthless before he started it. From these data I infer that the Western Union owes me 75 cents; that is to say, the amount paid for combined wire and land transportation—a recoup provided for in the printed paragraph which heads the telegraph-blank.

By these humane and Christian stages we now arrive at the complaint proper. We have had a grave case of illness in the family, and a relative was coming some six hundred miles to help in the sick-room during the convalescing period. It was an anxious time, of course, and I wrote and asked to be notified as to the hour of the expected arrival of this relative in Boston or in York Harbor. Being afraid of the telegraph—which I think ought not to be used in times of hurry and emergency—I asked that the desired message be brought to me by some swift method of transportation. By the milkman, if he was coming this way. But there are always people who think they know more than you do, especially young people; so of course the young fellow in charge of this lady used the telegraph. And at Boston, of all places! Except York Harbor.

The result was handed to the h. c. of the Boston office at 9 this morning. It said, "Shall bring A. S. to you eleven forty-five this morning." The distance traveled by the dispatch is forty or fifty miles, I suppose, as the train-time is five minutes short of two hours, and the trains are so slow that they can't give a W. U. telegram two hours and twenty minutes start and overtake it. As I have said, the dispatch was handed in at Boston at 9. The expected visitors left Boston at 9.40, and reached my house at 12 noon, beating the telegram 2 solid hours, and five minutes over.

The boy brought the telegram. It was bald-headed with age, but still legible. The boy was prostrate with travel and exposure, but still alive, and I went out to condole with him and get his last wishes and send for the ambulance. He was waiting to collect transportation before turning his passing spirit to less serious affairs. I found him strangely intelligent, considering his condition and where he is getting his training. I asked him at what hour the telegram was handed to the h. c. in Boston. He answered brightly, that he didn't know.

I examined the blank, and sure enough the wary Boston h. c. had thoughtfully concealed that statistic. I asked him at what hour it had started from Boston. He answered up as brightly as ever, and said he didn't know.

I examined the blank, and sure enough the Boston h. c. had left that statistic out in the cold, too. In fact it turned out to be an official concealment—no blank was provided for its exposure. And none required by law, I suppose. "It is a good one-sided idea," I remarked; "They can take your money and ship your telegram next year if they want to—you've no redress. The law ought to extend the privilege to all of us."

The boy looked upon me coldly.

I asked him when the telegram reached York Harbor. He pointed to some figures following the signature at the bottom of the blank—"12.14." I said it was now 1.45 and asked—

"Do you mean that it reached your morgue an hour and a half ago?"

He nodded assent.

"It was at that time half an hour too late to be of any use to me, if I wanted to go and meet my people—which was the case—for by the wording of the message you can see that they were to arrive at the station at 11.45. Why did your h. c. send me this useless message? Can't he read? Is he dead?"

"It's the rules."

"No, that does not account for it. Would he have sent it if it had been three years old, I in the meantime deceased, and he aware of it?"

The boy didn't know.

"Because, you know, a rule which required him to forward to the cemetery to-day a dispatch due three years ago, would be as good a rule as one which should require him to forward a telegram to me to-day which he knew had lost all its value an hour or two before he started it. The construction of such a rule would discredit an idiot; in fact an idiot—I mean a common ordinary Christian idiot, you understand—would be ashamed of it, and for the sake of his reputation wouldn't make it. What do you think?"

He replied with much natural brilliance that he wasn't paid for thinking.

This gave me a better opinion of the commercial intelligence pervading his morgue than I had had before; it also softened my feelings toward him, and also my tone, which had hitherto been tinged with bitterness.

"Let bygones be bygones," I said, gently, "we are all erring creatures, and mainly idiots, but God made us so and it is dangerous to criticise."

Sincerely, S. L. Clemens

DAVID HUME TO ADAM SMITH
"It has Depth and Solidity and Acuteness"

British economist Adam Smith defined the basic principles and benefits of a free market economy with his seminal book The Wealth of Nations. *Smith described how the "invisible hand" of the profit motive leads to the most efficient use of labor and resources. Economist David Hume of Scotland was one of the first to recognize the importance of Smith's book.*

Edinburgh, 1 Apr. 1776

Euge! Belle! Dear Mr. Smith:

I am much pleas'd with your Performance, and the perusal of it has taken me from a State of great Anxiety. It was a Work of so much Expectation, by yourself, by your Friends, and by the Public, that I trembled for its Appearance; but am now much relieved. Not but that the Reading of it necessarily requires so much Attention, and the Public is disposed to give so little, that I shall still doubt for some time of its being at first very popular: But it has Depth and Solidity and Acuteness, and is so much illustrated by curious Facts, that it must at last take the public Attention. It is probably much improved by your last Abode in London. If you were here at my Fireside, I should dispute some of your principles. I cannot think, that the Rent of Farms makes any part of the Price of the Produce, but that the Price is determined altogether by the Quantity and Demand. It appears to me impossible, that the King of France can take a Seigniorage of 8 per cent upon the Coinage. No body would bring Bullion to the mint: It would be all sent to Holland or England, where it might be coined and sent back to France for less than two per cent. Accordingly Neckre says, that the French King takes only two per cent of Seingiorage. But these and a hundred other Points are fit only to be discussed in Conversation; which, till you tell me the contrary, I shall still flatter myself with soon. I hope it will be soon: For I am in a very bad State of Health and cannot afford a long Delay.

I fancy you are acquainted with Mr. Gibbon: I like his Performance extremely and have ventured to tell him, that, had I not been personally acquainted with him, I should never have expected such an excellent Work from the Pen of an Englishman. It is lamentable to consider how much that Nation has declined in Literature during our time. I hope he did not take amiss the national Reflection....

I wrote you about six Weeks ago, which I hope you received: You may certainly at present have the Subject of a Letter to me; and you have no longer any pressing Occupation. But our Friendship does not depend on these Ceremonials.

D H

CLYDE BARROW TO HENRY FORD

"I have drove Fords exclusively when I could get away with one"

Six weeks before being gunned down with his partner Bonnie Parker, gangster Clyde Barrow wrote the following letter to Henry Ford complimenting him on the reliability of his automobiles. The charming letter from the popularly romanticized couple belies the fact that Barrow and Parker were accused of murdering twelve people during the previous two years.

Tulsa Okla
10th April [1934]
Mr. Henry Ford
Detroit Mich.

Dear Sir:—

While I still have got breath in my lungs I will tell you what a dandy car you make. I have drove Fords exclusively when I could get away with one. For sustained speed and freedom from trouble the Ford has got ever[y] other car skinned, and even if my business hasn't been strictly legal it don't hurt enything to tell you what a fine car you got in the V8.

Yours truly
Clyde Champion Barrow

PASCO KIWANIS CLUB TO DUPONT COMPANY

"One cent each to make up the difference"

The manufacturing company E. I. DuPont de Nemours & Co. secretly built the atomic bomb for the United States government as part of the massive Hanford Engineers Works near Pasco, Washington, during World War II. When the bomb was dropped on Hiroshima in early 1945, it effectively ended the war and saved thousands of American lives by extension. It was soon revealed that DuPont had done the project for a profit of one dollar. A thirty-two cents expense item, however, had reduced the profit margin to sixty-eight cents, prompting the local Kiwanis Club to praise the company for its work and make up the financial difference. The president of DuPont replied to the gesture in kind.

August 11, 1945
Mr. Walter S. Carpenter, Jr., President
E. I. DuPont de Nemours & co.
Wilmington, Delaware

Dear Mr. Carpenter:

At the last regular meeting of the Pasco Kiwanis Club a resolution was passed which reads as follows:

"An article in the local newspaper states that the DuPont Company received only One Dollar profit from the operations at the Hanford plant and that an expense item of thirty-two cents was not allowed by an accountant, leaving the balance of sixty-eight cents. Thirty-two members of this club are contributing one cent each to make up the difference and also placing their signatures to this letter."

We are proud to be so closely situated to the Hanford project, and all of us feel very sincerely that we have had a part in this magnificent enterprise. We also hope that the Lord will see fit to direct future efforts and achievements of this product into the right channel for the good of all mankind.

Sincerely yours,
Mel Swanson, President

August 30th 1945
Mr. Mel Swanson, President
Pasco Kiwanis Club
Pasco, Washington

Dear Mr. Swanson:

I appreciate sincerely the efforts of you and your associates to restore the solvency of our operation at Hanford. This good-humored gesture of friendliness on your part brings pleasure to all of us. We have always regarded our one dollar fee for the Hanford work as satisfactory compensation.

In fact, so highly do we prize the spirit which led you to write your amusing letter and send us the 32 cents, that we are placing both the letter and the contribution in our company museum for permanent record. It is a most appropriate addition to the various archives and mementoes of sentimental significance of DuPont history.

Please accept our thanks and assurances of appreciation for the cooperation and generosity shown us by the people of the Pasco area. The exacting industrial assignment carried out there, amid conditions calling for utmost discretion from the community, could not have been been fulfilled without your able and unstinting assistance. Your forebearance and understanding, under trying circumstances, have been invaluable.

We join fervently in your prayers that the future of atomic energy can be directed toward the benefit and advancement of the human race. We recognize, with you, the national responsibility involved. I am confident, however, that the unity and devotion of the many who had a part in the success of the project will in the end succeed also in turning to the good of all men.

Yours sincerely,
W. S. Carpenter, Jr.

DAVID OGILVY'S OBSERVATIONS ON TALENT
"One of the best headlines I ever read"

For better or worse, the advertising legend David Ogilvy was always direct in his opinions and frequently not shy about expressing them in print. The following three brief letters and memos reflect his directness and humor. The first is a memo to an employee, Joel Raphaelson, written in 1964. The second is a letter to the New Hampshire Vacation Center. And the final one is to a former copywriter of Ogilvy & Mather, Ray Taylor.

Joel:

I thought you promised to show me the Sears ad (with copy) last Tuesday.

It is now three months since Struthers picked them. Longer than the period of gestations in PIGS.

D.O.

April 12, 1971

Gentlemen:

"America is alive and well and living in New Hampshire." This is one of the best headlines I have ever read.

I offer humble congratulations to the man or woman who wrote it.

Yours sincerely,

D.O.

June 29, 1983

Dear Ray:

Nineteen years ago you wrote me the best job application letter I have ever received. I can still recite the first paragraph. ["My father was in charge of the men's lavatory at the Ritz Hotel. My mother was a chambermaid at the same hotel. I was educated at the London School of Economics."]

For the next three years you were one of the best copywriters ever employed in our New York office.

I was miserable when you returned to London, and still more miserable when you joined another agency.

But I cannot grudge Masius their good fortune in recruiting you, because it was Mike Masius who got me my first job in the United States.

Now I hear that you are retiring. What a waste of genius.

May your shadow never grow less.

Yours affectionately,

David Ogilvy

COCA-COLA CUSTOMERS TO COCA-COLA

"It was nice knowing you"

On April 23, 1985, the Coca-Cola Company unveiled New Coke, a revamped version of the most popular soda drink in the history of the United States. During World War II, General Dwight Eisenhower issued specific orders for millions of bottles of Coke. One soldier wrote home: "This week, Coca-Cola came to Italy. Seemingly everyone had heard the rumor, but no one put much faith in it. How could it be true? Coca-Cola is some vaguely familiar nectar, reminiscent of some far-off paradise land."

Forty years later, company officials believed they had a great new product to replace the traditional Coke, which was under pressure from competitors like Pepsi and diet sodas. By combining the brand name of "Coke" with what they believed was a better-tasting product, Coca-Cola Company thought it had a sure winner. In hand-delivered letters to the national media, the company wrote:

"Robert C. Goizueta, chairman of the board and chief executive officer of the Coco-Cola Company, and Donald Keough, president and chief operating officer, invite you to a news conference, which they will conduct on Tuesday, April 23, in New York City, at which time the most significant soft-drink marketing development in the company's nearly 100-year history will be announced."

But Coca-Cola was wrong. A hailstorm of criticism and complaints greeted New Coke. Coke customers bombarded the company with calls at a rate of 5,000 a day and sacks of letters. Consumers compared Coke to a friend, the U.S. Constitution, and an American icon. Excerpts from some of the letters are below.

Reversing one of the great gaffs in American marketing history, Coca-Cola nullified its decision to stop producing the traditional Coke. Instead, the company decided to produce two lines of its soda, Classic Coke and New Coke. This prompted a second wave of letters praising the company for restoring their beloved soft drink.

Letters about New Coke

Dear Sir:

Changing Coke is like God making the grass purple or putting toes on your ears or teeth on your knees.

It was nice knowing you. You were a friend for most of my 35 years. Yesterday I had my first taste of the new Coke and to tell the truth, if I would have wanted Pepsi, I would have ordered a Pepsi not a Coke.

It is absolutely TERRIBLE! You should be ashamed to put the Coke label on it…. This new stuff tastes worse than Pepsi.

Monkeying with the receipt is akin to diddling with the U.S. Constitution…. Many of us aren't interested in caffeine-free, NutraSweet, diet slop, fancy gimmicks or new formulas. After all these years, the original Coke practically runs through our veins.

I can only hope your daring spirit will come forth when you realize the mistake you have made and you can admit it publicly. And that you'll have the guts to go back to the original formula.

I do not drink alcoholic beverages, I don't smoke, and I don't chase other women, my only vise has been Coke. Now you have taken that pleasure from me.

Letters on restoring old Coke

With the return of "Coca-Cola Classic," you might say that the old coke has been "reincarbonated."

God does work in mysterious ways and I thank him for answering my prayers to bring back the "real" Coke.

We love you for caring! You have given us back our dream! We are grateful. You have made our hard lives easier to bear and have given us confidence in ourselves to change things for the better.

I feel like a lost friend is returning home.

SOUTHWEST AIRLINES CUSTOMERS TO HERB KELLEHER
"You are the talk of the town"

Daring to betray convention, Herb Kelleher built Southwest Airlines into one of the most admired companies in America. His seemingly screwball style has included painting planes to look like killer whales, implementing a policy to "hire people with a sense of humor," and making feuding departments switch places for a day to appreciate the challenges other company employees face.

In addition to keeping prices down, Southwest Airlines has consistently scored at the top among all airlines in terms of customer satisfaction. As the flow of complimentary letters to the company reflect, the company defied the industry's reputation for impersonal dealings with its customers.

Dear Mr. Kelleher,

… Another real bonus from flying Southwest is the ease of travel arrangements. I can honestly say I have never used an airline "ticket" to fly your airline. Quite frankly, it wasn't until my sister used one of my free passes that I realized there was such a thing as a Southwest Airlines ticket. Whenever I make my travel reservations, it is so easy. And because my schedule often changes, so do my flight plans. But your people make the changes I need quickly and always with a smile and thanks.

Dugald K. Winter
San Antonio, Texas

[To Southwest Airlines]

I flew in early May to Albuquerque, on a flight that began with the flight attendant welcoming us and then telling us that we have a VIP on board. He welcomed Leonard Nimoy, the actor who played Spock on "Star Trek." We all clapped and turned to see him—we were told this was all in fun. Instead, we were the VIPs on board! Then he graciously welcomed each of us to Southwest Airlines as the most important person…. He then treated us to the most entertaining flight announcement routine, telling us we were flying over 7,943 hot tubs, swimming pools, etc., so here was the water evacuation information. Please wave to his mother on cue. He had a great sense of humor and mixed fun several times into our flight. On arriving, he and the crew sang a song, and he closed by saying if we enjoyed our flight, their names were Reggie, Sam, and Pete. However, if we didn't enjoy his foolishness, their names were Fred, Tom, and Harry. Everyone was laughing and in a great mood by the time we deplaned.

Now I realize that not everyone has Reggie's personality and showmanship. But I think many people don't risk this kind of playfulness because they fear that it will be seen as unprofessional. There is a new kind of professionalism that Southwest is becoming known for; all over the world—great service with lots of fun mixed in.

[To Southwest Airlines]

Southwest is without a doubt the most responsive business today. As far as I know, it is the only business where you call and a human voice answers on the first ring.

Donelle Weiss
Hammond, Indiana

[To Southwest Airlines]

Please let your flight attendants and customer service agents know that every time you play games to generate some creative fun with Customers, you get free advertising. I hear wonderful stories about games, songs, poems, and skits on Southwest everywhere I go. I was in Orlando and people were talking about how flying Southwest was more fun than Disneyland and then told about a game of drawing a pumpkin on their head without looking or a scavenger hunt while waiting for a weather delay. You are the talk of the town.

Thank you, Southwest. You're terrific.

A Frequent Flyer

COMPLAINTS

JON SHUBERT TO SOUTHWEST AIRLINES EMPLOYEES
"Everyone deserves apologies"

While Southwest Airlines may get an unusually high dose of compliments from its customers, that doesn't mean it is immune to criticism. In a 1992 memo to employees, Jon Shubert, the company's manager of executive office communications, defined the different categories of complaints the airlines receives and offered commentary on how to respond.

December 1992

It is inevitable that we will not be able to please all of our Customers all of the time. The complaints we receive usually fall into two categories: (1) we didn't do something we should have; or (2) we did something we shouldn't have. So beware the pitfalls of, respectively, Omission and Commission!

Omission

• A Customer writes, "Your employees didn't apologize even once!" We've seen that complaint many times. That's Omission, because we didn't do something we should have.

• "We waited in the gate area for almost two hours, and no one updated us on our delayed flight." Omission.

Work on empathizing with our Customers. Let them know what, when, why, and how to the best of your knowledge. Keep them informed. Let them know we care and we're sorry. After all, everyone wants explanations—and everyone deserves apologies.

Commission

Commission, on the other hand, is when we do too much. How could that upset a Customer, you ask? Well, consider "verbal communication":

• Mr. Bigg arrives just as the flight closes and demands that you and your cohorts form a human bridge from the jetway to the aircraft door. This is not a good time to engage in off-the-cuff lecturing: "You should have been here sooner!" That's Commission. (And Customers routinely classify this as "verbal abuse" in their letters.) Save the "tsk,tsk"-ing for Rover when he gnaws on the corners of the Chippendale.

• Ms. Haverman's Guccis didn't arrive. Practicing armchair psychology will only make matters worse. "Maybe you just *thought* you handed them over at curbside to a Southwest employee. Are you sure he was wearing a Southwest uniform?" Commission. Engaging thusly is dangerous, and ranks up there with eating snakes.

CHARLES DICKENS TO CLOCKMAKER
"Enduring internal agonies of a most distressing nature"

Charles Dickens wrote this letter to a local clock shop in the hopes of getting a repairman to his house.

Gad's Hill Place, Higham by Rochester, Kent,
Monday Night, Fourteenth September, 1863

My dear Sir,

Since my hall clock was sent to your establishment to be cleaned it has gone (as indeed it always has) perfectly well, but has struck the hours with great reluctance, and after enduring internal agonies of a most distressing nature, it has now ceased striking altogether. Though a happy release for the clock, this is not convenient to the household. If you can send down any confidential person with whom the clock can confer, I think it may have something on its works that it would be glad to make a clean breast of.

Faithfully yours,
Charles Dickens

MARK TWAIN TO HARTFORD GAS COMPANY

"Your present idea is to leave us a little more in the dark"

Mark Twain made frequent complaints to his gas company in Hartford, Connecticut.

Gentlemen,

There are but two places in our whole street where lights could be of any value, by any accident, and you have measured and appointed your intervals so ingeniously as to leave each of those places in the center of a couple of hundred yards of solid darkness. When I noticed that you were setting one of your lights in such a way that I could almost see how to get into my gate at night, I suspected that it was a piece of carelessness on the part of the workmen and would be corrected as soon as you should go around inspecting and find it out. My judgment was right. It is always right when you are concerned. For fifteen years, in spite of my prayers and tears, you persistently kept a gas lamp exactly half-way between my gates so that I couldn't find either of them after dark, and then furnished such execrable gas that I had to hang a danger signal on the lamp post to keep teams from running into it, nights. Now I suppose your present idea is to leave us a little more in the dark.

Don't mind us—out our way. We possess but one vote apiece, and no rights which you are in any way bound to respect. Please take your electric light and go to—but never mind, it is not for me to suggest. You will probably find the way. And anyway you can reasonably count on divine assistance if you lose your bearings.

S. L. Clemens

Hartford, February 12, 1891

Dear Sirs:

Some day you will move me almost to the verge of irritation by your chuckle-headed Goddamned fashion of shutting your Goddamned gas off without giving any notice to your Goddamned parishioners. Several times you have come within an ace of smothering half of this household in the beds and blowing up the other half by this idiotic, not to say criminal, custom of yours. And it has happened again to-day. Haven't you a telephone?

Ys, S L Clemens

DISSATISFIED CUSTOMER TO FRENCH TYPEWRITER SHOP
"Vous pourrxz ravoir cx damné instrumxnt"

Illustrating his point of contention beautifully, a very dissatisfied French customer uses the faulty typewriter he bought to type his complaint to the shop from which he made his purchase. Among other problems, the typewriter apparently refused to type the letter "e," preferring "x" instead.

Monsixur,

Il y a quxlquxs sxmainxs jx mx suis offxrt unx dx vos machinxs à écrix. Au début j'xn fus assxz contxnt. Mais pas pour longtxmps. Xn xffxt, vous voyxz vous-mémx lx défaut. Chaqux fois qux jx vxux tapxr un x, c'xt un x qux j'obtixns. Cxla mx rxnd xnragé. Car quand jx vxux un x, c'xst un x qu'il mx faut xt non un x. Cxla rxndrait n'importx qui furixux. Commxnt fairx pour obtxnir un x chaqux fois qux jx desirx un x? Un x xst x, xt non un x. Saisissxz-vous cx qux jx vxux dirx?

Jx voudrais savoir si vous étxs xn mxsurx dx mx livrxr unx machinx à écrirx donnant un x chaqux fois qux j'ai bxsoin d'un lorsqu'on tapx un x, vous pourrxz ravoir cx damné instrumxnt. Un x xst trés bixn tant qux x, mais, oh xnfxr!

Sincérxmxnt à vous, un dx vox clixnts rxndu xnragé.

Xugénx X

Sir:

Sxvxral wxxks ago I was offxrxd onx of your typxwritxrs. At first I was plxasxd, but not for long. In fact, you can sxx thx problxm right hxrx. Xvxry timx I want to typx n x, I gxt an x instxad. This xnragxs mx. Whxn I want an x, an x is what I nxxd, and not an x. This would xnragx anyonx. What should I do to gxt an x xvxry timx I want an x? An x that is an x, not an x. Do you undxrstand what I'm trying to say?

I'd likx to know if you'd bx ablx to sxll mx a typxwritxr that gavx mx an x xach timx I nxxd an x whxn I typx an x, you can havx this damnxd instrumxnt. An x is vxry good as an x, but, oh hxll!

Yours sincxrxly, onx of your customxrs drivxn to ragx.

Xugxnx X.

UNHAPPY OPERA FAN TO VERDI
"This money troubles my rest like a frightful spectre"

Disappointed by an opera written by Verdi, Signor Prospero Bertani wrote the composer an extraordinary letter announcing his dislike of Aida and demanding his money back for the two performances that he paid to attend, along with reimbursement for railroad tickets and dinner.

Verdi wrote his publishers, Messrs Ricordi in Milan, asking them to pay Bertani 27 lire 80 centimes. "It is not the amount he demands," Verdi noted, "but that in addition I should be expected to pay for his supper, certainly not! He might well take his meals at home.

"It is understood that he will give you an acknowledgement, and further a short letter in reply, undertaking to hear my new operas no more, exposing himself no more to the menace of spectres, and sparing me further traveling expenses."

Bertani wrote a letter back, pledging to not attend a new opera by Verdi again, and that if he does, and is dissatisfied, he would bear the costs of the expenditure.

Much honored Signor Verdi,

The 2nd of this month I went to Parma, drawn there by the sensation made by your opera *Aida*. So great was my curiosity, that half an hour before the commencement of the piece I was already in my place, No. 120. I admired the *mise en scène*, I heard with pleasure the excellent singers, and I did all in my power to let nothing escape me. At the end of the opera, I asked myself whether I was satisfied, and the answer was "No." I started back to Reggio and listened in the railway to the opinions given upon *Aida*. Nearly all agreed in considering it a work of the first order.

I was then seized with the idea of hearing it again, and on the 4th I returned to Parma; I made unheard-of efforts to get a reserved seat; as the crowd was enormous, I was obliged to throw away five lire to witness the performance in any comfort.

I arrived at this decision about it: it is an opera in which there is absolutely nothing which causes any enthusiasm or excitement, and without the pomp of the spectacle, the public would not stand it to the end. When it has filled the house two or three times, it will be banished to the dust of the archives.

You can now, dear Signor Verdi, picture to yourself my regret at having spent on two occasions thirty-two lire; add to this the aggravating circumstances that I depend on my family, and that this money troubles my rest like a frightful spectre. I therefore frankly address myself to you, in order that you may send me the amount. The account is as follows:

	Lire
Railroad—going......................	2.60
Railroad—returning................	3.30
Theater............................	8
Detestable supper at the station...	2
Twice..............................	15.90
	31.80

Hoping that you will deliver me from this embarrassment, I salute you from my heart.

Bertani

My address: Bertani Prospero, Via San Domenico, No. 5.

TAXPAYERS TO INTERNAL REVENUE SERVICE
"If we did this to a customer, we'd lose their business"

Fairly or not, the U.S. Internal Revenue Service has held a poor reputation in its handling of taxpayers for many decades. Here are two letters to the agency from taxpayers complaining of problems they had encountered.

Dear Sir:

I received the notice from your "idiot box, commonly called computer" indicating that I owe you $5.00 plus $.11 interest on my 1963 tax return.

I know it is common practice for your service to charge the taxpayers for information rendered to them about their returns. I am enclosing herewith a bill for my services, and telling you that your computer forgot to apply the $5.00 filed with my estimated tax return. Please refer to line 19-b.

Inasmuch as my time is extremely valuable, it seems to me that the charge I have made for my services to straightening out your computer is most reasonable. Your prompt remittance will be appreciated so that I will not have to start charging interest on the amount you owe me.

Sir:

You had better check your records of your data processing system again and if you don't come up with the right answer you better have the robot overhauled.

The records of my processing system, which is by the way myself, shows that I wrote and mailed a check, together with depository receipts, in the amount of $60.57 on April 15. Your dept. endorsed it on May 5. Where it was all that time, I'll be damned. But I have the cancelled check to prove it.

Get it straightened out once and for all. You people have made more errors with our account in the past few months than is necessary.

If we did this to a customer we'd lose their business

NORMAN ROCKWELL TO PERSONAL SECRETARY
"My honest sentiment about those damn figurines"

Paintings of America's premier 20th-century illustrator Norman Rockwell were often used for commercial purposes. Most of his images first appeared on magazine covers and calendars. Many companies wanted to use Rockwell's images for other objects, such as plates and figurines. Rockwell, however, was less than enthused about it, and in some cases, he hated the results. In this memo to his personal secretary, Rockwell wrote a draft letter to a figurine manufacturer. It is not known whether the letter was actually mailed.

Clair:

Enclosed you'll find a letter expressing my honest sentiment about those damn figurines. You must have seen them and you must agree with me they're pretty terrible. Please write and tell me if I'm doing it the right way.

Bernard,

I don't know what to say but I think I should be honest. I think the figurines are awful and I just don't think they bring any credit to me as representing my work.

These are harsh words but I do think I should tell the truth.

Norman Rockwell

"Lazlo Toth" to Gold Seal Co.
"My Mother doesn't even get a capital for her *M*!"

Comedian Don Novello frequently wrote to politicians, generals, and business leaders under the assumed name "Lazlo Toth" inquiring about the most preposterous issues in very serious terms. Novello sent one of the letters to the makers of Mr. Bubble asking why the box instructed users to keep the soap dry.

The manufacturer, The Gold Seal Company, dutifully responded that the soap was most effective if the box was kept away from moisture. The letter ended with promotional comments about the company's new product "SNOWY" BLEACH. "Toth" responded with mock indignity, which drew a final letter of apology from the company.

February 18, 1974
Mr. Bubble
Gold Seal Co.
Bismark, N.D. 58501

Dear Gentlemen:

I want you to know first of all that I enjoy your product. It's always refreshing to spend some time in the tub with some bubbles.

However, I must confess I am puzzled by some of the instruction on the box. It says: "KEEP DRY". How can you use it if you keep it dry?

Thought you'd be interested to know someone caught the mistake.

I thought you'd like to know.

Sincerely,
Lazlo Toth

164 Palm

San Rafael, California

March 1, 1974

M. Hershey

Consumer Relations Dir.

Gold Seal Company

10303 Northwest Freeway

Houston, Texas 77018-ZIP

Dear M. Hershey,

I was being nice to tell you about the error you have on your box and you send me coupons and tell me to give an educational bulletin about stains to my Mother.

To begin with, I wouldn't give your lousy educational bulletin #22 to nobody! Everybody I know knows more about stains and that stuff than your fancy company will ever know! Why you don't even know how to thank someone when they offer you an intelligent suggestion! And then you have the nerve to try to give me some pitch about your BLEACH!

I was writing about MR. BUBBLE, I don't care about BLEACH! What does BLEACH have to do with it! Come on!

And how come the only words in capitals are SNOWY BLEACH and MR. BUBBLE while my Mother doesn't even get a capital for her *M*!

This is a warning that I'm thinking of moving on to another bubble bath.

Stand by our President!

With a right to be angry,

Lazlo Toth

Encl.

Bulletin #22

SNOWY and MR. BUBBLE

Coupons

DEALS

PROPOSALS

DIONYSARION TO PROTARCHUS
"A dowry of clothes to the value of 240 silver pieces"

From as far back as ancient Greece, marriage has often been more about a financial arrangement between families than about affection. Dowries reflect the financial "value" of the wife and her family, as well as the "cost" of the husband's support of his wife, and appear in print as far back as the Book of Genesis.

Girls and young women often saved money for their dowries to enhance their marriage prospects and escape the curse of remaining single. The following letter, dating from the first century B.C., is from a Roman woman with money troubles arranging the terms of her dowry.

To Protarchus, from Dionysarion, the daughter of Protarchus, with her brother Protarchus as guardian, and from Hermione, daughter of Hermias, a citizen, on the authority of her brother's son, Hermias:

Dionysarion agrees that the contract is invalidated which the son of Hermione, Hermias, made with her, with Hermione serving as bondsman. . . . It is agreed, on behalf of her deceased husband, that Dionysarion take from Hermione's house by hand the dowry which she brought to Hermias, with Hermione serving as bondsman: a dowry of clothes to the value of 240 silver pieces, earrings, and a ring. . . . The contract is invalidated with all documents sealed by her. Dionysarion is not to enter suit against Hermione, nor is any man acting on her behalf, not for any of the deceased Hermias' possessions nor concerning the dowry or support nor about any other written or unwritten agreement made in the past up the present day. Since Dionysarion has become pregnant, she is not to sue for childbirth, because she is more persuasive on that account; she is permitted to expose her baby or to join herself in marriage to another husband. She agrees that if she breaks this authorized agreement she is subject to damages and the established fine.

JEANNE BÉCU (DU BARRY) TO M. DUVAL, AN ADMIRER
"I will tell you what I suggest now: pay attention"

Blond and charming, Jeanne Bécu learned at a young age how to leverage her alluring qualities among 18ᵗʰ-century French royalty. As a shop attendant in Paris, she attracted the attention of some of the nation's leading young aristocratic men. For business reasons, she used the surname (Rançon) of the man her mother married late in life. Early in her ascent to the highest circles of French power, she learned how to negotiate the best deal for herself, as this letter to an admiring young French noble, written when Du Barry was a teenager, demonstrates. Thirty-two years later, Bécu was among the first to be executed by guillotine during the French Revolution's Reign of Terror.

April 6ᵗʰ, 1761

Yes, my dear friend, I have told you, and repeat it: I love you dearly. You certainly said the same thing to me, but on your side it is only impetuosity; directly after the first enjoyment, you would think of me no more. I begin to know the world. I will tell you what I suggest, now: pay attention. I don't want to remain a shopgirl, but a little more my own mistress, and would therefore like to find someone to keep me. If I did not love you, I would try to get money from you; I would say to you, You shall begin by renting a room for me and furnishing it; only as you told me that you were not rich, you can take me to your own place. It will not cost you any more rent, not more for your table and the rest of your housekeeping. To keep me and my headdress will be the only expense, and for those give me one hundred livres a month, and that will include everything. Thus we could both live happily, and you would never again have to complain about my refusal. If you love me, accept this proposal; but if you do not love me, then let us each of us try his luck elsewhere. Good-by, I embrace you heartily.

Rançon

Thomas Jefferson to Samuel H. Smith
"Make me the tender of it to the library committee of Congress"

Shortly after British troops sacked Washington, D. C., during the War of 1812, Thomas Jefferson offered to sell his extraordinary collection of books to the federal government and create the new Library of Congress. Compiled meticulously over the course of half a century in America and Europe, the books filled nearly 20 wagons. Congress accepted Jefferson's offer, starting one of the world's most impressive and complete libraries.

Monticello, September 21, 1814

Dear Sir,

I learn from the newspapers that the Vandalism of our enemy has triumphed at Washington over science as well as the arts, by the destruction of the public library with the noble edifice in which it was deposited. Of this transaction, as of that of Copenhagen, the world will entertain but one sentiment. They will see a nation suddenly withdrawn from a great war, full armed and full handed, taking advantage of another whom they had recently forced into it, unarmed, and unprepared, to indulge themselves in acts of barbarism which do not belong to a civilized age. . . .

I presume it will be among the early objects of Congress to re-commence their collection. This will be difficult while the war continues, and intercourse with Europe is attended with so much risk. You know my collection, its condition and extent. I have been fifty years making it, and have spared no pains, opportunity or expense, to make it what it is. While reading in Paris, I devoted every afternoon I was disengaged, for a summer or two, in examining all the principal bookstores, turning over every book with my own hand, and putting by everything which related to America, and indeed whatever was rare and valuable in every science. Besides this, I had standing orders during the whole time I was in Europe, on its principal book-marts, particularly Amsterdam, Frankfort, Madrid and London, for such works relating to America as could not be found in Paris. So that in that department particularly, such a collection was made as probably can never again be effected, because it is hardly probable that the same opportunities, the same time, industry, perseverance and expense, with some knowledge of the bibliography of the subject, would again happen to be in concurrence. During the same period, and after my return to America, I was led to procure, also, whatever related to the duties of those in the high concerns of the nation. So that the collection, which I suppose is of between nine and ten thousand volumes, while it includes what is chiefly valuable in science and literature generally, extends more particularly to whatever belongs to the American statesman. In the diplomatic and parliamentary branches, it is particularly full. It is long since I have been sensible it ought not to continue private property, and had provided that at my death, Congress should have the refusal of it at their own price. But the loss they have now incurred, makes the present the proper moment for their accommodation, without regard to the small remnant of time and the barren use of my enjoying it. I ask of your friendship, therefore to make me the tender of it to the library committee of Congress, not knowing myself of whom the committee consists. I enclose you the catalogue, which will enable them to judge of its contents. Nearly the whole are well bound, abundance of them elegantly, and of the choicest editions existing.

They may be valued by persons named by themselves, and the payment made convenient to the public. It may be, for instance, in such annual installments as the law of Congress has left at their disposal, or in stock of any of their late loans, or of any loan they may institute at this session, so as to spare the present calls of our country, and await its days of peace and prosperity. They may enter, nevertheless, into immediate use of it, as eighteen or twenty wagons would place it in Washington in a single trip of a fortnight. I should be willing indeed, to retain a few of the books to amuse the time I have yet to pass, which might be valued with the rest, but not included in the sum of valuation until they should be restored at my death, which I would carefully provide for, so that the whole library as it stands in the catalogue at this moment should be theirs without any garbling. Those I should like to retain would be chiefly classical and mathematical. Some few in other branches, and particularly one of the five encyclopedias in the catalogue. But this, if not acceptable, would not be urged. I must add, that I have not revised the library since I came home to live, so that it is probable some of the books may be missing, except in the chapters of Law and Divinity, which have been revised and stand exactly as in the catalogue. The return of the catalogue will of course be needed, whether the tender be accepted or not. I do not know that it contains any branch of science which Congress would wish to exclude from their collection; there is, in fact, no subject to which a member of Congress may not have occasion to refer. But such a wish would not correspond with my views of preventing its dismemberment. My desire is either to place it in their hands entire, or to preserve it so here. I am engaged in making an alphabetical index of the author's names, to be annexed to the catalogue, which I will forward to you as soon as completed. Any agreement you shall be so good as to take the trouble of entering into the committee, I hereby confirm. Accept the assurance of my great esteem and respect.

Thomas Jefferson

EDWARD DRAKE TO JAMES M. TOWNSEND
"We beg to offer you our services"

Shortly after discovering oil in western Pennsylvania, Edward Drake started receiving orders from all over the world to market it. F. Streng & Company of Manchester, England, sent a letter to Drake offering to sell petroleum on his behalf in England and Europe.

Drake, who may not have appreciated the full importance of his discovery, passed the inquiry on to one of his sponsors, James Townsend, whose faith in oil's prospects were equally uncertain.

Titusville March 11th 1860

Friend Townsend

I last evening recd. A Letter from F Streng & Co Manchester England who represent themselves as being Commission Merchants. But I will give you a copy verbatim ad literatim (as the saying is)

Mr. Drake. Titusville Pa

Dear Sir

Having heard of your extraordinary discovery of oil possessing such superior qualities we beg to offer to you our services for its sale both in England and on the continent of Europe. Our business is that of commission Merchants & we have correspondents and Agents in all the manufacturing Districts and places of Commerce &c &c. Should be enabled to give to your Oil the most extensive sale by introducing it almost simultaneously in all parts of Europe. We are confident of great success and should be very glad to be entrusted with your general Agency for Europe. Hoping soon to be favoured with your kind reply we remain yours &c.

References

Thos Hoyle & Son Manchester Messrs Conlon & Co London

Messrs Conlon & Co London Brugobenan & Co Bussells besides some Dutch and French names I cant make out.

I wish you would let me know what your Brother William has done and what you think best to do. I think it would be best to open a correspondence with them I shall write them that I will send them an answer by next of the following Steamer with regard to the Agency if we satisfy ourselves with regard to their responsibility. If your Brother is in N H or N York you can get all the information we want and if he is in Europe write him to call and see these folks At last I have recd. A small Order from the Cleveland & Erie Rail Road and the Mast Machinist on the Sunbury & Erie pronounces it first rate Lubricator and will work anywhere. It takes time and work to introduce it but I shall succeed I know

E L Drake

Mch 11/60

Mr. Ferris was here and offered the enormous sum of 20¢ pr Gall for the Oil at the works. He did not call upon me at all but devoted his whole time to Brewer and Watson but it did not amount to any thing he is a gas Bag I have been shut up in the House the past 5 days about half sick shall get out as soon as the weather clears up it is storming now. Smith has gone to Butler on business of his own will be back next Saturday
My family all got colds but not sick

Yours &c
E L Drake

JACOB W. DAVIS TO LEVI STRAUSS
"I wish to make you a proposition"

Jacob W. Davis, a tailor in Reno, Nevada, wanted to patent a new type of pants he had invented using rivets to secure the seams and pockets. His wife, however, wouldn't spend the money for the expense, believing him to have wasted enough money already on another patent for a steam-powered ore crusher.

Davis asked his supplier of denim, Levi Strauss & Co., to pay for the costs of the patent ($68) in exchange for half the revenues for sales generated in the Pacific Coast. Impressed that miners were willing to spend up to three times the cost of other trousers for Davis's pants, Strauss seized the offer. More than 100 million pairs of Levi's pants were sold over the next century.

July 2, 1872

. . . I also send you by Express 2 ps. Overall as you will see one Blue and one made of the 10 oz Duck which I have bought in greate many Peces of you, and have made it up in to Pensts, such as the sample.

The secratt of them Pents is the Rivits that I put in those Pockets and I found the demand so large that I cannot make them up fast enough. I charge for the Duck $3.00 and the Blue $2.50 a pear. My nabors are getting yealouse of these success and unless I secure it by Patent Papers it will soon become a general thing. Everybody will make them up and thare will be no money in it.

Therefore Gentleman, I wish to make you a Proposition that you should take out the Latters Patent in my name as I am the inventor of it, the expense of it will be about $68, all complit and for these $68 will give you half the right to sell all such clothing Revited according to the patent, for all the Pacific States and Teroterious, the balince of the United States and half of the Pacific Coast I resarve for myself. The investment for you is but a trifle compaired with the improvement in all Coarse Clothing. I use it in all Blankit Clothing such as Coats, Vests and Pents, and you will find it a very salable article at a much advenst rate. . . .

These looks like a trifle hardly worth speakeing off but nevertheless I knew you can make a very large amount of money on it. If you make up Pents the way I do you can sell Duck Pents such as the Sample at $30. Per doz. and they will readly retail for $3. a pair.

Jacob Davis

P.T. Barnum to Ulysses S. Grant

"I will give you one hundred thousand dollars cash"

"The Greatest Showman on Earth," P. T. Barnum knew a crowd pleaser when he saw it. Barnum filled his famous 19th-century circuses with attractions, low and high (but mainly low), ranging from exotic elephants to bearded ladies. High on his list of attractions were historic relics, which he pursued tirelessly and with great imagination.

When Union soldiers captured Jefferson Davis, the former president of the Confederacy, fleeing in disguise at the end of the Civil War in 1865, Barnum offered five days later to buy for $500 the petticoats Davis used in his ill-fated escape.

Twenty years later, Barnum made a much more generous offer to General Ulysses S. Grant to purchase his Civil War relics for the staggering sum of $100,000. Barnum's offer came after he learned that Grant was broke and owed $250,000 to W. H. Vanderbilt. Grant politely turned down Barnum's offer, saying that Vanderbilt promised the relics would be given to a museum. Grant worked his way out of debt, instead, by writing his Personal Memoirs, which he completed four days before dying of throat cancer, but soon enough to get his family out of debt.

Telegram to Secretary of War Edwin M. Stanton

Bridgeport, 15 May [1865]

I will give five hundred dollars to the Sanitary Commission or Freedman's Association for the petticoats in which Jeff Davis was caught.

P. T. Barnum

New York, January 12, 1885

To General U.S. Grant, twice President of the United States, etc.:

Honored Sir: The whole world honors and respects you. All are anxious that you should live happy and free from care. While they admire your manliness in declining the large sum recently tendered you by friends, they still desire to see you achieve financial independence in an honorable manner. Of the unique and valuable trophies with which you have been honored, we all have read, and all have a laudable desire to see these evidences of love and respect bestowed upon you by monarchs, princes and people throughout the globe.

While you would confer a great and enduring favor on your fellow-men and women by permitting them to see these trophies you could also remove existing embarrassments in a most satisfactory and honorable manner. I will give you one hundred thousand dollars cash, besides a proportion of the profits, if I may be permitted to exhibit these relics to a grateful and appreciative public, and I will give satisfactory bonds of half a million dollars for their safe-keeping and return.

These precious trophies of which all your friends are so proud, would be placed before the eyes of your millions of admirers in a manner and style at once pleasing to yourself and satisfactory to the best elements of the entire community. Remembering that the mementoes of Washington, Napoleon, Frederick the Great and many other distinguished men have given immense pleasure to millions who have been permitted to see them, I trust you will in the honorable manner proposed, gratify the public and thus inculcate the lesson of honesty, perseverance and true patriotism so admirably illustrated in your career.

I have the honor to be truly your friend and admirer,

P. T. Barnum

DEAL NEGOTIATIONS

MARGERY BREWS TO JOHN PASTON
"My father will no more money part with"

Negotiations over dowries for wives during medieval times could become intensely personal. Margery Brews implores her prospective husband, John Paston, to accept her father's offer of a dowry in this 1477 letter. Paston, however, held out and received an extra 150 marks for the stalling tactic.

I let you plainly understand that my father will no more money part with in that behalf, but £100 and 50 marks, which is right far from the accomplishment of your desire.

Wherefore, if you could be content with that good [money] and my poor person, I would be the merriest maiden on earth; and if you think yourself not satisfied, or [think] that you might have much more good, as I have understood by you before, good, true, and loving Valentine, [I ask] that you take no such labor upon you, but let it pass, and never more to be spoken of, as I may be your lover and bedeswomen [servant who prays for you] during my life. No more unto you at this time, but Almighty Jesus preserve you, both body and soul, &c. by your Valentine,

Margery Brews

MICHELANGELO TO THE ARCHITECT TO THE POPE
"It will be a work without equal in all the world"

Michelangelo's spectacular paintings at the Vatican in Rome came about after intense, difficult and highly political negotiations—that Michelangelo lost. Michelangelo's talents as an artist reached the attention of Rome when he was in his early twenties and he proposed a gigantic painting called "The Tragedy of the Tomb" to Pope Julius II. Although the Pope liked the idea, his head architect, Bramante, stopped Michelangelo once he had begun, and instead Bramante tried to hire his nephew, Raphael of Urbino, to work on it.

Furious at the interference, Michelangelo left Rome and went to Florence, where he wrote the letter below to another papal architect, setting the terms for his return to Rome to complete the work. Threatening war, Julius II got Michelangelo to return. The artist, however, was forced to instead paint a mural on the ceiling of the Sistine Chapel depicting the creation and fall of man. The Pope died a year later, but his successors never let Michelangelo complete his original proposal for "The Tragedy of the Tomb." Pope Paul III ordered Michelangelo to instead paint "The Last Judgment" on the wall of the Sistine Chapel.

Florence, May 2, 1506

Maestro Giuliano, Architect to the Pope

Giuliano, I learn from a letter sent by you that the Pope was angry with my departure, that he is willing to place the money at my disposal and to carry out what was agreed between us; also, that I am to come back and fear nothing.

As far as my departure is concerned, the truth is that on Holy Saturday I heard the Pope, speaking at table with a jeweler and the Master of the Ceremonies, say that he did not want to spend another *baiocco* on stones, whether small or large, which surprised me very much. However, before I set out I asked him for some of the money required for the continuance of my work. His Holiness replied that I was to come back again on Monday: and I went on Monday, and on Tuesday, and on Wednesday, and on Thursday—as His Holiness saw. At last, on the Friday morning, I was turned out, that is to say, I was driven away: and the person who turned me away said he knew who I was, but that such were his orders. Thereupon, having heard those words on the Saturday and seeing them afterwards put into execution, I lost all hope. But this alone was not the whole reason for my departure. There was also another cause, but I do not wish to write about it; enough that it made me think that, if I were to remain in Rome, my own tomb would be prepared before that of the Pope. This is the reason for my sudden departure.

Now you write to me on behalf of the Pope, and in similar manner you will read this letter to the Pope. Give His Holiness to understand . . . that if he really wishes to have this tomb erected it would be well for him not to vex me as to where the work is to be done, provided that within the agreed period of five years it be erected in St. Peter's, on the site he shall choose, and that it be a beautiful work, as I have promised: for I am persuaded that it will be a work without equal in all the world if it be carried out.

If His Holiness wishes to proceed, let him deposit the said money here in Florence with a person whose name I will communicate to you. . . . With regard to the aforesaid money and work, I will bind myself in any way His Holiness may direct, and I will furnish whatever security here in Florence he may require. Let it be what it may, I will give him full scrutiny even though it be the whole of Florence. There is yet one thing I have to add: it is this, that the said work could not possibly be done for the price in Rome, but it could be done here because of the many conveniences which are available, such as could not be had in Rome. . . . I beg of you to let me have an answer, and quickly. I have nothing further to add.

Your Michelangelo,
Sculptor, in Florence

WILLIAM BLAKE TO GEORGE CUMBERLAND
"I cannot Print more Except at a great loss"

An extraordinary poet, artist and printer, William Blake wrote this letter to his patron George Cumberland giving a price list for his illuminated books, which he engraved, printed and colored himself. The "Little Card" Blake refers to was to be his last engraving—he died soon afterward.

Dear Cumberland,

I have been very near the Gates of Death & have returned very weak & an Old Man feeble & tottering, but not in Spirit & Life, not in The Real Man
The Imagination which Liveth for Ever. In that I am stronger & stronger as
this Foolish Body decays. I thank you for the Pains you have taken with Poor Job. . . .

You are desirous I know to dispose of some of my Works & to make them Pleasing. I am obliged to you & to all who do so. But having none remaining of all that I had printed I cannot Print more Except at a great loss, for at the time I printed those things I had a whole House to range in: now I am shut up in a Corner therefore am forced to ask a Price for them that I scarce expect to get from a Stranger. I am now Printing a Set of the Songs of Innocence & Experience for a Friend at Ten Guineas which I cannot do under six Months consistent with my other Work, so that I have little hope of doing any more of such things. The Last Work I produced is a Poem Entitled Jerusalem the Emanation of the Giant Albion, but find that to Print it will Cost my time the amount of Twenty Guineas once I have finish'd. It contains 100 Plates but it is not likely that I shall get a Customer for it.

As you wish me to send you a list with the Prices of these things they are as follows

	£	s	d
America	6.	6.	0
Europe	6.	6.	0
Vision &c	5.	5.	0
Thel	3.	3.	0
Songs of Inn. & Exp.	10.	10.	0
Urizen	6.	6.	0

The Little Card I will do as soon as Possible but when you Consider that I have been reduced to a Skeleton from which I am slowly recovering you will I hope have Patience with me.

Flaxman is Gone & we must All soon follow, every one to his Own Eternal house, leaving the

Delusive Goddess Nature & her Laws to get into Freedom from all Law of the Members into The Mind, in which every one is King & Priest in his own House. God send it so on Earth as it is in Heaven.

I am, Dear Sir, Yours Affectionately

William Blake
12 April 1827
N 3 Fountain Court Strand

ALFRED KRUPP TO GERMAN WAR MINISTER

"An object which I have pursued for several years"

Alfred Krupp developed a new type of crucible steel at his German factory in the 1840s that was stronger and more durable than other steels to date. Convinced that his product could produce better guns and breastplates for the German army, he tried repeatedly to convince military officials to use his steel for their weaponry.

Despite demonstrations of the superiority of his product, military officials kept rejecting his inquiries, as this 1847 letter from Krupp to the War Minister, Von Rohr, in Berlin demonstrates. Krupp decided against trying to promote his armaments abroad for fear of their being used against Germany.

The German army did not even seriously consider using Krupp's steel products for another decade, by which time Krupp had an international reputation for manufacturing materials for the railroad industry. In the end, the superiority of Krupp's crucible steel played a major role in a string of major battlefield victories by German armies, especially the Franco–Prussian War of 1870.

Essen, 23.10.1847

Your Excellency,

I take the liberty of begging your kind attention for an object which I have pursued for several years, and your favor in regard thereto, if the matter appears to deserve it.

It concerns the manufacture of weapons from crucible steel, particularly of muskets, rifles, breastplates, loophole-shutters, cannon and the like.

His Excellency the War Minister, Herr von Boyen, to whose post your Excellency has now succeeded, very readily submitted my sample supplies to test.

On 20th Jan. 1845, a sheet 0.20" thick was fired at with rampart guns, as regards which test an account, dated 27th Febr. 1845, sent to me by the War Office, contains results which confirmed the strength previously shown by my material in breastplates, and which demonstrated its usefulness for loophole-shutters. I have since supplied the material for two loophole-shutters, and still await information as to the results obtained with this last consignment to the management of the Principal Artillery Workshop on 20th March of this year, and a decision whether I shall be required to make supplies for fortification works.

A very detailed report, from the Royal Firearm Revisal Committee at Potsdam, dated 6th May 1845, regarding experiments, which were undertaken at the establishment there, at the instance of the

War Office, with my crucible steel and with musket and rifle barrels produced therefrom, concludes with the following expression of opinion: "The Committee gives it as its opinion with regard to the crucible-steel barrels, as well as the Krupp crucible steel, that nothing better and more excellent is yet in existence, and that equipments of this material promise to last three times as long as at present. As, however, the cost of the general adoption of this material is against it, a good deal would be gained from using it for rifled barrels, in which it offers a greater effectiveness; for the barrels of the cavalry arms, whereby greater lightness can be attained; for the inner parts of locks, in order to avoid repairs and increase safety; for swords, on account of the stability and hardness which it possesses; for breastplates and loophole-shutters, on account of its ductility."

In view of this and other brilliant results, I hoped, even if the cost of the material has not up to the present permitted its use for musket, that rifles, ordinary rifled and lighter cavalry barrels made of it might soon be introduced, since the cost-price of the barrels, especially of the rifled ones, can be amply compensated for by the certain success of every specimen in respect to inner cleanness and to standing the firing test. . . .

As long ago as 1844, breastplates of my material referred to above were supplied by Herr Wilh. Jäger of Elberfeld to the War Office for test, and were found entirely satisfactory. I have recently decided to carry out the complete manufacture of these in my Works, under my own supervision, since in the case of a direct test consignment sent to the War Office (Military Supply Department) on 6th July of last year it was proved that a breastplate manufacturer, to whom I supplied my best material for the purpose, so spoiled it that the breastplates lacked resistance, and since my request that the breastplates might be finished in the Royal Musket Factory has been refused. I have therefore pushed on as much as possible with all the arrangements, and now count positively on completing and dispatching some breastplates within a fortnight; I hope the delay has not been so long as to cause dissatisfaction at the War Office. . . .

Lastly, I beg most obediently to refer to the discussion, commenced as early as 1844, regarding the supply of a cannon of the same material. Instead of a solid gun-barrel, which War Office minute of 22nd April 1844 decided to order, I have constructed, under approval given on 24th August of this year, a 3-pounder gun with a completed inner tube of crucible steel and a jacket (still to be completed) of iron, dispatched it to the War Office (General War Department), and proposed, in my obedient communication of 24th August, that the further completion of the gun in accordance with the opinion of the experts charged with the matter, particularly the experiment with a new jacket, should be carried out with a tenacious variety of iron. I am in receipt of the agreeable assurance that this experiment shall be carried out quickly and thoroughly, and await an intimation as to when the gun will be so far ready and this test will take place, as I should much like to be present.

Having now made your Excellency acquainted with the object which I have pursued for years, and which has cost me thousands but borne no fruit as yet, I repeat my most obedient request for your gracious notice and favor for my zealously offered services, if the more exact testing of my material shows me to be deserving of such a privilege.

JACOB H. SCHIFF, ON THE BUYER OF *THE NEW YORK TIMES*
"The very man who might be able to resurrect the paper"

In 1896, the struggling New York Times *sought an infusion of cash and energy to restore the newspaper's prominence. Adolph S. Ochs, the energetic publisher of the Chattanooga Times, emerged as a prospective buyer. Uncertain about whether to accept an offer from the rustic businessman from Tennessee, shareholders balked. Ochs's persuasiveness and letters of support, such as this one from financier Jacob H. Schiff, however, convinced Charles R. Flint—who held a controlling interest in the stock of the newspaper—to sell. Ochs and his descendents have controlled the newspaper ever since.*

New York April 6th 1896

Dear Mr. Flint:

I have your letter of the 4th inst., enclosing receipt for my stock in the New York Times.

Mr. Trask has inquired of me as to Mr. Adolph S. Ochs, of the Chattanooga Times, and I have taken special pains to make careful inquiries as to the latter's standing and capabilities for the position which he seeks in connection with the New York Times. From what I learn I am strongly impressed that he is a man of exceptional energy, experience and talent in the journalistic line, and, so far as I can judge from the information I have about Mr. Ochs, he appears to be the very man who might be able to resurrect the paper.

I much hope your Committee will be able to make arrangements with Mr. Ochs mutually satisfactory, and I am,

Yours truly,

Jacob H. Schiff

R. R. LINGEMAN TO MONOCLE PERIODICALS
"Must have raise or count me out"

Telegrams compelled negotiators to keep their words spare, as this unsuccessful plea for a raise and its response demonstrate.

Publisher
Monocle Periodicals
80 Fifth Avenue
New York NY

Must have raise or count me out.

Lingeman
Executive Editor

R. R. Lingeman
305 East 17 Street
New York NY

One, two, three, four, five, six, seven, eight, nine, ten.

Monocle Periodicals

WILLIAM RANDOLPH HEARST TO WHITELAW REID
"How much will you take for the Tribune?"

William Randolph Hearst's bid to buy the New York Tribune *was brief in the following exchange of telegrams.*

Whitelaw Reid, Owner
New York Tribune
154 Nassau Street
New York NY

How much will you take for the Tribune?

W. R. Hearst

William Randolph Hearst
New York Journal
Park Row
New York NY

Three cents on weekdays, five cents on Sundays.

Reid

GEORGE S. KAUFMAN TO PARAMOUNT PICTURES
"Disregard my offer. Have changed my mind."

Apparently disgruntled, George S. Kaufman, the Hollywood screenwriter and director, counters an offer made by telegram for his screenplay of the 1932 film Once in a Lifetime, *and then takes it back.*

George S. Kaufman
14 East Street
New York NY

Offer $40,000 for screen rights to "Once in a Lifetime."
Lasky, Paramount

Jesse Lasky
Paramount Publix Corporation
1501 Broadway
New York NY

Offer $40,000—For Paramount Company.
Kaufman

Jesse Lasky
Paramount Publix Corporation
1501 Broadway
New York NY

Disregard my offer. Have changed my mind.
Kaufman

GEORGE S. KAUFMAN TO AUGUSTUS AND RUTH GOETZ
"A new idea that I rather like"

The great classic director George S. Kaufman was also a famous playwright. His works included You Can't Take It with You *and* The Man Who Came to Dinner, *which he co-wrote with Moss Hart. All told, he wrote 45 plays and won two Pulitzer Prizes. In this letter to his friends Augustus and Ruth Goetz, he recalls a very favorable and unusual business deal that he made in a dream.*

Tuesday

Dear Goetzes,

I had a chance to dispose of the movie rights to Franklin Street the other night, so I thought I'd better do it. This was in a dream induced by two sleeping pills, which is the reason I went right ahead without communicating with you.

This was in a large store which seemed to handle a good many things besides movie rights—shirts, nails, custard. Everything. I had a good deal of trouble getting waited on. "Miss, would you mind . . . Miss, I've been waiting longer than . . . I think it's my turn now, Miss."

But once I got attention everything went very nicely. I sold it an act at a time, which is a new idea that I rather like. The first act went for $30,000, and the second act for $60,000, which I thought was doing pretty well. The girl who was waiting on me knew all about these two acts, but the third act was all new to her. However, she took my word for it. I said there were two nice situations in it, and that it should bring $35,000. I remember her saying, "Well, as long as we've got the other two . . ."

Don't bother to thank me for this—anyone in my place would have done the same. I imagine they're delivering the money, like Saks.

And incidentally, how's tricks?

George

FRANK LLOYD WRIGHT AND EDGAR J. KAUFMANN

"You won't be let down so don't let me down"

Architect Frank Lloyd Wright designed perhaps the world's most famous private home, Fallingwater, in the 1930s for Edgar J. Kaufmann and his family, the owners of prominent department stores in Pittsburgh. Perched on a rocky ledge of a waterfall called Bear Run, the Laurel Highlands, Pennsylvania, house was an act of creative genius by Wright and a major logistical challenge.

During the course of design and construction of the residence, the correspondence between Wright and Kaufmann reflected the sometimes tempestuous relationship between a client and an architect— or any professional-service provider for that matter. Kaufmann had his own ideas regarding how to build the house, and questioned aspects of Wright's design. Wright, who was known for his supreme confidence, took this as meddling.

In the first exchange of letters below, Kaufmann suggests using a specific wall he had helped design for the structure, prompting a lecture from Wright. The next letter was written by Wright after the original supporting stone walls had to be rebuilt and Kaufmann had an engineer check Wright's calculations. The engineer suggested that Wright's proposed concrete slab might not be sufficient to carry the structure. This prompted an angry response (although years later, the concrete slabs needed replacing). The final letter is a request from Wright for payment of his services.

Despite the conflicts and questions over payment, Wright and Kaufmann kept a lifelong friendship.

April 3, 1936

Mr. Frank Lloyd Wright

Taliesin

Spring Green, Wis.

Dear Mr. Wright:

Upon my return I found Pittsburgh in the throes of the flood condition, details of which no doubt you have heard. We are just coming through it, but in spite of it all I have had time to look at the plans and study them with no end of thrills.

We are constructing a sample wall and as soon as you return to Taliesin I think you should arrange to come to Pittsburgh as there will be a number of things to discuss.

This letter must suffice for this time as I am far behind with my correspondence and store duties.

Warm personal greetings, remain

Sincerely, Edgar J. Kaufmann

May 4ᵗʰ, 1936

Mr. Edgar J. Kaufmann

Kaufmann Department Stores

Pittsburgh, Pennsylvania

Dear E.J.:

You seem to forget all I said about building an extraordinary house in extraordinary circumstances. Having been through it scores of times I know what we are up against and decline to start unless I can see our way. The same to you.

Now suppose I were a sculptor and you would say "carve me an extraordinary statue."

I would accept.

Then you would hand me a pantagraph and say—"use this." I have found the use of the pantagraph a good way to carve statues. It saves me time and money.

Then I would say—"but in this case it will waste both time and money and ruin the statue."

You would come back with "but when I have statues made I have the pantagraph used."

Well, E.J., you would have the sculptor where you have me now with your Thumb. I can't build an extraordinary house with a Thumb. Read the enclosed correspondence and note the pantagraph punctilio for only one thing. There is no sense whatever of the things he should know after studying the plans.

Now a pickaxe is more suited to my style of labor than a pantagraph. But, for a fact, I can't use either.

Your Thumb won't do. I must have my own fingers. I want to make a success of this house if I have a chance. A chance means very largely having my own way with my own work using my own fingers.

Your Thumb might be helpful in his place. His place wouldn't be trying to use me (fools rush in where angels fear to tread) to get your house built but letting me use him.

This ought to clear up point one and get me a modest builder with brains—not too anxious to show off—willing to learn new ways of doing old things. Able but wise to the fact that his previous experience might fool him in this case.

I know the type. I've worked with scores of them. Can't you send somebody here to me for a few days that I can initiate?

Again if I were a sculptor you could say "all right bring your own tools." But being an architect hundreds of miles away and a house for you in question I have to find my tools near you. I have explained all this to you many times.

Now about money.

You seem suspicious when I ask for it, and use the scissors to clip the sum. Don't be afraid. You aren't going to pay too much nor pay much too soon. You won't be let down so don't you let me down.

Sincerely yours,
Frank Lloyd Wright

August 30, 1936
Mr. E.J. Kaufmann
Kaufmann's Department Stores
Pittsburgh, Pennsylvania

If your engineer was consistent in his checkup of our details he would have had to reject not only the reinforcement in the beams he questioned but throughout the building from start to finish—not only steel but concrete as well.

For this reason—

I have learned from experience with the earthquake-proof Imperial Hotel and other buildings that the fibre stress in steel is safe at 25 to 30,000 lbs and that the compression on concrete of 1500 is entirely safe.

We have had those stresses in order to save you waste because we are not operating under contract conditions to meet the hazards of which the assumptions of your engineer were made. So why waste money to actually weaken structure by excess weight.

Also it had never been the practice of Adler and Sullivan with whom I served an apprenticeship of seven years (nor my own practice since—the earthquake-proof Imperial Hotel included) to assume a live load on reinforced concrete constructions in dwellings.

By these assumptions we have not only saved you more than two thousand five hundred dollars but given you a stronger building.

Now if you had been above board in your dealing with your architect you might have saved your own engineer from demonstrating his incompetence and saved your money as well. Incompetence because by applying the standards set for him he put his finger upon only two spots in the structure where the sheer waste of standardized ignorance should be applied whereas he should have condemned the whole structure if he was consistent and reliable.

In interfering as you have you have set up a condition where we have no recourse but to accept an accusation that we do not know how to build our building without your help—and deliberately given current gossip a good break against us. Why? I thought I had found a man and a client.

But is this your usual method in dealing with men?

If so I will make a prophecy—in ten years time no one will work for you for either love or money.

I have worked for much of one in your case and a little of the other. So damned little of the other (money) that it hardly matters in the consideration of the whole. And for this you hand me this betrayal to solve your own fear—if you were afraid why didn't you say so?

In short Mr. E.J. Kaufmann (client No. 199) these assumptions of your engineer, to wit: 750 lbs for concrete—plus a 40 live load—20,000 for steel would double the cost of your construction because not only is there double the cost of your structure but the increase to carry the increase in weight would be considerably more.

Now maybe these pearls of wisdom gained by experience have been cast before swine, and not only do the swine refuse to eat the pearls but turn and rend us.

What do you think?

Does any client really know when he is well off?

Frank Lloyd Wright, Architect

September 2, 1939
Mr. Edgar J. Kaufmann
Kaufmann's Fifth Avenue Department Store
Pittsburgh, Pennsylvania
Dear Edgar,

I hope this letter won't make you mad or anything like that but . . . I've been driven by the failure of the Lansing group of professors to get money—(seven houses for which we can yet get only a 3% preliminary for, although all the plans are made) to see what I can do to tide over the emergency created in the Fellowship by their failure. As one hope I've been going over the work we've done for you.

Facts are, about $100,000.00 has been spent on House, Guest Wing, and Office. Fee on House ten percent plus travel and cost of resident superintendent. House cost so far as I know $71,000.00 furniture, fixtures, etc, included—far too low.

Fee of office—20%—cost $6,000.00.

Total—say—$110,000.00.

I meant to be generous with our resources where your work went and I have been—to the limit and beyond and always will be—I am now designing chairs, etc., etc., and getting a decent lighting for the place. I think I have it—meantime I've dug up five schemes I've drawn before—all lost in execution.

But E.J. . . . to date, including the $500.00 you have just so kindly sent us—we have received from you $7100.00 to cover Office, House and Furniture and Guest and Servant House, etc., etc. Included in this sum is traveling expenses—$186.36 and seven weeks superintendence only—$175.00.

It isn't enough E.J. and I am asking not for justice but mercy. So far you have paid me all I've asked but I haven't asked enough. You have no idea how much of our resources went into your work. If I had more I would have gladly given it to get you and give you the top—I am giving it here right now. I think you believe that.

The traveling expenses to date not counting six or seven trips when I was going by anyway is

	$310.00
Bob and Edgar—54 weeks	1,100.00
Fee on House (too low)	7,100.00
Fee on Guest extension (too low)	2,800.00
Total	$11,310.00

Therefore there is clearly a balance due at this time of

$11,310.00

7,100.00

$4,209.40

Would you in view of the amount of extra work on the items of furnishing and refurnishing the house make this sum $5,000.00, giving us $2,500.00 now and $2,500.00 November 1st. I will include all my own services needed to get you settled as I would like to have you.

Truth is, no money can be made by us to show for our time and effort at that figure, but we've all got much besides to show for our time and effort—and—forever—

Will you give us the lift?

Faithfully,

Frank Lloyd Wright

Helene Hanff to Marks & Company
"I'm sending it c/o you, FPD, whoever you are"

Starting as a simple exchange of business letters for secondhand books, New York City freelance writer Helene Hanff and Marks & Company employee Frank Doel ended up having a twenty-year trans-Atlantic correspondence. The relationship, which became one of friends and spread to include other Marks & Company employees, ended when Doel died from a ruptured appendix in 1969.

Hanff, who never actually met Doel, published the letters in a charming and very successful book entitled 84, Charing Cross Road. *Anne Bancroft and Anthony Hopkins starred in a film depicting their relationship. Some of the early letters in the exchange follow.*

October 5, 1949
Marks & Co.
84, Charing Cross Road
London, W.C. 2
England
Gentlemen:

Your ad in the Saturday Review of Literature says that you specialize in out-of-print books. The phrase "antiquarian booksellers" scares me somewhat, as I equate "antique" with expensive. I am a poor writer with an antiquarian taste in books and all the things I want are impossible to get over here except in very expensive rare editions, or in Barnes & Noble's grimy, marked-up schoolboy copies.

I enclose a list of my most pressing problems. If you have clean secondhand copies of any of the books on the list, for no more than $5.00 each, will you consider this a purchase order and send them to me?

Very truly yours,
(Miss) Helene Hanff

25th October, 1949
Miss Helene Hanff
14 East 95th Street
New York 28, New York
U.S.A.
Dear Madam,

In reply to your letter of October 5th, we have managed to clear up two thirds of your problem. The three Hazlitt essays you want are contained in the Nonesuch Press edition of his Selected Essays and the Stevenson is found in Virginibus Puerisque. We are sending nice copies of both these by Book Post and we trust they will arrive safely in due course and that you will be pleased with them. Our invoice is enclosed with the books.

The Leigh Hunt essays are not going to be so easy but we will see if we can find an attractive volume with them all in. We haven't the Latin Bible you describe but we have a Latin New Testament, also a Greek New Testament, ordinary modern editions in cloth binding. Would you like these?

Yours faithfully,
FPD
For Marks & Co.

November 3, 1949
Marks & Co.
84, Charing Cross Road
London, W.C. 2
England
Gentlemen:

The books arrived safely, the Stevenson is so fine it embarrasses my orange-crate bookshelves, I'm almost afraid to handle such soft vellum and heavy cream-colored pages. Being used to the dead-white paper and stiff cardboardy covers of American books, I never knew a book could be such a joy to touch.

A Britisher whose girl lives upstairs translated the £1/17/6 for me and says I owe you $5.30 for the two books. I hope he got it right. I enclose a $5 bill and a single, please use the 70¢ toward the price of the New Testaments, both of which I want.

Will you please translate your prices hereafter? I don't add too well in plain American, I haven't a prayer of ever mastering bilingual arithmetic.

Yours,
Helene Hanff
I hope "madam" doesn't mean over there what it does here.

December 8, 1949
Sir:

(It feels witless to keep writing "Gentlemen" when the same solitary soul is obviously taking care of everything for me.)

Savage Landor arrived safely and promptly fell open to a Roman dialogue where two cities had just been destroyed by war and everybody was being crucified and begging passing Roman soldiers to run them through and end the agony. It'll be a relief to turn to Aesop and Rhodope where all you have to worry about is a famine. I do love secondhand books that open to the page some previous owner read oftenest. The day Hazlitt came he opened to "I hate to read new books," and I hollered "Comrade!" to whoever owned it before me.

I enclose a dollar which Brian (British boy friend of Kay upstairs) says will cover the /8/ I owe you, you forgot to translate it.

Now then. Brian told me you are all rationed to 2 ounces of meat per family per week and one egg per person per month and I am simply appalled. He has a catalogue from a British firm here which flies food from Denmark to his mother, so I am sending a small Christmas present to Marks & Co. I hope there will be enough to go around, he says the Charing Cross Road bookshops are "all quite small."

I'm sending it c/o you, FPD, whoever you are.

Noel.

Helene Hanff
20th December, 1949
Miss Helene Hanff
14 East 95th Street
New York 28, New York
U.S.A.
Dear Miss Hanff,

Just a note to let you know that your gift parcel arrived safely today and the contents have been shared out between the staff. Mr. Marks and Mr. Cohen insisted that we divide it up among ourselves and not include "the bosses." I should just like to add that everything in the parcel was something that we either never see or can only be had through the black market. It was extremely kind and generous of you to think of us in this way and we are all extremely grateful.

We all wish to express our thanks and send our greetings and best wishes for 1950.

Yours faithfully,
Frank Doel
For Marks & Co.

7th April, 1950
Dear Miss Hanff,

Please don't let Frank know I'm writing this but every time I send you a bill I've been dying to slip in a little note and he might not think it quite proper of me. That sounds stuffy and he's not, he's quite nice really, very nice in fact, it's just that he does rather look on you as his private correspondent as all your letters and parcels are addressed to him. But I just thought I would write to you on my own.

We all love your letters and try to imagine what you must look like. I've decided you're young and very sophisticated and smart-looking. Old Mr. Martin thinks you must be quite studious-looking in spite of your wonderful sense of humor. Why don't you send us a snapshot. We should love to have it.

If you're curious about Frank, he's in his late thirties, quite nice-looking, married to a sweet Irish girl, I believe she's his second wife.

Everyone was so grateful for the parcel. My little ones (girl 5, boy 4) were in Heaven—with raisins and egg I was actually able to make them a cake!

I do hope you don't mind my writing. Please don't mention it when you write to Frank.

With best wishes,
Cecily Farr

P.S. I shall put my home address on the back of this in case, you should ever want anything sent you from London.

Feuding Correspondence over RJR Nabisco
"You have no basis to lecture me"

In the largest takeover in Wall Street history up to that time, the most aggressive investment banks and corporate raiders engaged in a competitive frenzy to acquire the food and tobacco giant RJR Nabisco in 1988. The $25 billion deal proved to be the climactic takeover deal of the Reagan era, and a precursor to a new wave of even more gargantuan mergers that followed in the late 1990s.

As the following exchange of letters from officials illustrate, deal makers, publicity flacks, competing industrial giants and financial wizards engaged in fierce struggles for dominance, throwing insults and accusations along the way. These letters were exchanged by competing investment bankers at Shearson Lehman Hutton, representing RJR Nabisco's management, and Goldman Sachs & Co. and Forstmann Little & Co., representing a rival bidder. In the end, Kohlberg Kravis Roberts & Co. (KKR) won the Wall Street war.

November 7, 1988

Dear Ted:

I am deeply disappointed, in fact dumbfounded, by published reports that you may be leading a group whose purpose would be to seek to acquire RJR Nabisco, Inc.

You will recall that two weeks ago you approached Jim Robinson, Ross Johnson, and me with a view towards becoming an important member of the management-led group which was considering an offer for RJR Nabisco. I am sure you remember you expressed reasons for wanting to join us.

In view of your strong desire to become our partner, and in reliance upon the specific representations outlined below, we agreed to discuss all aspects of our proposed transaction with you fully and frankly, including our economic models, our detailed financing arrangements, our proposed bidding strategy and our preliminary thoughts regarding possible divestitures. . . .

We allowed Goldman Sachs, as your agent, to participate in our conversations based upon your and their expressed assurances that they would likewise be bound by the terms of the confidentiality agreement which you had signed. It would appear that Goldman Sachs nonetheless induced certain food companies to join your group, presumably using the confidential information which you obtained from us to induce them.

I strongly urge you to very carefully consider your actions. Our business relationships, including our recent discussions, presumes a code of conduct which should not include either ethical lapses or breaches of contractual relations. Shearson and the executives of RJR Nabisco intend to honor the commitments they have made. We expect you will do so as well. . . .

I very much hope that you will carefully consider the contents of this letter.

Very truly yours,
Peter

November 8, 1988
Dear Mr. Cohen:

Through your letter of November 7, 1988 and your apparent distribution of that letter to the press, you have begun a program of irresponsible and false attacks against the ethics of Goldman, Sachs & Co. and Forstmann Little. By implication, you also attack the ethics of Procter & Gamble, Ralston Purina and Castle & Cooke, which have joined with us in considering the acquisition of RJR Nabisco. As you are aware, by attacking our reputation, you attack that which is most valuable to us. We believe that the motivation for your actions is to drive us out of the bidding process for RJR Nabisco in order to permit Shearson Lehman and certain RJR executives to buy the company at a reduced price. It is particularly disappointing that you should pursue this "tactic" because the RJR Nabisco management with whom you are working is obligated to protect the interests of RJR Nabisco shareholders. . . .

As I am sure you recall, we expressly informed you during the course of our discussions that, if we could not reach agreement with you, we reserved the right to consider our own transaction. We repeatedly made clear to you that we maintained three options: first, to participate in the transaction you were proposing if it were amended to comply with our standards; second, to walk away from any involvement with RJR; or third, to formulate our own proposal if such a proposal was invited by the Special Committee. After the Special Committee indicated to us that they would welcome our group's interest, we determined to pursue the option of considering such a proposal. . . .

The Forstmann Little group's interest in RJR Nabisco works to the clear benefit of RJR's shareholders and has been expressly welcomed by the company's Special Committee. We will not make a proposal if, after careful review this transaction fails to meet our strict financial standards. However, under no circumstances will we permit your efforts at intimidation to impair the interests of Forstmann Little and its capital partners.

The firm of Forstmann Little & Co. has been built carefully, with the highest possible business standards and with total integrity. We have acted in all respects consistent with those standards throughout this transaction; we need no advice from you in this regard.

I hope this puts to rest the phony controversy which you have manufactured. Unlike you, we do not intend to release this letter to the press.

Very truly yours,
Theodore J. Forstmann

November 8, 1988
Dear Peter:

I received your letter of November 7, 1988 at approximately the same time I received a call from the press, and thus it is clear to me that your letter was for purposes of public relations rather than communication with us. It is also clear that you don't know me very well; otherwise you wouldn't have wasted your and my time with insults or threats—particularly when you have not gotten your facts straight.

In my judgment your letter is not worthy of reply. However, my colleagues have persuaded me that it is appropriate to give you a written response.

Your letter is factually erroneous and totally unwarranted. Goldman Sachs has not violated any of the terms of the confidentiality agreements which Forstmann Little signed with RJR Nabisco. As you know, I was not personally present, but I am categorically advised by my colleagues that our clear message to you has been that we might proceed independently of management or Shearson and were actively considering that possibility. Goldman Sachs is not precluded by any agreement with Shearson or RJR Nabisco from pursuing that alternative or making proposals for RJR Nabisco that would be received favorably by the Company and its shareholders.

This view is clearly shared by the Company's committee of independent directors. As it publcly reaffirmed today, the committee has welcomed the potential interest of Forstmann Little, Goldman Sachs and the highly respected companies with which we are working.

I find it difficult, if not impossible, to take seriously your professed interest in a good relationship with Goldman Sachs. It is not conducive to any relationship between our firms for you to make charges such as those in your November 7 letter, or to seek to exploit them by releasing them to the press before you have even communicated them to us or received our response. We do not believe it is in anyone's interest to escalate this exchange and therefore we are not planning at this time to send copies of this letter to the press.

I strongly object to the tone and substance of your letter; you have no basis to lecture me, Geoff Boisi or Goldman, Sachs & Co. about anything. Moreover, your tactical maneuvers can only contribute to the negative impression of our industry that many people have. I trust those tactics will ease.

Sincerely,
John L. Weinberg

SEALED DEALS

LUDWIG VAN BEETHOVEN TO CHARLES NEATE
"I am satisfied with the fee of 100 guineas"

This letter by Beethoven to Charles Neate, director of the Philharmonic Society in London, sets the terms for three musical compositions that became part of what was known as Beethoven's late quartets. There were a total of five late quartets. The reference to the "new symphony" was about Beethoven's Ninth Symphony and the overture was "The Consecration of the House." Though he mentions his desire to travel to the British Isles, Beethoven never made it to England.

Vienna, February, 1823

My dear and valued Friend!

As Ries has written to tell me that you would like to have three quartets from me, I am writing to ask you to be so kind as to let me know when you would like to receive them. I am satisfied with the fee of 100 guineas which you offer. But, as soon as you hear from me that the quartets are ready, please send a draft for the 100 g[uineas] to a Viennese banking house *where I shall also deliver* the quartets and at the same time receive the 100 guin[eas]. I trust that you are leading a pleasant and happy life in the bosom of your small family. But why are you not in Vienna so that I might have the pleasure of witnessing your happiness?— I have sent Ries a new overture for the Philharmonic Society; and I am only waiting for the arrival of the draft to dispatch immediately the new symphony from Vienna and, what is more, by an opportunity provided by our Imperial and Royal Embassy.

The bearer of this letter is Herr von Bauer, who is as intelligent as he is amiable and who can tell you a good deal about me—If my health, which has been very poor for the last three years should improve, I hope to go to London in 1824. Let me know what compositions the Philharmonic Society would like to have, for I would gladly compose for it. I should like to visit England and meet all the splendid artists there. Such a visit would benefit me materially too, for I shall never be able to achieve anything in Germany—You need only write my name on a letter to me and I shall certainly receive it—That all good and beautiful things may be your portion is the wish of your sincere friend.

Beethoven

ANDREW CARNEGIE TO HENRY PHIPPS JR.
"It is closed, all fixed"

Concluding a classic rags to riches story, Andrew Carnegie cashed in on his behemoth steel company in 1901, selling Carnegie Steel to J. P. Morgan. After a game of golf at the Saint Andrews Golf Club in Westchester County in New York, Morgan asked Carnegie to name his price for the steel company. Carnegie scribbled down "$480 million" and asked that the payment be made in bonds, not stock in the new merged company, U. S. Steel. Morgan said: "I accept the price." The deal was finalized a few weeks later.

Carnegie later had misgivings about the price, suggesting to Morgan that he had set the price $100 million too low. Morgan responded "Very likely, Andrew."

Nonetheless, Carnegie was relieved to be out of the business, as he wrote to his longtime business partner, Henry Phipps Jr., after the sale was finalized. Carnegie promptly set about giving the money away in a binge of philanthropic gestures that lasted until his death eighteen years later. He gave away more than $350 million during his lifetime, a sum that was all the more extraordinary a century ago.

5 West 51st Street

Sunday eve.

My dear H. P.

Mr. Stetson has just called to tell me it is closed, all fixed—big times on Stock Exchange tomorrow.

Well, this is a step in my life—a great change, but after a time, when I get down to new conditions, I shall become I believe a wiser and more useful man, and besides live a dignified old age as long as life is granted, something few reach.

Yours,

A. C.

ANGLO-PERSIAN OIL COMPANY TO
HIS EXCELLENCY SHAIKH SIR AHMAD AL JABIR
"Your Excellency's most obedient servants"

Although business negotiations are often marked by standoffs and acrimony, this often gives way to mutual admiration once the deal is sealed, and it would likely be difficult to find letters signaling the conclusion of an agreement more gracious than this exchange between officials at the Anglo-Persian Oil Company and Kuwait's ruler, Shaikh Ahmad—regarding a deal that took two decades to conclude. Ironically, many officials at the Anglo-Persian Company thought the concession would yield little oil in Kuwait or neighboring Bahrain. Even the company's chief geologist was skeptical, promising he "would drink any commercial oil found in Bahrain." It was a pledge he couldn't keep.

Abadan

25th June, 1932

H. E. Shaikh Sir Ahmad Al Jabir

As-Subah, K.C.I.E., C.S.I.

Ruler of Koweit

Koweit,

Your Excellency,

We will have the honour to refer to our letter of the 15th June last and to inform Your Excellency that we have now received a telegram from our Chairman, Sir John Cadman, in which he directs us to express to Your Excellency the very deep sense of gratification it has given to him personally to receive Your Excellency's message.

In deference to Your Excellency's wishes, Sir John Cadman has given immediate instructions for an Agreement embodying a comprehensive concession to explore, prospect and mine for oil within Your Excellency's territory to be prepared and submitted to Your Excellency for consideration. The preparation and translation of this document will necessarily take a short time but we desire to assure Your Excellency that it will be undertaken without delay and submitted as soon as possible.

Sir John Cadman has made, in his telegram, a particular reference to the grateful recollections he retains of the hospitality and courtesy he received from the Rulers and people of Koweit during his visit to Koweit 20 years ago and he expresses the earnest hope that the contact so happily inaugurated then, and continued since may develop shortly into a still closer association between Your Excellency's State and this Company.

The cordial reception accorded to the undersigned by Your Excellency prompts us to add with what pleasure we shall look forward to continuing the discussions on lines which Your Excellency desired.

We have the honour to be,

Your Excellency's most obedient servants,

For Anglo-Persian Oil Company Ltd.,

N. A. Gass

DY. General Manager

Kuwait

20/6/32

The General Manager,

Messrs. A.P.O.C. Ltd.,

Abadan.

After compliment.

I have received with much pleasure your kind and courteous letter of 15th June 1932 under No. C.7/72 in which you had thanked me for the reception afforded to Mr. N. A. Gass during his visit to Kuwait. I have done nothing beyond my duty, and his appreciation of my assistance to him is out of his generosity and courtesy. His communicating my views regarding oil fields in my territory and your referring to Company's principals and your proceeding to London noted. I wish you continuous success and a very pleasant voyage.

Yours truly,

Ahmed Aljabar Alsabah

WALTER WANGER TO LELAND HAYWARD
"The other 90 percent"

Producer Walter Wanger sent this congratulatory telegram to the theatrical agent Leland Hayward,
who had just eloped with Margaret Sullavan, a client.

November 16, 1936
Lelan Hayward
654 Madison Avenue

Congratulations on acquiring the other 90%.
Walter Wanger

CHINESE PUBLISHER'S REJECTION LETTER
"With fear and trembling I return your writing"

Writing rejection letters for proposed manuscripts is part of a publishing company's job. While many editors try to be gracious in their responses to unsuccessful submissions, it is difficult to imagine a more gilded rejection letter than the following one, written by a Chinese publisher.

Illustrious brother of the sun and moon—

Behold thy servant prostrate before thy feet. I kow-tow to thee and beg of thy graciousness thou mayest grant that I may speak and live. Thy honored has deigned to cast the light of its august countenance upon me. With raptures I have pursued it. By the bones of my ancestry, never have I encountered such wit, such pathos, such lofty thoughts. With fear and trembling I return your writing. Were I to publish the treasure you sent me, the Emperor would order that it should be made the standard, and that none be published except such as equaled it. Knowing literature as I do, and that it would be impossible in ten thousand years to equal what you have done, I send your writing back. Ten thousand times I crave your pardon. Behold my head is at your feet. Do what you will.

Your servant's servant
The Editor

EMPLOYMENT

GETTING A JOB

Leonardo da Vinci Seeks Job from the Duke of Milan
"In painting I can do as much as anyone else"

Thirty years old, bored yet eager to leave his native city of Florence, Leonardo da Vinci wrote the Duke of Milan, Lodovico Sforza, in 1482 looking for work. He offered his talents as an inventor, sculptor and artist—and could have added geologist, biologist, botanist, philosopher and author.

Although Da Vinci was an intellectual colossus of his time, he did not gain fame for many years. Reputation alone would not get him the job. Here, he plainly states the martial and mechanical services he can provide in a tone that reflects his lifelong motto—and daily routine—of "obstinate rigor."

Da Vinci got the job and held it for 16 years, until a French army captured Milan and imprisoned his employer. Da Vinci died in France in 1519, frustrated that his "greatest schemes in science remained unrealized" and that his "quest for perfection in art" was unsuccessful.

1482

Having, most illustrious lord, seen and considered the experiments of all those who pose as masters in the art of inventing instruments of war, and finding that their inventions differ in no way from those in common use, I am emboldened, without prejudice to anyone, to solicit an appointment of acquainting your Excellency with certain of my secrets.

I can construct bridges which are very light and strong and very portable, with which to pursue and defeat the enemy; and others more solid, which resist fire or assault, yet are easily removed and placed in position; and I can also burn and destroy those of the enemy.

In case of a siege I can cut off water from the trenches and make pontoons and scaling ladders and other similar contrivances.

If by reason of the elevation or the strength of its position a place cannot be bombarded, I can demolish every fortress if its foundations have not been set on stone.

I can also make a kind of cannon which is light and easy of transport, with which to hurl small stones like hail, and of which the smoke causes great terror to the enemy, so that they suffer heavy loss and confusion.

I can noiselessly construct to any prescribed point subterranean passages either straight or winding, passing if necessary underneath trenches or a river.

I can make armoured wagons carrying artillery, which shall break through the most serried ranks of the enemy, and so open a safe passage for his infantry.

If occasion should arise, I can construct cannon and mortars and light ordnance in shape both ornamental and useful and different from those in common use.

When it is impossible to use cannon I can supply in their stead catapults, mangonels, *trabocchi*, and other instruments of admirable efficiency not in general use—In short, as the occasion requires I can supply infinite means of attack and defense.

And if the fight should take place upon the sea I can construct many engines most suitable either for attack or defense and ships which can resist the fire of the heaviest cannon, and powders or weapons.

In time of peace, I believe that I can give you as complete satisfaction as anyone else in the construction of buildings both public and private, and in conducting water from one place to another.

I can further execute sculpture in marble, bronze or clay, also in painting I can do as much as anyone else, whoever he may be.

Moreover, I would undertake the commission of the bronze horse, which shall endue with immortal glory and eternal honour the auspicious memory of your father and of the illustrious house of Sforza.

And if any of the aforesaid things should seem to anyone impossible or impracticable, I offer myself as ready to make trial of them in your park or in whatever place shall please your Excellency, to whom I commend myself with all possible humility.

JAMES BURBAGE TO THE EARL OF LEICESTER
"You humble Servants and daily Orators your players"

The Elizabethan era of 16th-century England may have been a high point in theater and literature, but it was a low point for the actors who performed the plays. Highly dependent on aristocrats to serve as their patrons, actors, such as those who signed this letter, stooped very low indeed to retain their tenuous jobs in the theater business.

James Burbage and his manager Cuthbert Burbage built the Globe Theatre in 1599, and the venue was made famous by hosting performances of Shakespeare's plays. James's son, Richard Burbage, is considered the first great leading British actor.

3rd January, 1572

To the right honourable Earl of Leicester, their good Lord and Master

May it please your honour to understand that foreasmuch as there is a certain Proclamation out for the reviving of a Statute as touching retainers, as your Lordship knoweth better than we can inform you thereof:

We therefore, your humble Servants and daily Orators your players for avoiding all inconvenience that may grow by reason of the said Statute, are bold to trouble your Lordship with this our Suit, humbly desiring your honour that (as you have been always our good Lord and master) you will now vouchsafe to retain us at this present as your household Servants and daily waiters (not that we mean to crave any further stipend or benefit at your Lordship's hands but our liveries as we have had, and also your Honour's license to certify that we are your household Servants when we shall have occasion to travel amongst our friends as we do usually once a year, and as other noblemen's players do and have done in time past) whereby we may enjoy our faculty in your Lordship's name as we have done heretofore.

Thus being bound and ready to be always at your Lordship's commandment, we commit your Honour to the tuition of the Almighty.

Long may your Lordship live in peace,
A peer of noblest peers:
In health, wealth and prosperity
Redoubling Nestor's years.

Your Lordship's Servants most bounden,

James Burbage

John Perkinne

John Laneham

William Johnson

Robert Wilson

Thomas Clarke

BENJAMIN FRANKLIN'S MODEL LETTER OF RECOMMENDATION
"I must refer you to himself for his character"

Benjamin Franklin wrote the following recommendation from France for an acquaintance about to sail to America.

Paris April 2, 1777

Sir

The Bearer of this who is going to America, presses me to give him a Letter of Recommendation, tho' I know nothing of him, not even his Name. This may seem extraordinary, but I assure you it is not uncommon here. Sometimes indeed one unknown person brings me another equally unknown, to recommend him; and sometimes they recommend one another! As to this Gentleman, I must refer you to himself for his Character and merits, with which he is certainly better acquainted than I can possibly be; I recommend him however to those Civilities which every Stranger, of whom one knows no Harm, has a Right to, and I request you will do him all the good Offices and show him all the Favour that on further Acquaintance you shall find him to deserve. I have the honour to be, &c.

Benjamin Franklin

SAMUEL SLATER TO MOSES BROWN
"I flatter myself that I can give the greatest satisfaction"

Samuel Slater is widely credited with introducing the mill factory system to the United States. At the age of 21, he sailed to the United States in 1789 looking for a new start after spending a few years working in British textile mills.

Shortly after arriving, he learned that Moses Brown—who would later found Brown University—had bought two pieces of expensive spinning machinery that he could not get to work properly. Seeing an opportunity, Slater wrote the following letter introducing himself and his services. Brown took on Slater, who spent the winter building a new mill from scratch. The enterprise flourished. By the time Slater died in 1835, he was recognized as the leading textile industrialist in the United States.

New York, December 2d, 1789
Sir,—

A few days ago I was informed that you wanted a manager of cotton spinning, etc., in which business I flatter myself that I can give the greatest satisfaction, in making machinery, making good yarn, either for stockings or twist as any that is made in England; as I have had opportunity, and an oversight of Sir Richard Arkwright's works, and in Mr. Strutt's mill upwards of eight years. If you are not provided for, I should be glad to serve you; though I am in the New York manufactory, and have been for three weeks since I arrived from England. But we have but one card and spinning. (Meaning the Arkwright patents). If you please to drop a line respecting the amount of encouragement you wish to give, by favor of Captain Brown, you will much oblige, sir, your most obedient humble servant.
Samuel Slater

FRANZ SCHUBERT TO FRANCIS II

"The undersigned humbly begs Your Majesty graciously to bestow upon him the vacant position"

Born into abject poverty, Franz Schubert was an extraordinarily gifted musician who spent his brief 31 years writing songs, symphonies, sonatas, quartets and masses so fast that copyists couldn't keep pace. Despite his musical prowess and ambitions for professional success, he was confronted by one obstacle after another throughout the course of his career.

Schubert tried many times to gain minor musical positions in Vienna, without success. At one point, Schubert worked as a teacher for the family of a Hungarian count who treated him like a servant and housed him with the estate gardeners.

In 1826, at the age of 29, Schubert wrote the letter below desperately seeking a position in the court of the Austrian emperor Francis II. Despite Schubert's entreaties, Francis II did not even acknowledge Schubert, who had no friends to advise the court of his musical gifts. The position was given to someone else after a year's delay.

Your Majesty!

Most gracious Emperor!

With the deepest submission the undersigned humbly begs Your Majesty graciously to bestow upon him the vacant position of Vice-Kapellmeister to the Court, and supports his application with the following qualifications:

The undersigned was born in Vienna, is the son of a schoolteacher, and is 29 years of age.

He enjoyed the privilege of being for five years a Court Chorister at the Imperial and Royal College School.

He received a complete course of instruction in composition from the late Chief Kapellmeister to the Court, Herr Anton Salieri, and is fully qualified, therefore, to fill any post as Kapellmeister.

His name is well known, not only in Vienna but throughout Germany, as a composer of songs and instrumental music.

He has also written and arranged five Masses for both smaller and larger orchestra, and these have already been performed in various churches in Vienna.

Finally, he is at the present time without employment, and hopes in the security of a permanent position to be able to realize at last those high musical aspirations which he has ever kept before him.

Should Your Majesty be graciously pleased to grant this request, the undersigned would strive to the utmost to give full satisfaction.

Your Majesty's most obedient humble servant,
Franz Schubert

LETTER OF RECOMMENDATION FOR ALBERT EINSTEIN
"One of the most original minds that we have ever met"

During his spare time while employed by the Swiss patent office, Albert Einstein published in 1905 The Special Theory of Relativity. *Few had the slightest idea of the importance of Einstein's work, but one who did was Max Planck, discoverer of the original quantum theory. Planck wrote Einstein an encouraging letter hailing his theory of relativity as "a revolution in human thought."*

Einstein's ability to reconstruct the universe on paper did him little good at securing a job at a university. Finally, in 1911, after applying for a faculty position at the Federal Institute of Technology at Zurich, and armed with the letter of recommendation below from two of the leading mathematicians and physicists of the day—Henri Poincaré and Marie Curie—the university gave Einstein the job.

Herr Einstein is one of the most original minds that we have ever met. In spite of his youth he already occupies a very honorable position among the foremost savants of his time. What we marvel at him, above all, is the ease with which he adjusts himself to new conceptions and draws all possible deductions from them. He does not cling to classical principles, but sees all conceivable possibilities when he is confronted with a physical problem. In his mind this becomes transformed into an anticipation of new phenomena that may some day be verified in actual experience. . . . The future will give more and more proofs of the merits of Herr Einstein, and the University that succeeds in attaching him to itself may be certain that it will derive honor from its connection with the young master.

Henri Poincaré
Marie Curie

DOROTHY THOMPSON TO AN ADMIRER OF HER HUSBAND
"Mrs. Sinclair Lewis to you"

When Sinclair Lewis became the first American to win the Nobel Prize in Literature, in 1930, he received a deluge of fan mail. The correspondence included one letter from a woman offering to work as his secretary. "Dear Mr. Lewis," she wrote, "I'll do everything for you—and when I say everything I mean everything." Sinclair's wife came upon the letter and wrote the following response.

My dear Miss—:

My husband already has a stenographer who handles his work for him. And, as for "everything" I take care of that myself—and when I say everything I mean everything.

Dorothy Thompson
(Mrs. Sinclair Lewis to you.)

Jim Clark to Marc Andreessen

"I plan to form a new company"

As the founder of Silicon Graphics in the 1980s, Jim Clark took computers out of the realm of words and numbers and into the world of three-dimensional graphics. In 1994, he wanted to form a new company using the latest technology, and he stumbled upon 24-year-old Marc Andreessen while looking for talented computer engineers.

Andreessen had developed the Mosaic technology as a student at the University of Illinois. Clark recognized the potential of the application as a browser system for the Internet. "I knew a good thing when I saw it," Clark later wrote of his meeting with Andreessen. He wrote the e-mail below asking to meet with Andreessen and received a response in less than 10 minutes.

The two men went on to start Netscape. Mosaic revolutionized information technology over the Internet. The company Netscape completely changed the way technology start-ups were financed. Prior to Netscape, computer programmers were considered well-paid and talented hired help, but venture capitalists and financiers called the shots. And, few people considered taking a company public without first establishing a track record of profits. Jim Clark broke both these standards with Netscape. Suddenly, young computer whiz kids were making the decisions at the hottest companies, and the need to show profits before taking a company public became an old-fashioned idea.

Marc:

You may not know me, but I'm the founder and former chairman of Silicon Graphics. As you may have read in the press lately, I'm leaving SGI. I plan to form a new company. I would like to discuss the possibility of your joining me.

Jim Clark

Jim:

Sure. When would you like to meet?

Marc

CAREER CHOICES

DAVID GARRICK TO PETER GARRICK
"I have the genius for an actor"

Before becoming one of the greatest actors to ever grace a British stage, David Garrick was a struggling wine merchant. In this letter to his brother, he describes how he keeps losing money in the wine business, but has excellent prospects as an actor—which he also happens to enjoy doing.

October, 1741

I received my shirt safe and am now to tell you what I suppose you may have heard of before this. But before I let you into my affair, 'tis proper to premise some things, that I may appear less culpable in your opinion than I might otherwise do.

I have made an Exact Estimate of my stock of wine, and what money I have out at interest, and find that since I have been a Wine Merchant I have run out near four hundred pounds, and trade not increasing. I was very sensible some way must be thought of to redeem it. My mind (as you must know) has always been inclin'd to the Stage; nay, so strongly so that all my Illness and lowness of Spirits was owing to my want of resolution to tell you my thoughts when here; finding at last both my Inclination and Interest requir'd some new way of Life, I have chose the most agreeable to myself; and though I know you will be much displeas'd at me, yet I hope when you shall find that I have the genius for an actor without the vices, you will think less severe on me, and not be asham'd to own me for a Brother.

Last night I played the Richard the Third to the surprise of Everybody; and as I shall make very near £300 per annum by it, and as it is really what I dote upon, I am resolv'd to pursue it. Pray write me an answer immediately.

[No signature]

[Postcript] I have a farce, Ye Lying Varlet, coming out at Drury Lane.

JOHN KEATS TO SISTER FANNY
"He mentioned Tea Brokerage"

The pursuit of business as a career is a fine enterprise for most people. But there are some for whom it was better for them, and for the rest of the world, that they turned their backs on the world of commerce. In 1819, the British poet John Keats pursued an offer from his guardian to enter the tea brokerage business. As this letter to his sister Fanny shows, the venture withered.

December 20, 1819

Wentworth Place, Monday Morn

My Dear Fanny,

When I saw you last, you ask'd me whether you should see me again before Christmas. You would have seen me if I had been quite well. I have not, though not unwell enough to have prevented me—not indeed at all—but fearful le[s]t the weather should affect my throat which on exertion or cold continually threatens me. By the advice of my Doctor I have had a wa[r]m great Coat made and have ordered some thick shoes—so furnish'd I shall be with you if it holds a little fine before Christmas day.

I have been very busy since I saw you especially the last Week and shall be for some time, in preparing some Poems to come out in the Spring. . . . My hopes of success in the literary world are now better than ever. Mr. Abbey, on my calling on him lately, appeared anxious that I should apply myself to something else—He mentioned Tea Brokerage. I suppose he might perhaps mean to give me the Brokerage of his concern, which might be executed with little trouble and good profit; and therefore said I should have no objection to it especially as at the same time it occur[r]ed to me that I might make over the business to George—I questioned him about it a few days after. His mind takes odd turns. When I became a Suitor, he became coy. He did not seem so much inclined to serve me. He described what I should have to do in the progress of business. It will not suit me. I have given it up. . .

Mr. Brown and I go on in our old dog trot of Breakfast, dinner (not tea for we have left that off), supper, Sleep, confab, stirring the fire and reading. . . . On Tuesday I am going to hear some schoolboys Speechify on breaking up day—I'll lay you a pocket pi[e]ce we shall have "My name is norval." . . . This moment Bentley brought a Letter from George for me to deliver to Mrs. Wylie—I shall see her and it before I see you. The direction was in his best hand, written with a good Pen and sealed with Tassi[e]'s Shakespeare such as I gave you—We judge of people's hearts by their Countenances; may we not judge of Letters in the same way? If so, the Letter does not contain unpleasant news—Good or bad spirits have an effect on the handwriting. This direction is at least unnervous and healthy. Our sister is also well, or George would have made strange work with Ks and Ws. The little Baby is well or he would have formed precious vowels and Consonants—He sent off the Letter in a hurry, or the mail bag was rather a wa[r]m birth, or he has worn out his Seal, for the Shakespeare's head is flattened a little. This is close muggy weather as they say at the Ale houses—

I am, ever, my dear Sister
Yours affectionately
John Keats

WILLIAM RANDOLPH HEARST TO HIS FATHER
"I am convinced that I could run a newspaper successfully"

A towering giant in American newspapers for more than 50 years, William Randolph Hearst outlined in 1885 the basic guidelines for his future media empire, and he was merely 22 years old. In this letter to his father, the junior Hearst asked to be given control of The San Francisco Examiner, which his father had acquired for repayment of a bad debt and which Hearst senior had called a "limp rag of a newspaper."

The son's main credentials at the time were being dismissed from Harvard for "overindulgence in a passion for pranks" and a fertile mind. The letter, however, proved convincing enough to his father. In 1887, the young Hearst took control of The San Francisco Examiner, beginning one of the world's most spectacular careers in journalism.

Hearst carried out most of the promises and ideas of the letter over the following decades, building a network of newspapers, magazines, film studios, gold mines, real-estate companies and other enterprises. Known by his employees as "the Chief," Hearst was widely considered not only a hard-driving businessman, but also a first-rate newspaper writer.

[Washington] 1885

Dear Father:

I have just finished and dispatched a letter to the Editor of the *Examiner* in which I recommended Eugene Lent to his favorable notice, and commented on the illustrations, if you may call them such, which have lately disfigured the paper. I really believe that the *Examiner* has furnished what is thus far the crowning absurdity of illustrated Journalism, in illustrating an article on the chicken show by means of the identical Democratic roosters used during the late campaign. In my letter to the editor, however, I did not refer to this for fear of offending him, but I did tell him that in my opinion the cuts that have recently appeared in the paper bore an unquestionable resemblance to the Cuticura Soap advertisements; and I am really inclined to believe that our editor has illustrated many of his articles from his stock on hand of cuts representing before and after using that efficacious remedy.

In case my remarks should have no effect and he should continue in his career of desolation, let me beg of you to remonstrate with him and thus prevent him from giving the finishing stroke to our miserable little sheet.

I have begun to have a strange fondness for our little paper—a tenderness like unto that which a mother feels for a puny or deformed offspring, and I should hate to see it die now after it had battled so long and so nobly for existence; in fact, to tell the truth, I am possessed of the weakness, which at some time or other of their lives, pervades most men; I am convinced that I could run a newspaper successfully.

Now if you should make over to me the *Examiner*—with enough money to carry out my schemes—I'll tell you what I would do!

In the first place I would change the general appearance of the paper and make seven wide columns where we now have nine narrow ones, then I would have the type spaced more, and these two changes would give the pages a much cleaner and neater appearance.

Secondly, it would be well to make the paper as far as possible original, to clip only when absolutely necessary and to imitate only some such leading journal as the *New York World* which is undoubtedly the best paper of that class to which the *Examiner* belongs—that class which appeals to the people and which depends for its success upon enterprise, energy and a certain startling originality and not upon the wisdom of its political opinions or the lofty style of its editorials: And to accomplish this we must have—as the *World* has—active, intelligent and energetic young men; we must have men who come out West in the hopeful buoyancy of youth for the purpose of making their fortunes and not a worthless scum that has been carried there by the eddies of repeated failures.

Thirdly, we must advertise the paper from Oregon to New Mexico and must also increase our number of advertisements if we have to lower our rates to do it, thus we can put on the first page that our circulation is such and our advertisements so and so and constantly increasing.

And now having spoken of the three great essential points let us turn to details. The illustrations are a detail, though a very important one. Illustrations embellish a page; illustrations attract the eye and stimulate the imagination of the masses and materially aid the comprehension of an unaccustomed reader and thus are of particular importance to that class of people which the *Examiner* claims to address. Such illustrations, however, as have heretofore appeared in the paper, nauseate rather than stimulate the imagination and certainly do anything but embellish a page.

Another detail of questionable importance is that we actually or apparently establish some connection between ourselves and the *New York World*, and obtain a certain prestige in bearing some relation to that paper. We might contract to have important private telegrams forwarded or something of that sort, but understand that the principal advantage we are to derive is from the attention such a connection would excite and from the advertisement we could make of it. Whether the *World* would consent to such an arrangment for any reasonable sum is very doubtful, for its net profit is over one thousand dollars a day and no doubt would consider the *Examiner* as beneath its notice. Just think, over one thousand dollars a day and four years ago it belonged to Jay Gould and was losing money rapidly.

And now to close with a suggestion of great consequence, namely, that all these changes be made not by degrees but at once so that the improvement will be very marked and noticeable and will attract universal attention and comment.

There is little to be said about my studies. I am getting on in all of them well enough to be able to spend considerable time in outside reading and in Journalistic investigation. There is, moreover, very little to be said about Washington, for Congress is as stupid as it is possible to conceive of and has been enlivened only once during our stay and that the other day when Wise of Virginia sat on Boutelle of Maine for attempting to revive the dissensions of the war. So heavily, indeed, did Mr. Wise sit on Boutelle that I fear the latter gentlemen has not even yet recovered his characteristic rotundity of form.

Well, good-by. I have given up all hope of having you write me, so I suppose I must just scratch along and trust to hearing you through the newspapers. By the way, I heard you had bought 2000 acres of land the other day and I hope some of it was the land adjoining our ranch that I begged you to buy in my last letter.

Your affectionate son,
W. R. Hearst

LOUISA MAY ALCOTT TO HER FAMILY
"Pay small at first, but it is a beginning & honest work"

Ten years before publishing the beloved book Little Women, *Louisa May Alcott had a difficult time making ends meet. This letter to her family describes her struggles as a young governess. Among other tasks, she oversaw a girl whom Alcott would later describe as "a demonic little girl who don't digest her food & does rave & tear & scold & screech like an insane cherubim."*

(1858)
To the Alcott Family
Boston Sunday evening

Dear People

You will laugh when you hear what I have been doing. Laugh, but hear, unless you prefer to cry, & hear.

Last week was a busy, anxious time, & my courage most gave out, for every one was so busy, & cared so little whether I got work or jumped into the river that I thought seriously of doing the latter. In fact did go over the Mill Dam & look at the water. But it seemed so mean to turn & run away before the battle was over that I went home, set my teeth & vowed I'd make things work in spite of the world, the flesh & the devil.

Lovering sent no answer about Alice, & nothing else could I find. I waited till Friday, then rushed out & clamored for work. Called on Mrs. Lovering, she was out. Tore across the Common to Mrs. Reed. She had no sewing but would remember me if she had. Asked Mr. Sargent, had nothing for me to do. Then I said "Damn!" & after a tempestuous night got up, went straight to Mr. Parker's & demanded him. You may judge what desperate earnest I was in to go to people I knew so little. Mr. P. was out also Miss L. But Mrs. P. was in. . . . I don't know what she thought of me for I was muddy & shabby, pale & red-eyed, grim one minute & choky the next. Altogether a nice young person to come bouncing in & demanding work like a reckless highway woman.

I told her in a few words that we were poor, I must support myself & was willing to do anything honest; sew, teach, write, house work, nurse, &c.

She was very kind, said she would confer with Theodore & Hannah; & came away feeling better, for, though she gave me no work a little sympathy was worth its weight in gold just then, & no one else offered me a bit.

Today went to church, heard a sermon on "Good is set against evil." Tried to apply it, but didn't do it very well. At noon Hannah H. called & offered me a place as seamstress at the Reform School Winchester. Sew 10 hours a day, making & mending for 30 girls. Pay small at first, but it is a beginning & honest work.

Miss H. evidently thought I wouldn't take it for she said "Mrs. P. told me of your visit, was it in earnest or only a passing idea?" "I was in desperate earnest, & shall be glad of any thing, no matter how hard or humble," said I in my tragic way. "May I depend on you, & do you like sewing?" "You may depend on me if my health holds out with the 10 hours work. As for liking, it was not what I *want* but what I can get that I must take & be grateful for." She seemed satisfied, gave me a ticket, said, "Try it a week," & told me to go on Monday.

So I shall go & try my best, though it will be hard to sit patching & darning day after day with a dozen stories bubbling in my brain & "knocking proudly on the lid demanding to be taken out & sold." Knocking about is good for me I suppose. I get so much of it, I shall grow mellow & fit to eat in the fullness of time, though I think peacefully growing on the parent tree with plenty of sun an easier way.

Monday eve

Now what do you think? Last eve when my mind was all made up to go out to W[inchester] in comes a note from Lovering saying that on talking it over they concluded to have me come & governess Alice for the winter.

I skipped for joy, & dear Molly said "Stay here & sew for me & that will pay your board, you help so much in many ways & make it so lively." I agreed at once, & there I am. Allyluyer! I went & told Hannah H. and she was glad & said, "I knew it wasn't the thing for you & only offered it as a little test of your earnestness, meaning to get you something better in time." Mr. P. said "the girl has got true grit," & "we were all pleased with you." So that is right, & the ten hours will dwindle to four, with walking, playing & lessons to vary the time.

It has been a hard week but it is all right now, & I guess the text will prove true in the end, for my despair found me friends, & duty was made easier when I had accepted the hardest. Amen.

I begin tomorrow & am in fine spirits again. "Here we go up up up—And here we go down down downy" is a good song for me.

With love your tragic comic, Lu

JAMES RUSSELL LOWELL TO W. D. HOWELLS
"If you can reckon on your own temperament, accept"

James Russell Lowell offered the following advice to his friend and fellow writer W. D. Howells on whether to accept a job as a professor. As with any job decision, Lowell urges him to consider his own temperament, financial needs, and interests in making the decision.

Ashridge, Berkhampstead, Dec. 21, 1882

Dear Howells,—

I was very glad to get your letter, though it put me under bonds to be wiser than I have ever had the skill to be. If I remember rightly, Panurge's doubts were increased by consulting the oracle, but how did the Oracle feel? Did it ever occur to you that a certain share of our sympathy should go in that direction?

My best judgment is this, and like all good judgment is this, and like all good judgment it is to a considerable degree on both sides of the question. If you are able now, without overworking mind or body, to keep the wolf from the door and to lay by something for a rainy day—and I mean, of course, without being driven to work with your left hand because the better one is tired out—I should refuse the offer, or should hesitate to accept it. If you are a systematic worker, independent of moods, and sure of your genius whenever you want it, there might be no risk in accepting. You would have the advantage of a fixed income to fall back on. Is this a greater advantage than the want of it would be a spur to industry? Was not the occasion of Shakespeare's plays (I don't say the motive of 'em) that he *had* to write? And are any of us likely be better inspired than he? Does not inspiration, in some limited sense at least, come with the exercise thereof, as the appetite with eating? Is not your hand better for keeping it in, as they say? A professorship takes a great deal of time, and, if you teach in any more direct way than by lectures, uses up immense stock of nerves. Your inevitable temptation (in some sort your duty) will be to make yourself learned—which you haven't the least need to be as an author (if you only have me at your elbow to correct your English now and then, naughty boy!). If you can make your professorship a thing apart—but can you and be honest? I believe the present generation doesn't think I was made for a poet, but I think I could have gone nearer convincing 'em if I had not estranged the muse by donning a professor's gown. I speak of myself because you wanted my experience. I am naturally indolent, and being worked pretty hard in the College, was willing to be content with the amount of work that was squeezed out of me by my position, and let what my nature might otherwise have forced me into go. As I said before, if you can reckon on your own temperament, accept. If you have a doubt, *don't*. I think you will divine what I am driving at. . . .

Inexorable lunch has sounded, and I must say goodby. I should say, on the whole—it is safe to ask my advice, but not to follow it. But then people never do.

Affectionately yours,

J. R. L.

ELINORE RUPERT STEWART TO MRS. CONEY
"Homesteading is the solution of all poverty's problems"

Elinore Rupert left Denver, Colorado, for Wyoming in 1909 with a young daughter to become a homesteader. Her husband had been killed in a train accident. She wanted to work on a ranch to learn how to run her own homestead. Four years later she was married and had realized her dream. Stewart wrote this letter to her old boss describing the wisdom of her decision.

January 23, 1913

Dear Mrs. Coney,

I am afraid all my friends think I am very forgetful and that you think I am ungrateful as well, but I am going to plead not guilty. Right after Christmas Mr. Steward came down with la grippe and was so miserable that it kept me busy trying to relieve him. Out here where we can get no physician we have to dope ourselves, so that I had to be housekeeper, nurse, doctor, and general overseer. That explains my long silence.

And now I want to thank you for your kind thought in prolonging our Christmas. The magazines were much appreciated. They relieved some weary night-watches, and the boos did Jerrine more good than the medicine I was having to give her for la grippe. She was content to stay in bed and enjoy the contents of her box.

When I read of the hard times among the Denver poor, I feel like urging them every one to get out and file on land. I am very enthusiastic about women homesteading. It really requires less strength and labor to raise plenty to satisfy a large family than it does to go out to wash, with the added satisfaction of knowing that their job will not be lost to them if they care to keep it. Even if improving the place does go slowly, it is that much done to stay done. Whatever is raised is the homesteader's own, and there is no house-rent to pay. This year Jerrine cut and dropped enough potatoes to raise a ton of fine potatoes. She wanted to try, so we let her, and you will remember that she is but six years old. We had a man break the ground and cover the potatoes for her and the man irrigated them once. That was all that was done until digging time, when they were ploughed out and Jerrine picked them up. Any woman strong enough to go out by the day could have done every bit of the work and put in two or three times that much, and it would have been so much more pleasant than to work so hard in the city and then be on starvation rations in the winter.

To me, homesteading is the solution of all poverty's problems, but I realize that temperament has much to do with success in any undertaking, and persons afraid of coyotes and work and loneliness had better let ranching alone. At the same time, any woman who can stand her own company, can see the beauty of the sunset, loves growing things, and is willing to put in as much time at careful labor as she does over the washtub, will certainly succeed; will have independence, plenty to eat all the time, and a home of her own in the end.

Experimenting need cost the homesteader no more than the work, because by applying to the Department of Agriculture at Washington he can get enough seed and as many kinds as he wants to make a thorough trial, and it doesn't even cost postage. Also one can always get bulletins from there and the Experiment Station of one's own State concerning any problem or as many problems as may come up. I would not, for anything, allow Mr. Stewart to do anything toward improving my place, for I want the fun and the experience myself. And I want to be able to speak from experience when I tell others what they can do. Theories are very beautiful, but facts are what must be had, and what I intend to give some time.

Here I am boring you to death with things that cannot interest you! You'd think I wanted you to homestead, wouldn't you? But I am only thinking of the troops of tired, worried women, sometimes even cold and hungry, scared to death of losing their places to work, who could have plenty to eat, who could have fires by gathering the wood, and comfortable homes of their own, if they but had the courage and determination to get them.

I must stop right now before you get so tired you will not answer. With much love to you from Jerrine and myself, I am

Yours affectionately,
Elinore Rupert Stewart

MANAGEMENT

ELIZABETH I TO RICHARD COX, BISHOP OF ELY
"Proud Prelate"

Queen Elizabeth I of England has recently been put forth as an instructive model for corporate leaders. Two of Elizabeth's outstanding traits were the firmness of her decision-making and her support of loyal court favorites.

As the British monarch, Elizabeth I controlled the properties of the Church of England. These included a house in London known for a garden overflowing in roses and strawberries. Richard Cox, Bishop of Ely, operated the house. Sir Christopher Hatton, a favorite of Elizabeth, coveted the home and offered to occupy it for a nominal rent in 1573. The Bishop of Ely refused, so Hatton appealed to the queen. Elizabeth's response was swift and sure. The Bishop of Ely gave in.

Proud prelate:

You know what you were before I made you what you are now. If you do not immediately comply with my request, I will unfrock you, by God.

Elizabeth

THE RUSSIAN AMERICAN COMPANY TO ALEKSANDR ANDREEVICH BARANOV

"The pigs which are on Kad'iak are not company property"

Managing employees from afar has always been an especially difficult task. The fur trappers that worked for the Russian American Company in Alaska two hundred years ago may have been history's most remote collection of employees. Twelve time zones away from their home Moscow office across frozen tundra of Siberia, the trading outpost was so distant it would often take eighteen months to deliver a letter, and more than three years for a simple exchange of information to take place.

In 1818 a new supervisor, L.A. Hagemeister, arrived in Alaska and discovered that the first manager had raised so many pigs that they had overrun the island. Hagemeister issued the following directive to Baranov to dispose of the pigs.

January 17, 1818

Having learned from you that the pigs which are on Kad'iak are not common property, but belong to you and other private persons, and that, judging by the report of the Kad'iak office, they have multiplied to such a degree as to have become a burden on the company to maintain, I must ask you to sell to the company from your said property a certain number of both sows and boars, so that henceforth this type of livestock will be established as company property. This livestock is useful for feeding the people, and its maintenance, in moderate numbers, is not burdensome. At your discretion, please inform me of your decision, so that when I send a vessel to kad'iak I may among other things issue proper orders on this matter.

ABRAHAM LINCOLN TO "FIGHTING JOE" HOOKER
"I am not quite satisfied with you"

Abraham Lincoln was very skilled at handling people. One of his most difficult challenges as President during the Civil War was selecting and managing his generals. No expert in the military, Lincoln had to rely on his generals to get the most pressing task of his presidency accomplished—win the Civil War.

Lincoln often wrote to his generals seeking information, offering support, and setting standards of accountability. In the first letter below, Lincoln states in very clear terms to the recently appointed General Joseph Hooker why he has been named commander of the army, in spite of some potential shortcomings. Hooker proved to be a disappointment, discharged from command after being routed at the Battle of Chancellorsville less than four months after Lincoln's words of advice.

Lincoln was much more pleased with General Ulysses S. Grant's performance as commanding general, however. At the outset of the spring campaign of 1864 Lincoln wrote Grant of his satisfaction and support for the pending invasion of Virginia. Grant's campaign proved to be very bloody, with one inconclusive battle after another ending with the extended siege of Petersburg. Tens of thousands of soldiers were killed or injured, prompting calls for Lincoln to sack Grant. But Lincoln stood by Grant, and within a year, the war was over.

Executive Mansion
Washington, January 26, 1863
Major-General Hooker:
General:

I have placed you at the head of the Army of the Potomac. Of course I have done this upon what appear to me to be sufficient reasons. And yet I think it best for you to know that there are some things in regard to which, I am not quite satisfied with you. I believe you to be a brave and skillful soldier, which, of course, I like. I also believe you do not mix politics with your profession, in which you are right. You have confidence in yourself, which is a valuable, if not an indispensable quality. You are ambitious, which, within reasonable bounds, does good rather than harm. But I think that during Gen. Burnside's command of the Army you have taken counsel of your ambition, and thwarted him as much as you could, in which you did a great wrong to the country, and to a most meritorious and honorable brother officer. I have heard, in such a way as to believe it, of your recently saying that both the Army and the Government need a Dictator. Of course, it was not *for* this, but in spite of it, that I have given you the command. Only those generals who gain successes, can set up dictators. What I now ask of you is military success, and I will risk the dictatorship. The government will support you to the utmost of its ability, which is neither more nor less than it has done and will do for all commanders. I much fear that the spirit which you have aided to infuse into the Army, of criticising their Commander and withholding confidence from him, will now turn upon you. I shall assist you as far as I can, to put it down. Neither you, nor Napoleon, if he were alive again, could get any good out of an army, while such a spirit prevails in it. And now, beware of rashness. Beware of rashness, but with energy, and sleepless vigilance, go forward and give us victories.

Yours very truly,
A. Lincoln

Executive Mansion, Washington
April 30, 1864
Lieutenant-General Grant:

Not expecting to see you again before the spring campaign opens, I wish to express in this way my entire satisfaction with what you have done up to this time, so far as I understand it. The particulars of your plans I neither know nor seek to know. You are vigilant and self-reliant; and, pleased with this, I wish not to obtrude any constraints or restraints upon you. While I am very anxious that great disaster or capture of our men in great numbers shall be avoided. I know these points are less likely to escape your attention than they would be mine. If there is anything wanting which is within my power to give, do not fail to let me know it. And now, with a brave army and a just cause, may God sustain you.

Yours very truly,
A. Lincoln

BUFFALO BILL ON STAR COWBOYS
"They git the big head"

The legendary cowboy William F. Cody earned his nickname for his prowess as a buffalo hunter for western railroad crews in the 1860s. But Buffalo Bill gained international fame as the owner and manager of the Buffalo Bill Wild West Show, an extravaganza of cowboys and Indians, mock lawmen and desperadoes, horses and horses, all recreating wild scenes of the Old West for audiences in the eastern United States and Europe.

Cody, who was also a rider in the Pony Express and one of the best scouts in the cavalry, started his career in show business in a traveling theater company, which he enjoyed immensely. Before long he started his own company. He employed some of his rootin' tootin' cowboy companions and it grew into the Wild West show. In addition to the logistical nightmare of moving his highly involved show around, one of his biggest management headaches was handling the egos of his star cowboys, many of whom were enjoying celebrity for the first time.

North Platte

July 5th [18]79

My Dear Sam

Just came in from branding calves tired out feeling bully otherwise. Rained to beat h—. Sorry you were feeling so blue and if I was not so hard pushed for scads [money] I would just send you a hundred for luck. But I am pushed to the wall until I can ship beeves [cattle] or get to work. If I were not going away to soon would have you to come out but I will make a brake next week first to Colorado then to N.Y. back to Davenport Iowa where I open Sep. 1st. In regard to you going on the boards again. I must think of it I have no part in either my dramas that would be suitable for you to play as I did say that I would never again have another Scout or western man with me. That is one whom I would work up. For just as soon as they see their names in print a few times they git the big head and want to start a company of their own. I will name a few. Wild Bill Texas Jack John Nelson Oregon Bill Kit Carson Capt. Jack all busted flat before they were out a month and wanted to come back. Because I would not take them then they talked about me. But old pard I don't realy believe you are that kind of a hair Jim and I will see what can be done. I see in a Chicago paper the other day where Kit Carson (Jr.) was arrested for strikeing his wife with intent to kill. Was bound over to the next court. I expected as much when he married that old dame. Kit by the way aint a bad fellow but he thought at one time that he

was a little K Christ He is out of luck. had better stick to the old man. run out of paper good by
Cody,
With Kind Wishes

ANDREW CARNEGIE, J. P. MORGAN & CHARLES M. SCHWAB GAMBLING CONTROVERSY
"Go ahead and have a bully time"

When Andrew Carnegie sold his steelworks to J. P. Morgan in 1901 he recommended his young protégé Charles M. Schwab as president of the merged U. S. Steel Corporation. But within a year Schwab had sparked a huge furor in the newspapers when he was spotted gambling in Monte Carlo during a business trip to Europe.

A strait-laced Scotsmen, Carnegie was mortified and wrote a letter to Morgan apologizing for recommending Schwab and urging Morgan to fire him. Schwab—who had only played a few hands of cards with friends—was stunned by the barrage of telegrams he was getting in Monte Carlo. He sent back a telegram to Morgan's right-hand man, George W. Perkins, explaining the situation, and offering to resign. Morgan—who was known to seek pleasures of his own—was unmoved by the publicity and stood by Schwab.

Confidential

5 West Fifty-first Street, New York

Jany 14th, 1902

My Dear Mr Morgan,

I feel in regard to the enclosed as if a son had disgraced the family. What the Times says is true. He is unfit to be the head of the United States Steel Co.—brilliant as his talents are. Of course he would never have so fallen when with us. His resignation would have been called for instanter had he done so.

I recommended him unreservedly to you. Never did he show any tendency to gambling when under me, or I should not have recommended him you may be sure. He shows a sad lack of *solid* qualities, of good sense, & his influence upon the many thousands of young men who naturally look to him will prove pernicious in the extreme.

I have had nothing wound me so deeply for many a long day, if ever.

Sincerely yours,

Andrew Carnegie

George Perkins,

Am advised that there have been sensational publications regarding gambling. Did play but sensational statements of great winnings and losses absolutely false. Friends advise by cable that should resign, of course will do so if Morgan thinks I should. Sorry. Cable me at Bristol Hotel Vienna any advice or instructions.

Charles M. Schwab

Charles Schwab,

Everything all right. Andrew Carnegie and several others were very much excited but they did not make the slighest impression on Mr Morgan. Do not give the matter any further thought or consideration. Go ahead and have a bully time.

George Perkins

JOHN D. ROCKEFELLER, JR. TO JOHN D. ROCKEFELLER, SR.
"A salary and bonus based on earnings"

Sixty years before compensation packages based on company earning and stock performance started to become all the rage, John D. Rockefeller Jr. proposed a similar arrangement for Standard Oil officers. His father, however, opposed the idea because of the cost. Giving a gold watch upon the retirement of a long-time employee, however, proved a more appealing idea.

26 Broadway
New York
December 16, 1926

Dear Father:

Your letter of the 13th is received. I am glad to have this further reflection of yours on the question of compensation for the higher officials of the various companies. It is undoubtedly true that a fixed salary, even if high, would be less costly to a company than a salary and bonus, the latter being based on earnings. I am not sure, however, that the total paid compensation in the latter plan would be larger in proportion to the total earnings of the company. Unless a percentage basis stimulates to increased earnings for the stockholders, it would not increase the compensation of the officer.

I am enclosing a clipping from a recent issue of the Wall Street Journal, which is very interesting and kindly. I am sure you will enjoy it. . . .

As you know, Mr. Cary is retiring at the end of the year. He has been with us many, many years. I have thought that it would be a nice thing for you and me to give him a gold watch. This I am sure he would appreciate enormously. Does the suggestion appeal to you? If so I will go ahead with it.

Affectionately
John

E. B. White to Harold Ross

"I resented the idea of having to give a gift to my employer"

As the founding publisher of The New Yorker *in the 1920s, Harold Ross was beloved by many of his writers and editors, some of the finest scribes of that era. At Christmas, 1927, E. B. White wrote the following letter to accompany a gift he was giving Ross. In contemplating the relationship between employer and employee, White repeatedly insults Ross. Though it may be hard to tell at times, it was all in good fun. The two men remained friends for many years. (White's address given at the end of the letter was intentionally wrong.)*

Dear Mr. Ross:

Here is the address book you were hinting for. Perhaps a few words of explanation would not be amiss. It was bought at Brentano's and cost seven fifty, a little more than I had expected to pay. It is of hand-tooled leather, as opposed to the ordinary machine-tooled kind which is every bit as good probably. It is a "red" book with a decorative border of "gold" and has a little pencil at the side which you will never use because it isn't practical. There is a good chance that you will never use the book either, but I took that into consideration when I bought it and will not be emotionally affected one way or the other. The filler or "pack" is removable, which is a handy wrinkle except that Brentano's have none of them in stock and it would be a lot of work to hunt one up any place else. The filler is indexed, the letters of the alphabet being alternately blue and red, possibly for some reason which you can figure out.

Now as to the spirit of the gift. The spirit of the gift is very good. At first I resented the idea of having to give a gift to my employer. I don't owe you anything! Everything I have had at your hands I have worked for, often twice. But then it occurred to me that it might be worth my while to give you an address book in order to "get in strong" with you. And I might add that all my previous employers, when Christmas came round, received from me a little package of ground glass and porcupine quills. But my relations with you have always been pleasant, and as Ring Lardner so aptly put it you are a wonderful friend. With a lot of hard work and honest effort on your part, I see no reason why we cannot continue on this friendly basis almost indefinitely. Please enter my name in your address book 12 W. 113 St. Chelsea 5276 and believe me

Merry Christmas,

E. B. White

Thank you for your many courtesies, which I often brood over.

EDDIE CANTOR AND FLORENZ ZIEGFELD
"Yessir"

*Florenz Ziegfeld, the legendary "glorifier of the American girl"—via his extravagant Ziegfeld Follies—
did most of his business communication by telegram. This often included his relations with employees
in his own building. The following is an exchange between Ziegfeld and the entertainer Eddie Cantor
following a twelve-page wire of instructions from Ziegfeld to Cantor for an upcoming show.*

Florenz Ziegfeld
New Amsterdam Theatre Building
New York NY

Yes.

Cantor

Eddie Cantor
Ziegfeld Follies
New Amsterdam Theater
New York NY

Yes what?

Ziegfeld

Florenz Ziegfeld
New Amsterdam Theatre Building
New York NY

Yessir!

Cantor

Eddie Cantor
Ziegfeld Follies
New Amsterdam Theatre
New York NY

What do you mean, Yessir? Do you mean Yessir you'll take out the song, or Yessir you will put in the line, or Yessir you will fix that scene or Yessir you have talked to those actors?

Ziegfeld

Florenz Ziegfeld
New Amsterdam Theatre Building
New York NY

No Sir.

Cantor

GERMAN PRINCE TO HESSIAN GENERAL
"Glory is true wealth"

The British army hired Hessian soldiers from Germany to fight for the crown during the American Revolution. The German prince Count de Schaumburg supplied many of these soldiers using a fee structure that included 30 guineas for each of his mercenaries killed in battle. The prince relied on this income for financing his lavish court, tours of the Riviera, and cultural pursuits.

Assuming the count's voice, Benjamin Franklin wrote the following letter as a satire of his motives, portraying Schaumberg as eager to fill his treasury's coffer with new revenues.

Rome, February 18, 1777
General, Baron Hohenhorf:

On my return from Naples, I received at Rome your letter of the 27th December of last year. I have learned with unspeakable pleasure the courage our troops exhibited at Trenton, and you cannot imagine my joy on being told that of the 1,950 Hessians engaged in the fight, but 345 escaped. There were just 1,605 men killed, and I cannot sufficiently commend your prudence in sending an exact list of the dead to my minister in London. This precaution was the more necessary, as the report sent to the English ministry does not give but 1,455 dead. This would make 483,450 florins instead of 643,500 which I am entitled to demand under our convention. You will comprehend the prejudice which such an error would work in my finances, and I do not doubt you will take the necessary pains to prove that Lord North's list is false and yours correct.

The court of London objects that there were a hundred wounded who ought not to be included in the list, nor paid for as dead; but I trust you will not overlook my instructions to you on quitting Cassel, and that you will not have tried by human succor to recall the life of the unfortunates whose days could not be lengthened but by the loss of a leg or an arm. That would be making them a pernicious present, and I am sure they would rather die than live in a condition no longer fit for my service. I do not mean by this that you should assassinate them; we should be humane, my dear Baron, but you may insinuate to the surgeons with entire propriety that a crippled man is a reproach to their profession, and that there is no wiser course than to let every one of them die when he ceases to be fit to fight.

I am about to send to you some new recruits. Don't economize them. Remember glory before all fit to fight.

I am about to send to you some new recruits. Don't economize them. Remember glory before all things. Glory is true wealth. There is nothing degrades the soldier like the love of money. He must care only for honour and reputation, but this reputation must be acquired in the midst of dangers. A battle gained without costing the conqueror any blood is an inglorious success, while the conquered cover themselves with glory by perishing with their arms in their hands. Do you remember that of the 300 Lacedaemonians who defended the defile of Thermopylae, not one returned? How happy should I be could I say the same of my brave Hessians!...

Count de Schaumburg
February, 1777

ROBERT BENCHLEY TO ART SAMUELS
"Am being inducted into Indian tribe"

Excuses, excuses, excuses. Managers of employees have heard them all. But the editor at Harper's Bazaar *in 1933 heard them all on the same day from Robert Benchley. Benchley was known to the public for his humorous writings, but to his editors as being unreliable in meeting deadlines. Aware of this shortcoming, Benchley would often come up with excuses such as this series of telegrams sent to* Harper's Bazaar *on the deadline for an article he was supposed to submit.*

May 29, 1933
Worcester Massachusetts

Collect
Art Samuels, Editor
Harper's Bazaar
572 Madison Avenue
New York NY

Am taking care of my sick mother.

Benchley

May 29, 1933
Presque Isle Maine

Collect
Art Samuels, Editor
Harper's Bazaar
572 Madison Avenue
New York NY

Am acting as guide for hunting party.

Benchley

May 29, 1933
Detroit Michigan

Collect
Art Samuels, Editor
Harper's Bazaar
572 Madison Avenue
New York NY

Am inspecting new Packard engines.

Benchley

May 29, 1933
Miami Beach Florida

Collect
Art Samuels, Editor
Harper's Bazaar
572 Madison Avenue
New York NY

Am judging orange blossom carnival.

Benchley

May 29, 1933
Sante Fe New Mexico

Collect
Art Samuels, Editor
Harper's Bazaar
572 Madison Avenue
New York NY

Am being inducted into Indian tribe.

Benchley

May 29, 1933
Hollywood California

Collect
Art Samuels, Editor
Harper's Bazaar
572 Madison Avenue
New York NY

Am working on picture with Greta Garbo.

Benchley

May 29 1933
New York NY

Collect
Robert Benchley
Royalton Hotel
44 West 44 Street
New York NY

Gather you haven't done the piece.

Samuels

BERNARD MILES TO KIRSTEN FLAGSTAD
"To be obedient, tractable, sweet-tempered and helpful"

Opera producer Bernard Miles put on a fund-raising event for his new theater, the Mermaid Theatre in London, in 1950. Soprano Kirsten Flagstad and Miles's wife, Josephine Wilson, agreed to help with the event. Miles and Flagstad wrote a letter to each other as mock agreement of terms.

Mermaid Theatre
Duff House
Acacia Road
London N.W. 8
19th April, 1951

ARTICLES OF AGREEMENT between KIRSTEN FLAGSTAD, Soprano, hereinafter called "the Singer" and THE MERMAID COMPANY, hereinafter called "the Management."

The Singer undertakes:

1. To sing for 20 (twenty) performances the part of Dido in the opera DIDO AND AENEAS.

2. To assist in the production of the opera and to lend all such aid, help and assistance as may be deemed necessary to the successful presentation thereof.

3. To use only her best quality voice, fully supported by the breath throughout the performance.

4. To sing all her notes in time and in tune, but not to add any notes, grace notes, acciaccaturas, appoggiaturas, upper and lower mordents, shakes, trills, turns, titillations or other embellishments.

5. To let the management or any part thereof look down her throat with laryngoscope whenever they need encouragement.

6. To sing to the Management or any part thereof any or all of the songs of Schubert, Schumann, Beethoven, Handel, Bach, Grieg as often as requested.

7. To be obedient, tractable, sweet-tempered and helpful in every possible way, and not to brag about the Vikings.

On their side, the Management undertake:

1. To treat the Singer in the manner worthy of her great name and fame, to look after her, to nourish, cherish, care for and make much of her. Also to hold her dear, to prize, treasure, cling to, adore, idealise and dote upon her.

2. To appoint as her personal slaves their three youngest members, to whit, Sarah, Biddy and John, who shall wait upon her hand, foot and finger.

3. To supply the Singer with all necessary scores, bars, notes, and parts of notes, key signatures, ledger lines, etc. as shall be deemed necessary for the adequate interpretation of her role.

4. To find her in board-lodging throughout the run of the opera.

5. To supply her with two pints of oatmeal stout per diem, at the following times and in the following quantities, viz. Lunch one half pint, dinner one half pint, and one pint following each performance.

6. To give her plenty of little surprises, presents of flowers, fruit, fish and fresh foliage; to recite to her; to write letters and little poems to her; also to take every opportunity of making her laugh.

Given under all our hands and with all our hearts, this tenth day of February, one thousand nine hundred and fifty.

Sealed with a kiss.

RAYMOND CHANDLER TO ALFRED HITCHCOCK

"Nobody can be adequately paid for wasting his time"

In 1950, hard-boiled mystery writer Raymond Chandler wrote a screenplay for Alfred Hitchcock's film Strangers on a Train. Invoking the director's privilege, Hitchcock made wholesale changes to Chandler's script. Chandler's response expresses the rage of any employee or contractor who has done his best, only to see the effort demolished through decisions beyond his control.

Dear Hitch,

In spite of your wide and generous disregard of my communications on the subject of the script of Strangers on a Train and your failure to make any comment on it, and in spite of not having heard a word from you since I began the writing of the actual screenplay-—or all of which I might say I bear no malice, since this sort of procedure seems to be part of the standard Hollywood depravity—in spite of this and in spite of this extremely cumbersome sentence, I feel that I should, just for the record, pass you a few comments on what is termed the final script. I could understand your finding fault with my script in this or that way, thinking that such and such a scene was too long or such and such a mechanism was too awkward. I could understand you changing your mind about the things you specifically wanted, because some of such changes might have been imposed on you from without. What I cannot understand is your permitting a script which after all had some life and vitality to be reduced to such a flabby mass of clichés, a group of faceless characters, and the kind of dialogue every screen writer is taught not to write—the kind that says everything twice and leaves nothing to be implied by the actor or the camera. Of course you must have had your reasons but, to use a phrase once coined by Max Beerbohm, it would take a "far less brilliant mind than mine" to guess what they were.

Regardless of whether or not my name appears on the screen among the credits, I'm not afraid that anybody will think I wrote this stuff. They'll know damn well I didn't. I shouldn't have minded in the least if you had produced a better script—believe me. I shouldn't. But if you wanted something written in skim milk, why on earth did you bother to come to me in the first place? What a waste of money! What a waste of time! It's no answer to say that I was well paid. Nobody can be adequately paid for wasting his time.

Raymond Chandler

Thomas J. Watson, Jr. to Thomas J. Watson

"I have got to make good"

All chief executive officers are subject to second-guessing and criticisms, but when Thomas J. Watson, Jr. took over at IBM in 1956, he discovered that his most pressing criticisms came from his own parents. His father, Thomas J. Watson, founded the company as a penniless sewing-machine salesman and built it into a leading technology company by the 1950s. The son had mighty shoes to fill when he succeeded his father.

The following letter was prompted by an inquiry from his mother about the firing of a low-level manager. The wife of the employee wrote her to complain about her husband's treatment. Watson's letter in response reflects the weight of issues that confront any company president—among them, trying to balance conflicting pressures, often making decisions with only partial information.

Watson remained head of the company through 1971. His faith in IBM proved justified and it became the largest computer company in the world.

... All of the thoughts which you, Dad, have expressed to me . . . about the possibilities of things not going well in IBM—the fact that we must watch expenses—the fact that if the business starts slipping, it's hard to stop—these are all facts which I knew about before you mentioned them. In truth, they are possibilities which I go to bed with every night. If they should come about my reputation as a businessman is vanished—my reputation as a successful son is finished. No wonder I think about them frequently. I have got to make good.

There are literally hundreds of incidents throughout the year like the Smith situation. That Mrs. Smith saw fit to write you, Mother, is unfortunate. But before she did, the matter had been fairly & well settled. Therefore I don't believe we should panic or be rushed into decisions because of a dishonest man who has been fired. I would tend to discount his threats and allegations. Let's suppose though that Mrs. Smith had not written you & let's suppose we handled the matter as we did. Isn't it vital that we be capable as a team of handling these matters well because you both can't know of all of them nor can I. If the present team . . . isn't operating to your satisfaction, I believe you should make adjustments until you have a group in which you have complete faith—a group who can give you peace of mind about the IBM Co.

Nothing would please me more or help me more than to have your advice on every matter which comes to my attention—much of the time, I'm somewhat in the dark. . . . [But] I don't share your fears about IBM. I believe the company is as strong as it has ever been—with as competent a management as ever, and as well run as ever! This is because you have trained me to think along the lines you think and because you have permitted me to pick a team of the strongest men in the business.

If I am right in my beliefs about IBM, then it ought to be possible for the builder of this great business to drop around and chat with us about our really important problems: Our Department of Justice case—how much of our capital investment should go into electronics—how we should improve the Time division—how we can find and upgrade more executive possibilities from the field. This rather than getting involved in criticizing . . . our operations as in the Smith matter or the general administration of the company.

Can you not by looking at our annual Report . . . convince yourself that we are not doing too bad a job? Can you not take some pride in the fact that the job is being done by T. J. Watson trained men? Can you not find some personal satisfaction and peace of mind in watching this wonderful business enterprise which you have built, grow on to greater heights & move forward on all fronts with a continuing fine profit directed by your team?

Love to you both,
Tom

FRANCIS T. FOX TO THE MANAGER OF THE BEATLES
"The airport cannot permit a public airport reception here"

Soon after a handful of young British musicians formed the Beatles, the band burst onto the world stage as a new cultural phenomenon. Teenage riots broke out at concerts in England as hysterical fans clamored to hear, see and touch the Fab Four. When the Beatles came to tour in the United States in 1964, excited fans mobbed airports to greet the band.

In preparation for the Beatles' trip to Los Angeles, Francis T. Fox, the city's general manager of airports, sent Brian Epstein, manager of the Beatles, instructions on how to arrive in a way that avoided unsafe conditions. The Beatles followed the suggestions and arrived without incident. Eventually, the Beatles stopped giving concerts altogether, in large part because of the dangerous conditions their mere presence on stage created.

Concerns about safety in publicly accessible locations would become more and more of an issue for businesses in the United States. A combination of heightened awareness of safety in the workplace and a rash of lawsuits prompted an increasing emphasis on avoiding potentially dangerous conditions.

CITY OF LOS ANGELES
DEPARTMENT OF AIRPORTS
1 WORLD WAY
LOS ANGELES, CALIFORNIA 90009
TELEPHONE 646-5252

August 17, 1964

Mr. Brian Epstein
Manager, The Beatles
5/6 Argyll
London W1, England

Delivered to Mr. Derek Taylor
    Assistant Manager of the Beatles

Dear Mr. Epstein:

Due to the dangerous conditions which have been created at airports where the Beatles have landed, the Department of Airports has held conferences with the several agencies responsible for the safety of persons, property and aircraft. Included in these meetings have been representatives of the Los Angeles Police and Fire Departments, the Federal Aviation Agency, the sponsors of the Beatles' Los Angeles appearance, and Airport Security and Operations' personnel.

We therefore advise you, as manager of the Beatles, and as a person vitally concerned with their physical welfare, as well as the safety of the Beatles' youthful fans, of the following conditions and recommendations:

(1) The Los Angeles Police Department cannot guarantee the safety of the Beatles should thousands of youngsters be urged by Beatle publicists to greet them at the airport. Only those officers who can be spared from essential duties throughout this vast city may be made available.

(2) The airport cannot permit a public airport reception here. Children have been crushed and injured at other airports when over-excited at the sight of the Beatles.

Therefore, should you elect to arrive at Los Angeles International Airport, the aircraft, be it a chartered or scheduled airline, will be directed to a restricted area to which there is no public access.

(3) We recommend that you use a charter aircraft to its best advantage for the safety of all concerned. In this area as well as in most other cities, there are numerous airports in which you can land with destination unannounced.

It is entirely within your jurisdiction to keep both the time and place of arrival unannounced in order to avoid the dangerous congregation of many thousands of children.

You might also want to consider the possibility that unsafe ground conditions brought on by uncontrolled and emotional crowds can force closure of the airport and diversion of your aircraft.

We sincerely hope you will follow our recommendation. If you have any questions please contact this office. It is a simple procedure to arrive without fanfare. I'm quite certain fellow airport operators join with us in urging such a policy on your part.

Very truly yours,
Francis T. Fox, General Manager

DAVID OGILVY TO "SYNDICATE HEADS"
"Get people alongside you who make up for your weaknesses"

Advertising man David Ogilvy, author of the book Principles of Management, wrote advice to his department heads at his firm, Ogilvy & Mather, on hiring people who complement one's own skills and interests. One of the department heads responded by asking what types of people he should be seeking. An excerpt from Ogilvy's reply follows the initial letter.

April 29, 1971

A Word to the Wise

Long ago I realized that I lack competence, or interest, or both in several areas of our business. Notably television programming, finance, administration, commercial production and marketing.

So I hired people who are strong in those areas where I am weak.

Every one of you Syndicate Heads is strong in some areas, weak in others. Take my advice: get people alongside you who make up for your weaknesses.

If you are strong in production and weak in strategy, have a strategist as your right arm.

If your taste is uncertain—or nonexistent—have someone as your right hand whose taste is impeccable.

If you are a print writer and inept in television, get someone beside you who is the reverse. (Some of you are good at TV but haven't a clue about print.)

If you are weak in package goods, have someone at your right hand who is strong in this area. . . .

Don't compound your own weaknesses by employing people in key positions who have the *same* weakness. . . .

Who wants to admit, even to himself, that he has no taste, or is bored by television production, or inadequate on strategy?

Ah, that is the question.

David Ogilvy

June 9, 1971

Dear _____

You are the only one of the Syndicate Heads who has asked me this question. Which says a lot about you . . .

It would be easier for me to answer the question specifically for certain other Syndicate Heads:

A has terrible taste, so should get someone who has good taste

B is a mere execution man—he should get a strategist

C is blind to graphics and so are his art directors

D ditto

E is a shit and should hire an angel

I am making a speech next week to the grand American Chamber of Commerce in London. I'm so nervous that I'm having nightmares about it.

Yours,

David

Cargill CEOs to Cargill Employees
"If a practice cannot be discussed openly, it must be wrong"

Damage control is one of the more challenging aspects of running a company. In the mid-1970s, the American grain industry was wracked by charges of corruption. Grain companies were accused of bribing inspectors within the United States and companies abroad. Congressional investigations eventually led to new laws making it illegal for American companies to pay off foreign officials, which placed U.S. businesses on a higher ethical plane than most developed countries.

Cargill, the world's largest private company, responded to the crisis with a series of letters to employees, outlining the nature of the controversy, stating the company's position, and asserting Cargill's policy of upright dealings. The first letter below was written by President Fred Sneed shortly after the controversy broke. Sneed's successor, Whitney MacMillan, wrote the second letter six months later.

Both letters place the controversy—which had more to do with other companies—in the context of Cargill's interests. Despite the intense competition of the grain industry, Cargill reaffirmed its corporate ethic of integrity.

June 16, 1975

To All Employees:

Serious charges have been made in Congress and in the national press about irregularities in vessel inspection and in grain weighing and grading at some ports. These charges range from bribery to inspectors and weighman—which our own investigation of our port facilities indicate Cargill is not involved in—to mixing and blending practices that are important features of normal commercial activity. . . .

While we do not know all of the facts, Cargill shares with farmers and foreign customers . . . [a desire to see] that all necessary steps are taken to eliminate irregularities where they are found and to restore confidence in the grain marketing system. . . .

The charges of a "grain inspection scandal" rest on evidence that federally licensed grain inspectors and weighmen have intentionally misgraded or misweighed grain shipments. Such practices—if committed—would prove very damaging to the grain industry. They undermine foreign confidence in U.S. grain exports and willingness to rely on U.S. inspections.

All grain going to overseas customers is sold on the basis of weights and grades established by inspection as the grain is loaded on the ships. These inspections may be performed by individuals licensed by the U.S. Department of Agriculture or directly by USDA employees; . . . the overseas buyer assumes the risk of deterioration in transit. Our obligation as an exporter is satisfied by supplying a certificate showing that the shipment met contract specifications at the time of loading. Allegations of scandal threaten the integrity of weight and grade certificates on which exporters like Cargill must rely in enforcing outstanding contracts. . . .

Many foreign customers are complaining about the quality of U.S. grain shipments. Such complaints underline the seriousness of the current
problem, but they may also result from factors totally unrelated to accurate grain inspection. . . .

Large losses on these contracts could encourage some overseas buyers to raise questions about the condition of grain delivered and about the integrity of origin grades in an effort to avoid taking delivery.

The coincidence of these factors promises continued controversy. No one suffers more than Cargill from lack of confidence in the marketing system. For more than a year we have known of and cooperated with authorities in their investigations of grain inspections at the Gulf. Congressional interest is more recent and extends to much wider issues. Hopefully the result of these investigations will be a better grain marketing system and renewed confidence on the part of customers for American grains.

Sincerely,
Fred M. Sneed
President

November 5, 1975
Fellow Employees:

During the past year, all of us have been made aware through the news media of various illegal or questionable corporate practices, ranging from illegal campaign contributions in the U.S. to payoffs made to foreign officials. Grain industry firms have been charged with bribing weighers and inspectors at U.S. gulf export elevators. Such events compel me to reaffirm certain corporate policies of Cargill as they apply to all of our activities around the world.

Our corporate goals and objectives state: "Continue to make certain that all employees of the Cargill companies recognize and adhere to the principles of integrity which have always been basic to our philosophy and upon which the Cargill companies' reputation is founded."

This means we have a deep responsibility to conduct ourselves and our business under the highest standards of ethics, integrity, and in compliance with the laws of all countries and communities in which we have been granted the opportunity to perform our services.

This means should there be a question concerning a particular practice, open discussion will surely resolve the issue. If a practice cannot be discussed openly, it must be wrong.

This means business secured by any means other than legal, open, honest competition is wrong.

This means if a transaction cannot be properly recorded in the company books, subject to an independent audit, it must be wrong.

This means that Cargill does not want to profit on any practice which is immoral or unethical. Should we discover our business being done in any other than an absolutely proper manner, disciplinary action will be taken.

A company with a good reputation is a good place to work. Cargill has enjoyed 110 years of a fine reputation built on integrity. We must maintain our honor and self-respect as a basis of our continued growth and pride in the Cargill Companies.

Sincerely,
Whitney MacMillan
President

AL NEUHARTH TO GANNETT PUBLISHERS
"For even happier Holiday Inning"

As the hard-driving chairman of the Gannett newspaper chain, Al Neuharth's job included visiting newspapers across the country. Time was short and he was a man who didn't want to waste it. Making his expectations crystal clear on the logistical aspects of his visits, Neuharth sent the following memo to his publishers during the 1980s.

To Gannett Publishers:

Based on our travels for regional or subsidiary meetings of recent weeks and in view all of us will be doing even more such in the future . . .

Here are some purely personal preferences and/or prejudices which, if catered to, will make me even more charming and effective on these visits:

1. When arriving at local airport, I like to be met by publisher himself or herself. That permits business talk en route to office or motel-hotel.

2. We should not waste time checking into and out of hotels. Preregistration, keys, billings, etc., should all be arranged.

3. A suite is essential for me so that I can have any desired business meetings without guests or associates sitting on bed or floor.

4. That suite should contain latest editions of local newspapers. Ice and fruit helps. Booze is not necessary, but a bottle of Montrachet or Pouilly-Fuissé wine never hurt anybody.

5. En route to office, I need list of names of persons I will be seeing first—starting with receptionist and/or publisher's secretary. This, of course, should include the department heads with whom we'll be meeting. Noting any recent important personal items about any of them helps.

6. The meeting room must include the last week's editions of the local newspaper.

7. If, in the infinite and autonomous wisdom of the local editor or publisher, an interview is desired with me, okay. But, it is a waste of time for all to have most recent recruit off the street do the interview. If it's worth doing, it's worth having reasonably intelligent reporter with some knowledge of Ganett [sic] and Newhart [sic] do the interviewing.

8. For social functions, advance list of attendees with first names is essential. A notation about babies, birthdays, anniversaries, girlfriends, boyfriends, etc., helps. Nametags are a must.

9. Breakfast meetings are a waste of time for me. I prefer those early morning hours for jogging,

reading morning papers, telephone calls, and preparation for the day's meetings and/or travels.

10. Whether we publish a morning paper in that city or not, a copy of the nearest a.m. publication (including The Wall Street Journal, if possible) should be at the hotel room door before 6 a.m. No questions will be asked as to whether the publisher or circulation manager delivered it on the way home from saloon or on the way to work.

Yours for even happier Holiday Inning . . .

Al Neuharth

DEPARTING WORK

VICAR OF BAULKING DISMISSES PENELOPE BETJEMAN
"Your playing has got worse and worse"

Dismissing a friend from a job can be a very difficult task, requiring a blend of tact and bluntness. In the following letter, the Vicar of Baulking tries to soften the blow of relieving Penelope Betjeman of her musical duty, but at the same time makes it plain that she lacks a central ingredient for a piano player—talent.

My Dear Penelope,

I have been thinking over the question of the playing of the harmonium on Sunday evenings here and have reached the conclusion that I must no take it over myself.

I am very grateful to you for doing it for so long and hate to have to ask you to give it up, but, to put it plainly, your playing has gotten worse and worse and the disaccord between the harmonium and the congregation is becoming destructive of devotion. People are not very sensitive here, but even some of them have begun to complain, and they are not usually given to doing that. I do not like writing this, but I think you will understand that it is my business to see that divine worship is as perfect as it can be made. Perhaps the crankiness of the instrument has something to do with the trouble. I think it does require a careful and experienced player to deal with it.

Thank you ever so much for stepping so generously into the breach when Sibyl was ill; it was the greatest possible help to me and your results were noticeably better then than now.

Yours ever,
F. P. Harton

MICHEL SAINT-DENIS TO LONDON THEATRE STUDIO
"I have to leave at short notice"

Duty sometimes intervenes in business. When World War II broke out, millions of men and women were compelled to stop or change their business activities. Here, the French actor and producer Michel Saint-Denis submits a letter announcing his withdrawal from the London Theatre Studio to serve in the French army.

2nd September 1939

To the Chairman of the Board of Directors of London Theatre Studio:

I had to repay the sum of £72.14.3 to the Studio; this sum was going to be repaid on the 21st August when the rehearsals for The Cherry Orchard started and when by contract I was going to have £150.0.0. I have to leave at short notice because of general mobilisation in France, and the abnormal circumstances have naturally stopped the management of the Globe Theatre paying me the £150.0.0. I am, therefore, unable to repay the Studio, at present, and I will be during the length of the war, because I have only my salary as a French officer to live on.

M. St. Denis

JACK WELCH TO LAID-OFF EMPLOYEE'S WIFE
"I'm sorry we were so slow to get our act together"

Considered one of the great managers in American business history, John F. ("Jack") Welch became CEO of General Electric Company, forging the manufacturing company into a behemoth multinational corporation. GE's stock value soared at an annualized rate of 23.5 percent over the next 20 years.

But if Welch's arrival meant profits for shareholders, it also brought turmoil to many GE workers. Welch demanded strong earnings from all GE's various divisions. This often meant wholesale layoffs and closed factories, particularly in the mid-1980s. Welch became known as "Neutron Jack" because of his propensity to wipe out large numbers of workers while leaving the buildings intact. In all, his actions resulted in 130,000 GE employees losing their jobs.

The following exchange of letters was between the wife of a laid-off worker—caught in business decisions beyond his control—and Welch. Although GE had nearly 400,000 employees at the time, Welch sometimes responded personally to letters in cases where unfair situations were brought to his attention.

c.c.: John F. Welch Jr.

August 14, 1985

To: Division Vice president & General Manager

From: [Employee's Spouse]

Dear Mr.___:

I am giving you an opportunity to read this letter and respond before I share my story publicly. I am in a very traumatic situation that I can't fully comprehend. Here are the details:

A man interviews with one of the top 100 corporations in America for a sales position. He is offered the job. The man presently lives in ___, a booming metropolis. The job offer will require him to relocate to ___, a small seaside community. The man and his wife decide that the job is worth the relocation. They are at this conclusion based on several facts: 1) The position is with a stable, reputable company. 2) The man knows that he will enjoy the job and be successful at it. 3) He foresees opportunity for upward career mobility. 4) The job offers adequate salary and benefits for family support. The man accepts the job. He sells his home in ___. His wife quits her well-paying job, and they move to ___.

In ___, they rent a place to live and he purchases a company car. Six months pass and they buy a home. The wife becomes pregnant and the couple joyfully await the birth of their first child.

The man works very hard for the company. He frequently works 12 hours a day, arriving home at 7:30 p.m. or later. But he enjoys his job. The hard work pays off, and he meets his sales objectives. He has established new dealers, increased business with old ones and developed large sales with OEM's. After eight months in the field, he reaches 127% of his sales objective. This he accomplished without any hands-on assistance from management. He was an eight-month rookie and he produced! He succeeded in spite of his not knowing how his performance was stacking up by company standards. You see, he was never given a performance evaluation.

Now the man has to sell the home in ____ that he bought two months ago. He and his pregnant wife must prepare to move back to ___, where he will stand a better chance to secure a job to provide for his family.

Why does the man have to move again? He *has just been informed that as of November 1, he will no longer be employed with the company due to "lack of work."* He asks himself, "How can there be a lack of work when I could not get the order department to fill a countless number of orders due to product unavailability?" He wonders, "Why me? What about my family? What about my career? I trusted these people."

This is a true story. The man is ____, *my husband.* The company is the General Electric Company, ____ Division. I realize that you may not know my husband, but I was compelled to write this letter because I can't believe that you are fully aware of your current policies. My husband is intelligent, sharp, ambitious and hardworking. Your ____ management will attest to his attributes on the grounds that they hired him. *It seems to me our family is a victim of General Electric's lack of planning and integrity.* How would you explain this situation?

At this point I feel that the decent and fair thing for GE to do is to purchase our house in ___ and assume responsibility for our moving back to ____. These requests are quite minimal compared to what we have given you and what we stand to lose because of your actions.

If our experience is indicative of General Electric's regard for the American family, then it's no wonder that the institution of family continues to disintegrate with every height of corporate prosperity.

Sincerely,
Mrs. ____

September 5, 1985

Dear Mrs. _____:

Thanks for your direct and thoughtful letter of August 14.

I wish I could say that no component of General Electric is ever too optimistic in setting its goals, or falls short . . . but clearly you know better. In this case, the _____ industry price collapse was far greater than the management of the business anticipated. In fact, the business will lose more than thirty billion dollars in 1985.

"Fair and decent" is precisely what we want to be to each of the individuals affected by cutbacks in _____, or any of our businesses effecting reduction in force in the struggle to deal with an increasingly competitive environment.

By the time you receive this letter, I believe the _____ program to assist your husband in finding a new job and relocating will be known to you. I hope you both will find it helpful.

Thanks again for your letter. I'm sorry we were so slow in getting our act together.

Sincerely,

Jack Welch

STEVEN JOBS TO A. C. "MIKE" MARKKULA
"The decision to resign as Chairman was mine"

Demanding and brilliant, Apple Computer co-founder Steven Jobs could also be mercurial and arrogant. Many employees found it very difficult to work with him. In 1985, less than a decade after Jobs helped start the company that revolutionized personal computers, Apple's management and board of directors had isolated him from the daily operation of the company, even though he was still chairman.

Around this time, Jobs decided to start a new company to address the needs of higher education and attempted to resign from Apple. His board of directors asked him to delay the decision while Apple considered purchasing a piece of Jobs's new company. Over the next few days, however, Apple learned that Jobs intended to take with him some of Apple's top engineers and marketing personnel—who were privy to Apple's next generation of computers.

Apple's top management considered removing Jobs as chairman, but Jobs beat them to the punch, submitting the following letter to the company's vice chairman, A. C. "Mike" Markkula, and simultaneously sending it to the press.

September 17, 1985

Dear Mike:

This morning's paper carried suggestions that Apple is considering removing me as Chairman. I don't know the source of these reports but they are both misleading to the public and unfair to me.

You will recall that at last Thursday's Board meeting I stated I had decided to start a new venture and I tendered my resignation as Chairman.

The Board declined to accept my resignation and asked me to defer it for a week. I agreed to do so in light of the encouragement the Board offered with regard to the proposed new venture and the indications that Apple would invest in it. On Friday, after I told John Sculley who would be joining me, he confirmed Apple's willingness to discuss areas of possible collaboration between Apple and my new venture.

Subsequently the Company appears to be adopting a hostile posture toward me and the new venture. Accordingly, I must insist upon the immediate acceptance of my resignation. I would hope that in any public statement it feels it must issue, the company will make it clear that the decision to resign as Chairman was mine.

I find myself both saddened and perplexed by the management's conduct in this matter which seems to me contrary to Apple's best interest. Those interests remain a matter of deep concern to me, both because of my past association with Apple and the substantial investment I retain in it.

I continue to hope that calmer voices within the Company may yet be heard. Some Company representatives have said they fear I will use proprietary Apple technology in my new venture. There is no basis for any such concern. If that concern is the real source of Apple's hostility to the venture, I can allay it.

As you know, the company's recent reorganization left me with no work to do and no access even to regular management reports. I am but 30 and want still to contribute and achieve.

After what we have accomplished together, I would wish our parting to be both amicable and dignified.

Yours sincerely,
Steven P. Jobs

GILBERT F. AMELIO TO APPLE EMPLOYEES
"I'll be cheering from the sidelines!"

Nearly 12 years after Steve Jobs resigned as chairman and CEO of Apple Computer, he returned to Apple to replace Gilbert F. Amelio. Amelio sent the following resignation letter via e-mail to Apple employees on July 9, 1997.

Amelio had taken over the company a mere 523 days earlier. Prior to his arrival, Apple had suffered from years of poor management and indecisive leadership. Amelio implemented a series of initiatives to cut costs, simplify the product line, spin off accessory divisions, replace key personnel and develop a new operating system strategy. The result was a much better run company and the release of the world's fastest laptop and desktop computers.

Unfortunately for Amelio, sales did not rebound. Apple lost $1.6 billion in revenues under his watch. Although Amelio argued that sales would be the last piece of the equation to recover, his board of directors would not wait and they forced him to resign to make way for Jobs's return. Soon afterward, Apple returned to profitability.

[July 9, 1997]

Today, Apple announced my resignation as Chairman and CEO of Apple Computer effective immediately. I will remain an employee, but not an officer, until September 27, 1997, in order to effect a smooth transition.

I joined Apple on February 2, 1996, following a successful tenure as Chairman, President and CEO of National Semiconductor Corporation. I did so because as a Board member of Apple it had become increasingly clear that the company was entering a period of extreme crisis and the very survival of the company as an independent entity was in question. Someone had to take on the task of trying to bring Apple back to health.

As we came to discover, Apple actually faced five crises from the outset: (1) a shortage of cash and liquidity, (2) poor quality products, (3) lack of viable operating system strategy, (4) a corporate culture lacking in accountability and discipline, and (5) fragmentation—trying to do too much and in too many directions. These issues persisted notwithstanding a number of extremely talented contributors. Much of my time at Apple has been about confronting these and other matters. I am very confident that the decisions and actions taken have been the right ones. Today, these problems are either resolved or well on the way to being addressed. Today, Apple has the strongest product line-up in the history of the company. Today, we have an exciting operating system strategy and we are on the eve of announcing Mac OS 8 which has received very favorable reviews during beta testing. Rhapsody, our industrial strength operating system, is close behind and will establish a new paradigm in operating system architecture. Today, we have the strongest management team in recent history. And today, we have a cost structure more in line with achievable revenues.

It has been very difficult, but much has been accomplished in the last 17 months as I believe will become increasingly evident in the months and quarters ahead. Apple's next phase, and remaining challenge, is to follow through flawlessly on the programs we have launched and to rebuild the sales volume. I am confident that the team in place can handle this mission. On a personal note, I look forward to once again being able to spend a little more time with my family.

My time at Apple has been exciting and fulfilling. We have made great progress. It is now time to realize the value made possible by this work for all Apple stakeholders. Thank you for your unwavering support during my time here . . . it made the demands less formidable. I lovingly leave Apple in your care. Good luck, I'll be cheering from the sidelines!

Respectfully,
Gil

FINANCE

GEORGE WASHINGTON TO ALEXANDER HAMILTON
"I do hereby authorize you to borrow on behalf of the United States"

George Washington launched the Treasury market in 1790 with this letter to Treasury Secretary Alexander Hamilton authorizing him to borrow $14 million on behalf of the new federal government of the United States.

At the time of this letter, the United States was considered an extremely risky credit. The previous government, chartered under the Articles of Confederation, was a financial disaster, having defaulted on multiple debts incurred during the American Revolution. Hamilton wanted to make good on those loans and bolster the nation's fiscal soundness. This meant restructuring past debts and raising taxes to pay for them. In spite of fierce public opposition (and a tax revolt in western Pennsylvania), Hamilton prevailed.

The United States has never defaulted on its bonds since and its Treasury bonds are considered the world's safest investment. Hamilton's portrait is on the $10 bill and he is considered by many to be the best Treasury secretary in the history of the United States.

George Washington, President of the United States of America, to the Secretary of the Treasury for the time being:

By virtue of the several acts, the one entitled "An act making provision for the debt of the United States" and the other entitled "an act making provision for the reduction of the public debt," I do hereby authorize and empower you, by yourself or any other person or persons, to borrow on behalf of the United States, within the said States or elsewhere, a sum or sums not exceeding in the whole $14,000,000, and to make or cause to be made for that purpose such contract or contracts as shall be necessary and for the interest of the said States, subject to the restrictions and limitations in the said several acts contained; and for so doing this shall be your sufficient warrant.

In testimony whereof I have caused the seal of the United States to be hereunto affixed.

Given under my hand, at the city of New York, this 28th day of August, A.D. 1790.

G. Washington
By the president:
Th. Jefferson

NICHOLAS BIDDLE TO JOHN WHITE
"The whole evil therefore lies in an overbanking"

After Alexander Hamilton, Nicholas Biddle, head of the National Bank, was the most important financial figure in the early history of the United States. A brilliant student who graduated from the University of Pennsylvania at the age of thirteen, Biddle understood the importance and impact of banks in financing the young economy.

As the letter below shows, he deplored the easy credit that state banks provided in the early 1800s. One year after writing this letter, financial panic swept through the nation because of wild investments fueled by speculative loans. Although proven right, Biddle's tight-money policies were still very unpopular.

Biddle ultimately lost a showdown in 1832 with President Andrew Jackson (who despised him) when it came time to renew the charter of the Second Bank of the United States. The country went without a central bank until the Federal Reserve Bank was created in 1913.

March 3, 1818

John White, Esqr.

Cashier, Off. Dt. Dept.

Baltimore

Your favor of the 28th ult. was duly received, and I avail myself of the opportunity of answering it, to state precisely what is the present situation of the Bank and the views entertained of its proper course in the present posture of the affairs of the country.

For some months past, the importations from France and England have been very extensive, and without great caution, the results may prove highly disastrous. The low price of our exported articles and tardiness with which the crop of Exchange from the South comes into the market this year, have diminished the means of paying for these importations, and resort has been of course had to the exportation of coin. The natural correction of this evil—for, beyond a certain limit, it is an evil—is the diminution of the business of those institutions which are the depositories of the coin, which by rendering bank credits less easy, makes them more valuable, and by depriving the importers of these artificial facilities to obtain money, diminishes the means & the temptations to continue these importations, and of course lessens the demand for, and the price of, Exchange. This course which all prudent Banking companies should adopt, is the only true & ultimate restraint on excessive importations. It is therefore a matter of equal surprize and regret that the Banks of New York on whom the pressure of specie has now continued for several months have not until now diminished their discounts one dollar but have gone on discounting as freely as hitherto. The obvious consequence is this. The importers ship specie, or they buy bills from those that do—their goods arrive—are sent immediately to auction. The Banks discount the auction notes, the proceeds of which are drawn out in specie & shipped, thus furnishing the means of continuing indefinitely the circle of operations. As long as they do so—they themselves furnish the means of making the very demands of which they complain. The whole evil therefore lies in an overbanking which occasions an overtrading, and the whole remedy lies in preventing this overbanking. One of our most respectables & extensive merchants trading to France assured me a few days ago, that he was alarmed at these excessive importations & had written to France to send no more, as he anticipated a great glut of French goods with all its train of ruinous consequences. Against these it is the business of the Bank of the U. States to guard. It has accordingly placed itself in an attitude of security and strength, so as to interpose whenever it may be necessary to protect the community. The precise point of that interposition is the interesting question. While the State Banks go on in their present career, it is hardly fair to throw on the Stockholders of the Bank of the U. S. the burden of protecting them against the effects of their own improvidence—of releasing them at the first moment of difficulty by incurring a heavy debt in Europe bearing an interest of five per cent. It seems more just that the Bank of the U. S. should reserve its strength—and let the State Banks feel the pressure which their thoughtlessness occasions. Such is the present position of this Bank. It keeps within its limits—discounts cautiously—and when demands for specie come, turns them over to the State Banks. These operations are coming to their natural result. The State Banks of Phila. are already uneasy, & are adopting a prudent course of restrictions. Those of New York will shortly follow the example—and the effect will be a reduction in the rate of Exchange and a stoppage of specie shipments. If those should fail in producing their effect—or if the operation threatens great inconveniences to the community the Bank can and will immediately interfere. But it seems premature to do at the present moment—while the first effect will be to induce the State Banks to continue their present course—and while the remedy is in their own hands if they have only the prudence to adopt it.

In regard to your Office our impression has been that as the demand for money is habitually small with you and you were more out of reach of the operations which press on New York & Phila.—it was not necessary to recommend to you any particular course of restriction. Nevertheless the course of things at present may before long reach you and it would be a very judicious and acceptable co-operation on your part in our present course of measures, if for the present you would abstain from increasing your discounts, and particularly if you would avoid giving facilities to those whose operations are most inconvenient to us. This mutual understanding of our objects will perhaps be more advantageous than any precise stipulation of the mutual credits between the Bank & the Office. The occasion for the restriction will we trust pass when the immediate result expected from it, shall be produced—and it was in this point of view that I regarded our present need of coin as temporary in its duration. It is a fortunate circumstance after the great exhaustion which the country has undergone that the demand for the Canton trade promises to be very small this Spring, and will enable us to return to a more settled state after this immediate crisis is over. Of this of course the earliest intimation will be given to you. In the mean time I have thought it best to state precisely our present position and views.

With great regard
Yrs
Nicholas Biddle
Prest.

LEVI WOODBURY TO DEPOSIT BANKS
"Complaints have been made of frauds, speculations, and monopolies"

One of the greatest banking booms in the history of the United States followed the demise of the Second Bank of the United States. State legislatures no longer required bank charters. It was as easy to start a bank as to open a butcher shop. Trading posts in obscure corners of the frontier issued loans with little or no gold, silver or other financial backing.

Speculative fever reached such a pitch that in 1836 Andrew Jackson had Treasury Secretary Levi Woodbury issue the Specie Circular, a letter to banks informing them that the federal government would require hard currency for the purchase of western public lands. The requirement tested the quality of bank notes, crimping bank lending and convincing British banks to call in their American loans. This set off financial panic that plunged the country into depression for six years and led to a new wave of much stricter banking regulation.

Circular to Receivers of Public Money, and to the Deposite Banks
Treasury Department, July 11, 1836

In consequence of complaints which have been made of frauds, speculations, and monopolies, in the purchase of public lands, and the aid which is said to be given to effect these objects by excessive bank credits, and dangerous if partial facilities through bank drafts and bank deposites, and the general evil influence likely to result to the public interests, and especially the safety of the great amount of money in the Treasury, and the sound condition of the currency of the country, from the further exchange national domain in this manner, the President of the United States has given directions, and you are hereby instructed, after the 15th day of August next, to receive in payment of the public lands nothing except what is directed by the existing laws, viz: gold and silver, and in the proper cases, Virginia land scrip; provided that till the 15th of December next, the same indulgences heretofore extended as to the kind of money received, may be continued for any quantity of land not exceeding 320 acres to each purchaser who is an actual settler or bona fide resident in the state where the sales are made.

In order to ensure the faithful execution of these instructions, all receivers are strictly prohibited from accepting for land sold, any draft, certificate, or other evidence of money, or deposite, though for specie, unless signed by the Treasurer of the United States, in conformity to the act of April 24, 1820.

The principal objects of the President in adopting this measure being to repress alleged frauds, and to withhold any countenance or facilities in the power of the Government from the monopoly of public lands in the hands of speculators and capitalists, to the injury of the actual settlers in the new States, and of emigrants in search of new homes, as well as to discourage the ruinous extension of bank issues, and bank credit, by which those results are generally supposed to be promoted, your utmost vigilance is required, and relied on, to carry this order into complete execution

Levi Woodbury

SALMON P. CHASE TO HORACE GREELEY
"I borrowed money every way I could"

The outbreak of the Civil War in 1861 put severe financial stress on the United States government. The annual expenses of the U. S. government soared from $67 million in 1860 to $1.3 billion in 1865. Much to his annoyance, Treasury Secretary Salmon Chase (who strongly believed he should have been president) was charged with financing the costs of the North's war effort.

Chase turned to two innovations, both of which are commonplace today but were considered very risky at the time. One was issuing "greenbacks," or paper money, as a national currency backed by the full faith and credit of the United States Treasury. The second involved issuing hundreds of millions of dollars in bonds, borrowing money at an unprecedented rate. Chase explained some of the details of his actions in a letter to the newspaper publisher Horace Greeley.

Although Chase's innovations were extraordinarily successful, irony intruded. In a twist of fate, Chase was appointed to the U.S. Supreme Court, and was a member when a case was brought challenging the constitutionality of paper money. Amazingly, Chase deemed greenbacks unconstitutional.

Washn. Nov. [19], 1867

My dear Mr. Greeley,

I feel as the Quakers say impressed to write you about the Finances.

There are few who understand what my work was. It may be set under three heads.

1. To establish satisfactory relations between the public credit and the productive industry, of the country—in other words to obtain supplies.

The suspension of the banks put an end to the first & most obvious resort, loans of gold, & made new methods indispensable.

Then I resorted to legal Tender Notes, made them a currency, & borrowed them as cash.

The patriotism of the people came in aid of the plans of the treasury & the legislation of Congress, and the first great object was made secure.

2. To provide against disastrous [*illegible*] [on the return] of peace.

This could only be done by providing a National Currency.

There were about 1500 state Banks in existence who wanted to make their own paper the currency of the country.

This I resisted & confined my loans to greenbacks but I could not drive out their currency, nor indeed did I think it exactly honest to deprive them of it without giving an equivalent.

To neutralize their opposition to a national currency and make them allies as far as possible instead of enemies in my endeavor to secure one I proposed the National Banking System: and before I left the Department its success was assured.

The National Banks were certain to be useful in many ways but my main object was the establishment of a National currency.

This saved us from panic & revulsion at the close of the war, and is of inestimable value to the men of labor & the men of business indeed to every class.

3. The third division of my work was the provision of a funding system.

It was unavoidable that every resource of credit should be used. I borrowed money every way I could at reasonable rates. The form which suited one lender did not suit another, and the Army & Navy wanted every dollar that could be raised in every form.

Hence many temporary loans—Certificates of deposit/Certificates of Indebtedness, 7.30 notes, compound interest notes, Treasury notes payable after 1 & 2 years &c &c.

But it was necessary to have funding loans into which all these temporary loans might be ultimately merged. To this end I established the 5-20 loan and the 10-40 loan. My belief was that after the 4,000,000 of the 5-20 loan had been taken, that the additional amounts needed could be obtained by the 10-40 loan & the temporary loans; but was ready to resort to the 5-20s in case of emergency. I did get 73 millions on the 10-40 loan, & my successors got about 120 millions more at par, & I have never been able to any good reason for making the 7.30 currency notes subsequently issued convertible, at the holders option, into 5-20s instead of 10-40s. Lenders of course preferred the former, bearing 6% in gold to the latter bearing only 5%; and lenders were rather more favored after I left the Department than before. And so indeed were brokers; for Jay Cooke got nearly or quite twice as large commissions under Fessenden & McCulloch as I allowed him.

You can see how this funding system of mine has worked if you take up the last Statement of the Public Debt. . . .

Can there be a better funding system? I don't believe it.

Yet there is talk of a new funding loan!

The object is to catch grudgeons by apparently yielding to the popular clamor for taxation on bonds.

The way is to offer a new 6% loan, with reservation or right of tax not exceeding 6%—in other words a non-taxable 5% loan: and it is proposed to make this a long loan say 30 years. It will be magnificent for brokers, bankers, & lenders, but death to the people. Of course such a loan can be negotiated; for a 5%, 30 year loan untaxable is worth more in the market than any loan now outstanding; and nothing is more certain in the future than Government will be paying within five years 5, 10 & even 15% for the privilege of paying its debt before maturity.

I want specially to call your attention to this. It may be well enough to make the loan, in the form proposed, if the clamor for taxation will be satisfied by it; but why make it for 20 or 30 years, instead of adhering to the 10-14 plan, by which the debt is redeemable at any time after 10 years & thus kept under the control of [the public]. I have no doubt that, if our finances are properly managed, we can borrow within 10 years at 4%, or 5 with right to tax 1/5, as easily as we can now borrow at 5 or 6 with right to tax 1/6. Why bind ourselves to pay interest for 30 years, when it is not only unnecessary, but certain to entail a heavy additional expence, in the form of premiums for redemption.

But enough though I could add much more.

Yours cordially
S P Chase

GROVER CLEVELAND TO E. ELLERY ANDERSON
"I am glad that the business interests of New York are at last to be heard"

The United States reversed its loosened currency standards after the Civil War, redeeming greenbacks for gold and dropping silver dollars from coinage. Advocates of strong-money policies fiercely endorsed using gold as the sole medium of payment.

The late years of the 19th century, however, were marked by deflation, especially in farming prices. Although beneficial to banks and creditors, it imposed severe strains on farmers and debtors who had to produce more and more goods to meet loan payments. A "free silver" movement emerged, particularly in agrarian regions, calling for the minting of silver coins, which would increase the money supply.

The Eastern business establishment firmly opposed the silver movement. Controversy raged. This letter was one of the highlights of the struggle. The U.S. Senate passed a free silver bill in January 1891, with Democratic support. Cleveland, a Democrat, was believed to be wavering in his pro-gold position. However, the content of this correspondence declining an invitation to speak at the Reform Club clearly stated his alliance with the conservative eastern wing of the Democratic Party.

New York, February 10, 1891

I have this afternoon received your note inviting me to attend tomorrow evening the meeting called for the purpose of voicing the opposition of the business men of our city to the "free coinage of silver in the United States."

I shall not be able to attend and address the meeting as you request, but I am glad that the business interests of New York are at last to be heard from on this subject.

It surely cannot be necessary for me to make a formal expression of my agreement with those who believe that the greatest peril would be initiated by the adoption of the scheme embraced in the measure now pending in Congress for the unlimited coinage of silver at our mints. If we have developed an unexpected capacity for the assimilation of a largely increased volume of this currency, and even if we have demonstrated the usefulness of such an increase, these conditions fall far short of insuring us against disaster, if in the present situation we enter upon the dangerous and reckless experiment of free, unlimited and independent silver coinage.

J.P. MORGAN PREVENTS FINANCIAL DISASTER
"$30,000,000 N.Y. City Revenue Bonds"

Financial panic struck Wall Street in the fall of 1907. The failure of a copper speculator was followed by the collapse of an affiliated bank, The Knickerbocker Trust. The ripple effect of buckling banks soon infected all of Wall Street. Loans were called. Stock prices collapsed. Credit markets came to a halt.

Financiers turned to J. P. Morgan Sr. to intervene. His bank had the resources and he had the credibility to pull together enough other banks and lenders to engineer a series of bailout loans to stem the crisis. One of the most important of these deals was a $30 million bond issue that prevented New York City from going into bankruptcy. Worked out in an all-night meeting, he jotted down the terms of the deal and initialed the memo from his library on October 29, 1907, at seven o'clock in the morning.

Morgan's intervention worked—he braved financial disaster, steered the market to safety, and he made a lot of money out of it. But more than anything else, his actions convinced the business community that the United States needed centralized oversight of the national financial system. Six years later, Congress created the Federal Reserve System.

Oct. 29, 1907

$30,000,000 N.Y. City Revenue Bonds

Running 9 to 12 months or as long as can be legally issued at option of syndicate with option of $20,000,000 additional until 15 January at par.

The bonds to be issued $1000 or multiples thereof payable in Sterling @ $483 at option of holder.

The rate of 6% per annum

JPM 7 a.m.

Henry P. Davison to Thomas Lamont
"The credit of all Europe has broken down absolutely"

The outbreak of World War I in Europe in the summer of 1914 marked the end of Europe's dominance of financial markets and the rise of the United States as the center of world finance. Henry P. Davison, J. P. Morgan, Jr.'s. top man in Europe, immediately grasped the opportunities for his bank to step in as a source of credit. He wired these telegrams to Thomas Lamont about the breakdown of Europe's credit markets. Davison later secured a $3 billion loan to England and France to help them finance the war.

    Although the bank's profitable loans led to accusations of J. P. Morgan being a "merchant of death," Morgan himself urged peace efforts, predicting financial disaster and warning that people would "pay for war with their blood and property."

August 4, 1914

    THE CREDIT OF ALL EUROPE HAS BROKEN DOWN ABSOLUTELY SPECIE PAYMENTS SUSPENDED AND MORATORIUM IN FORCE IN FRANCE AND PRACTICALLY IN ALL COUNTRIES THOUGH NOT OFFICIALLY IN ENGLAND.

August 7, 1914

    PROBABLY COULD DO LITTLE IF YOU WERE HERE THE ONLY POINT BEING THAT IS FILLED WITH EXTRA ORDINARY INTEREST AND OF COURSE GREAT POSSIBILITYS.... PERHAPS I MIGHT EXPRESS THE SITUATION BY STATING THAT IT IS AS IF WE HAD HAD AN EARTHQUAKE ARE AS YET SOMEWHAT STUNNED BUT WILL SOON GET TO RIGHTING THINGS.

BERNARD BARUCH TO SENATOR WILLIAM H. KING, PREDICTING THE 1929 STOCK MARKET CRASH

"They should have acted very promptly in raising the rate"

In early 1929, economist Bernard Baruch wrote Senator William H. King of Utah warning of a pending financial crisis on Wall Street from inflated stock prices. He pinned the blame of the problem on the Federal Reserve for its loose monetary policy that he believed had careened out of control.

Dear Senator King:

The original difficulty started in 1927 when the Federal Reserve System reduced its rate to 3_% for the purpose of forcing gold out or stimulating our exports. Whether that was wise or not, they evidently had in mind the accomplishment of some definite, constructive purpose. But they overlooked the fact that when they artificially reduced the rate . . . there would be a re-evaluation of securities and an artificial stimulus to business. Whatever their purpose was, they should have acted very promptly in raising the rate and that would have stopped the things they are now objecting to and which they directly caused.

Bernard Baruch

Earnest Elmo Calkins to *The New York Times*
"My losses last week are paper losses"

The stock market boom of the 1920s helped bring the world of finance to the general public. The Dow Jones Industrial Average soared from 63.9 in 1921 to 381.17 in the fall of 1929. The six-fold increase both brought prosperity to a broad base of the population and opened the privileged corridors of Wall Street to a wider range of investors.

But it proved to be a perilous place. At the end of October, the stock market crashed, dropping almost 50 percent in a week. Despite the initial panic, many people downplayed the significance of the crash, such as advertising man Earnest Elmo Calkins in this letter to The New York Times.

Sure enough, within two weeks, the market rallied. It regained about half its losses, reaching a postcrash high of 294.07 points. But the good times were short-lived. The market renewed its descent and did not reach a bottom until the summer of the 1932 when the Dow Jones scraped its floor at 41.22 points. Speculators, investment banks, brokerage houses, major corporations and many others were wiped out.

The Crash of 1929 proved to be the precursor to the Great Depression. Some economists insist it did not cause the decline in the real economy. They argue that isolationist trade policies and tightened monetary policies were the true culprits. Nevertheless, within the next three years, the national income dropped by almost 50 percent, unemployment reached 25 percent, and more than 5,500 banks went out of business.

October 29, 1929

To the Editor of the *New York Times:*

I have a feeling that fewer person are affected by the stock market drop than one would infer from the figures, just as fewer persons were affected by the previous rises. I am judging by my own situation. Among the stocks I happen to own are some that suffered the greatest losses last week, such as Tel. and Tel., American Tobacco, Union Pacific and Western Union, but my income from them remains the same as before.

As far as I am concerned a group of men, technically known as the Stock Exchange, gets together and decides that my Tel. and Tel. stock is worth $310 a share, and I experience a momentary glow of elation. A few days or weeks later they get together and decide that it is worth only $232, and I have a feeling of disappointment, also momentary. It is unlikely that the slump will affect the continued use of the telephone or that the company will be unable to continue to pay the $9 a share. I bought my stock at an average price of $98 a share, so even at the present low—or high, according to the point of view—it is worth even more than double what I paid for it.

Doesn't it seem probable that mine is the situation of a great majority of holders of this and other good stocks? That they have merely lost some of their spectacular gains, but their stocks are still quoted at and worth more than they paid for them?

It seems to be the practice to compute the total loss in such a recession, and multiply it by the total number of shares outstanding, and imply that somebody or the country has lost that vast amount. Headlines last week said that the loss was about $4,000,000,000. In Monday's market only 87,100 shares of Tel. and Tel. were traded in. That is a very small percentage of the 13,203,093 shares outstanding. How many of the holders of these shares have actually lost anything? I am just where I was a few weeks ago. When Tel. and Tel first crossed 232 I thought that was pretty good, and I still think so now that it has receded to 232, and I felt the same about American Tobacco when it first touched 196, Union Pacific when it first touched 240, and Western Union when it first touched 191. My profits the last few weeks have been paper profits, and my losses last week are paper losses, and one cancels the other.

It reminds me of the farmer who told a neighbor that Josh Stebbins had offered two hundreds dollars for his horse.

"Josh Stebbins ain't got no two hundred dollars."

"Yes, I know, but ain't it a good offer?"

Earnest Elmo Calkins
New York, October 29, 1929

JOHN KENNETH GALBRAITH TO JOHN F. KENNEDY
"The stock market slump is of consequence"

John Kenneth Galbraith served as an economic adviser to President John F. Kennedy. A liberal economist, he had previously written a book about the stock market crash of 1929. When the market dipped in 1962 after a prolonged advance, he wrote the following letter to Kennedy explaining the causes of the stock plunge and the possible impacts on the economy.

Newfane, Vermont

May 29, 1962

Memorandum for the President

Subject: The Stock Market

The stock market slump is of consequence, and I venture some suggestions.

1) The cause of the drop is that people have ceased to see an unlimited prospect for capital gains. This is partly out of respect for the Administration anti-inflation measures. That means that common stocks will not rise forever for reasons of inflation. And as the inflation danger lessens, so does the demand for stock as an inflation hedge. However, as always, speculation has vastly exaggerated this movement. The great reality is that you can make money out of the market when it is going up if you sell when it starts going down. Lots of people have been making money. They are now trying to sell. Yesterday's movement was one of the inevitable results.

2) The argument as to whether stock movements foretell economic movements is a footless one. As you said rightly the other day, sometimes they do and sometimes they don't. But there is no question that a bad crack-up in the market can have serious repercussions on the economy. Although it was considered highly uncouth to say so—and almost no one did—the 1929 crash was a major factor in the collapse in the economy that followed. Investment decisions are sensitive to the market. Also people spend capital gains and are influenced in their spending by what is happening to capital gains. There was a readily traceable effect from the market to other middle-class spending in 1929 and the impact on all consumer spending was quantitatively considerable.

3) Similar effects also significant in their effect must be expected as a result of recent market behavior. These will have a depressing effect on investment and on consumer spending. I would expect housing, real estate investment, automobiles, home furnishing to be especially affected.

4) The Administration should adhere to the following rules in the present situation:

a) keep down the number of reassuring statements. Everyone will be tempted to rush in with magic words to calm the fever. The words will quickly be discounted to zero, or—as in the case of Mr. Hoover—to something less. Very soon everyone will look foolish.

b) hold rigidly to the explanation that the market is accommodating itself to the end of inflation, the diminished prospect for capital gain, and the speculative disappointment associated with the latter. Say that for these reasons the termination of inflation was bound to bring a sharp readjustment. This explanation has the advantage of being valid; of separating the issue of inflation from that of employment, profit and production levels, and minimizing uneasiness about the latter; and it is the explanation most conducive in the dollar abroad.

c) at the same time, everyone must recognize that the effect of the stock market drop will be depressing on the economy. Accordingly all forms of budget liberalization and any needed steps to keep money rates easy and encourage investment are of increased urgency. As usual, I would be against a tax cut. I am sending you a copy of my history of the 1929 episode which, by the kind of foresight that can only inspire confidence, has just become available in a new and inexpensive edition.

J. K. Galbraith

E. B. White to Consolidated Edison Company
"A very odd letter indeed"

Long before famed Fidelity fund manager Peter Lynch advised people to trust their own knowledge of companies in deciding what stocks to buy, humorist E. B. White recognized a questionable stock based on his experience with his own refrigerator, as related here in a letter to Consolidated Edison Company.

The fact that a writer of relatively modest means was involved in the stock market reflected that despite the trauma of market crashes, stock investment had become an ordinary part of personal financial portfolios.

Dear Mr. Aiken,

I am a stockholder in the Consolidated Edison Company, and I rent an apartment at 229 East 48 Street in which there is a gas refrigerator. So I have a double interest in your letter of December 19. It seems to me a very odd letter indeed.

You say that my refrigerator, even if it seems to be operating properly, may be producing poison gas, and you suggest that I open a window. I do not want to open a window. It would be a very unpopular move with the cook. Furthermore, I haven't the slightest intention of living under the same roof with a machine that discharges poison gas. Your recommendation is that I get plenty of fresh air— enough to counteract the effect of the gas. But I cannot believe that you are serious.

Will you be good enough to let me know what sort of poison gas is generated by a Servel gas refrigerator, and in what quantity, and how discharged. I know that there is a vent at the top of the machine and that some sort of warm air flows from the vent. I have always assumed it was hot air. Is it something else?

I also know that a gas refrigerator poses a carbon problem, and I ask the landlord to remove the carbon about once a year, which he does. But your letter makes me think that the matter is not so simple and I am anxious to be enlightened.

If gas refrigerators are, as your letter suggests, discharging poison gases into people's homes I don't want to own a gas refrigerator and I shall certainly sell my stock.

Sincerely,
E. B. White

GROUCHO MARX TO FRANKLIN CORPORATION
"No one named Prosswimmer can possibly be a success"

Responding to a glossy annual report from the Franklin Corporation in 1961, Groucho Marx wrote a letter to the president expressing his concerns as an investor in the company.

Dear Mr. Goodman:

I received the first annual report of the Franklin Corporation and though I am not an expert at reading balance sheets, my financial advisor (who, I assure you, knows nothing) nodded his head in satisfaction.

You wrote that you hope I am not one of those borscht circuit stockholders who get a few points' profit and hastily scram for the hills. For your information, I bought Alleghany Preferred eleven years ago and am just now disposing of it.

As a brand new member of your family, strategically you made a ghastly mistake in sending me individual pictures of the Board of Directors. Mr. Roth, Chairman of the Board, merely looks sinister. You, the President, look like a hard worker with not too much on the ball. No one named Prosswimmer can possibly be a success. As for Samuel A. Goldblith, PhD., head of Food Technology at MIT, he looks as though he had eaten too much of the wrong kind of fodder.

At this point I would like to stop and ask you a question about Marion Harper, Jr. To begin with, I immediately distrust any man who has the same name as his mother. But the thing that disturbs me about Junior is that I don't know what the hell he's laughing at. Is it because he sucked me into this Corporation? This is not the kind of face that inspires confidence in a nervous and jittery stockholder.

George S. Sperti, I dismiss instantly. Any man who is the President of an outfit called Institutum Dive Thomae will certainly bear watching. . . . James Sullivan, I am convinced, is Paul E. Prosswimmer photographed from a different angle.

Offhand, I would say that I have summed up your group fairly accurately. I hope, for my sake, that I am mistaken.

In closing, I warn you, go easy with my money. I am in an extremely precarious profession whose livelihood depends upon a fickle public.

Sincerely yours,
Groucho Marx
(temporarily at liberty)

ALAN GREENSPAN TO FEDERAL HOME LOAN BANK

"Lincoln clearly merits the exemption it seeks"

Future Federal Reserve Bank Chairman Alan Greenspan wrote the following letter of support in 1985 on behalf of the Lincoln Savings & Loan for a waiver of a federal regulation on direct investments by S&Ls. At the time, Greenspan headed a consulting firm on Wall Street, his most impressive credential being the time he had spent as chairman of the Council of Economic Advisors for President Gerald Ford.

But economic prospects changed quickly, and with it the Lincoln's balance sheet. Lincoln Savings & Loan's collapse three years later was the most spectacular in the wave of failed S&Ls that swept the country.

Ironically, when the S&L crisis hit, Greenspan had been named chairman of the Federal Reserve. He acted decisively to clean up the mess, righting the nation's financial sector and putting it in a position to fuel the decade-long expansion of the national economy, the longest in American history.

February 13, 1985
Mr. Thomas F. Sharkey
Principal Supervisory Agent
Federal Home Loan Bank
600 California Street
San Francisco, California 91420
Re: Application of Lincoln Savings and Loan Association for permission to Exceed Ten Percent Limitation in "Direct Investments"

Dear Mr. Sharkey,

I am writing on behalf of Lincoln Savings and Loan Association and in support of its application for an exemption from the 10 percent limitation on direct investments that will be imposed by the new direct investment rule, 12 C.F.R.563.9-6, announced by the Federal Home Loan Bank board on January 31, 1985.

I have reviewed and commented on the direct investment rule in its earlier forms, and I have reviewed the rule in the form announced on January 31. I note that it contains a provision expressly allowing an association to apply for an exemption raising the limit on the percentage of its assets which it may place in direct investments. I note, too, that the Board states in its notice of the rule (at p. 4) that the prior proposed rule added a "presumption" in favor of approval of applications and that the January 31 rule preserves that presumption (at p. 43). The rule requires that a Principal Supervisory Agent "shall approve an application" unless he makes one of four specific findings.

The Board's notice states (at p. 8) that "direct investments can be prudent and desirable" when they are "supported by adequate capitalization, a sound business plan, managerial expertise and proper diversification." On the basis of my review of Lincoln's application and of its audited financial statements and the criteria established in the new rule, I believe that Lincoln Savings and Loan has demonstrated that it has the adequate capitalization, sound business plans, managerial expertise and proper diversification to which the Board refers.

I have reviewed the application Lincoln has submitted to your office, and it is my opinion that Lincoln clearly merits the exemption it seeks. Its application established the critical and dispositive facts:

1. Lincoln's new management, and that of its parent, American Continental Corporation, is seasoned and expert in selecting and making direct investments;

2. the new management has a long and continuous track record of outstanding success in making sound and profitable direct investments;

3. the new management succeeded in a relatively short period of time in reviving an association that had become badly burdened by a large portfolio of long-term, fixed-rate mortgages and unfavorably structured adjustable rate mortgages whose relatively low yields had been forcing large losses on the association and pushing it nearer the point of insolvency;

4. the new management effectively restored the association to a vibrant and healthy state, with a strong net worth position, largely through the expert selection of sound and profitable direct investments;

5. the new management is devoting a large proportion of its assets to the financing, servicing and construction of residential housing; and

6. the new management has developed a series of carefully planned, highly promising, and widely diversified projects—a high percentage of which involve the development and construction of residential housing—requiring sizeable amounts of direct investments.

Given these facts, Lincoln in my judgment meets the requirements that the new direct investment rule establishes for granting a waiver of the 10 percent limit.

Finally, I believe that denial of the permission Lincoln seeks would work a serious and unfair hardship on an association that has, through its skill and expertise, transformed itself into a financially strong institution that presents no foreseeable risk to the Federal Savings and Loan Corporation. Consequently, Lincoln should be allowed to pursue new and promising direct investments as and when they become available, in accordance with the plans and proposals outlined in its application.

It is my opinion that Lincoln's record and its application satisfy the requirements for an exemption that the new direct investment rule establishes. I strongly support Lincoln's application and urge that it be granted.

In closing, let me thank you for giving my letter your attention.

Very truly yours,
Alan Greenspan

ANONYMOUS TO MERRILL LYNCH
"Two of your executives … are trading with inside information"

On May 25, 1985, Richard Drew, vice president of the compliance department at Merrill Lynch, found an anonymous letter on his desk. Fraught with spelling and grammatical errors, it appeared to be written by someone who did not speak English very well. The information, however, does reflect knowledge about insider trading in the financial industry, the role of the Securities Exchange Commission (SEC) and accounting procedures for trading securities.

Drew followed up on the tip, unleashing an investigation that ultimately led to the unraveling of a high-powered network of Wall Street bankers dealing in inside information, the conviction of junk bond king Michael Milken and others, and the demise of the firm Drexel Burnham Lambert.

May 22, 1985

Dear Sir: please be informed that two of your executives from the Caracas office are trading with inside information. A copie with description of their trades so far has been submitet to the S.E.C. by separate mail. As is mantion on that letter if us customers do not benefit from their knoledg, we wonder who surveils the trades done by account executives. Upon you investigating to the last consequencies we will provide with the names of the insider on their owne hand writing.

Executives max hoffer 14899052

Carlos zubillaga 14899073

mr frank granados might like to have a copie

JOHN W. MERIWETHER TO INVESTORS
"Losses of this magnitude are a shock"

A fantastically successful Wall Street trader and partner at the investment bank Salomon Brothers, John Meriwether gathered together a handful of supereconomists in 1993 to form a hedge fund called Long-Term Capital Management. The secretive investment fund for the ultrarich applied esoteric "risk management" strategies devised by the company's Nobel Prize–winning economists.

Placing enormous bets based on their computer models, Long-Term Capital leveraged their investors' money by borrowing billions and billions of dollars. But in the summer of 1998, Long-Term Capital's investments went bust. Russia defaulted on its bonds, triggering a global meltdown in bond prices. The company's investment model had not taken into consideration the ensuing panic. In fact, it encouraged the fund to invest more money as prices dropped. But when the ensuing decline turned into a plunge, it took Long-Term Capital with it.

With a balance sheet of more than $100 billion, however, Long-Term Capital's collapse could have brought down the entire financial market. In an unprecedented move, the Federal Reserve Bank stepped in to organize Wall Street's leading banks—some of which had investments in the fund—to bail the company out. Meriwether wrote this letter informing his investors about the fund's collapse and efforts to salvage the firm. The firm never recovered, and was eventually taken over by other investment banks.

September 2, 1998
To: Investors in the Investment Vehicles of Long-Term Capital Portfolio, LP
Re: Impact on Net Asset Value of August Market Conditions

Dear Investor:

As you are all too aware, events surrounding the collapse in Russia caused large and dramatically increasing volatility in global markets throughout August, capped by a last-day decline in the Dow Jones Industrial Average of 513 points. The resulting dislocations in markets and greatly increased uncertainty have driven investors to safer and more liquid assets. With increases in both risk and liquidity premia—investment funds widely, many Wall Street firms, and money-center banks have reported large trading losses with resulting sharp declines in their share prices. Investors everywhere have experienced large declines in their wealth.

Unfortunately, Long-Term Capital Portfolio ("Fund") has also experienced a sharp decline in net asset value. As you know our formal procedure for releasing our official net asset value normally takes about ten days after month end. Following our usual practice to give you an early estimate of the Fund's performance, it is down 44 percent for the month of August and 52 percent for the year-to-date. Losses of this magnitude are a shock to us as they surely are to you, especially in light of the historical volatility of the Fund. The losses arising from the event-driven major increase in volatility and the flight to liquidity were magnified by the time of year when markets were seasonally thin. . . .

With the large and rapid [fall] in our capital, steps have been taken to reduce risks now, commensurate with our level of capital. We have raised the risk-return tradeoff requirements for positions. Risk and position reduction is occurring in some strategies that do not meet the new standard. This is a prudent step given the level of capital and uncertainties in the market place.

On the other hand, we see great opportunities in a number of our best strategies and these are being held by the Fund. As it happens, the best strategies are the ones we have worked on over many years. We will focus on these high expected return-to-risk positions and, thereby we can manage them more aggressively.

A cornerstone of our investment management philosophy is the availability and efficiency of financing to support the long horizon for many of our investment strategies. Our capital base is over $2.3 billion, and it is quite liquid. Our financing is in place, including secured and unsecured term debt and long-dated contractual arrangements. These term agreements provide time to reduce our positions, if needed, as markets become more settled. We continue to work closely with counterparts. . . .

The poor performance of the Fund, year-to-date and especially in August, has been very disappointing to us all. However, I would ask in assessing the performance going forward, that you keep in mind that the Fund's relative-value strategies may require a relatively long convergence horizon. The expected horizon for convergence on our trades range from six months to two years, or even longer. Implementation of these strategies involves large positions that take significant time to accumulate and to reduce efficiently. The convergence return pattern of these core strategies normally implies that the day-to-day volatility is much greater in proportion to time than the month-to-month or year-to-year volatility of their performance. This does not imply, however, that the reported short-term performance of the Fund is in any way an inaccurate or invalid measure of actual returns. The mark-to-market valuations on positions in the Fund reported to you are always derived from actual dealer and broker quotations.

The Fund returned approximately $2.7 billion of its capital at year-end 1997 when it appeared that the existing investment opportunities were not large and attractive enough to warrant its retention. Many of the trades had converged producing profits and were unwound. Over the past several months, however, these trades that had converged once again diverged. The Fund added to its positions in anticipation of convergence, yet largely because of last month's market events, the trades diverged dramatically. As a result, the opportunity act in these trades at this time is believed to be among the best that LTCM has ever seen. But, as we have seen, good convergence trades can diverge further. In August, many of them diverged at a speed and to an extent that had not been seen before. LTCM thus believes that it is prudent and opportunistic to increase the level of the Fund's capital to take full advantage of this unusually attractive environment. . . .

I cannot close without telling you about the remarkable performance of the LTCM employees during this particularly difficult month. Over the first four years of the Fund, we had the great good fortune of consistent return performances resulting in larger-than-expected returns with lower-than-expected volatility. We expected that sooner or later that this good fortune could not continue uninterrupted and that we as a firm would be tested. I did not anticipate, however, how severe the test would be. I am happy to report the magnificent performance of our employees operating as a team—administration, technology, operations, legal and strategies—coordinating across our Greenwich, London, and Tokyo offices during this extreme period. August has been very painful for all of us, but I believe that as a consequence, LTCM will emerge as a stronger and better firm.

Sincerely,
John W. Meriwether

Warren E. Buffett to
Berkshire Hathaway Shareholders
"Treating both [managers and shareholders] as we would wish to be treated"

Considered by many to be the world's greatest stock picker, Warren E. Buffett has steered his holding company, Berkshire Hathaway, to one of the most extraordinary records of success in financial history. Using Berkshire Hathaway to buy shares in a variety of different companies ranging from McDonald's to Disney to GEICO insurance company, Buffett parlayed a $45 investment in the company in 1969 into nearly $70,000 in early 2001.

Buffett's success comes from a highly disciplined "value" approach to investing that places an emphasis on quality of management, transparent accounting and long-term earnings potential. Based in Omaha, Nebraska, Buffett's style is decidedly homespun. His annual shareholder meetings include a picnic and softball game. His annual letter to shareholders typically includes self-deprecating jokes, wholesome compliments to his favored managers and simple explanations of often obscure accounting procedures. And despite the guffaws of some of the slicker financiers on Wall Street, Buffett insists on not investing in any products that he does not thoroughly understand, such as computer technology.

When Buffett wrote his annual letter to shareholders in his 2000 annual report, Berkshire Hathaway had suffered its worst loss ever in the previous year, largely because of his refusal to invest in technology companies. Buffett entirely missed one of history's greatest stock manias when he refused to invest in the Internet, telecommunications and technology companies that soared in value in the late 1990s. He preferred to hold cash.

Ironically, the timing of this letter in March 2000 coincided almost precisely with the top of the technology-laden NASDAQ index, peaking above 5,000 points before plunging 50 percent over the next year. Berkshire Hathaway's stock, however, soared, chalking up a better than 70-percent gain from its March low of slightly more than $40,000 to about $70,000 a year later.

To the Shareholders of Berkshire Hathaway Inc.:

Our gain in net worth during 1999 was $358 million, which increased the per-share book value of both our Class A and Class B stock by 0.5%. Over the last 35 years (that is, since present management took over) per-share book value has grown from $19 to $37,987, a rate of 24.0% compounded annually.

The numbers on the facing page show just how poor our 1999 record was. We had the worst absolute performance of my tenure and, compared to the S&P, the worst relative performance as well.

Relative results are what concern us: Over time, bad relative numbers will produce unsatisfactory absolute results.

Even Inspector Clouseau could find last year's guilty party: your Chairman. My performance reminds me of the quarterback whose report card showed four Fs and a D but who nonetheless had an understanding coach. "Son," he drawled, "I think you're spending too much time on that one subject."

My "one subject" is capital allocation, and my grade for 1999 most assuredly is a D. What most hurt us during the year was the inferior performance of Berkshire's equity portfolio—and responsibility for that portfolio, leaving aside the small piece of it run by Lou Simpson of GEICO, is entirely mine. Several of our largest investees badly lagged the market in 1999 because they've had disappointing operating results. We still like these businesses and are content to have major investments in them. But their stumbles damaged our performance last year, and it's no sure thing that they will quickly regain their stride.

The fallout from our weak results in 1999 was a more-than-commensurate drop in our stock price. In 1998, to go back a bit, the stock outperformed the business. Last year the business did much better than the stock, a divergence that has continued to the date of this letter. Over time, of course, the performance of the stock must roughly match the performance of the business.

Despite our poor showing last year, Charlie Munger, Berkshire's Vice Chairman and my partner, and I expect that the gain in Berkshire's intrinsic value over the next decade will modestly exceed the gain from owning the S&P. We can't guarantee that, of course. But we are willing to back our conviction with our own money. To repeat a fact you've heard before, well over 99% of my net worth resides in Berkshire. Neither my wife nor I have ever sold a share of Berkshire and—unless our checks stop clearing—we have no intention of doing so.

Please note that I spoke of hoping to beat the S&P "modestly." For Berkshire, truly large superiorities over that index are a thing of the past. They existed then because we could buy both businesses and stocks at far more attractive prices than we can now, and also because we then had a much smaller capital base, a situation that allowed us to consider a much wider range of investment opportunities than are available to us today.

Our optimism about Berkshire's performance is also tempered by the expectation—indeed, in our minds, the virtual certainty—that the S&P will do far less well in the next decade or two than it has done since 1982. A recent article in *Fortune* expressed my views as to why this is inevitable, and I'm enclosing a copy with this report.

Our goal is to run our present businesses well—a task made easy because of the outstanding managers we have in place—and to acquire additional businesses having economic characteristics and managers comparable to those we already own. We made important progress in this respect during 1999 by acquiring Jordan's Furniture and contracting to buy a major portion of MidAmerican Energy. We will talk more about these companies later in the report but let me emphasize one point here: We bought both for cash, issuing no Berkshire shares. Deals of that kind aren't always possible, but that is the method of acquisition that Charlie and I vastly prefer.

Guides to Intrinsic Value

I often talk in these pages about intrinsic value, a key, though far from precise, measurement we utilize in our acquisitions of businesses and common stocks. ...

In our last four reports, we have furnished you a table that we regard as useful in estimating Berkshire's intrinsic value. In the updated version of that table, which follows, we trace two key components of value. The first column lists our per-share ownership of investments (including cash and equivalents but excluding assets held in our financial products operation) and the second column shows our per-share earnings from Berkshire's operating businesses before taxes and purchase-accounting adjustments (discussed on page 61), but after all interest and corporate expenses. The second column excludes all dividends, interest and capital gains that we realized from the investments presented in the first column. In effect, the columns show how Berkshire would look if it were split into two parts, with one entity holding our investments and the other operating all of our businesses and bearing all corporate costs.

Year	Investments Per Share	Pre-tax Earnings (Loss) Per Share With All Income from Investments Excluded 1969
	$45	$4.39
1979	577	13.07
1989	7,200	108.86
1999	47,339	(458.55)

Here are the growth rates of the two segments by decade:

Decade Ending	Investments Per Share	Pre-tax Earnings Per Share With All Income from Investments Excluded
1979	29.0%	11.5%

1989	28.7%	23.6%
1999	20.7%	N.A.
Annual Growth Rate, 1969-1999	25.4%	N.A.

In 1999, our per-share investments changed very little, but our operating earnings, affected by negatives that overwhelmed some strong positives, fell apart. Most of our operating managers deserve a grade of A for delivering fine results and for having widened the difference between the intrinsic value of their businesses and the value at which these are carried on our balance sheet. But, offsetting this, we had a huge—and, I believe, aberrational—underwriting loss at General Re. Additionally, GEICO's underwriting profit fell, as we had predicted it would. GEICO's overall performance, though, was terrific, outstripping my ambitious goals.

We do not expect our underwriting earnings to improve in any dramatic way this year. Though GEICO's intrinsic value should grow by a highly satisfying amount, its underwriting performance is almost certain to weaken. That's because auto insurers, as a group, will do worse in 2000, and because we will materially increase our marketing expenditures. At General Re, we are raising rates and, if there is no mega-catastrophe in 2000, the company's underwriting loss should fall considerably. It takes some time, however, for the full effect of rate increases to kick in, and General Re is therefore likely to have another unsatisfactory underwriting year.

You should be aware that one item regularly working to widen the amount by which intrinsic value exceeds book value is the annual charge against income we take for amortization of goodwill—an amount now running about $500 million. This charge reduces the amount of goodwill we show as an asset and likewise the amount that is included in our book value. This is an accounting matter having nothing to do with true economic goodwill, which increases in most years. But even if economic goodwill were to remain constant, the annual amortization charge would persistently widen the gap between intrinsic value and book value.

Though we can't give you a precise figure for Berkshire's intrinsic value, or even an approximation, Charlie and I can assure you that it far exceeds our $57.8 billion book value. Businesses such as See's and Buffalo News are now worth fifteen to twenty times the value at which they are carried on our books. Our goal is to continually widen this spread at all subsidiaries.

A Managerial Story You Will Never Read Elsewhere

Berkshire's collection of managers is unusual in several important ways. As one example, a very high percentage of these men and women are independently wealthy, having made fortunes in the businesses that they run. They work neither because they need the money nor because they are contractually obligated to—we have no contracts at Berkshire. Rather, they work long and hard because they love their businesses. And I use the word "their" advisedly, since these managers are truly in charge—there are no show-and-tell presentations in Omaha, no budgets to be approved by headquarters, no dictums issued about capital expenditures. We simply ask our managers to run their companies as if these are the sole asset of their families and will remain so for the next century.

Charlie and I try to behave with our managers just as we attempt to behave with Berkshire's shareholders, treating both groups as we would wish to be treated if our positions were reversed. Though "working" means nothing to me financially, I love doing it at Berkshire for some simple reasons: It gives me a sense of achievement, a freedom to act as I see fit and an opportunity to interact daily with people I like and trust. Why should our managers—accomplished artists at what they do—see things differently?

In their relations with Berkshire, our managers often appear to be hewing to President Kennedy's charge, "Ask not what your country can do for you; ask what you can do for your country." Here's a remarkable story from last year: It's about R. C. Willey, Utah's dominant home furnishing business, which Berkshire purchased from Bill Child and his family in 1995. Bill and most of his managers are Mormons, and for this reason R. C. Willey's stores have never operated on Sunday. This is a difficult way to do business: Sunday is the favorite shopping day for many customers. Bill, nonetheless, stuck to his principles—and while doing so built his business from $250,000 of annual sales in 1954, when he took over, to $342 million in 1999.

Bill felt that R. C. Willey could operate successfully in markets outside of Utah and in 1997 suggested that we open a store in Boise. I was highly skeptical about taking a no-Sunday policy into a new territory where we would be up against entrenched rivals open seven days a week. Nevertheless, this was Bill's business to run. So, despite my reservations, I told him to follow both his business judgment and his religious convictions.

Bill then insisted on a truly extraordinary proposition: He would personally buy the land and build the store—for about $9 million as it turned out—and would sell it to us at his cost if it proved to be successful. On the other hand, if sales fell short of his expectations, we could exit the business without paying Bill a cent. This outcome, of course, would leave him with a huge investment in an empty building. I told him that I appreciated his offer but felt that if Berkshire was going to get the upside it should also take the downside. Bill said nothing doing: If there was to be failure because of his religious beliefs, he wanted to take the blow personally.

The store opened last August and immediately became a huge success. Bill thereupon turned the property over to us—including some extra land that had appreciated significantly—and we wrote him a check for his cost. And get this: Bill refused to take a dime of interest on the capital he had tied up over the two years.

If a manager has behaved similarly at some other public corporation, I haven't heard about it. You can understand why the opportunity to partner with people like Bill Child causes me to tap dance to work every morning.

A footnote: After our "soft" opening in August, we had a grand opening of the Boise store about a month later. Naturally, I went there to cut the ribbon (your Chairman, I wish to emphasize, is good for something). In my talk I told the crowd how sales had far exceeded expectations, making us, by a considerable margin, the largest home furnishings store in Idaho. Then, as the speech progressed, my memory miraculously began to improve. By the end of my talk, it all had come back to me: Opening a store in Boise had been my idea.

MARKETING

P.T. Barnum to Moses Kimball

"I must have the fat boy or the other monster"

The great showman P. T. Barnum raised the art of traveling amusement shows to a new level by using spectacle and sensation to draw customers. To Barnum, who courted the press wherever he went, the event doubled as the promotion.

Moses Kimball, the proprietor of the Boston Museum, was a close friend of Barnum's. The two frequently shared each other's exhibitions, including the improbable Feejee Mermaid—the torso and head of a monkey attached to the body of a large fish.

In the letter below, Barnum refers to "The General," a midget named Charles S. Stratton, then only four years old, who Barnum dubbed "General Tom Thumb." Yan Zoo was a Chinese juggler. Peale's Museum was a rival show.

American Museum [New York], 30 January 1843

Dear Moses,

… My business averaged but $70 per day last week. Sorry you[rs] is not better than that. As I have to raise $500 to pay a private loss before the 22 Feb., I send the General to Philadelphia on Sunday next. I shall run on & make arrangements next Thursday. He will probably be ready for you about 1st or 10th of March. In a few days I will send you some fine lithographs of him so that you can be giving him notoriety….

I must have the fat boy or the other monster [or] something new *in the course of this week* so as to be sure to put them in the General's place *next Monday, so don't fail!* I don't want Yan Zoo unless he can perform on 8 feet stage & will come for $15 per week for two weeks with a privilege on my part, and he pays expences—indeed, I don't want him at all if you send the fat boy or something as good. Mrs. Smith will answer me *anytime* as well as Miss Mills, from whom I have heard nothing. I hope you will get the Mother Carys chickens for me. Now more about the *General.* I pay him and his father $7 per week and board & travelling expences for all three—father, mother, & son—and I have engaged my good friend parson Hitchcock at $12 per week, board & travelling expenses, to go with him and shew him off…. He will do the same at Philadelphia & Baltimore. When the Genl. Goes to Boston the Parson may continue with him, or he may remain here and attend to Peale's Museum while the boy & parents go to Boston, and you pick up some genteel person in Boston to do it. Just as you please. I dare not trust my singer with him, lest he may tamper with the parents and try to hire them away. Indeed, I fear the same from any person you might employ. Hitchcock's wages may seem high, but he is genteel, industrious, and knowing the ways of the boy well; I think he will earn all I pay him, and of course before returning from Phil. & Baltimore he will be thoroughly rehearsed. So do as you please about Hitchcock; only if he don't go to Boston, you must employ some person who won't tamper with the parents. Peale's took $60 last week.

Don't fail to send me some attraction in time for next week.

Yours forever & a day,
Barnum

KENTUCKY DISTILLERS TO ALCOHOLICS' SANATORIUM
"Our customers are your prospective patients"

In a letter of extraordinary brazenness, the president of a liquor company wrote to a sanatorium for alcoholics, offering to sell his mailing list of customers. The Anti-Saloon League used the letter as a leaflet to demonstrate the depravity of the liquor industry.

Kansas City, Mo.

Dec. 3, 1913.

Keeley Institute

Dwight, Illinois

Gentlemen: Our customers are your prospective patients. We can put on your desk a mailing of over 50,000 individual consumers of liquor. The list is the result of thousands of dollars of advertising.

Each individual on the list is a regular user of liquor. The list of names is new, live and active. We know this because we have circularized it regularly. We furnish this list in quantities at the prices listed below. Remittances to accompany each order.

      40,000 to 50,000.................$400

      20,000...........................$300

      10,000...........................$200

We will not furnish this list in lots less than 10,000. Discontinuance of business January 1, is the occasion for selling our mailing list.

Yours truly,

Kentucky Distillers' Co.

W. Franklin, President

STURGIS DORRANCE TO CONGRESS
"The Rise of Advertising"

Advertising in the United States exploded during the 1920s. The boom in marketing came about from a combination of the expertise gained from a massive government propaganda effort in support of American involvement in World War I and the development of a wide range of consumer products such as radios and automobiles.

Savvy manufacturers realized that style could matter as much as substance in the selling of a product. They hired marketing staffs and developed advertising budgets to boost sales. As the following letter reflects, even the U.S. government began to see the value in advertising as Congress considered allocating money for an advertising budget to promote its own services.

January 20, 1925
Hon. William E. Wood
House Representatives Office Building
Washington D. C.

My dear Mr. Wood:

As promised you at the time of our talk on Saturday, I am attaching herewith a list of large national Advertisers and the amounts expended for advertising in these various industries, in relation to their gross business.

You will see that these figures bear out the statement given you that they range from 1% to 10% depending upon the product and the advertising problem.

I trust that these will be of some value to you and your colleagues on the appropriation committee in establishing a basis for the advertising of the Fleet Corporation and the United States Shipping board.

It would seem to me that the figure asked for in the 1926 budget is far from being out of line. In fact, it is lower than most big corporations would consider necessary to merchandise a product or a service, and of course the Shipping Board problem is to merchandise a service recognised by passenger and freight traffic, to say nothing of securing the cooperation of the American Public as represented by their good will expressed in both passenger and freight patronage, as well as confidence.

If I can be of any further service you may rest assured that I will be glad to have you call on me.

I am looking forward to seeing you in Washington in the near future.

Sincerely yours,
Sturgis Dorrance
President

Stromberg Carburator	3.5%
Studebacker automobiles	2%
Union Pacific Railroad	2 1/2 %
Universal Portland Cement	2%
Velvet Tobacco	6%
Vister Talking Machine	5%
Welch Grape Juice	10%
White Motor Truck Co.	1%
Wooltex Clothes	2%

The above figures are on the authority of the Periodical Publishers Association and Alexander Hamilton Institute.

Some of the percentages vary a little bit from year to year, but on the whole they are accurate indices of the current appropriations of these companies.

The following are figures compiled by the Sheffield Scientific School of Yale University, supplemented by estimates given by the Alexander Hamilton Institute, showing the average percentage of sales expended for advertising by commodity groups:

Automobile Accessories	4.2%
Automobiles	1.5%
Building Materials	2.4%
Cement	1.2%
Candies & Chewing Gum	8.1%
Men's Clothes	1.5 to 2%
Men's Collars	2.5 to 3.5%
Fountain Pens	5.3%
Office Supplies	5.1%
Optical Goods	7.3%

Paints & Varnishes	3.5%
Phonographs	5%
Soaps	2 to 3%
Tobacco	5 to 8%
Department Stores	2.5% to 3%
Mail Order Houses	10 to 12%

UNITED ARTISTS PUBLICITY STUNT
"This story will simply be written by Quarlberg"

Some publicity agents are known for the extremes to which they will go in order to get stories in the press. The New Yorker *magazine once wrote that "a press agent who worries about taste is as badly miscast as a soldier who faints at the sight of blood." The following excerpt from an internal memo at the United Artists film studio shows how outright fabrication can result in front-page news.*

The actor Louis Wolheim was a well-known actor in the 1920s whose looks were distinguished by a large pug nose that had been broken three times. Publicists decided to make up a story in which Wolheim goes to a plastic surgeon to fix his nose, against the objections of United Artists. Headlines such as "COURT MAY HALT SCHEME TO RE-ETCH ACTOR'S BUM RAP" told the story for two weeks as Wolheim and the studio went to court to fuel the fake stunt.

Suppose, for instance, the UPI [United Press International] is given a tip that Wolheim is thinking about having his face remodeled—that he has been playing roles such as "The Hairy Ape" and "Capt. F." and only more recently the role in "Two Arabian Knights" that show his face in a way that makes people laugh. The tip further states that he has conferred with Dr. Balsinger in Los Angeles, and that it is rumored it will be one of the strangest facial operations—that of remaking a man's face that is so ugly. The tip might further state that it represents a $10,000 fee, etc. etc. etc.

Then suppose UPI release a big story on the day wire which hits as many if not more papers than the AP, with four papers in New York, including the *World* and *Telegram*.

The story will be an exclusive interview with Wolheim by the UPI and will carry a byline over the wire. This is all set. If you recollect, I have on my staff a certain young chap named Quarlberg who formerly was the LA Bureau manager for the UP. The present Bureau Manager won his job there through Quarlberg, and is a very near and dear pal. In fact, this story, will simply be written by Quarlberg and shot, as is, over the entire UP system.

ALFRED P. SLOAN, JR. TO H. H. BASSETT
"Are we as advanced from the standpoint of beauty of design?"

One of the great innovations of General Motors was bringing a sense of style to its cars. In contrast to Henry Ford's famous comment that customers could buy a Ford in any color they wanted "so long as it was black," General Motors President Alfred P. Sloan, Jr., realized that a car's design was a selling point. He saw the importance of offering the public "a car for every purse and purpose" and of upgrading cars for an increasingly prosperous, consumer-oriented society. General Motors' success in overtaking Ford as the largest car manufacturer came about in part because of Sloan's understanding and manipulation of the growing consumer market. Sloan expressed his desire to see more sense of style in General Motors' cars, as this letter to H. H. Bassett, general manager of GM's Buick division, attests.

July 8, 1926

My dear Harry:

...[For] The first Cadillac car that I ever had ... I purchased small wire wheels in order to get the car down nearer the ground and I never could see why, as motor car people, we have apparently been so loath to do a thing which contributed probably more to the appearance of the car from the attractive standpoint than any other single thing. Chrysler, in bringing out his original car, certainly capitalized that idea to the fullest possible extent and I think a great deal of his success ... was due to that single thing. Slowly but surely we are ... getting our cars nearer to the ground.... This, of course, is to a certain extent a mechanical feature but nevertheless it involves the appearance as well.

I am sure we all realize ... how much appearance has to do with sales; with all cars fairly good mechanically it is a dominating proposition and in a product such as ours where the individual appeal is so great, it means a tremendous influence on our future prosperity. When it comes to our body design,

I am sure we all recognize the quality, the wonderful workmanship and the constructiveness from every standpoint of Fisher bodies. They speak for themselves...

Irrespective of all this, however, the question arises—Are we as advanced from the standpoint of beauty of design, harmony of lines, attractiveness of color schemes and general contour of the whole piece of apparatus as we are in the soundness of workmanship and the other elements of a more mechanical nature? That is the point I am raising and I believe it is a very fundamental one...

At the present time one of our very important lines is being revamped from the appearance standpoint....

Alfred P. Sloan Jr.

MARIANNE MOORE TO AND FROM
THE FORD MOTOR COMPANY
"All we want is a colossal name"

Three years after winning the Pulitzer Prize, poet Marianne Moore was approached by Ford Motor Company's Marketing Research Department to assist in the naming of a new series of cars. In a delightful exchange of letters, Moore took the challenge of coming up with a distinctive name, devising lists and lists—which, unfortunately, all went for naught.

October 19, 1955

Dear Miss Moore:

This is a morning we find ourselves with a problem which, strangely enough, is more in the field of words and the fragile meaning of words than in car-making. And we just wonder whether you might be intrigued with it sufficiently to lend us a hand.

Our dilemma is a name for a rather important new series of cars.

We should like this name to be more than a label. Specifically, we should like it to have a compelling quality in itself and by itself. To convey, through association or other conjuration, some visceral feeling of elegance, fleetness, advanced features and design. A name, in short, that flashes a dramatically desirable picture in people's minds.

Over the past few weeks this office has confected a list of three hundred-odd candidates which, it pains me to relate, are characterized by an embarrassing pedestrianism. We are miles short of our ambition. And so we are seeking the help of one who knows more about this sort of magic than we.

As to how we might go about this matter, I have no idea. One possibility is that you might care to visit with us and muse with the new Wonder which now is in clay in our Advance Styling Studios. But, in any event, all would depend on whether you find this overture of some challenge and interest.

Should we be so fortunate as to have piqued your fancy, we will be pleased to write more fully. In summary, all we want is a colossal name (another "Thunderbird" would be fine). And, of course, it is expected that our relations will be on a fee basis of an impeccably dignified kind.

Respectfully,

Robert B. Young

Marketing Research Department

November 13, 1955

Some other suggestions, Mr. Young for the phenomenon:

THE RESILIENT BULLET

or intelligent bullet

or bullet cloisoné

or bullet lavolta

(I have always had a fancy for THE INTELLIGENT WHALE—the little first Navy submarine shaped like a sweet-potato; on view in our Brooklyn Yard).

THE FORD FABERGÉ (That there is also a perfume Fabergé seems to me to do no harm for here, allusion is to the original silversmith).

THE ARC-en-CIEL (the rainbow)

ARCENCIEL?

Please do not feel that memoranda from me need acknowledgment. I am not working day and night for you; I feel that etymological hits are partially accidental.

Sincerely yours,

Marianne Moore

The bullet idea has possibilities, it seems to me, in connection with mercury (with Hermes and Hermes trismeistus) and magic (white magic).

November 28, 1955

To: Mr. Robert B. Young

From: Marianne Moore

MONGOOSE CIVIQUE

ANTICIPATOR

REGNA RACER (couronne à couronne) sovereign to sovereign

AEROTERRE

Fée rapide (aerofée, aero faire, fée aiglette, magi-faire) comme il faire

tonnère alifère (wingèd thunder)

aliforme alifère (wing-slender a-wing)

TURBOTORC (used as an adjective by Plymouth)

THUNDERBIRD allié (Cousin Thunderbird)

THUNDER CRESTER

DEARBORN diamanté

MAGIGRAVURE

PASTELOGRAM

I shall be returning the sketches very soon—

M. M.

December 8, 1955

Mr. Young:

May I submit UTOPIAN TURTLETOP?

Do not trouble to answer unless you like it.

Marianne Moore

November 8, 1956

Dear Miss Moore:

Because you were so kind to us in our early and hopeful days of looking for a suitable name, I feel a deep obligation to report on events that have ensued.

And I feel must do so before the public announcement of same come Monday, November 19.

We have chosen a name out of the more than six-thousand-odd candidates that we gathered. It has a certain ring to it. An air of gaiety and zest. At least, that's what we keep saying. Our name, dear Miss Moore, is—Edsel.

I know you will share your sympathies with us.

Cordially,

David Wallace, Manager

Marketing Research

P.S. Our Mr. Robert Young, who corresponded with you earlier, is now and temporarily, we hope, in the services of our glorious U.S. Coast Guard. I know he would send his best.

NORMAN ROCKWELL ENDORSES PAINT-BRUSHES
"I don't think I have always been completely honest about some of my endorsements"

Norman Rockwell often supplemented his income as an illustrator with paid endorsements for products ranging from Skippy Peanut Butter to Coca-Cola. Rockwell's famous name could help sell products, especially paintbrushes. In his enthusiasm to compliment two rival manufacturers, however, Rockwell inadvertently got into trouble.

The following three letters illustrate the matter. The first two were published as advertisements by rival paintbrush companies. The third letter comes from the president of the smaller company, who asked Rockwell to intervene on his behalf.

December 15, 1959
Mr. Robert Simmons, President
Robert Simmons, Inc.
555 Sixth Avenue
New York, N. Y.

Dear Mr. Simmons:

As you know it was with some hesitation that I accepted the idea of a gift of your brushes and a following endorsement. Because I don't think I have always been completely honest about some of my endorsements, and I am trying to endorse only those things I find to be really top notch quality.

But when I received your generous gift of brushes, and after using them for a week, I can wholeheartedly and honestly endorse them. Not since I used those wonderful "Rubens" brushes (which before the war were made in Germany), have I found such beautifully made and perfect brushes. They not only can stand the wear and tear I give them, but also have the texture and resilience I enjoy.

I certainly wholeheartedly endorse these brushes, and thank you again for your generous gift.

Sincerely,
Norman Rockwell

[January, 1961]

M. Brumbacher, Inc.

460 West 34th Street

New York, N. Y.

Gentlemen:

The superior quality of the bristle, together with the expert craftsmanship that is required to make such superb brushes, have made the Rubens brushes the symbol of perfection.

I always look for the Brumbacher Rubens name to be sure of obtaining the same high quality, perfect brushes, which I have always used.

Very truly yours,

Norman Rockwell

January 31, 1961

Mr. Norman Rockwell

Stockbridge,

Mass.

Dear Mr. Rockwell,

Am enclosing a copy of the letter you sent us, which with your permission, we used as a national Advertisement in its original form with a specific layout and format as designed by our agency.

To our extreme consternation we have just noticed that Grumbacher is advertising a letter of endorsement from you using the EXACT SAME FORMAT as OUR ad ... and we have learned that they will continue to run this ad in National Magazines on a monthly basis. ...

We were really proud when we received your letter. It was spontaneous, warm and enthusiastic, confirming our belief that we manufacture the finest brushes possible. To hear this from America's Number One Artist, was a feather in our hat.

Now, in effect we look and feel extremely foolish. Your endorsement of an imported brush in direct competition of ours ... and in an ad which copies of the format of ours EXACTLY, has led to a great deal of confusion, and artists are wondering which brush is which. Does Grumbacher make

Robert Simmons' Bristle Brushes or vice versa?

Note also that Grumbacher, a giant concern which spends a considerable amount of money for advertising as compared to our small limited budget has only allotted a small quarter page to your endorsement ... while we, on the other hand felt it important enough to devote and pay for a half page space.

We can readily understand that this is a minor matter as far as you're concerned ... in trying to be obliging you have unwittingly placed yourself in the middle of an unsavory situation. However, if you will ask Brumbacher to stop using this endorsement letter ... particularly in its present format, it would help us save face and regain some of the prestige which we have lost as a result of this confusing maneuver.

Am extremely sorry to have to trouble you with a matter of this sort, especially since you were nice enough to give our brushes such a hearty endorsement originally.

Very truly yours,
Robert Simmons, Pres.

J. F. Hind to C. A. Tucker
"Tomorrow's cigarette business"

In a memo marked "Secret," a market research official at the tobacco company R. J. Reynolds wrote the following letter to the company's vice president of marketing. The correspondence described the marketing strategy that would ultimately lead to the creation of the advertising cartoon character Joe Camel. In this approach, teenagers were specifically targeted.

January 23, 1975

Mr. C. A. Tucker:

Our attached recommendation to expand nationally the successfully tested "Meet the Turk" ad campaign and new Marlboro-type blend is another step to meet our marketing objective: To increase our young adult franchise. To ensure increased and longer-term growth for CAMEL FILTER, the brand must increase its share penetration among the 14-24 age group which have a new set of more liberal values and which represent tomorrow's cigarette business.

Presently, almost two-thirds of the CAMEL FILTER business is among smokers over 35 years of age, more than twice that for Marlboro. While "Meet the Turk" is designed to shift the brand's age profile to the younger age group, this won't come over night. Patience, persistence, and consistency will be needed. There may even be temporarily a softness in CAMEL FILTER'S growth rate as some of the older, more conservative CAMEL FILTER smokers are turned off by the campaign and younger, more liberal smokers begin to come into the brand's franchise. Test market results suggest, though, that this risk is small.

The current media spending level will be maintained since test market shipments indicate no significant short-term volume gains from increased spending. Other competitive brands, such as VANTAGE, Newport, and Virginia Slims with sharply directed advertising have demonstrated significant growth rates attainable with CAMEL FILTER's media spending level. We would prefer, as we did for VANTAGE, to demonstrate an increased growth rate with this campaign/blend and then give consideration to asking for extra monies.

Jim

E. B. WHITE TO XEROX CORPORATION
"Whenever money changes hands something goes along with it"

The potential influence of advertisers on the editorial content of newspapers, magazines, television and other media is an ever-present issue. Advertisers frequently try to exert their financial leverage to encourage favorable press coverage.

In 1975, Xerox Corporation initiated an unusual arrangement in which it would directly pay a well-known and highly respected journalist for an article in Esquire *magazine on the relatively innocuous topic of traveling in the United States.* New Yorker *writer E. B. White raised objections to the arrangement as a potential threat to the concept of the free press. In a letter to his local weekly Maine newspaper and a follow-up letter to Xerox Corporation, below, he describes the potential dangers of concentrated corporate control of the press.*

W. B. Jones, the Xerox Director of Communications, thanked White for "telling me what I didn't want to hear." A few months later, Jones informed White that Xerox would no longer underwrite articles in the press, noting they were convinced it was "the right decision."

To The Editor of the Ellsworth [Maine] American

January 1, 1976

To the Editor:

I think it might be useful to stop viewing fences for a moment and take a close look at Esquire magazine's new way of doing business. In February, Esquire will publish a long article by Harrison E. Salisbury, for which Mr. Salisbury will receive no payment from Esquire but will receive $40,000 from the Xerox Corporation—plus another $15,000 for expenses. This, it would seem to me, is not only a new idea in publishing, it charts a clear course for the erosion of the free press in America. Mr. Salisbury is a former associate editor of the New York Times and should know better. Esquire is a reputable sheet and should know better. But here we go—the Xerox-Salisbury-Esquire axis in full cry!

A news story about this amazing event in the December 14th issues of the Times begins: "Officials of Esquire magazine and of the Xerox Corporation report no adverse reactions, so far, to the announcement that Esquire will publish a 23-page article [about travels through America] in February 'sponsored' by Xerox." Herewith I am happy to turn in my adverse reaction even if it is the first one across the line.

Esquire, according to the Times story, attempts to justify its new payment system (get the money from a sponsor) by assuring us that Mr. Salisbury will not be tampered with by Xerox; his hand and his pen will be free. If Xerox likes what he writes about America, Xerox will run a "low keyed full-page ad preceding the article" and another ad at the end of it. From this advertising, Esquire stands to pick up $115,000, and Mr. Salisbury has already picked up $40,000, traveling, all expenses paid, through this once happy land....

Apparently Mr. Salisbury had a momentary qualm about taking on the Xerox job. The Times reports him as saying, "At first I thought, gee whiz, should I do this?" But he quickly compared his annoying doubts and remembered that big corporations had in the past been known to sponsor "cultural enterprises," such as opera. The emergence of a magazine reporter as a cultural enterprise is as stunning a sight as the emergence of a butterfly from a cocoon. Mr. Salisbury must have felt great, escaping from his confinement.

Well, it doesn't take a giant intellect to detect in all this the shadow of disaster. If magazines decide to farm out their writers to advertisers and accept the advertiser's payment to the writer and to the magazine, then the periodicals of this country will be far down the drain and will become so fuzzy as to be indistinguishable from the controlled press in other parts of the world

E. B. White

North Brooklin
January 30, 1976
Dear Mr. Jones:

In extending my remarks on sponsorship, published in the Ellsworth American, I want to limit my discussion to the press—that is, to newspapers and magazines. I'll not speculate about television, as television is outside my experience and I have no ready opinion about sponsorship in that medium.

In your recent letter to me, you ask whether, having studied your ground rules for proper conduct in sponsoring a magazine piece, I still see something sinister in the sponsorship. Yes, I do. Sinister may not be the right word, but I see something ominous and unhealthy when a corporation underwrites an article in a magazine of general circulation. This is not, essentially, the old familiar question of an advertiser trying to influence editorial content; almost everyone is acquainted with that common phenomenon. Readers are aware that it is always present but usually in a rather subdued or non-threatening form. Xerox's sponsoring of a specific writer on a specific occasion for a specific article is something quite different. No one, as far as I know, accuses Xerox of trying to influence editorial opinion. But many people are wondering why a large corporation placed so much money on a magazine piece, why the writer of the piece was willing to get paid in so unusual a fashion, and why Esquire was ready and willing to have an outsider pick up the tab. These are reasonable questions.

The press in our free country is reliable and useful not because of its good character but because of its great diversity. As long as there are many owners, each pursuing his own brand of truth, we the people have the opportunity to arrive at the truth and to dwell in the light. The multiplicity of ownership is crucial. It's only when there are a few owners, or, as in a government-controlled press, one owner, that the truth becomes elusive and the light fails. For a citizen in our free society, it is an enormous privilege and a wonderful protection to have access to hundreds of periodicals, each peddling its own belief. There is safety in numbers: the papers expose each other's follies and peccadillos, correct each other's mistakes, and cancel out each other's biases. The reader is free to range around the whole editorial bouillabaisse and explore it for the one claim that matters—the truth.

When a large corporation or a rich individual underwrites an article in a magazine, the picture changes: the ownership of that magazine has been diminished, the outline of the magazine has been blurred. In the case of the Salisbury piece, it was as though Esquire had gone on relief, was accepting its first welfare payment, and was not its own man anymore. The editor protests that he accepts full responsibility, he somehow did not get around to paying the bill. This is unsettling and I think unhealthy. Whenever money changes hands, something goes along with it—an intangible something that varies with the circumstances. It would be hard to resist the suspicion that Esquire feels indebted to Xerox, that Mr. Salisbury feels indebted to both, and that the ownership, or sovereignty, of Esquire has been nibbled all around the edges.

Sponsorship in the press is an invitation to corruption and abuse. The temptations are great, and there is an opportunist behind every bush. A funded article is a tempting morsel for any publication— particularly for one that is having a hard time making ends meet. A funded assignment is a tempting dish for a writer, who may pocket a much larger fee than he is accustomed to getting. And sponsorship is attractive to the sponsor himself, who, for one reason or another, feels an urge to penetrate the editorial columns after being so long pent up in the advertising pages. These temptations are real, and if the barriers were to be let down I believe corruption and abuse would soon follow. Not all corporations would approach subsidy in the immaculate way Xerox did or in the same spirit of benefaction. There are a thousand reasons for someone's wishing to buy his way into print, many of them unpalatable, all of them to some degree self-serving. Buying and selling space in news columns could become a serious disease of the press. If it reached epidemic proportions, it could destroy the press. I don't want IBM or the National Rifle Association providing me with a funded spectacular when I open my paper. I want to read what the editor and the publisher have managed to dig up on their own—and paid for out of the till....

My affection for the free press in a democracy goes back a long way. My love for it was my first and greatest love. If I felt a shock at the news of the Salisbury-Xerox-Esquire arrangement, it was because the sponsorship principle seemed to challenge and threaten everything I believe in: that the press must not only be free, it must be fiercely independent—to survive and to serve. Not all papers are fiercely independent, God knows, but there are always enough of them around to provide a core of integrity and an example that others feel obliged to steer by. The funded article is not in itself evil, but it is the beginning of evil and it is an invitation to evil. I hope the invitation will not again be extended, and, if extended, I hope it will be declined.

About a hundred and fifty years ago, Tocqueville wrote: "The journalists of the United States are generally in a very humble position, with a scanty education and a vulgar turn of mind." Today, we chuckle at this antique characterization. But about fifty years ago, when I was a young journalist, I had the good fortune to encounter an editor who fitted the description quite closely. Harold Ross, who founded the New Yorker, was deficient in education and had—at least to all outward appearances—a vulgar turn of mind. What he did possess, though, was the ferocity of independence. He was having a tough time finding money to keep his floundering little sheet alive, yet he was determined that neither money nor influence would ever corrupt his dream or deflower his text. His boiling point was so low as to be comical. The faintest suggestion of the shadow of advertising in his news and editorial columns would cause him to erupt. He would explode in anger, the building would reverberate with his wrath, and his terrible swift sword would go flashing up and down the corridors. For a young man, it was an impressive sight and a memorable one. Fifty years have not dimmed for me either the spectacle of Ross's ferocity or my own early convictions—which were identical to his. He has come to my mind often while I've been composing this reply to your inquiry.

I hope I've clarified a little bit my feelings about the anatomy of the press and the dangers of sponsorship of articles. Thanks for giving me the chance to speak my piece.

Sincerely,
E. B. White

DAVID OGILVY TO OGILVY & MATHER
"You cannot bore people into buying your product"

British advertising man David Ogilvy wrote the following letter to department heads of his agency Ogilvy & Mather, where he served at that time as creative head. In the letter, Ogilvy contends that the best kinds of advertisements not only increased sales, but also embraced "big ideas."

July 18, 1977

Confusion?

I am told that some of you are confused by what you perceive as a change in my creative philosophy.

For many years you heard me inveigh against "entertainment" in TV commercials and "cleverness" in print advertising. When the advertising world went on a "creative" binge in the late 1960s, I denounced award winners as lunatics. Then I started the David Ogilvy Award—for the campaign which produced the biggest increase in *sales*.

You got the word.

Then, two years ago, you began to receive memos from me, complaining that too much of our output was stodgy and dull. Sometimes I circulated commercials and advertisements which I admired, but which appeared to violate my own principles.

Have I gone mad?

My original Magic Lantern started with the assertion that *Positioning* and *Promise* were more than half the battle. You accepted that, and proceeded accordingly.

But another slide in my dear old Lantern states that "unless your advertising contains a *Big Idea* it will pass like a ship in the night." Very few of you seem to have paid attention to that.

Three years ago I woke up to the fact that the majority of our campaigns, while impeccable as to positioning and promise, contained no big ideas. They were too dull to penetrate the filter which consumers erect to protect themselves against the daily deluge of advertising. Too dull to be remembered. Too dull to build a brand image. Too dull to *sell*. ("You cannot *bore* people into buying your product.")

In short, we were still *sound*, but we were no longer *brilliant*. Neither soundness nor brilliance is any good by itself, each requires the other....

So the time had come to give the pendulum a push in the other direction. If that push has puzzled you, caught you on the wrong foot and confused you, I can only quote Ralph Waldo Emerson:

"A foolish consistency is the hobgoblin of little minds.... Speak what you think today in words as hard as cannonballs, and tomorrow speak what tomorrow thinks in hard words again, though it contradict everything you said today."

I want all our offices to create campaigns which are second to none in positioning, promise—and brilliant ideas....

D.O.

AL NEUHARTH TO ADVERTISING AND CIRCULATION MANAGERS

"One helluva impression to make"

The former chairman of Gannet Company and founder of USA TODAY *newspaper, Al Neuharth placed a strong emphasis on advertising and marketing his newspapers—especially the groundbreaking* USA TODAY *in the 1980s. The following internal memos from his autobiography,* Confessions of an S.O.B., *reflect the importance he placed on attention to detail in making a successful newspaper. Cathie Black was the publisher of* USA TODAY. *Frank Vega was first vice president of circulation.*

To Cathie Black:

I know you are busy, BUT I have had no response to my memo asking you how we are doing with Hilton and Procter & Gamble.

My Hilton question and the answer are important because I will be with Barron Hilton Saturday evening in Washington and I want to know what I am talking about.

In fact, all my memos and questions are important, or I wouldn't send them or ask them. Therefore, quick action by you is important and expected. Please fix.

To Cathie Black:

After my constant preaching about the importance of the presentation of our ads, and after your assuring me that you had allegedly fixed the alphabetizing of the lines in classified, how much longer am I going to have to wait before you get it done so that it will stay done?

Don't you care how often you screw things up?

To Frank Vega:

This morning, at 9:00 AM, the vending machine kitty-corner across from the White House at Pennsylvania and Executive Avenue still had yesterday's USA TODAY in the window and in the box.

Directly across the street, the vending machine had its door ripped off, stashed along the side, and the machine was empty. This is the second consecutive day it has been in this condition. I did not report it yesterday because I wanted to see how quickly your efficient street crew would repair it.

This is one helluva impression to make on those hundreds who mill around the White House every day, and many of whom get their first impression of USA TODAY on those street corners.

Some swift and solid ass-kicking is necessary around here. I have started mine. Now it's your turn.

NIGEL CARROLL TO EBAY CUSTOMERS
"Hi, my name is Nigel Carroll"

The arrival of the Internet in the 1990s brought with it a revolution in the way business is conducted. The introduction of eBay, the Internet auction site, made it possible for individuals and small businesses to reach their markets with very little cost. The eBay model was ideal for niche markets in which highly specialized products could be marketed and sold to targeted audiences over the Internet. In the formula for matching product and consumer, geography was all but eliminated.

EBay exploded in popularity with more than 10 million registered users signing on within three years of its initial launch. To create a more personal connection, the company introduced a feature called About Me that allowed registered users to describe themselves and even post their own picture. The following letter to prospective buyers from Nigel Carroll was typical of the About Me postings.

Hi, my name is Nigel Carroll

WELCOME TO MY SALE!

I hope that the information on this page will help you to decide to bid on my item. You are probably looking at a motor vehicle, and considering bidding for it. Before you do, please read on.

BUYING A CAR ON THE INTERNET

Buying anything on the Internet without seeing it can be a little scary, so I will attempt to put your mind at rest! I have been a collector, buyer, and seller of motor vehicles for thirty-three years. It started as a hobby and became a business. My company is called INTERNATIONAL CLASSIC CARS INC. My associate Richard Mitchell and I have over fifty years of combined experience in the classic car market place, both in the United States and in Europe. ICC is licensed and bonded in the State of California. We specialize in providing motor vehicles to the film industry for use in commercials, music videos, and movies. Occasionally we have vehicles for sale, either purchased by us or consigned to ICC by the owner for sale on his or her behalf.

Based in Los Angeles, California, the vast majority of our vehicles have spent their entire motoring lives in our sunny dry climate. In 1999 ICC offered close to thirty classic cars for sale on eBay, most of them sold first time out, others took a little longer, but so far I have had no complaints and I am grateful to those customers who left me feedback, which speaks for itself. Our cars have been shipped as far away as Europe, and have been collected by customers who have flown into Los Angeles from all over the United States to drive their purchases home. Our listings on eBay include a

Volkswagen Bug, which sold at $1,600 all the way up to a Ferrari Testarossa with a high bid of $53,500.00. Our goal is to offer quality cars at a price that is generally lower than you will find in your local paper.

We will be more than happy to answer as many questions as possible, and send more photographs to you via e-mail. If you are the successful high bidder we will send you a video of the vehicle if requested so you will get a better idea of the condition of your purchase prior to making your travel arrangements to pick it up. We urge you to ask questions BEFORE bidding, and please don't bid if you do not have the funds available at the auction close to complete the purchase. We have added a link below to Kelley Blue Book Used Car Values for your convenience. We also buy classic cars. If you have a vehicle that you think might be of interest to us, for sale or use in a commercial, e-mail details. We can also help you find what you are looking for.

WE ARE NOT SALESMEN, REMEMBER YOU SET THE PRICE! GOOD LUCK WITH YOUR BID! Thank you for visiting my page.

A Message From Warren E. Buffett
"Drop me a line, not e-mail though; I haven't made that much progress"

Even the well-known technophobe stock investor Warren Buffett could use the Internet to directly reach potential customers, investors, and others. Here he urges visitors to the website of his company, Berkshire Hathaway, to use products and goods offered by the companies owned by Berkshire Hathaway.

Dear Reader,

Thanks for visiting our website. Being a lifelong technophobe, I tiptoed into the computer world only a few years ago. If you have any ideas about how we can make these pages more useful, just drop me a line (not e-mail though; I haven't made that much progress).

You probably know that I don't make stock recommendations. However, I have three thoughts regarding your personal expenditures that can save you real money. I'm suggesting that you call on the services of three subsidiaries of Berkshire: GEICO, Borsheim's and Berkshire Hathaway Life Insurance Company of Nebraska (BHLN).

I estimate that about 40% of all auto drivers in the country can save money by insuring with GEICO. The figure is not 100% because insurers differ in their underwriting judgments, with some favoring drivers who live in certain geographical areas and work in certain occupations more than GEICO does. I believe, however, that GEICO more frequently offers the lower price than does any other national carrier selling insurance to all comers. You can quickly find out whether you can save money by calling 800-555-2756.

Fine jewelry, watches and giftware will almost certainly cost you less at Borsheim's. I've looked at the figures for all publicly-owned jewelry companies and the contrast with Borsheim's is startling. Our one-store operation, with its huge volume, enables us to operate with costs that are fully 15-20 percentage points below those incurred by our competitors. We pass the benefits of this low-cost structure along to our customers.

Every year Borsheim's sends out thousands of selections to customers who want a long-distance opportunity to inspect what it offers and decide which, if any, item they'd like to purchase. We do a huge amount of business in this low-key way, which allows the shopper to conveniently see the exceptional values that we offer. Call Scot Caniglia or Marvin Cohn at Borsheim's (800-642-4438) and save substantial money on your next purchase of jewelry.

Finally, BHLN sells annuity products directly over the internet at its website www.brkdirect.com.

Like GEICO and Borsheim's, BHLN maintains a low cost structure and, thus, can offer savings to many customers. By visiting the web-site, you can evaluate the specific products, get quotes and actually make a purchase. Check to see whether one or more of the products meet your financial planning needs.

Sincerely,
Warren E. Buffett

Amazon.com to New Customer
"A little bird told us …"

In addition to being able to post letters for passing readers, the Internet allows companies to gather data from past purchases and use this information to tailor their pitches to individual customers. It also allows companies to transmit these pitches in an instant. Amazon.com, the world largest internet retailer, or "e-tailer," has developed some of the most sophisticated of these marketing techniques. In this letter to an Amazon customer, the company's general manager uses very chatty language to overcome the inherent anonymity of e-mail communication between strangers.

Dear Amazon Customer,

A little bird told us you just placed your first order at Amazon.com. (Actually it was an ultrasecure, heavily guarded computer system—but the bird sounds friendlier.) At any rate, I'd like to take this opportunity to welcome you to Amazon.com and introduce you to some fun, free services every Amazon shopper should know about.

First off, sign up for Deliveries. Our expert editors will send you information-packed e-mails about the topics that interest you most. Choose from over 100 subjects—from DVD New Releases and Mystery Books to Bargain Music and Children's Software.

Next, are there authors you adore, musicians you admire, actors or directors you absolutely love? Then sign up for Amazon.com Alerts. We'll send you an e-mail to let you know when a new release from that person first becomes available.

Last order of business—send an e-Card. It's a fun way to keep in touch with friends. Our wacky e-Card creative team has come up with clever greetings for every occasion under the sun. When they run out of holidays, they create their own—such as Bad Hair Day.

That's it. Thanks again for shopping at Amazon.com. We hope you'll stop in again soon and put these special services to work for you.

Sincerely,

Jennifer Cast

General Manager and Avid Amazon Shopper

We hope you enjoyed receiving this message. Prefer not to receive these e-mails or want to adjust your e-mail preferences? Please visit your Amazon.com Account page and click the "Update your communications preferences" link.

THE MONEY
CHASE

RICHARD QUINCY TO WILLIAM SHAKESPEARE
"Yow shal nether loase creddytt nor money by me"

Richard Quincy was the bailiff of Stratford-upon-Avon, William Shakespeare's hometown. On October 25, 1598, Quincy wrote this letter to Shakespeare seeking money for his own use while on a mission on behalf of the Stratford Corporation, which was having trouble paying its tax bills.

To my loveinge good ffrend and contreymann Mr. Wm. Shackespere deliver thees

Loveinge contreyman, I am bolde of yow, as of a ffrende, craveinge yowr helpe with £30 uppon Mr. Bushells and my securytee, or Mr. Myttons with me. Mr. Rosswell is nott come to London as yeate, and I have especiall caws. Yow shall ffrende me muche in helpeing me out of all the debettes I owe in London, I thancke God, & muche quiet my mynde, which wolde nott be indebted. I am now towardes the Courte, in hope of answer for the dispatche of my buysenes. Yow shal nether loase creddytt nor money by me, the Lorde wyllinge; & nowe but perswade yowrselfe soe, as I hope, & yow shall nott need to feare, butt, with all hartie thanckefullenes, I wyll holde my tyme, & content yowr ffrende, & yf we bargaine farther, yow shal be the paie-master yowrselfe. My tyme biddes me hastene to an ende, & soe I commit thys night ffrom the Cowrte. Haste. The Lorde be with yow & with us all, Amen! Ffrom the Bell in Carter Lane, the 25 october, 1598.

Yowrs in all kyndenes
Ryc Quynet

DANIEL DEFOE TO ROBERT HARLEY
"You would be Mov'd to hasten My Relief"

This letter written by novelist and journalist Daniel Defoe years before he would write Moll Flanders *and* Robinson Crusoe, *seeks payment for services that were five months overdue. Defoe served in Edinburgh in the early 1700s as the agent of Robert Harley, first Earl of Oxford, Secretary of State for the Northern Department. Defoe wrote this letter for his work promoting the Act of Union between England and Scotland on Harley's behalf.*

Sir

You have Always Allow'd me The Freedome of a plain and Direct Stateing things to you. If I Should Not do it Now I should not be just to you. Much less Faithfull to My Self; and I Entreat your Pardon for This from the True and Necessary part of it.

If I Were where I have had the honor to be Sir, in your Parlour, Telling you my Own Case, and what a Posture my Affaires are in here, it would be too Moveing a Story; you Could Not, I am Perswaded, pardon my Vanity, you have too much Concerne for me and too much Generosity in your Nature, you Could Not bear it—I have allwayes Sir been bred like a Man, I Would Say a Gentleman if Circumstances Did Not of late Alter that Denomination, and tho' my Missfortunes and Enemies have Reduced me, yet I allwayes struggled with the World So as Never to want, till Now—Again Sir I had the honour to Come hither in a Figure Suitable to your Design, whom I have the honor to Serv; while you Supply'd me Sir, I can Appeal to him that knows all things, I Faithfully Serv'd. I baulk't No Cases. I Appeared in print when Others Dared not to Open Their Mouths, and without boasting I Ran as Much Risq of my life as a Grenadr in storming a Counterscarp;—It is Now five Months since you were pleased to Withdraw your Supply;—and yet I had Never your Ordr to Return;—I knew My Duty better Than to quitt my post without your Command; But Really Sir if you supposed, I had lay'd up a Bank Out of your former, It is my Great Misfortune that such a Mistake happens; I Depended too much on your Goodness to withold any Reasonable Expence, to form a Magazine for my Last Resort.

Tis true I spend you a Large Summe. But you will Remember how often I entreated your Restraint in that Case, and perticular Directions, but as left to my liberty, I acted as I Concluded I Ought to Do, Pushing Every work as Thoro'ly as I Could,—And in stead of Forming a Magazine for My Self. If you were to See Me Now, Entertaind of Courtisy, without Subsistence, almost Grown shabby in Cloths, Dejected &c, what I Care Not to Mention; you would be Mov'd to hasten My Relief, in a Manner Suitable to that Regard you were Allways pleased to show for me.

I Was Sir Just on the brink of Returning, and that of Meer Necessity, when Like life From the Dead I recd your last, with My Ld Treasurers letter; But Sir Hitherto, his Ldships Goodness to Me, Seems like Messages from an Army to a Town besieged, That Relief is Comeing; which heartns and Encourages the Famished Garrison, but does not Feed them: and at Last They Are Obliged to Surrender for want, when perhaps One week would ha' Delivred them.

What shall I farther liken my Case to? Tis like a Man hang'd, Upon an Appeal, with the Queens Pardon in his Pocket; Tis Really the Most Disscourageing Circumstance that Ever I was in; I Need Not Tell you Sir that this is Not a place to Get Money in. Pen and Ink and Printing will Do Nothing here. Men Do Not live here by Their Witts—When I look on my present Condition, and Reflect that I am Thus, with my Ld T—s Letter promiseing Me an Allowance for Subsistence in My Pocket, and Offring me Comfortable Things, Tis a Very Mortifying Thought that I have Not One friend in the World to Support me Till his Ldship shall think Fitt to begin That allowance.

The prayer of this Petition Sir is Very Brief, That I may be helped to wait, or that you will please Sir to Move my Ld T—r That Since his Ldship has thought Fitt to Encourage Me to Expect Assistance in Order to Serve the Governmt in this place;—his Ldship will be pleased to Make Such steps Towards it, as may prevent My being Oblig'd to abandone an Employ of Such Consequence, to My Own Ruine and the loss of the Capascity I am Now in of Doeing his Ldship Service.

I Need Say No More to Move you to This Sir. I entreat a speedy Reply and Supply to
Sir, Your Faithful Tho' Discouraged Servt
DF
Sept. 11 1707

THOMAS JEFFERSON RESTRUCTURES HIS DEBTS
"My plan for payments of my great debts"

As gifted a writer, thinker, architect, horticulturist and politician as Thomas Jefferson was, he was a dreadful businessman. Assigned the post of ambassador to France, in 1787, Thomas Jefferson wrote to Nicholas Lewis with a plan for handling his debts, which were largely incurred purchasing slaves for his Monticello estate. Torn whether to hire out or sell his slaves, Jefferson wrestled with the significant problem of how to raise money at a time of economic distress in the fledgling United States.

Paris July 29, 1787

Dear Sir,

In my letter of Dec. 19, 1786, I informed you that, as you had supposed in yours of March 14, that the balance of bonds & profits of the estate to that time would pay all the debts then known to you except my sister Nancy's, I was desirous of laying our shoulder seriously to the paiment of Farrell & Jones' & McCaul's debts; & that I should make propositions to them on that subject. I did so. These propositions were, to pay to Jones 400 £ sterl. a year & to McCaul 200 £ sterl., or to the former if he preferred it two thirds of the profits of my estate & to the latter one third. 2. That the crop of 1787, should commence these paiments. 3. That no interest should be allowed on their debts from Apr. 19, 1775 to Apr. 19, 1783 (being 8 years) 4. That their accounts should remain perfectly open to settlement & rectification, notwithstanding the paiments which should be made. McCaul has acceded very contentedly to these proposals; I added some other conditions to Jones, not worth mentioning as he does not accede as yet, I think however he will accede. I consider myself as so much bound in honor to the sacred execution of this agreement that when the profits fall short of enabling us to pay at any time, I would chuse to have made up by a sale of something or another. . . .

So far I had settled in my own mind the plan for extinguishing as fast as we could those two great debts, when I received from Mr. Eppes a letter of May 1, 1787, wherein he tells me he had been with you in Sep. 1786, that you had computed together, all the former debts (except my sister Nancy's) due from the estate & all due to it; and that there was still a balance of 1200£ against it, to pay which there would be nothing but the crop of 1786, two thirds of which would be consumed by negroes clothing & taxes. This account threatens a total derangement of my plan for payment of my great debts. I had observed that by a statement in your letter of March 14 of the probable proceeds of the crop of 1785, (about 50 hogsheads of tobacco) that the profits of the few house servants & tradesmen hired out were as much as those of the whole estate, & therefore suggested to you the hiring out the whole estate. The torment of mind I endure till the moment shall arrive when I shall not owe a shilling on earth is such really as to render life of little value. I cannot decide to sell my lands. I have sold too much of them already, and they are the only sure provision for my children, nor would I willingly sell the slaves as long as there remains any prospect of paying my debts with their labor. In this I am governed solely by views to their happiness which will render it worth their while to use extraordinary exertions for some time to enable me to put them ultimately on an easier footing, which I will do the moment they have paid the debts due from the estate, two thirds of which have been contracted by purchasing them. I am therefore strengthened in the idea of renting out my whole estate; not to any one person, but in different parts to different persons, as experience proves that it is only small concerns that are gainful, & it would be my interest that the tenants should make a reasonable gain. . . .

I must pray of you to make all the arrangements possible for enabling me to comply with the first years paiment of my debts, that is to say the paiment for this present year, which is to be made in the city of London the next spring. Apologies for all the trouble I give you would only show you how sensible I am of your goodness. I have proposed the extraordinary trouble of the leases with less reluctance, because it will be taken once for all, & will be a relief in the end. Be so good as to assure Mrs. Lewis of my attachment and my wishes for her health & happiness as well as that of your whole family.

GEORGE COLMAN NEEDS TO BORROW MONEY
"[Money transactions] are damned, nauseous, nasty, sour things"

In 1789, dramatist George Colman started managing the Haymarket Theatre in London before buying the famous theater in 1794. Three years later, Colman found himself short of cash when an edict prohibited the production of plays during Lent, depriving him of ticket revenues. Colman turned to a friend "more blessed with affluence than I" for a loan. As the following letters to his patron, Arnold, show, the request was first turned down, but then met.

Sunday Night, Piccadilly

My dear Arnold,

I feel more unpleasantly than I can tell you . . . in writing to you on money subjects. Take, therefore, a plain tale: though tales, nowadays, according to Lord Bishops and Lord Chamberlains, are of ill-omen. I am so thrown back in consequence of the failure of our Lenten entertainment (which I reckoned on as a certainty) that I am obliged to apply to those who are more blessed with affluence than I am.

Can you, my dear Arnold, lend me two hundred pounds? For the repayment of which, in summer (or before), I give you the word of an old friend and any other security in my power. I am in need of this occasional supply to take up a bill which is soon becoming due. . . .

Please send me a line in the course of tomorrow.

Truly yours,

G. Colman

Piccadilly, March 7, 1797

My dear Arnold,

I cannot leave town . . . without sending you a line to thank you, my dear Arnold, for your letter. Alas! We are two unlucky dogs! Could you have assisted me now, it would have rejoiced me; and I am sure you would if you could. I feel your explanations and intentions to be most kind and friendly.

Ever truly yours,

G. Colman

My Dear Arnold,

...let me thank you (although I am awkward at thanks and say much less than I feel) for your goodness and real friendship on this occasion. I hate all money transactions in general; they are damned, nauseous, nasty, sour things that go against my stomach. But you have contrived to throw into your draughts such a mixture of warmth and kindness that I shall never think of it without pleasure...

I am my dear Arnold,
Yours truly and affectionately,
G. Colman

SIR WALTER SCOTT TO JOHN GIBSON LOCKHART
"I would rather bear my own burden"

In 1825, Sir Walter Scott's investments in Ballantyne, his own publishing company, and Constable, another publisher, went sour. Scott had borrowed heavily to pay for the investments, as well as expenses for his estate, Abbotsford. When his financing agent, Hurst & Robinson, collapsed, Scott's finances went with it.

One of the great British writers of the early 19th century, Scott refused to declare bankruptcy, preferring to work out debts totaling £130,000. He delivered the news of his financial plight to his friend and son-in-law, John Gibson Lockhart.

Four days after writing this letter, Scott told his creditors: "I will be their vassal for life, and dig in the mine of my imagination to find diamonds . . . to make good my engagements, not to enrich myself." In the remaining six years of his life, Scott cut the debt to £54,000, all of which was paid by life insurance and copyright earnings upon his death.

Edinburgh, January 20, 1826

My Dear Lockhart:

I have your kind letter. Whenever I heard that Constable had made a *cessio fori*, I thought it became me to make public how far I was concerned in these matters, and to offer my fortune so far as it was prestable, and the completion of my literary engagements (the better thing almost of the two); to make good all claims upon Ballantyne & Co.; and even supposing that neither Hurst & Co. nor Constable & Co. ever pay a penny they owe me, my old age will be far from destitute—even if my right hand should lose its cunning. This is the *very worst* that can befall me; but I have little doubt that, with ordinary management, the affairs of those houses will turn out favourably. It is needless to add that I will not engage myself, as Constable desires, for £20,000 more—or £2000—or £200. I have advanced enough already to pay other people's debts, and now must pay my own.

If our friend C. had set out a fortnight earlier nothing of all this would have happened; but he let the hour of distress precede the hour of provision, and he and others must pay for it. Yet don't hint this to him, poor fellow; it is an infirmity of nature.

I have made my matters public, and have had splendid offers of assistance, all which I have declined, for I would rather bear my own burden than subject myself to obligation. There is but one in such cases.

It is easy, no doubt, for my friend to blame me for entering into connection with commercial matters at all. But I wish to know what I could have done better, excluded from the Bar, and then from all profits for six years, by my colleague's prolonged life. Literature was not in those days what poor Constable has made it; and, with my little capital, I was too glad to make commercially the means of supporting my family. I got but £600 for the *Lay of the Last Minstrel*, and—it was a price that made men's hair stand on end—£1000 for *Marmion*. I have been far from suffering by James Ballantyne. I owe it to him to say, that his difficulties, as well as his advantages, are owing to me. I trusted too much Constable's assurances of his own and his correspondents' stability, but yet I believe he was only sanguine. The upshot is just what Hurst & Co. and Constable may be able to pay me; if 15S. is in the pound; I shall not complain of my loss, for I have gained thousands in my day. But while I live I shall regret the downfall of Constable's house, for never did there exist so intelligent and liberal an establishment.

They went too far when money was plenty, that is certain; yet if every author in Britain had taxed himself half a year's income, he should have kept up the house which first broke in upon the monopoly of the London trade, and made letters what they now are.

I have had visits from all the monied people, offering their purses—and those who are creditors, sending their managers and treasurers to assure me of their joining in and adopting any measures I may propose. I am glad of this for their sake, and for my own; for although I shall not desire to steer, yet I am the only person that can *conn*, as Lieutenant Hatchway says, to any good purpose.

A very odd anonymous offer I had of £30,000, which I rejected, as I did every other. Unless I die, I shall beat up against this foul weather. A penny I will not borrow from any one. Since my creditors are content to be patient, I have the means of righting them perfectly, and the confidence to employ them. I should have given a good deal to have avoided the *coup d'etat*; but that having taken place, I would not give sixpence for any other results. I fear you will think I am writing in the heat of excited resistance to bad fortune. My dear Lockhart, I am as calm and temperate as ever you saw me, and working at *Woodstock* like a very tiger. I am grieved for Lady Scott and Anne, who cannot conceive adversity can have the better of them, even for a moment. If it teaches a little of the frugality which I never had the heart to enforce when money was plenty, and it seemed cruel to interrupt the enjoyment of it in the way they liked best, it will be well.

Kindest love to Sophia, and tell her to study the song and keep her spirits up. Tyne heart, tyne all; and it is making more of money than it is worth to grieve about it. Kiss Johnnie for me. How glad I am fortune carried you to London before these reverses happened, as they would have embittered parting, and made it resemble the boat leaving the sinking ship.

Your, dear Lockhart, affectionately,
Walter Scott

ANNA MATILDA KING TO TRUSTEE
"Creditors have seized and taken from him all his property"

Anna Matilda King, the mother of nine and wife to a bankrupt plantation owner, turned to the trustee of her father's will for financial assistance.

Waverley, 3d March 1842

My dear Sir

It cannot be unknown to you that the unfavorable seasons for some years past, and the almost annual ravages of the Caterpillar have cut short the crop of Sea Island cotton on the coast of Georgia, and in some locations almost destroyed it. My husband has probably been one of the greatest sufferers from these successive disasters. At a time when negroes were selling from five to six hundred dollars round in gangs—he unfortunately purchased largely; relying on the proceeds of his cotton crops to enable him to make payment, but the almost total failure in some years, short crops and low prices in others have prevented him from realizing the means to meet his engagements. The result is that his creditors have seized and taken from him all his property which in the condition of the country and at present Prices will probably not pay his debts: This may render it necessary for me to call on your friendly aid as one of my Trustees, to protect the property bequethed in my Fathers will for the benefit of myself and children.

I do not impute any blame, or mismanagement to my husband, nor has his misfortunes, in the slightest degree impaired my confidence in his integrity, or his ability to manage property. Nor is it my desire to give you unnecessary trouble. I simply ask that you will stand the friend of my fathers child in case my husbands creditors shall after taking all his property attempt to seize that upon which I can alone rely for the support of a family of nine children most of them small and at that peculiar age when instruction and parental support are essential and necessary. I do not know that my husbands creditors will disturb me but in case they attempt it I desire permission to call on you and Mr Joseph Jones—my other trustee—to protect my property—as my husband cannot act and I can rely alone upon my Trustees.

It is my desire that my husband be left as your or my agent, in the management of my plantations and business generally.

If my memory serves me a copy of my Fathers will was sent to you soon after his decease. If you cannot lay your hand upon it I will send you another immediately.

I send you enclosed, a list of the 50 negroes left to me in the will, with their increase. Pray let me hear from you as soon as convenient. Direct your letter to Waynesville. My kind regards to Mrs. Couper

Very respectfully
Your obt Servt, Anna Matilda King

ABRAHAM LINCOLN TO HIS FATHER AND BROTHER
"I very cheerfully send you the twenty dollars"

On Christmas Eve, in 1848, Abraham Lincoln, then a successful Illinois lawyer, responded to two requests for money from close family members. One was to his father, who needed $20 to pay for a past judgment on his land. Although Lincoln "cheerfully" sent the money, his accompanying note suggests that Lincoln may be a little dubious about the real need for the money.

The second letter was to his older stepbrother, declining to lend him $80, on the grounds that he is an "idler," offering instead some harsh advice on how to earn the money.

Decr. 24th, 1848

My dear father:

Your letter of the 7th. was received night before last. I very cheerfully send you the twenty dollars, which sum you say is necessary to save your land from sale. It is singular that you should have forgotten a judgment against you; and it is more singular that the plaintiff should have let you forget it so long, particularly as I suppose you have always had property enough to satisfy a judgement of that amount. Before you pay it, it would be well to be sure you have not paid it; or, at least, that you can not prove you have paid it. Give my love to Mother, and all the connections.

Affectionately your Son

[December 24, 1848]

Dear Johnston:

Your request for eighty dollars, I do not think it best, to comply with now. At the various times when I have helped you a little, you have said to me, "We can get along very well now," but in a very short time I find you in the same difficulty again. Now this can only happen by some defect in your conduct. What that defect is, I think I know. You are not *lazy*, and still you are an *idler*. I doubt whether since I saw you, you have done a good whole day's work, in any one day. You do not very much dislike to work, and still you do not work much, merely because it does not seem to you that you could get much of it.

The habit of uselessly wasting time, is the whole difficulty; it is vastly important to you, and still more so to your children, that you should break this habit. It is more important to them, because they have longer to live, and can keep out of an idle habit before they are in it, easier than they can get out after they are in.

You are now in need of some ready money; and what I propose is, that you shall go to work, "tooth and nail," for somebody who will give you money for it.

Let father and your boys take charge of your things at home—prepare for a crop, and make the crop, and you go to work for the best money wages, or in discharge of any debt you owe, that you can get. And to secure you a fair reward for your labor, I now promise you that for every dollar you will, between this and the first of May, get for your own labor either in money or in your own indebtedness, I will then give you one other dollar.

By this, if you hire yourself at ten dollars a month, from me you will get ten more, making twenty dollars a month for your work. In this, I do not mean you shall go off to St. Louis, or the lead mines, or the gold mines, in California, but I mean for you to go at it for the best wages you can get close to home—in Coles County.

Now if you will do this, you will soon be out of debt, and what is better, you will have a habit that will keep you from getting in debt again. But if I should now clear you out, next year you will be just as deep in as ever. You say you would almost give your place in Heaven for $70 or $80. Then you value your place in Heaven very cheaply, for I am sure you can with the offer I make you get the seventy or eighty dollars in four or five months' work. You say if I furnish you the money you will deed me the land, and if you don't pay the money back, you will deliver possession—

Nonsense! If you can't now live with the land, how will you then live without it? You have always been kind to me, and I do not mean to be unkind to you. On the contrary, if you will but follow my advice, you will find it worth more than eight times eighty dollars to you.

Affectionately
Your brother
A. Lincoln

NATHANIEL HAWTHORNE TO G. S. HILLARD
"The miserable pinch is over"

Nathaniel Hawthorne wrote this letter accompanying a payment for a loan extended to him by anonymous friends when he was in financial straits. Hawthorne was the first American literary figure to earn his living exclusively from income derived from his writing

Liverpool, Dec. 9, 1853

Dear Hillard,—

I herewith send you a draft on Ticknor for the sum (with interest included) which was so kindly given me by unknown friends, through you, about four years ago.

I have always hoped and intended to do this, from the first moment when I made up my mind to accept the money. It would not have been right to speak of this purpose before it was in my power to accomplish it; but it has never been out of my mind for a single day, nor hardly, I think, for a single working hour. I am most happy that this loan (as I may fairly call it, at this moment) can now be repaid without the risk on my part of leaving my wife and children utterly destitute. I should have done it sooner; but I felt that it would be selfish to purchase the great satisfaction for myself, at any fresh risk to them. We are not rich, nor are we ever likely to be; but the miserable pinch is over.

The friends who were so generous to me must not suppose that I have not felt deply grateful, nor that my delight at relieving myself from this pecuniary obligation is of any ungracious kind. I have been grateful all along, and am more so now than ever. This act of kindness did me an unspeakable amount of good; for it came when I most needed to be assured that anybody thought it worth while to keep me from sinking. And it did me even greater good than this, in making me sensible of the need of sterner efforts than my former ones, in order to establish a right for myself to live and be comfortable. For it is my creed (and was so even at that wretched time) that a man has no claim upon his fellow-creatures, beyond bread and water, and a grave, unless he can win it by his own strength or skill. But so much the kinder were those unknown friends whom I thank again with all my heart.

R. D. Leonard to A. Pierpont

"We had hired you and we would see you paid"

This letter from a drilling contractor brims with excitement about the discovery of oil in northwestern Pennsylvania that will lead to the "2nd California" gold rush. But the writer also reminds the Seneca Oil Company that it owes him money and is past due in making the payment.

Titusville March 26 1860

Mr A Pierpont

Secy of Seneca Oil Co

Sir

The week again comes around to fill my promise to write you once a week.

We are not carting much oil now owing to the conditions of the roads also the other wells are paying $1.25 pr Bbl to Union The highest we have paid is $1.00.

Mr Smith has returned from his trip to Butler Co and has the 2d Well down 55 ft with very favorable indications.

The pipe is down 39 ft 8 in and at 40 feet he struck a very fair show of oil and still continues to find small veins. And has now every evidence to expect a good well The Crosley well situated 1/2 mile below us on the opposite side of the creek, and the Barnsdall Well are still atracting a good deal of attention And I have no doubt are holding large quantities of oil at least they have advanced on the price of Barrells to $1.60.

The Excitement still continues and the effect will probably be that you will have a 2d California in North Western Pennsylvania.

It has now arrived to the point where moneyd men are looking for investments, and what will be the results time alone can tell.

Real estate in town is rapidly advancing in price and many improvements are in actual progress and many more contemplated.

I cannot close this letter without calling your attention to my bill of Labor sent you over one month ago and from which I have received not even a reply.

I cannot avoid telling you Sir that I am surprised after your telling me here that "We had hired you and we would see you paid." Mr Drake informs me that he has received no directions in relation to the matter from you.

And I certainly have had no orders from you or any member of the Seneca Oil Co to ask Mr

Drake for my pay And with whom I have made no contract although I believe my part of the business has been performed in a manner perfectly Satisfactory to Mr Drake by whose directions I was to be guided.

I received a letter last week from Mr Townsend saying "he was surprised that I should send for money and supposed that Mr Drake would pay all bills here" I replied to him by saying that I had made no contract with Mr Drake, that my contract was made with the members of the Seneca Oil Co at New Haven.

I also enclosed my bill to April 1st amounting to $175—and which I hope will claim your immediate attention—Also telling Townsend to say to the Members of the Co that it will be necessary for them to provide some one to take my place on or before April 10th next.

Trusting that you will find some one who will be more faithful to you than I have been and who will fill the Situation more satisfactorily to you

I am
Respectfully Yours
R D. Leonard

RICHARD WAGNER TO VON HORNSTEIN
"I hear that you have become rich"

Regarded by many as arrogant and egotistical, Richard Wagner was in desperate straits when he wrote this letter demanding money from a patron, Baron Robert von Hornstein. At the time of the writing, Wagner's opera Tristan und Isolde *had been abandoned after fifty-seven rehearsals as "a hopeless production." His career seemed ruined. When he learned that Hornstein had come into some money, he pounced on him, later saying that the request was "conferring an honor" upon the baron.*

Hornstein declined the demand. Many years later, Hornstein's son Ferdinand kept Wagner's obnoxious correspondence secret when he published his father's memoirs. But when Wagner made a bitter reference about Hornstein in his autobiography, Ferdinand made the following exchange public.

19, Quai Voltaire, Paris,

12th December 1861

Dear Hornstein,

I hear that you have become rich. In what a wretched state I myself am you can easily guess from my failures. I am trying to retrieve myself by seclusion and a new work. In order to make possible this way to my preservation—that is to say, to lift me above the most distressing obligations, cares, and needs that rob me of all freedom of mind—I require an immediate loan of ten thousand francs. With this I can again put my life in order, and again do productive work.

It will be rather hard for you to provide me with this sum; but it will be possible if you WISH it, and do not shrink from a sacrifice. This, however, I desire, and I ask it of you against my promise to endeavor to repay you in three years out of my receipts.

Now let me see whether you are the right sort of man!

If you prove to be such for me,—and why should not this be expected of someone someday?—the assistance you give me will bring you into very close touch with me, and next summer you must be pleased to let me come to you for three months at one of your estates, preferably in the Rhine district.

I will say no more just now. Only regards the proposed loan I may say that it would be a great relief to me if you could place even six thousand francs at my disposal immediately; I hope then to be able to arrange to do without the other four thousand francs until March. But nothing but the immediate provision of the whole sum can give me the help which I so need in my present state of mind.

Let us see, then, and hope that the sun will for once shine a little on me. What I need now is a success; otherwise—I can probably do nothing more!

Yours,
Richard Wagner

Dear Herr Wagner,

You seem to have a false idea of my riches. I have a modest fortune on which I can live in plain and decent style with my wife and child. You must therefore turn to really rich people, of whom you have plenty among your patrons and patronesses all over Europe. I regret that I cannot be of service to you.

As for your long visit to "one of my estates," at present I cannot contrive a long visit; if it should become possible later I will let you know.

I have read in the papers with great regret that the production of "Tristan und Isolde" will not take place this winter. I hope that it is only a question of time, and that we shall yet hear the work. Greetings to you and your wife.

From yours,
Robert von Hornstein

ROBERT LOUIS STEVENSON TO FATHER
"I appeal, in fine, to your purse"

Asking for money from one's parent can be a delicate exercise. Robert Louis Stevenson, author of classics such as Treasure Island *and* The Strange Case of Dr. Jekyll and Mr. Hyde, *wrote this request of his parent in this 1866.*

Respected Paternal Relative:

I write to make a request of the most moderate nature. Every year I have cost you an enormous—nay, elephantine—sum of money for drugs and physician's fees, and the most expensive time of the twelve months was March.

But this year the biting Oriental blasts, the howling tempests, and the general ailments of the human race have been successfully braved by yours truly.

Does this not deserve renumeration?

I appeal to your charity, I appeal to your generosity, I appeal to your justice, I appeal to your accounts, I appeal, in fine, to your purse.

My sense of generosity forbids the receipt of more—my sense of justice forbids the receipt of less—than half-a-crown.

Greeting from, Sir, your most affectionate and needy son.

CHARLOTTE HAWKINS BROWN TO MR. GALEN STONE

"I haven't the first dollar to pay on it"

Charlotte Hawkins Brown started the Palmer Memorial Institute, a school for African-American girls, in North Carolina in 1902. After years of dedication and setbacks, it became one of the leading schools for Southern blacks. Brown, an outstanding educator and national women's leader, wrote hundreds of letters to plead and cajole for funds for her school. One of her staunch supporters was the Boston attorney Galen L. Stone. This letter was written a year after a fire had destroyed part of the school; there was so little money, Brown could not even buy food for her students.

June 17, 1921

My dear Mr. Stone:

For the last four years either you or Mrs. Stone has made us a contribution in June to help with the current expenses.

I didn't want to write you, but I've tried for three weeks to raise a little money, for one day, two weeks ago, we had overdrawn our accounts $35.00. I know that is bad business, but two or three local checks given us were returned.

This is the darkest hour I have ever known, last week we had neither meat or sugar, because deep in debt as we are, I don't want to go into debt for food. I had a little money ($135) saved up to assist me in the course of study I planned to take up this summer, but I've spent every dollar for the school. I know times are hard everywhere, I've just talked with Mrs. Bright—our trustees will meet next week.

May I tell you that plans are developing whereby we are going to ask The American Missionary Association of New York that sent me here twenty years ago, to take us under the board. It will give a permanence to the work, and although like Fisk, we shall have to help look out for ourselves, it will give stability to the work—I am working to that end. The first step has been taken, my Uncle who has come to the work is soon to sign a contract with the Association to take charge of the community church (Congregational) joining school and church. A conference is arranged for August at which time I hope to present the plans of our Trustee Board to that effect.

Mr. Stone, I must try to raise some money to tide us over this summer, please don't turn me down, the dear Lord knows I've called on everybody and we are almost living from "hand to mouth," this summer. The fire put us so far behind for although the club raised $80, they had pledged toward current expense, $500, that used up before it came.

It takes $500 a month to keep things going here. We have two men and two boys on the farm, three girls who help to do the work, the head of the Agricultural Department, and a Mechanic, the other place is being filled this summer by one of our boys at $35.00 per month.

Now is the time to buy coal. I haven't the first dollar to pay on it—I want to put in 50 tons—if I wait until fall it will cost one-third more. I can secure the amount by putting in $100. We can't even arrange to have the accountant put in the budget system until we have some money with which to pay him. I'm at my wit's end—everything looks dark, but I am bound to believe that help must soon [arrive].

I thank you for sending Mr. Totman. He was very interesting and instructive, we are following his suggestions to the letter. Mr. Stone if you good folks will help us now, it will tide us over the crisis while I busy myself to make plans for cooperation with the church agency herein mentioned. Let me hear from you please. . . .

L. Q. WHITE AND FEDERAL RESERVE CORRESPONDENCE
"Mortgaging the future earnings of the people of the United States"

The boom times of the 1920s were fueled by a new era of modern inventions, such as radios, electricity and—especially—automobiles. Loose credit standards by banks and new innovations such as installment plans greased the wheels of consumption. Although easier credit helped many people buy goods they could not otherwise afford, some people viewed the lax lending standards with uneasy concern.

L. Q. White, a bank president and owner of a Massachusetts shoe company, expressed his alarm on the subject in a letter to Everett Sanders, secretary to President Calvin Coolidge. Sanders forwarded the correspondence to the Federal Reserve Board for a response. As the exchange illustrates, the Federal Reserve acknowledged the problem but felt powerless to impose checks on credit standards.

When the stock market crash took place four years later, however, one of the most significant impacts was a collapse in people's capacity to repay loans, which subsequently led to hundreds of banks going out of business, further exacerbating economic conditions.

August 7, 1925

My dear Mr. Sanders,

I would like to bring to the attention of the President a matter which I think is affecting all industries outside of the automobile and manufacturing industries allied with it. At the present time, every industry except the above is badly affected for reasons that nobody seems able to explain.

My impression is on account of the tremendous loans that every bank all over the country is extending to buyers of automobiles, that such loans are handicapping every other industry. The buyer of even the cheapest automobile obligates himself, for instance, to pay twelve notes maturing a month apart, $15 a month besides making an initial payment of perhaps $25 or $50 on a low priced car. This is only an example. As I am president of a bank here, I find this to be the practice.

If this is a Ford car or tractor, the dealer in town endorses this paper and puts it in for discount. If he does not care to take too much of that kind of paper, he takes it to a finance corporation in Boston. . . . This finance corporation may be run by a National Bank or Trust Company. They, in turn, as I understand it, endorse this paper and use the Federal Reserve by guaranteeing the discount.

If I am mistaken on this, it would change the conditions quite a good deal but as I understand it, if this paper is finally used in any way as a means of receiving a loan from the Federal Reserve, then the Federal Reserve is handicapping every other industry for the benefit of the automobile industry.

It seems to me that no industry should be allowed to employ excessive amounts of money thru the Federal Reserve by taking on this tremendous amount of small loans, which seems to be the manner of buying automobiles today. The very fact that the workman perhaps earning $20 to $25 a week is handicapped by having these payments to meet each month, certainly means a hardship for every other industry, and in time, would bring nothing but disaster to the automobile business as well as other businesses and I think there should be some limit to just how much of these kind of loans the Federal Reserve should be allowed to have anything to do with. Any business using the Federal Reserve for such propositions should be restricted to the amount and the total amount loaned thru the whole series of Federal Reserve banks should be kept to some maximum. At the present time, as I understand it, there is no limit.

I feel as though the depression we have had here the last two years is caused by just this condition, as we have it in the small town of Bridgewater and this is only a sample of what happens in all towns and cities. The buying of all merchandise on the installment plan and encouraged by banks and bankers, which is being done more and more, is certainly a dangerous position for the country and an extremely bad thing for the Federal Reserve to encourage in any way except for building a home, which can be handled thru, and is handled thru, the cooperatives banks more than any other way.

I feel that this is one of the reasons for the poor business conditions, for the whole country seems to be bound up in a frozen loan. I realize the President has a great many important matters on his mind but I consider this one of the most important that the country is facing at the present time, and if it is possible for you to have this brought to the President's attention, I would certainly appreciate it.

Sincerely yours,
L. Q. White

August 14, 1925
My dear Mr. Sanders,

I have your letter of August 13 enclosing the letter of L. Q. White, of Bridgewater, Mass, and requesting information.

Mr. White is concerned about the installment plan of paying for automobiles. The installment plan is not limited alone to automobiles; it has extended so far as to embrace the clothing that is worn in many parts of the United States. The automobile industry, financed as it is on the installment plan, is largely handled through discount corporations and not through the banks. It may be that there are some banks in some parts of the country that handle some of this paper, but I do not believe that a single instance can be cited where any of this paper comes into the Federal Reserve banks because I am of the opinion that it is ineligible as well as undesirable.

The practice of paying for automobiles in the manner suggested by Mr. White no doubt does affect other business and industry in the country. People will have an automobile and sacrifice paying their doctor bill, their grocery bill and clothing bill or will go without all of them rather than give up an automobile, and as long as this spirit prevails and as long as discount corporations operate this condition will continue. The discount companies find it extremely profitable because they have learned that the family will sacrifice every other convenience, every other luxury and often necessities rather than give up the automobile. This makes of course the assurance of payments to discount corporations that handle the paper at a large discount from the seller of automobiles, and the security is reasonably safe because the vendor of the automobile guarantees the loan in addition to this intense spirit to pay on the part of the buyer.

It may be possible, and I think it is quite likely, that member banks do loan to the dealers in automobiles, but that paper is not the kind that is rediscounted as a rule with the Federal Reserve banks. . . .

Mr. White's trouble is to be found in the local banks of the country and not in the Federal Reserve banks, and it is a condition over which the Federal Reserve Board and Federal Reserve banks have no control. The Board has no power under the Federal Reserve Act to say that a member bank shall not loan to an automobile dealer, and likewise they would have no power to say that money should not be loaned by a member bank to a shoe company.

I quite agree with Mr. White that the present method of mortgaging the future earnings of the people of the United States by installment plan is a subject that merits the careful consideration of all business men and all persons who have the welfare of the country at heart. . . .

One further thought: These discount corporations are not owned by national banks. There may be stockholders of national banks owners of discount corporations but they are not directly owned by national banks and can not be under the law.

I am returning Mr. White's letter as requested.

Respectfully,

D.R. Crissingor

Governor

CALVIN COOLIDGE TO *LOS ANGELES EVENING HERALD*
"The man who saves is the man who will win"

Ironically, the credit-induced consumer boom of the 1920s was presided over by President Calvin Coolidge, one of the great proponents of the benefits of thrift. Businesses and banks made frequent requests to Coolidge for statements about specific products and the advantages of saving money. Although Coolidge declined to endorse individual goods, he often provided general statements reflecting his strong belief in the value of financial prudence, such as in this 1925 letter from his personal secretary to the Los Angeles Evening Herald.

September 22, 1925

My dear Mr. Obern,

I have before me your request for an expression, by the President, on thrift, and I am enclosing a short statement by him on this subject, which I think will precisely suit your purpose.

Most sincerely yours,

C. Bascom Shemp

Secretary to the President

It is not so much what we earn today as what we save today that determines our position tomorrow. The people of past ages did not fail to work, oftentimes they put forth great effort, but what they produced they at once consumed. They did not get ahead. They made no progress. There came a time when they began to accumulate a surplus. From that hour civilization began to appear. The foundation of it all was thrift. On it was built character. It is the test of the power of self-control. Out of self-control by the individual grew the principle of self government by the people. But the basis of it all is thrift. No man is so poor that he cannot begin to be thrifty. No man is so rich that he does not need to be thrifty. The margin between success and failure, between a respectable place in life and comparative oblivion, is very narrow. It is measured by a single word, THRIFT. The man who saves is the man who will win.

Calvin Coolidge

A.G. TO FEDERAL EMERGENCY RELIEF ADMINISTRATION
"The mortgagee has been hot on my trail"

Millions of people lost their jobs during the Great Depression of the 1930s, with national unemployment running as high as 30 percent. Men and women who formerly held respectable jobs to sustain their families suddenly found themselves out of work and destitute. When Franklin D. Roosevelt became president in 1933, he implemented a series of relief programs. The following letter from an out-of-work man in Seattle, Washington, was sent to the Federal Emergency Relief Administration for a government loan to pay off his defaulted mortgage. The outcome is not known.

Seattle, Wash.

Dec. 12-1934

Federal Emergency Relief Administration

1734 New York Ave N.W.

Washington D.C.

Gentlemen:

When the Home Owners Loan Corporation first opened in Seattle, I made an application for a loan, the mortgage was for $2,000.00 on a 6 room house and nearly an acre of land, during the last two years conditions have been so adverse with me that I have been unable to make any payments on the interest neither have I been able to pay the taxes, the mortgages at first agreed to take the Government bonds, but when certain repairs were included, the total amount the Government would loan was not enough to pay the mortgagee all his money in fact it would show a loss of nearly $400.00 after all *accrued interest* together with all taxes and repairs, so the mortgagee refused to take the bonds, and consequently my loan was rejected although I was one of the first to apply. I took it up with the repair department, to let me do the painting and repair the roof myself and in that way give the extra money to the mortgage but just when it seemed I was about to get my loan through the Government stopped all loans, and since the mortgagee has been hot on my trail demanding me to give him a *deed* or he will foreclose at once.

Gentlemen, this is *all* I have in the *world* my home and family. I have four boys and a little girl all in school this is an Ideal place to raise my family to be good American citizens, we have enough good ground to raise lots of garden stuff and this goes a long way toward keeping the table, we are now forced on relief and it seems that everything comes at once, if they are allowed to take away my little home I don't know what I'll do. I understand the Government is planning to supply homes for those who have none, it would be 100 times better in my particular case if the Government would make it possible for me to keep my own little home.

I always have been able to give my family a decent living until economic conditions got so bad I was unable to make it go any longer.

I am inclosing the last letter I received from the mortgagee.

I sincerely believe if the Government will help me save my place, it wont be long before I will again be on my feet, I think, the worry and wear and tear for fear that the mortgagee would try and foreclose on me has kind of gotten me down a little, I have not been well for two or three weeks, but I'm sure if I can secure help from the Government at this time of my distress, it wont be long till I will again be on my feet.

I sincerely hope and pray you will come to my aid and help me save my home for my family, if I should loose it I don't know what I'll do as I have no other place to go, if I can save it, I will be able to raise my family to be good useful citizens.

My place is worth about $3,500.00 but to me it is my home. Where I have a lovely happy family, good loving wife, who is thrifty, energetic, and who makes a home what it should be, we teach our children to love God, go to Sunday school and train them to live to be proper Americans who love their country, and if needs be give their lives for it.

I believe God will see us through some way but it has been the hardest thing I have had to go through, this maybe His way so I'm writing to you asking and praying that you will do something to save our little home.

I am sure the President, if he only knew, would order that something be done, God Bless him. He is doing all he can to relieve the suffering and I am sure his name will go down in history among the other great men of our country.

Respectfully Yours
A.G.
Seattle
Wash

Frank Lloyd Wright to John Nesbitt

"A champagne appetite only to realize that his was a beer income"

Just before the outbreak of World War II, Hollywood producer John Nesbitt commissioned architect Frank Lloyd Wright to design a $50,000 house for him. By the time Wright finished the initial design, Nesbitt's could no longer afford to pay for the project. Nesbitt's prospects to recoup his finances ended with the bombing of Pearl Harbor, and his being called to military service in World War II.

Expecting he might not receive payment for his work, Wright wrote the letter below, going over the promises made and work performed. He offered a compromise solution, implying that if it was not accepted, he would go to court. Nesbitt—who in the meantime was drafted into the military—responded to Wright's letter in good spirits, promising to pay and work out a fair resolution.

December 22, 1941

My dear John:

When a man reaches the stage you have now reached there is no argument. Simply stated, he has undertaken something he now finds unprofitable but for which he must pay. He will pay as little as possible. How little he pays will depend on his character and the force of circumstances.

Apparently, we have both lost. I have lost because at this time of my life I can't afford to put dreams on paper to be left there for a sum of money that merely pays for time on a wage basis. Of course I am more than disappointed. I am frustrated. And I hate to see a young man like you pay money for something he can't use if he wanted to. But I hate, more than that, to see him try to reverse himself to save money, crawfish and lie.

Your first letter to me did mention a $50,000.00 house and incidentally a guest house "somewhere." A model of the ground came along. I submitted sketches for a house to cost $40,000.00 and a guest house to cost $10,000.00 (with which you were pleased) and suggested an enclosure of ground costing $7,500.00. These costs were guaranteed cost limits if not altered during construction. And I was prepared to stand back of them.

You approved this by word and act, also assuring me that when the plans were made from the sketches submitted you would promptly pay me for them according to schedule. The plans previously approved by you were duly made and you have them. A fine very complete set. You had previously suggested building as far as $50,000.00 would take you—in the whole venture. You repeated it again. This was o.k. with me.

Nothing whatever except the sketches has been done by me to push you along the road further than you wanted to go—only (as arranged) you could go by stages to where so far as I knew you now wanted to go.

Now, what others may have said to you or have to say to you about the cost of the proposed work means nothing to me. They have no measure that would apply to our effort. We have the true measure: experience. And we know the work controlled by us would be covered by our estimate of cost as given to you in perfect good faith. You would have then much faith in us also if you had any legitimate basis for employing me at all as your architect.

These, I swear, are the known and provable facts.

Now, however, the picture changes. A house on the Pacific Coast at the moment looks bad. Your employment (temporarily, I trust) deserts you. You cannot use these plans. The cost is now a definite deterrent.

Another promise you held out to me, meantime, was the rehabilitation of the F.L.W. opus you now inhabit. Your mind changed about that but you did not notify me. You let me go on with the work and waste myself upon it. Why you did not stop me while there was yet time is your own secret. You agreed definitely to give me $3500.00 to work with and pay me a fee of $700.00 to restore the place to the status of my original intentions. You now have no use for that either. Neither have I.

I understand your position as well I do my own.

Well, both horses are dead. Who wants to pay for dead horses? The horses are mine. You may not have deliberately killed the horses—and to look the gift horse in the teeth might get somebody something. But a dead one?

So, I have this solution to offer to you before returning the carcasses of the horses into court as evidence. We continually make plans for houses costing from $6,500.00 up to hundreds of thousands of dollars. There is no reason why we couldn't give you a house for any sum you wanted to spend on a house if that sum would reasonably pay for the house you wanted and would accept.

I do not want to see you waste your money even if you are quite willing now to have had me waste my time which was (in this case) actually myself. So if you pay up as agreed for this venture into the future I will engage in writing to supply you (and to your satisfaction) with completely new plans and we will proceed with no charge whatever for the additional scheme and additional work, except the two percent fee for superintendence.

You may never build. I may die. But reason can no further go with generosity in these circumstances where I am concerned with a young man who had a champagne appetite only to realize (suddenly after it was all over) that his was a beer income if any. And War came to grin at it all.

This loss to me is better, as I see it, than getting involved with the tedious meum and tuum of the Wisconsin courts—or even of Los Angeles courts. Either is probably "as worse as each other."

I make this offer for immediate acceptance and not for drawn out arguments or pettifoggery.

As far as the work on the Glendower house is concerned I suppose that ill-starred venture can remain with its ill-star, and I can add the loss on that to the rest.

This letter (in terms of immediate money) to be exact means that your check for $2,060.00 will release you now from your obligation and entitle you to an agreement with me for complete services for a house costing not more than $30,000.00 when you want to use it.

The experience gained in the first try at a noble house should be of more service to you in the second than it will have cost you in money. We learn by lessons. Not always as easy as this one.

I am (and more sorry than sore) your architect.

Frank Lloyd Wright

December 25, 1941
Frank Lloyd Wright
Taliesin West Ariz.

What big sharp teeth you have Grandfather. But don't worry Frank. Despite irregularities which make for irritation and wholesome combat we shall each receive what we want and what is due. And incidentally I'm about to be drafted into government service so you can't sue me. Ha Ha. But you won't have to for you will be loyal to your own greatness and my faith in it this Christmas and all others. Despite alarms and stormy seas much affection.

John Nesbitt

AL HIRSCHFELD TO LESTER MARKEL

"I should like more money for my drawings"

For more than seventy years starting in 1925, Al Hirschfeld drew theater caricatures for The New York Times. The distinctive and often humorous drawings were a staple of the newspaper's arts section. In 1962, however, Hirschfeld encountered a snag in a simple reimbursement request for expenses incurred on a business trip to Philadelphia. He responded with this letter to management. He ultimately got his 50¢ back.

Lester Markel, Esq.
New York Times
West 43rd Street
New York New York

Dear Lester,

I should like more money for my drawings. The realization that I am not a member of a Union, I have no agent, no boodle from a loving relative awaits me. Foundations ask ME for gifts, in short—gevalt! It also occurred to me that perhaps the Times management may never offer me a raise and so I make this belated request for myself.

I was thrown into this mercenary mood by a check I received from the Times for my expenses to Philadelphia and return on a drama assignment. My bill for the day in Philly was $20.35. The accounting department in its infinite wisdom deducted 50 cents for "meal disallowance" and forwarded to me the balance of $19.85. Needless to say, I have returned the offending draft with commendable restraint . . . offering no suggestion of ultimate disposal by shoving the promissory note up their alimentary canals.

It would be the height of folly to point out to these humorless drones that it was not my intention to rook the Times out of 50 cents. This knowledge gives me small comfort. I find it difficult to explain my sudden need for brooding darkly in corners, frustrated and furious . . . unhappy and sorry for myself . . . pride in my work no longer enough to satisfy my ego. . . . I take refuge in wife screaming and child yelling . . . even thought of shaving off my beard.

To get back on the rational trolley would it not be possible for the Times to put up the extra fare. Your friend and mine, Al Hirschfeld
May 30th 1962

WARREN E. BUFFETT TO KATHARINE GRAHAM
"Writing a check separates conviction from conversation"

For anyone seeking out investors, it is difficult to imagine a more welcome sight in the mail than a letter from Warren E. Buffett. In 1973, Katharine Graham, CEO of the Washington Post Company, received just such a letter. Virtually unknown to the general public at that time, Buffett sent the letter to Graham explaining that through his company, Berkshire Hathaway, he had bought more than 230,000 Class B shares of her company, intended to purchase more, and would not interfere in the operations of the company.

The letter initially spooked Graham, who had unexpectedly taken over the helm of The Washington Post Company a decade earlier after her husband's death and had become publisher of the paper, itself, in 1969. Colleagues feared Buffett's purchase may have been the first step in a hostile takeover. But further investigation and a subsequent meeting with Buffett eased her concern. "I have met the threat . . . and was conquered, unfortunately," she wrote to a friend at the time. Buffett and Graham forged a fast friendship. Buffett helped Graham get through her "priesthood approach" to business, demystifying finance and management. And Graham guided the company and its shareholders to enormous financial success.

Dear Mrs. Graham,

. . . This purchase represents a sizable commitment to us—and an explicitly quantified compliment to the Post as a business enterprise and to you as its chief executive. Writing a check separates conviction from conversation. I recognize that the Post is Graham-controlled and Graham-managed. And that suits me fine.

Some years back, a partnership which I managed made a significant investment in the stock of Walt Disney Productions. The stock was ridiculously cheap based upon earnings, asset values, and capability of management. That alone was enough to make my pulse quicken (and pocketbook open), but there was also an important extra dimension to the investment. In its field, Disney simply was the finest—hands down. Anything that didn't reflect his best efforts—anything that might leave the customer feeling shortchanged—just wasn't acceptable to Walt Disney. He melded energetic creativity with a discipline regarding profitability, and achieved something unique in entertainment.

I feel the same way about The Washington Post. The stock is dramatically undervalued relative to the intrinsic worth of its constituent properties, although that is true of many securities in today's markets. But, the twin attraction to the undervaluation is an enterprise that has become synonymous for quality in communications. How much more satisfying it is going to be to watch an investment in the Post grow over the years than it would be to own stock in some garden variety company which, though cheap, had no sense of purpose.

I am additionally impressed by the sense of stewardship projected by your communications to fellow shareholders. They are factual, complete and interesting as you bring your established newspaper standards for integrity to the newer field of corporate reporting.

You may remember that I was in your office about two years ago with Charles Munger, discussing the New Yorker. At the time I mentioned to you that I had received my financial start delivering the Post while attending Woodrow Wilson High in the mid-1940's. Although I delivered about 400 Posts per day, my record of loyalty is slightly tarnished in that I also had the Times-Herald route (much smaller—my customers were discriminating) in the Westchester. This was perhaps the first faint sign to keenly perceptive Washingtonians that the two organizations eventually would get together.

I should mention that Berkshire Hathaway has no radio or television properties, so that we will not be a complicating factor with the FCC. Our only communications property is the ownership of Sun Newspapers of Omaha, a group of financially (but not editorially) insignificant weekly newspapers in the metropolitan Omaha area. Last month our whole organization, seventy people counting printing, went into orbit when we won a Pulitzer for our reporting on Boys Town's undisclosed wealth. Incidentally, Newsweek and Time used approximately equal space in covering the story last year, but Newsweek's reporting job was far superior.

You can see that the Post has a rather fervent fan out in Omaha. I have hopes that, as funds become available, we will add to our holdings, at which time I will send along amended 13-D filings.

Cordially, Warren E. Buffett

NEW FRONTIERS

Christopher Columbus to Ferdinand and Isabella
"It abounds in various kinds of spices, gold and other metals"

Christopher Columbus' journey to the New World in 1492 was a speculative commercial voyage that paid off handsomely. In this letter written to the representative of his patrons, King Ferdinand and Queen Isabella of Spain, Columbus tells what he found in the lands he explored across the Atlantic Ocean (which he mistakenly believed to be India). It surely seemed like paradise.

Columbus not only found gold, spices, fertile fields, and towering trees bearing fruit all year long, but also natives who practically gave it all away to Columbus and his men "bartering like idiots." Each island proved to be wealthier in goods and more fertile than the last. Columbus noted that even if the native people's amiability did not last, it would be easy to control them because they were unarmed, naked and timid.

Claiming the islands for Ferdinand and Isabella, Columbus described harbors ideally suited for trade and left men behind to establish a fortress in the most commercially promising port. At the end of the letter, Columbus asks Ferdinand and Isabella to invest more money into the venture, which, of course, they did.

The description in this letter is mainly of Cuba (Juana) and the Dominican Republic/Haiti (Española). Columbus returned to the New World three more times. Although the commercial promise of the initial voyage proved accurate, the amicable relations between natives and Europeans quickly deteriorated. A brilliant navigator, Columbus proved to be an incompetent administrator of the new empire, ending his days in prison, despised by his men.

A Letter addressed to the noble Lord Raphael Sanchez, Treasurer to their most invincible Majesties, Ferdinand and Isabella, King and Queen of Spain, by Christopher Columbus, to whom our age is greatly indebted, treating of the islands of India recently discovered beyond the Ganges, to explore which he had been sent eight months before under the auspices and at the expense of their said Majesties.

Knowing that it will afford you pleasure to learn that I have brought my undertaking to a successful termination, I have decided upon writing you this letter to acquaint you with all the events which have occurred in my voyage, and the discoveries which have resulted from it. Thirty-three days after my departure from Cadiz I reached the Indian sea, where I discovered many islands, thickly peopled, of which I took possession without resistance in the name of our most illustrious Monarch, by public proclamation and with unfurled banners. To the first of these islands, which is called by the Indians Guanahani, I gave the name of the blessed Saviour (San Salvador), relying upon whose protection I had reached this as well as the other islands; to each of these I also gave a name, ordering that one should be called Santa Maria de la Concepcion, andother Fernandina, the third Isabella, the fourth Juana, and so with all the rest respectively. As soon as we arrived at that, which as I have said was named Juana, I proceeded along its coast a short distance westward, and found it to be so large and apparently without termination, that I could not suppose it to be an island, but the continental province of Cathay.

Seeing, however, no towns or populous places on the sea coast, but only a few detached houses and cottages, with whose inhabitants I was unable to communicate, because they fled as soon as they saw us, I went further on, thinking that in my progress I should certainly find some city or village. At length after proceeding a great way and finding that nothing new presented itself, and that the line of coast was leading us northward … I resolved not to attempt any further progress, but rather to turn back and retrace my course to a certain bay that I had observed, and from which I afterwards dispatched two of our men to ascertain whether there were a king or any cities in that province. These men reconnoitered the country for three days, and found a most numerous population, and great numbers of houses, though small, and built without any regard to order: with which information they returned to us. In the mean time I had learned from some Indians whom I had seized, that that country was certainly an island: and therefore I sailed towards the east, coasting to the distance of 322 miles, which brought us to the extremity of it; from this point I saw lying eastwards another island, 54 miles distant from Juana, to which I gave the name Española:…

This said island of Juana is exceedingly fertile, as indeed are all the others; it is surrounded with many bays, spacious, very secure, and surpassing any that I have ever seen; numerous large and healthful rivers intersect it; and it also contains many very lofty mountains. All these islands are very beautiful, and distinguished by a diversity of scenery; they are filled with a great variety of trees of immense height, and which I believe to retain their foliage in all seasons; for when I saw them they were as verdant and luxuriant as they usually are in Spain in the month of May—some of them were blossoming, some bearing fruit, and all flourishing in the greatest perfection, according to their respective stages of growth, and the nature and quality of each… There are besides in the same island of Juana seven or eight kinds of palm trees, which, like all the other trees, herbs, and fruits, considerably surpass ours in height and beauty. The pines are also very handsome, and there are very extensive fields and meadows, a variety of birds, different kinds of honey, and many sorts of metals, but no iron.

In that island also which I have before said we named Española, there are mountains of very great size and beauty, vast plains, groves, and very fruitful fields, admirably adapted for tillage, pasture, and habitation. The convenience and excellence of the harbors in this island, and the abundance of the rivers, so indispensable to the health of man, surpass anything that would be believed by one who had not seen it. The trees, herbage, and fruits of Española are very different from those of Juana, and moreover it abounds in various kinds of spices, gold and other metals. The inhabitants of both sexes in this island, and in all the others which I have seen, or of which I have received information, go always naked as they were born... None of them, as I have already said, are possessed of any iron, neither have they weapons, being unacquainted with, and indeed incompetent to use them, not from any deformity of body (for they are well-formed), but because they are timid and full of fear. They carry however in lieu of arms, canes dried in the sun, on the ends of which they fix heads of dried wood sharpened to a point, and even these they dare not use habitually; for it has often occurred when I have sent two or three of my men to any of the villages to speak with the natives, that they have come out in a disorderly troop, and have fled in such haste at the approach of our men, that the fathers forsook their children and the children their fathers....

As soon however as they see that they are safe, and have laid aside all fear, they are very simple and honest, and exceedingly liberal with all they have; none of them refusing any thing he may possess when he is asked for it, but on the contrary inviting us to ask them. They exhibit great love towards all others in preference to themselves: they also give objects of great value for trifles, and content themselves with very little or nothing in return. I however forbad that these trifles and articles of no value (such as pieces of dishes, plates, and glass, keys, and leather straps) should be given to them, although if they could obtain them, they imagined themselves to be possessed of the most beautiful trinkets in the world. It even happened that a sailor received for a leather strap as much gold as was worth three golden nobles, and for things of more trifling value offered by our men, especially newly coined blancas, or any gold coins, the Indians would give whatever the seller required; as, for instance, an ounce and a half or two ounces of gold, or thirty or forty pounds of cotton, with which commodity they were already acquainted. Thus, they bartered, like idiots, cotton and gold for fragments of bows, glasses, bottles, and jars;...

On my arrival at that sea, I had taken some Indians by force from the first island that I came to, in order that they might learn our language and communicate to us what they knew respecting the country; which plan succeeded excellently, and was a great advantage to us, for in a short time, either by gestures and signs, or by words, we were enabled to understand each other. These men are still traveling with me, and although they have been with us now a long time, they continue to entertain the idea that I have descended from heaven; and on our arrival at any new place they published this, crying out immediately with a loud voice to the other Indians, "come, come and look upon beings of a celestial race": upon which both women and men, children and adults, young men and old, when they got rid of the fear they at first entertained, would come out in throngs, crowding the roads to see us some bringing food, others drink, with astonishing affection and kindness....

The extent of Española is greater than all Spain.... This island is to be regarded with especial interest, and not be slighted; for although as I have said I took possession of all these islands in the name of our invincible King, and the government of them is unreservedly committed to his said Majesty, yet there was one large town in Española of which especially I took possession, situated in a remarkably favorable spot, and in every way convenient for the purposes of gain and commerce. To this town I gave the name of navidad del Señor, and ordered a fortress to be built there, which must by this time be complete, in which I left as many men as I thought necessary, with all sorts of arms, and enough provisions for more than a year. I also left them one caravel, and skillful workmen both in ship-building and other arts, and engaged the favor and friendship of the King of the island in their behalf, to a degree that would not be believed, for these people are so amiable and friendly that even the King took a pride in calling me his brother. But supposing their feelings should become changed, and they should wish to injure those who have remained in the fortress, they could not do so, for they have no arms, they go naked, and are moreover cowardly; so that those who hold the said fortress, can easily keep the whole island in check....

They assure me that there is another island larger than Española, whose inhabitants have no hair, and which abounds in gold more than any of the rest. I bring with me individuals of this island and of the others that I have seen, who are proofs of the facts which I state. Finally, to compress into few words the entire summary of my voyage and speedy return, and of the advantages derivable therefrom, I promise, that with a little assistance afforded me by our most invincible sovereigns, I will procure them as much gold as they need, as great a quantity of spices, of cotton, and of mastic (which is only found in Chios), and as many men for the service of the navy as their Majesties may require. I promise also rhubarb and other sorts of drugs, which I am persuaded the men whom I have left in the aforesaid fortress have found already and will continue to find;... Although all I have related may appear to be wonderful and unheard of, yet the results of my voyage would have been more astonishing if I had had at my disposal such ships as I required....

Therefore let the king and queen, our princes and their most happy kingdoms, and all the other provinces of Christendom, render thanks to our Lord and Saviour Jesus Christ, who has granted us so great a victory and such prosperity. Let processions be made, and sacred feasts be held, and the temples be adorned with festive boughs. Let Christ rejoice on earth, as he rejoices in heaven in the prospect of the salvation of the souls of so many nations hitherto lost. Let us also rejoice, as well on account of the exaltation of our faith, as on account of the increase of our temporal prosperity, of which not only Spain, but all Christendom will be partakers.

Such are the events which I have briefly described. Farewell.

Lisbon, the 14th of March.

Christopher Columbus,

Admiral of the Fleet of the Ocean

HENRY VII TO JOHN CABOT

"Letters patents of King Henry the seventh frante unto John Cabot"

After news of Columbus's discovery spread throughout Europe, other monarchs authorized voyages to the New World. Giovanni Caboto came to Bristol, England, in the 1480s as a merchant adventurer keen. He convinced Henry VII to grant him the patent to find undiscovered lands while taking a northern route across the Atlantic Ocean. He set sail from Bristol on May 2, 1497, and arrived in Labrador, claiming the region for England. The cost of the trip was borne by Bristol merchants.

March 5, 1496

The Letters patents of King Henry the seventh grante unto John Cabot and his three sonnes, Lewis, Sebastian and Sancius for the discoverie of new and unknowen lands.

Henry, by the grace of God, king of England and France, and lord of Ireland, to all to whom these presents shall come, greeting.

Be it knowen that we have given and granted, and by these presents do give and and grant for us and our heires, to our welbeloved John Cabot citizen of Venice, to Lewis, Sebastian, and Santius, sonnes of the sayd John, and to the heires of them, and every of them, and their deputies, full and free authority, leave, and power to saile to all parts, countreys, and seas of the East, of the West, and of the North, under our banners and ensignes, with five ships of what burthen or quantity soever they be, and as many mariners or men as they will have with them in the sayd ships, upon their owne proper costs and charges, to seeke out, discover, and finde whatsoever isles, countreys, regions or provinces of the heathen and infidels whatsoever they be, and in what part of the world soever they be, which before this time have bene unknowen to all Christians: we have granted to them, and also to every of them, and their deputies, and have given them license to set up our banners and ensignes in every village, towne, castle, isle, ore maine land of them newly found. And that the aforesayd John and his sonnes, or their heires and assignes may subdue, occupy and possesse all such townes, cities, castles and isles of them found, which they can subdue, occupy and possesse, as our vassals, and lieutenants, getting unto us the rule, title, and jurisdiction of the same villages, townes, castles, & firme land so found. Yet so that the aforesayd John, and his sonnes and heires, and their deputies, be holden and bounden of all the fruits, profits, gaines, and commodities growing of such navigation, for every their voyage, as often as they shall arrive at our port of Bristoll (at which port they shall be bound and holden onely to arrive) all manner of necessary costs and charges by them made, being deducted, to pay unto us in wares or money the fift part of the capitall gaine so gotten. We giving and granting unto them and to their heires and deputies, that they shall be free from all paying of customes of all and singular they shall bring with them from those places so newlie found.

And morever, we have given and granted to them, their heires and deputies, that all the firme lands, isles, villages, townes, castles and places whatsoever they be that they shall chance to finde, may not of any other of our subjects be frequented or visited without the licence of the foresayd John and his sonnes, and their deputies, under payne of forfeiture as well of their ships as of all them that shall chance to finde, may not of any other of our subjects be frequented or visited without the licence of the foresayd John and his sonnes, and their deputies, under payne of forfeiture as well of their ships as of all and singular goods of all them that shall presume to saile to those places so found. Willing, and most straightly commanding all and singular subjects as well on land as on sea, appointed officers, to give good assistance to the aforesaid John, and his sonnes and deputies, and that as well in arming and furnishing their ships or vessels, as in provision of queietnesse, and in buying victuals for their money, and all other things by them to be provided necessary for the sayd navigation, they do give them all their helpe and faver. In witnesse whereof we have caused to be made these our letters patents. Witnesse our selfe at Westminister, the fifth day of March, in the eleventh year of our reigne.

FUGGER CORRESPONDENT TO SIGNOR ADELGAIS
"A pepper store is a fine business"

After European explorers and adventurers first took the most valuable possessions they encountered in new lands, they often then set about developing permanent business enterprises. In the 1500s, Portugal extended a series of holdings along the African coast and southern Asia, including the Spice Islands in India.

Although German states did not colonize other parts of the world, the German banking house Fugger pursued commercial interests across the globe. One of its correspondents sent back the following letter describing the pepper business in India. Like other colonies, opportunities for new markets and products abounded.

From Cochin in India, the 10th day of January 1580.

Honourable, most kindly and dear Signor Adelgais!

Before my departure from Lisbon I informed you how I with my companions boarded our ships. Upon the 4th day of April 1579 all five vessels sailed from Lisbon at the same time; but we did not however, keep together for more than six days, but each soon struck out on its own course, since each captain or pilot believes he knows best how to arrive first at the goal. Although these ships are big and powerful, they strive not to stay together…. We arrived, thanks and praise be to the lord Almighty, upon the 10th day of October at the town of Goa, which belongs to the King of Portugal and is the finest capital in this country. Thus we have been on our way here from Lisbon six months and six days, and during that time have seen no land, only the sky and the sea. The lord god bestows on such journeys His special blessing and mercy, for otherwise it would not be possible to spend half a year between the planks. To sum up, whosoever is well equipped with provisions and a cook, both of which were mine, thanks to the Lord, feels the hardships of such a voyage less than the common people, who suffer great distress from lack of food and drink, especially water, which no money can buy. In such heat one cannot partake of much wine, only water of which, thanks be to God, I had in sufficient quantity with our food. There were about five hundred persons in our ship of whom not more than twenty-five altogether died on the way from Portugal to India….

Our ships have all five arrived from Lisbon, namely, three in Goa and two here. Now all five ships are here in Coshin. I made a sojourn of four weeks in the town of Goa and built me there a house. From thence I travelled one hundred miles onwards by sea. The voyage can be made in ten to twelve days. The ships are loaded with pepper here in Cochin, twenty miles from Calicut, wherefore they all have to come to this place. I shall maintain two establishments, one in Goa and the other here. I have not yet, however, resolved upon which shall fall my choice for remaining definitely. Although Goa is the capital in which the Viceroy of Portugal holds his Court, it is wearisome to journey back and forth every year, as I needs must be present in this our pepper store.

Such a pepper store is a fine business, but it requires great zeal and perseverance. It takes six weeks to receive the pepper from the heathen King of Cochin, who is our friend, and to load it into our ships. After the departure of these ships for Portugal I and my servants have but little to do. The pepper business is profitable indeed; when the Lord God grants by His mercy that none of the ships take damage either in coming or going, then the merchants wax rich....

This year, in my judgment, we shall not dispatch more than four ships with about twenty loads, although we ought to send thirty. We already possess the money, for so large a sum would not be obtainable by loan. What we are lacking this day can be bought, given a good opportunity, after the sailing of these ships for next year. Of all other spices such as cloves, nutmeg, flour and nuts, cinnamon, maces, and various drugs, this year's supplies are going to Portugal. In precious stones little was dispatched this year on account of the war, which the heathen Kings (of which there are many in this country) waged one upon another. Because of this, precious stones cannot come through from inland into our towns since all of them lie upon the shores of the sea.

All that lieth inland belongs to the Indians, heathens and Moors. We boast of the friendship of two or three of these Kings, but the majority are our enemies. Our fleet is continually fighting them at sea. The King of Portugal despite all his power is too weak for this vast country. The King of Spain, if he but took possession of Portugal, would be the right King for these lands. He should take over the whole of India, all the kingdoms and provinces right into China, where it adjoins Tartary, and unite under his rule his Spanish India with the Portuguese municipalities: this could be accomplished with fifty thousand men. Even though the Indian Kings have a goodly number of warriors, and there are many such Kings, they are not good fighters. One Christian can achieve more than six Indians. Besides, these Kings are continually involved in strife and quarrels amongst themselves.

JAN VAN RYEN TO THE DUTCH WEST INDIA COMPANY
"The blacks are more inclined to work than the Dutch"

The Dutch West India Company settled the New Netherlands (later New York and New Jersey) in the 1620s. This letter from a commander at one of three settlements shows the difficult and dangerous conditions faced by those attempting to start a commercial enterprise in the New World. In addition to sometimes hostile relations with local Native Americans, Jan van Ryen had to work with rotting equipment, feuding soldiers and lazy settlers.

The Honorable, Wise, Most Prudent Gentlemen, the Directors of the Chartered West India Company, at the Chamber of Zeeland

Honorable, most prudent Gentlemen:

After greetings, this serves to inform you that we arrived safely in the river of Wiapeco and landed there with our ammunition and other goods entrusted to us. Praise be to God. As soon as we came into the river, we learned that Captain Haudaen's men came here with a bark and divided themselves over three places. For some time they lived peacefully together, but as a quarrel had arisen between the Lieutenant and the Sergeant, it happened that the Lieutenant, coming from Cannaribo, and bringing with him much cassava and other provisions, was welcomed by the Sergeant, who at once took a pistol and shot him with it. The Sergeant was put in irons, but released again after a fortnight and made Lieutenant. Proceeding farther up the river, they fired a shot from the bark and forced the Indians to bring them cassava and other victuals, and, as the Indians were a little slow about it, the Sergeant beat them and threatened to shoot them. This provoked the Indians, who were, moreover, incited by the English to attack the Dutch. For when the Dutch had visited the English and asked what the Dutch had said, the English told them that the Dutch had come here to kill the Indians. So that the Indians, having been hurt in the first place by the arrogance of the Dutch, were on the other hand stirred up by the English, which were the principal reasons why the Indians attacked our people there in three places, first near the shore, thereafter here, where I am encamped now with my troop, and thirdly at Canaribo, so that of the fifty that were there but three escaped with their lives, of whom we have kept one with us and are sending over the others.

Concerning our plantation, I hope to send the gentlemen some of the products by the next ships, praise be to God. I have at present almost 2000 tobacco plants in the ground, which have already been transplanted and which are in fine condition. I hope daily to transplant more, but as it is impossible for me to cross the river without sloop or canoe, I am unable to get more plants. The Indians are not willing to barter a canoe, small or large, even if I offered them as many as 20 axes for it, for they fear and believe that we have come to avenge the other Dutchmen. I have tried my best to convince them of the contrary, but they have little confidence in this, and consequently I cannot procure on. I also need 20 more men to plant the sugar-cane, for there are too few of us here to start the plantation, and I do not like to divide my men as long as the times remain so uncertain. I would also request to have blacks sent rather than Dutchmen, for the blacks are more inclined to work than the Dutch.

As to the cotton, I have about 1000 plants in the ground, which grow up nicely, so that next year or with the first ships I shall send the Company some of the fruits. No more for the present, except to pray the very honorable and reverend gentlemen not to fail to send me a sloop similar to Captain Claude's, for I am here on an island and cannot go father than to the water's edge, and there I can only stand and look. Besides, the honorable gentlemen promised me a sloop at the time we made our agreement, and, furthermore, we cannot accomplish anything with the net that was given to us, without a sloop. Moreover, the net is half-rotten, and instead of having a new net, as was sent along for me, Jan Pieters has given me the aforesaid old rotten net, so that we shall hardly be able to make a haul with it without tearing it. Some day I hope to make him pay for that, as one who violated his oath. No more for the present, gentlemen, but to wish the Company all happiness and prosperity and to recommend myself to your honors. If you have any further order to give me, I pray your honors not to spare me. Actum, the 25th of Aprial, in Wiapeco, at Fort Nassau, year 1625.

Jan van Ryan

CH'IEN LUNG TO GEORGE III
"Strange and costly objects do not interest me"

Poet, scholar and one of the greatest emperors in Chinese history, Ch'ien Lung had led China for nearly 60 years when he received a British delegation sent by George III in 1793 to gain trade concessions in China for the East India Company. China at that time was one of the wealthiest and best-organized countries in the world. European merchants were eager to tap into its potentially lucrative markets.

Ch'ien Lung, however, had seen how trade concessions in neighboring India helped lead the transfer of power to British merchants and away from local authorities. Unimpressed by the entreaties of the British delegates, Ch'ien rejected the offer to expand trade relations.

You, O King, live beyond the confines of many seas, nevertheless, impelled by your humble desire to partake of the benefits of our civilization, you have dispatched a mission respectfully bearing your memorial. Your envoy has crossed the seas and paid his respects at my court on the anniversary of my birthday. To show your devotion you have also sent offerings of your country's produce.

I have perused your memorial: the earnest terms in which it is couched reveal a respectful humility on your part, which is highly praiseworthy. In consideration of the fact that your ambassador and his deputy have come a long way with your memorial and tribute I have showed them high favor and have allowed them to be introduced into my presence. To manifest my indulgence I have entertained them at a banquet and made them many gifts. I have also caused presents to be forwarded to the naval Commander and six hundred of his officers and men, although they did not come to Beijing, so that they too may share in my all-embracing kindness.

As to your entreaty to send one of your nationals to be accredited to my Celestial Court and to be in control of your country's trade with China, this request is contrary to all usage in my dynasty and cannot possibly be entertained. It is true that Europeans, in the service of the dynasty, have been permitted to live at Beijing, but they are compelled to adopt Chinese dress, they are strictly confined to their own precincts and are never permitted to return home. You are presumably familiar with our dynastic regulations. Your proposed envoy to my Court could not be placed in a position similar to that of European officials in Beijing who are forbidden to leave China, nor could he, on the other hand, be allowed liberty of movement and the privilege of corresponding with his own country; so that you would gain nothing by his residence in our midst.

Moreover our Celestial dynasty possesses vast territories, and tribute missions from the dependencies are provided for by the Department of for Tributary States, which ministers to their wants and exercises strict control over their movements. It would be quite impossible to leave them to their own devices. Supposing that your envoy should come to our Court, his language and national dress differ from that of our people, and there would be no place in which to bestow him. It may be suggested that he might imitate the Europeans permanently resident in Beijing and adopt the dress and customs of China, but it has never been our dynasty's wish to force people to do things unseemly and inconvenient. Besides, suppose I sent an ambassador to reside in your country, how could you possibly make for him the requisite arrangements? Europe consists of many other nations besides your own: if each and all demanded to be represented at our Court, how could we possibly consent? The thing is utterly impracticable. How can your dynasty alter its whole procedure and system of etiquette, established for more than a century, in order to meet your individual views?…

If you assert that your reverence for our Celestial dynasty fills you with a desire to acquire our civilization, our ceremonies and code of laws differ so completely from your own that, even if your envoy were able to acquire the rudiments of our civilization, you could not possibly transplant our manners and customs to your alien soil. Therefore, however adept the envoy might become, nothing would be gained thereby.

Swaying the wide world, I have but one aim in view, namely to maintain a perfect governance and to fulfill the duties of the state: strange and costly objects do not interest me. If I have commanded that the tribute offerings sent by you, O King, are to be accepted, this was solely in consideration for the spirit which prompted you to dispatch them from afar. Our dynasty's majestic virtue has penetrated into every country under heaven, and kings of all nations have offered their costly tribute by land and sea. As your ambassador can see for himself we possess all things. I set no value on objects strange and ingenious, and have no use for your country's manufactures. This then is my answer to your request to appoint a representative at my Court, a request contrary to our dynastic usage, which could only result in inconvenience to yourself. I have expounded my wishes in detail and have commanded your tribute envoys to leave in peace on their homeward journeys. It behooves you, O King, to respect my sentiments and to display even greater and loyalty in the future, so that, by perpetual submission to our throne, you may secure peace and prosperity for your country hereafter. Besides making gifts (of which I enclose an inventory) to each member of your mission, I confer upon you, O King, valuable presents in excess of the number bestowed on such occasions, including silks and curios—a list of which is likewise enclosed. Do you reverently receive them and take note of my tender good will toward you!

THOMAS JEFFERSON TO MERRYWEATHER LEWIS
"Instructions to Lewis"

When Thomas Jefferson decided to purchase the Louisiana Territory from France in 1803 for $15 million, it was the largest real estate transaction in American history, doubling the size of the country overnight. The 827,192-square-mile parcel stretched from Louisiana to Wyoming and included most of the Great Plains.

As this letter of instruction to Meriwether Lewis makes clear, Jefferson was interested in the commercial opportunities of the American West. Lewis and William Clark took three years to make their journey, the first cross-continental expedition across what is now the United States.

To Merryweather Lewis, Esq., Captain of the 1st Regiment of Infantry of the United States of America

Your situation as the Secretary of the President of the United States has made you acquainted with the object of my confidential message of Jan. 18, 1803, to the legislature. You have seen the act they passed, which, tho' expressed in general terms, was meant to sanction those objects, and you are appointed to carry them into execution....

The object of your mission is to explore the Missouri river, & such principal stream of it, as, by its course & communication with the water of the Pacific Ocean may offer the most direct and practicable water communication across this continent, for the purposes of commerce....

Your observations are to be taken with great pains & accuracy to be entered distinctly, & intelligibly for others as well as yourself, to comprehend all the elements necessary, with the aid of the usual tables to fix the latitude & longitude of the places at which they were taken, & are to be rendered to the war office, for the purpose of having the calculations made concurrently by proper persons within the U. S. Several copies of these as well as of your other notes, should be made at leisure times & put into the care of the most trustworthy of your attendants, to guard by multiplying them against the accidental losses to which they will be exposed. A further guard would be that one of these copies be written on the paper of the birch, as less liable to injury from damp than common paper.

The commerce which may be carried on with the people inhabiting the line you will pursue, renders a knolege of these people important. You will therefore endeavor to make yourself acquainted, as far as a diligent pursuit of your journey shall admit,

with the names of the nations & their numbers;

the extent & limits of their possessions;

their relations with other tribes or nations;

their language, traditions, monuments;

their ordinary occupations in agriculture, fishing, hunting, war, arts, & the implments of these;

their food, clothing & domestic accommodations;

the diseases prevalent among them, & the remedies they use;

moral and physical circumstances which distinguish them from the tribes they know;

peculiarities in their laws, customs & dispositions;

and articles of commerce they may need or furnish & to what extent.

Other objects worthy of notice will be

The soil & face of the country, its growth & vegetable productions especially those not of the U. S.

The animals of the country generally, & especially those not known in the U. S.

The remains & accounts of any which may be deemed rare or extinct;

The mineral productions of every kind; but more particularly metals, limestone, pit coal & saltpetre; salines & mineral waters, noting the temperature of the last & such circumstances as may indicate their character; volcanic appearances; climate as characterized by the thermometer, by the proportion of rainy, cloudy & clear days, by lightning, hail, snow, ice, by the access & recess of frost, by the winds, prevailing at different seasons, the dates at which particular plants put forth or lose their flowers, or leaf, times of appearance of particular birds, repitles or insects....

In all your intercourse with the natives treat them in the most friendly & conciliatory manner which their own conduct will admit; allay all jealousies as to the object of your journey, satisfy them of it's innocence, make them acquainted with the position, extent, character, peaceable & commercial dispositions of the U. S., of our wish to be neighborly, friendly & useful to them, & of our dispositions to a commercial intercourse with them; confer with them on the points most convenient as mutual emporiums, & the articles of the most desirable interchange for them & us....

President Thomas Jefferson

MOSES AUSTIN TO J. E. B. AUSTIN

"I shall take with me about 30 young men to commence the settlement"

Shortly after being wiped out by a financial panic in 1819, banker Moses Austin conceived the idea of starting an American settlement in the Mexican province of Texas. His previous experience had included stints as a dry goods merchant in Philadelphia and Richmond, and as owner of lead mines in Virginia and Missouri.

Austin wrote a letter to one of his sons explaining his goals shortly after asking the Mexican government for a land grant. Moses Austin, however, died before being able to realize his plan. Another son, Stephen Austin, followed through on his father's idea.

April 8, 1821

St. Louis, Missouri

... I much wish to see you return to this country before I leave it for the Spanish province of Texas. I have made a visit to St. Antonio and obtained liberty to settle in that country—*as I am, ruined in this*, I found nothing I could do would bring back my property again and to remain in a Country where I had enjoyed *welth* in a state of *poverty* I could Not submit to I therefore made an *exertion* and obtained what I asked for a right of settlement for myself and family the situation I have marked out is on the Colorado about 3 Days sale from New Orleans or rather from the Belise a most delightful situation.... I have asked for leave of settlement for 300 families and 200 Thousand Acres of Land to open a Port Town at the mouth of the River which has been granted me by the Governor of the Province of Texas and has gone on to the Vice King for his confirmation, I have been offered as many Names of respectable families as will make up the Number but until I return I shall not admit any as my wish is to have the lands surveyed before I introduce any families at all. I shall take with me about 30 young men to commence the settlement and return after your mother next years....

STEPHEN F. AUSTIN TO JAMES F. PERRY
"I have opened a fine field for human enterprise"

Stephen F. Austin became known as the Father of Texas because of his diligent efforts to enable pioneers from the United States to settle in what was then northern Texas in the 1820s and 1830s. One reason for his success was his reputation as an honest broker between settlers and the Mexican government.

In this letter to a friend in the northeast, he gives an update on the status of the settlement, places orders for goods that were diffiuclt or impossible to secure in the largely unsettled Texas, and suggests an opportunity to open a trading post.

Although Austin writes that his relations with Mexico were good, they soon deteriorated as American settlers bristled under Mexican rule. Austin was thrown in a Mexican prison shortly before Texas waged a successful war of independence against Mexico. As Austin predicts, he never made much money in Texas. Nevertheless, his contribution was acknowledged when the state's capital city was named after him.

San Felipe de Austin July 11 1830

Dr Brother

I wrote to you a few days ago to Potosi and to Philadelphia and now improve the opportunity presented by Cap Brown who goes direct to new york in the Sloop Nelson he is a settler here and has a good house at Brazoria, and intends returning immediately with a new vessel suitable for this trade—It would be a good opportunity for you to send out your goods. Col. Jesse Woodberry who was here with you goes out in the Nelson and will return in her should you wish for information write to Austin and Tayleur New York. The first of that house John P. Austin is a cousin of mine, a brother of Henry, Horace, etc. Woodberry will do his business with them.

Fisher the collector of Galveston has recd orders from govt to suspend the custom house at Galveston for the present[. T]he reason assigned is that no custom house is wanting, owing to the exemptions from duties and other laws in favor of Texas.

I made an engagement with Mr Morton to put me up a small brick house in this place that would do for you to winter in, but he has been sick, and I fear a total disappointment. The steam mill is going and does very well, and I will have a house ready, either here, or at the point on the bay—

I think it will not be material which place you land at, Brazoria or Harrisburgh, the water over red fish bar is about the same as over the Brazos far 5 feet—it will be convenient to send goods to Trinity from Harrisburgh—I think that you might bring out a considerable assortment and some indian goods among them one hundred troops are stationed on the brasos at the uppor or San Antonio road and a small store would do well there to supply them and the indians—there has been a great emigration and this fall it will be much greater than ever. I need some articles. I hold the commission of full colonel of the militia, the law requires that I should provide myself with a uniform. The uniform is that of a colonel of infantry of the Mexican Army, with gold epaulets and gold or yellow mounted sword etc.— The uniform coat and the epaulets ought to be made in a particular manner. And unless you could meet with some one in Pha who could give instructions about them, it would be difficult to get them of the right kind—Tho I must have a Sword, Sash, and belt, yellow Mounted. I also want a military surtout with a black silk cord and pantaloons trimmed in the same manner—All of navy blue clothe. Also a scarlet wescott with gold round cord on the edges, a pair of boots and yellow spurrs—As I am the highest militia officer of Texas it is expected that I should provide myself with these things and a handsome set of holsters. Also a yellow bitted bridle—I cannot use an american saddle, but should like a spanish saddle well rigged—that I can get here.

I want Vattel's law of nations in spanish, a portable writing desk, and a large plain secretary and book case to keep my private papers in—such a thing cannot be got here except at great cost.

If Tanner makes a good profit out of the Map I sent him he ought to give me one of his best bound and last American Atlass, it is the best now extant and would be very useful to teach the children geography—

I have sent the Texas gasette containing the law of 6 april to the Editor of the Nat. Gazette where you can see it. I wish you to subscribe for that paper and for the quarterly review for me, and have them sent in packages to an agent in new orleans to be sent out by provate conveyance by water, otherwise I shall not get the half of them, and if such an arrangement cannot be made it will be useless to take them.

Our colony matters are getting on very well, there is the utmost harmony among the settlers and between them and the Government. All the difficulties which appeared to be brewing when you were here about stopping emigration from the U. S. have passed away and I have been officially informed that I can go on and introduce the whole number of families I have contracted for and finish all my contracts—My standing with the Govt. has always been good and it is better now than ever, for they know more of me owing to the investigations which the stir in april created, by which it has appeared that I am the only empressario that has done any thing who has performed his duty and followed the law in good faith. The advertisements in the U. S. papers by D. A. Smith and others to sell millions of acres in Texas has done great harm for all that kind of speculation is fraudulent and it threw a shade of suspicion and censure at first, over all empressarios. My letter to Leaming that was published in the Nat. Gazette has made some of those speculating gentlemen my bitter and deadly enemies—and they are now secretly at work in Mexico to try to get revenge by injuring me—they will find themselves gnawing a file—

I wrote to Leaming to send me a genealogical account of my mothers family—call on him for it. Also bring or send me the number of the Nat. Gazette that has my letter about selling Texas lands—I wish for it to send to the Govt. in case those gentry should attempt to injure me, also get the newspapers that contain their advertisements on the subject.

Instead of roaming about in other countries to speculate I have devoted my life to the arduous task of trying to redeem this country from the wilderness and I have succeeded greatly beyond what was supposed possible, for I was ridiculed for attempting such a thing. I had no capital, and have supplied its defect by personal labor and attention, and by putting my shoulder to the wheel in earnest and in good faith. I have not made a fortune for my self (except in lands which now have no value) and probably shall not live to derive much personal benefit, but I have greatly benefited many others, hundreds of them, and made them and their families rich who were worth nothing before, and I have opened and enlarged a fine field for human enterprise and human happiness. This has always been the main object of my ambition and not a mere avaricious view to personal speculation. I have no fears that my motives or my acts will not receive the reward in public opinion which they merit, or that a few speculators can materially injure me, but they may harrass me. In a democratic republic enemies are sometimes more troublesome and dangerous than in any other form of Govt. for popular opinion is as often moved by whim or accident, as by reason or justice.

Farewell I long to see you that we may all settle down on a quiet Stock farm far from the reach of politics or popular whims—

S. F. Austin

LETTERS OF THE CALIFORNIA GOLD RUSH
"Reality exceeds our expectations"

The California gold rush of 1849 was one of the great economic manias in American history. Tens of thousands of prospectors, swindlers and legitimate enterprises descended on California in search of gold and profits. Almost overnight, San Francisco was transformed from a dusty village into a booming city.

The following three letters from participants illustrate the range of opportunities, pitfalls and challenges that confronted them. The first letter is from representatives of Macondray & Company to their eastern attorney, J. M. Forbes, describing the conditions and financial opportunities they found upon arrival.

The second letter is a series of requests for materials and money from Edward Austin to his brother to help him set up a bar in San Francisco, which would soon become known as one of the world's most sinful cities. Prospector Augustus West wrote the third letter to a friend describing the hard work involved in prospecting and the disappointments of many who arrived thinking that mining gold was an easy proposition.

The Macondary representatives' prediction of unsustainable manic business conditions proved accurate. The boom soon turned to bust. Most of the prospectors did not strike it rich. Nevertheless, the gold rush brought people and investments to California. And, as West wrote, many enjoyed "the comforts of California with good zest" and decided to stay. It marked the start of California's rapid growth as the most prosperous state in the United States.

1 September 1849

We arrived here on the 18th prepared to find an extraordinary state of things, and confess the reality exceeds our expectations. A speculation is going on here in real estate wilder than anything that we have known. Lots of land which sold for $1500 six months since have sold lately for $15,000 [to] $20,000, and the mania is not confined to this place alone. The old game of paper cities is playing through this whole place. Lots in Sacramento City 80 by 80 bring $15,000, and titles here are all worthless. Quit claims are the only transfer of property, and such a thing as a warranted deed is unknown, except a swindling warranted, which warrants and defends against one's self their heirs and executors.

It is all based upon credit, a small per centage only being paid down. We see nothing to warrant such a state of things except the enormous rates of rents. In some instances a man can pay these enormous rates, erect a building, and let rooms enough to pay the whole rent in one year. Gamblers infest the place, and by the enormous rates which they are able to pay—$1800 a month in some instances—establish the rents. Almost the entire population is involved in this mania, so that money is very scarce and brings enormous rates…. How long it may continue you can tell as well as we can, but it seems to us that there must be a wind up before long.

This state of things has embarrassed us somewhat in getting a place suitable to do our business in, but we have refused to purchase real estate, preferring to pay high rates for short leases believing that these prices must come down. The market is generally overstocked…. Of course there is no such thing as insurance here, and if a fire should take place during the high winds which prevail daily, the whole place would be swept.

We find a much better population than we expected. There is better security for property here than in N.Y. The streets in the evening or Sunday are as quiet as a New England village. Doors are left unlocked at night and large amounts of gold are left unguarded in counting rooms remote from dwellings, and goods unwatched on the beach. Immense quantities of good[s] are suffering for want of storage and must be ruined when the rainy season comes on, as it will be impossible to get storage for them, and we fear our friends will receive some Flemish accounts.

The receipts from the mines continue undiminished and new deposits are continually discovered. We can say to you what we would not to anyone else, that we believe the largest houses here are very much embarrassed and we should feel no confidence in consigning to them, and further, that business is generally conducted in a careless manner and with great unfaithfulness to the interests of the principals. This may seem to you presumptuous, after so short a residence here, but we cannot resist the evidence which come to our notice. It is perfectly idle for us to quote prices for anything and we refuse to do so, for the greatest irregularities exist in the market. No quotations can be relied on as a basis for future transactions. Everything must depend upon the amount of goods coming here.

We regret that we have not been able to do anything for you in Gold dust for this Steamer. She takes a large amount of specie no doubt, but shippers generally prefer sending the dust under insurance, and so much money is locked up here in real estate that merchants do not seem ready to make prompt remittances. Then we have been here but a short time and we have actually found some difficulty in drawing the whole amount placed in Appleton's hands…. There is no demand here for Exchange or London, we have not had one application, which is also the case with an agent of the Rothschild's who came out with us. We think we shall be able to do something for you by the next Steamer. We think a decided advantage might be gained if you would authorize us to draw at 60 ds. sight when we cannot ship the dust by the same steamer which takes the Bills, as they refuse freight for 24 hours before sailing day, and people often put off buying Exchange to the last moment. If we could draw up to the closing of the *mails*, we might often, we think, do so at an advanced rate and you could by a subsequent steamer get the dust nearly if not in time to meet the Bills. Sixty day Bills are the custom here.

The Mennon arrived on the 28th and is consigned to us. She is our first ship. Most of her cargo is well adapted to the market and we hope we shall be able to send her owners a good account of her. The labor scheme has been generally a failure. They break up almost without an exception immediately on arrival. We shall use what influence we have to prevent this [from taking] place when those in which you are interested arrive.

Edward Austin to his brother
24 September 1849

[Send] enough cherry boards for a good bar to the two story house. That house will rent for 60$ per day. Some fancy paper—say, some hunting scene or something like that—which will set it off to good advantage. I believe I wrote for paint and oil. The invoice I ordered before of tumblers, decanters, &c will answer for the fixtures. I am to have nothing to do with the concern except to collect the rents. And also send a few chairs—say, one dozen like those I had in my country room. Send out a few—say, four or six—chaste pictures of naked women with good frames. I put this in separate so that you can keep it "shady"—don't let the folks know any of this, not even Lucy, although I do not have any thing to do with it and would not, they might think hard of it....

I believe Frank can get any amount of goods, and tell him not to be bashful, I know the ropes of this country and the business. I have been in the country as long as most any one from the States. I arrived early, and should have been as rich had I funds on arrival. It is a hard place for one to accumulate money if he starts with out capital, but if you have money you can go it with a rush.

Oh George—it would make your eyes water as have mine, to see the noble chances slip by for a fortune, and you powerless for want of funds. If many had saved their money here and been prudent they could have gone home now rich. One young fellow in particular. He made $25,500 in four months in the mines up to last April. I saw him. Well, he came down to San Francisco and in five nights he was with out a cent, and had to work his passage up the river on the same vessel I came up on. He has sobered down and does not find it so easy to raise funds again. He has got now, he told me the other day, $1,400 and he was going to put it where the devil could not get it.

Augustus West to Peter DeWitt

31 August 1849

I have long since promised myself the pleasure of writing to you, in acknowledgement of your many esteemed favors of remembrance and regards so kindly extended since our sojourn here in this distant but none the less interesting country—and tho so long apparently remiss in doing so, I can but hope that even now I am still welcome, engrossed as I have been for months past in the exciting scenes and stirring events that have collected around us on every side, and at the same time an active participator and, as you may imagine, not a disinterested one.

I assure you that apart from those claims of a business character, I have had but a scanty respite to gratify the many wishes that I entertained to indulge myself in this more social and pleasing manner. But I am happy to say that now we have become more settled, and our affairs more in system and order, and duties that were at first without method are now defined so that I trust you, as well as many others, will hear from us two pioneers, rather more frequently. Both Alfred and myself have had a goodly share of this world's toil and trouble upon our hands, and with the inexperienced assistance we have had, you will readily conceive that our labors were but slightly lessened. If we have been fortunate perhaps in exceeding the expectations of our numerous friends, or if we have been successful in discharging the trust reposed in us, it has been accomplished, I may say literally, by the sweat of our brows.

Yet this is no more than all have to do at this time who would succeed and secure to himself a support for the future. This is truly no place for idlers or indolent men, and they make a great mistake who come out here bouyed up with the fallacious hopes created by the thousand and one rumors they hear of, about high rates, high prices &c; and how many are disappointed and become disgusted with the country, with themselves and everything else. And I dare say that ere this you may have heard the sorrowing representation of some unfortunates who, unfitted to combat with the realities that meet one here face to face, have sought again their less exacting homes. Instances easily occur that go to prove with how little reflection they embark to this country. Almost the first question asked is, "Well, I suppose there is plenty of gold?" You have "good times," "Making money," "getting rich"—supposing all a natural consequence, without toil or effort. Alas, they find the big lumps as well as the small are not to be had alone for the going for, and smarting hands, aching heads and sore limbs are more usually the results.

The mines still continue to yield abundance, and parties are fitting out to gather their share of the glittering dust, while others are returning quite content with getting back and satisfied, as tis termed, with the *Elephant*. Most of the associations have dissolved partnership and started on their own hook. Strange as it must seem, the old maxim of "Circumstances alter cases" annuls all previous engagements and of course breaks up, I may venture to say, every mining company that arrives.

Still there are many that are successful and who realize their expectations, but tis generally those of the hard working class, brought up to labor, tough as pine knots and case hardened. The Oregonians are the ones who make the most, for they can labor and toil and have no longings. As a class, I think they are the roughest, most hard working and penurious set of men I have ever seen—quite free from excess of any kind and saving to a penny, and I doubt if they have even an idea of what the comforts of life are.

Our City is growing up like magic, peopled with natives of every country and engaged in every profession and I question if there is ought that could be started that would be new. Our streets are fast becoming lined with houses—all stores or groghops or eating houses. Even the old sign-board is seen here and there to attract the passer by of "Cakes & Pies," "Pies & Cakes," "Hot Coffee," &c. During the day all is life and activity, wagons and carts, wheelbarrows, peddlars, musicians, and all sorts of things jostle you on every side. It is really wonderful to witness the great changes since last fall upon our arrival. One would scarce know the town, and at night when lit up by the numerous lights from the many dwellings that are scattered over a large space, presents to the eye a bright scene of a large City. Our harbour too wears the same busy, thriving look, quite in harmony with the confused appearance of the town—covering the whole front of the town, 6 and 7 deep, and so close that the eye can scarce find a break in the long line, and the many lighters passing to and fro from point to point along the beach, all tends to impress the stranger with the idea that this is a great place, tho a perfect anomaly to them.

But the papers you receive will give you a more general idea of our city than I can. But suffice it to say it has no equal for its age. Consider, but scarce nine months have elapsed and ships from every part of the globe almost, now lie in its harbour. Merchandise, also from every port, both Home and foreign, are now in the market and tho the business is now at the present time in my opinion at its lowest ebb, the time is fast approaching when it must assume a more healthy state. The state of the market here when known in N.Y. must cause a check as a general thing upon further shipments—and a revulsion in affairs must be the result. Notwithstanding the general stagnation in business, still scheming and speculation is carried on. To this there is no check and tis most surprising to see how successful are the operators. The state of scarcity here is hard to define, made up as it is of every material. I can only say that for its composition it does credit to the town. All is peace and quiet and no cause for apprehension....

We are all well with the exception of Henry who has a slight bilious attack, but he will be up again in a day or so. He is doing well with us and I find him a great assistance in our business. I can hardly say what I would wish to of our household affairs, but suffice it to say as far as I can speak we have a happy time of it and enjoy the comforts of California with good zest. It is now 12 o'c. Bidding you and all good night, with my best wishes for your continued health and prosperity. Believe me to be yrs truly Augustus.

JAMES M. TOWNSEND TO
CAPTAIN CHARLES HERVEY TOWNSEND
"[The oil business] may all fizzle"

Oil was first discovered and drilled for commercial purposes in western Pennsylvania in 1859. Although the new commodity seemed to offer promise, even the sponsors of the drill were skeptical of the long-term potential of oil, as this letter from James M. Townsend to his brother illustrates. Oil, however, boomed, and with it western Pennsylvania, ushering in a new era in industry and commerce.

New Haven, Conn., Dec. 16th, 1859

Dear brother Charles,

In haste but will drop you a few lines. Why don't you write? I thank you for your letter. Mother and all well, and everything so far as known all O.K. Last accounts from oil lands the oil had increased so that they were getting a gallon a minute. We have contracts with two parties who take one thousand gallons each a week, and everything looks very prosperous, but I don't calculate any upon it, it may all fizzle but so far it works well. I hope to get the agency and general agent in New York for brother William to manage. I am also managing to hire him to the other concern. If I do both sides will be nicely fixed I think. (Keep dark.) Then if it continues to work well, there will be some opening for George to manage I think, so that he can get out of the ice trade. But Charles this is all talk, for it may "fizzle." Now remember this, I don't count anything upon it and all I get I shall consider clear gain, so that if it all fizzles don't laugh at me, for I am determined not to count or depend anything upon it....

Your affectionate brother,

James

SIR ARNOLD WILSON TO BRITISH FOREIGN OFFICE
"See Psalm 104 verse 15"

As a young captain in the British Army, Arnold Wilson was stationed in southwest Persia (now Iran) looking for oil. On the morning of May 26, 1908, one of his team's two wells struck oil at a depth of 1,200 feet. The black liquid gushed 50 feet into the air. One of the largest oil finds in the Middle East had been discovered.

Wilson quickly sent the telegram below to the British Foreign Office, informing them of the discovery in an oblique message. The Biblical passages he refers to state: "That he may bring out of the earth oil to make him a cheerful countenance" and "the flint stone into a springing well."

Soon afterwards, Wilson wrote a letter to his father explaining the discovery's significance. "It is a great event," he wrote, "it remains to be seen whether the output will justify a pipe line to the coast, without which the field cannot be developed. It will provide all our ships east of Suez with fuel; it will strengthen British influence in these parts. It will make us less dependent on foreign-owned oil fields; it will be some reward to those who have ventured such great sums as have been spent. I hope it will mean some financial reward to the Engineers who have persevered so long, in spite of their wretched top-hatted directors in Glasgow, in this inhospitable climate. The only disadvantage is personal to myself—it will prolong my stay here!"

May 26, 1908

Bushire,

See Psalm 14 verse 15 third sentence and Psalm 114 verse 8 second sentence.

JEF RASKIN TO STEVE JOBS
"Starting with the abilities is nonsense"

Jef Raskin is credited with coming up with the original idea for the Apple Macintosh computer in 1979 and designing it with a small team of engineers. Envisioning a user-friendly computer that was light and portable, Raskin hoped to make the Macintosh relatively affordable at $500. It soon became obvious, however, that that would not be possible—it would be more like $1,500.

Apple founder Steve Jobs, however, told Raskin that the price was not his concern, but that he should tell him what the computer would include. Irked by the request, Raskin fired back a sarcastic memo with what at the time seemed to be a preposterous list of features. Twenty years later, the list doesn't seem ridiculous at all. Many of the components in Raskin's list eventually became standard features in Apple computers.

October 2, 1979

A small, lightweight computer with an excellent, typewriter style keyboard. It is accompanied by a 96 character by 66 line display that has almost no depth, and a letter-quality printer that also doesn't weigh much, and takes ordinary paper and produces text at one page per second (not so fast that you can't catch them as they come out). The printer can also produce any graphics the screen can show (with at least 1000 by 1200 points of resolution). In color.

The printer should weigh only a fraction of a pound, and never need a ribbon or mechanical adjustment. It should print in any font. There is about 200K bytes of main storage besides screen memory and a miniature, pocketable, storage element that holds a megabyte and costs $.50, in unit quantity.

When you buy the computer, you get a free unlimited access to the ARPAnet, the various timesharing services, and other informational, computer accessible data bases. Besides an unexcelled collection of application programs, the software includes BASIC, pascal, LISP, FORTRAN, APL, PL\1, COBOL, and an emulator for every processor since the IBM 650.Let's include speech synthesis and recognition, with a vocabulary of 34,000 words. It can also synthesize music, even simulate Caruso singing with the Mormon Tabernacle Choir, with variable reverberation.

Conclusion: starting with the abilities is nonsense. We must start with a price goal, and a set of abilities, and keep an eye on today's and the immediate future's technology. These factors must be all juggled simultaneously.

Jef Raskin

ERIC GREENBERG TO SCIENT EMPLOYEES
"Big dreams? Yes."

The Internet was the last great business frontier of the 20ᵗʰ century. Eric Greenberg, founder of the consulting services company Scient, reveals the exuberance and ambition of those on the cutting edge of the cyberspace frontier in this e-mail message to Scient employees at the end of 1998.

Greenburg's unabashed optimism was representative of the times. Over the next fifteen months, investors poured money into the e-tailing industry and Internet companies at a frantic pace. But in March 2000, the bubble burst. Internet company valuations came crashing down to earth, with many of the e-tailing companies going out of business, and most losing 75 percent or more of their value. Scient's stock plunged from a high of 133 to a low of 2 at the end of 2000.

To the Greatest Group of People I Have Ever Worked With,

We will accomplish things that would surprise the greatest optimist! The world is our oyster.

As my great friend and mentor, Bob Howe, says: "We have it all to play for."

Dreams come true. Our company is living proof. We are off to the greatest start in the history of our industry, but so what. It is about the journey and the end game: to buiod the greatest services firm on earth that is the preeminent influencer in the next stage of our economy. Big dreams?

Yes.

Look what Edison and Bell achieved through their innovations: GE and AT&T.

Let's shape the next 50 years of our economy together. We can. Bob cannot. I cannot. The Silicon Valley VCs cnnot. We together can. It is a collective effort of the best people doing their best work.

That is the only way we become legendary over time and build an enduring legacy. I know that I personally do not want to be forgotten by the world when I eventually pass on, and I hope you do not either. Scient is a means by which we can all make contributions and live forever—through our work-product and company longevity and quality.

This is the company we are building. Believe it. It is real. Recognize when momentum is going your way, and ride it!

NEW IDEAS

WILLIAM FICHET ON THE GUTENBERG PRINTING PRESS
"This man is worthy to be loaded with divine honors"

The invention of the printing press with movable type in about 1450 by Johannes Gutenberg of Mainz, Germany, revolutionized Europe. Suddenly, instead of writing out books and documents by hand, the printed word could be mass-produced. Gutenberg's invention set in motion dramatic social, economic, political, intellectual and religious changes in European society, as it made the written language accessible to all citizens.

William Fichet, who brought a Gutenberg printing press to Paris, writes of the invention to a friend.

. . . Great light has been thrown by the breed of new makers of books, whom, within our memory, Germany has sent broadcast into every quarter. For they say that there, not far from the city of Mainz, there appeared a certain John whose surname was Gutenberg, who first of all men, devised the art of printing, whereby books are made, not by a reed, as did the ancients, nor with a quill pen, as do we, but with metal letters, and that swiftly, neatly, beautifully. Surely this man is worthy to be loaded with divine honors by all the Muses, all the arts, all the tongues of those who delight in books, and is all the more to be preferred to gods and goddesses in that he has put the means of choice within reach of letters themselves and of mortals devoted to culture. . . .

But that great Gutenberg has discovered things far more pleasing and more divine, in carving out letters in such fashion that whatever can be said or thought can by them be written down at once and transcribed and committed to the memory of posterity.

MARTIN VAN BUREN TO ANDREW JACKSON
"A new form of transportation known as railroads"

Not all business innovations are welcomed by all parties. The construction of railroads in the early 1800s represented a threat to the entrenched interests of the booming canal industry. Shortly after the completion of the Erie Canal in New York State, Governor Martin Van Buren of New York wrote to President Andrew Jackson warning him of the dangers railroads brought with them.

Like many inventions that improve productivity, railroads posed a threat to existing industries and the jobs of canal workers, hay farmers, boat builders and others. Unstated was the potential (and subsequently realized) boon of a tremendous industrial and transportation revolution that resulted in the creation of many more jobs than those being displaced, even at the cost of the train engine's "roar and snort."

Van Buren, who would later be Jackson's vice president and would succeed him as president, accurately prophesied the decline of the canal industry. Some historians question this letter's is authenticity. Regardless, the sentiment it expresses is a time-honored one.

January 31, 1829

To: President Andrew Jackson

The canal system of this country is being threatened by the spread of a new form of transportation known as "railroads". The federal government must preserve the canals for the following reasons:

One. If canal boats are supplanted by "railroads" serious unemployment will result. Captains, cooks, drivers, hostlers, repairmen and lock tenders will be left without means of livelihood, not to mention the numerous farmers now employed in growing hay for horses.

Two. Boat builders would suffer and towlines, whip and harness makers would be left destitute.

Three. Canal boats are absolutely essential to the defense of the United States. In the event of the expected trouble with England, the Erie Canal would be the only means by which we could ever move the supplies so vital to waging modern war.

For the above-mentioned reasons the government should create an Interstate Commerce Commission to protect the American people from the evils of "railroads" and preserve canals for posterity.

As you may well know, Mr. President, "railroad" carriages are pulled at the enormous speed of 15 miles per hour by "engines" which, in addition to endangering life and limb of passengers, roar and snort their way through the countryside, setting fire to crops, scaring the livestock and frightening women and children. The almighty certainly never intended that people should travel at such breakneck speed.

Martin Van Buren
Governor of New York

The New-York Daily Times to Subscribers

"The Times is a very cheap paper"

The newspaper publisher Henry Raymond introduced The New-York Daily Times *to potential readers in New York City on September 21, 1851, with a letter offering subscriptions. This was followed a week later with a note to readers declaring the successful introduction of the newspaper.*

In 1896, Adolph Ochs bought the newspaper for $75,000. He vowed in a letter to readers to maintain the newspaper's integrity and "great history of right-doing." The newspaper has remained under the control of his family ever since.

September 21, 1851

The carrier of The New-York Daily Times proposes to leave it at this house every morning for a week, for the perusal of the family, and to enable them, if they desire it, to receive it regularly. The Times is a very cheap paper, costing the subscriber only SIXPENCE a week, and contains an immense amount of reading matter for that price.

The proprietors have abundant capital, able assistants and every facility for making it as good a paper as there is in the City of New York. It will contain regularly all the news of the day, full telegraphic reports from all quarters of the country, full city news, correspondence, editorials, etc., etc.

At the end of the week the carrier will call for his pay; and a continuance of subscription is very respectfully solicited.

September 27, 1851

This is the ninth number of the New-York Daily Times, and it has now a regular paying circulation of over TEN THOUSAND copies. If any other newspaper in this or in any other part of the world ever reached so large a circulation in so short a time, we should be glad to be informed of the fact. It is taken by business men at their stores, and by the most respectable families in town.

1896

To undertake the management of The New-York Times, with its great history for right-doing, and to attempt to keep bright the lustre which Henry J. Raymond and George Jones have given it, is an extraordinary task. But if a sincere desire to conduct a high-standard newspaper, clean, dignified and trustworthy, requires honesty, watchfulness, earnestness, industry and practical knowledge applied with common sense, I entertain the hope that I can succeed in maintaining the high estimate that thoughtful, pure-minded people have ever had of The New-York Times.

It will be my earnest aim that The New-York Times give the news, all the news, in concise and attractive form, in language that is parliamentary in good society, and give it as early, if not earlier, than it can be learned through any other reliable medium; . . . to make the columns of The New-York Times a forum for the consideration of all questions of public importance, and to that end to invite intelligent discussion from all shades of opinion.

… nor with there be a departure from the general tone and character and policies pursued with relation to public questions that have distinguished The New-York Times as a nonpartisan newspaper—unless it be, if possible, to intensify its devotion to the cause of sound money and tariff reform, opposition to wastefulness and peculation in administering the public affairs and its advocacy of the lowest tax consistent with good government, and no more government than is absolutely necessary to protect society, maintain individual vested rights and assure the free exercise of a sound conscience.

MARK TWAIN TO W. D. HOWELLS

"Now come! Don't fool away this treasure"

Not all business ideas are good ideas. While we often read about people with great notions for new businesses that flourish, we don't as often hear about the ones that flop. But more businesses fail than succeed, often because of poor planning, bad luck or inept management. Some people, focused more on the promise of possibility than the hard work of accomplishment, never seem to succeed in business.

Mark Twain's oldest brother, Orion, fell into this category, engaging in one failed enterprise after another. Mark Twain—who himself had a very checkered career as a businessman—relates some of Orion's feckless pursuits in this 1879 letter to his friend W. D. Howells.

Despite Twain's reservations, fraternal affection outweighed good sense. The next letter he sent to Orion included a check for $25 and a note stating, "You will have abandoned the project you wanted it for by the time it arrives but no matter, apply it to your newer and present project, whatever it is."

My dear Howells,

I have just received this letter from Orion. Take care of it, for it is worth preserving. . . .

Observe Orion's career—that is, a little of it: 1. He has belonged to as many as five different religious denominations. Last March he withdrew from the deaconship in a Congregational Church and the Superintendency of its Sunday School, in a speech which he said that for many months (it runs in my mind that he said 13 years) he had been a confirmed infidel and so felt it to be his duty to retire from the flock.

2. After being a republican for years, he wanted me to buy him a democratic newspaper. A few days before the Presidential election, he came out in a speech and publicly went over to the democrats. He prudently "hedged" by voting for 6 state republicans also.

The new convert was made one of the secretaries of the democratic meeting and placed in the list of speakers. He wrote me jubilantly of what a ten-strike he was going to make with that speech. All right—but think of his innocent pathetic candor in writing me something like this, a week later:

"I was more diffident than I had expected to be, and this was increased by the silence with which I was received when I came forward, so I seemed unable to get the fire into my speech which I had calculated upon, and presently they began to get up and go out, and in a few minutes they all rose up and went away."

How could a man uncover such a sore as that and show it to another? Not a word of complaint, you see—only a patient, sad surprise.

3. His next project was to write a burlesque upon *Paradise Lost*.

4. Then, learning that the *Times* was paying Harte $100 a column for stories, he concluded to write some for the same price. I read his first one and persuaded him not to write any more.

5. Then he read proof on the *N. Y. Eve. Post* at $10 a week and meekly observed that the foreman swore at him and ordered him around "like a steamboat mate".

6. Being discharged from that post, he wanted to try agriculture—was sure he could make a fortune out of a chicken farm. I gave him $900 and he went to a ten-house village 2 miles above Keokuk on the river bank. This place was a railway station. He soon asked for money to buy a horse and light wagon, because the trains did not run at church time on Sunday and his wife found it rather far to walk.

For a long time I answered demands for "loans" and by next mail always received his check for the interest due me to date. In the most guileless way he let it leak out that he did not underestimate the value of his custom to me, since it was not likely that any other customer of mine paid his interest quarterly, and this enable me to use my capital twice in 6 months instead of only once. But alas, when the debt at least reached $1800 or $2500 (I have forgotten which) the interest ate too formidably into his borrowings and so he quietly ceased to pay it or speak of it. At the end of two years I found that the chicken farm had long ago been abandoned, and he had moved into Keokuk. Later, in one of his casual moments, he observed that there was no money in fattening a chicken on 65 cents' worth of corn then selling it for 50.

Finally, if I would lend him $500 a year for two years (this was 4 or 5 years ago) he knew he could make a success as a lawyer, and would prove it. This is the pension which we have just increased to $600. The first year his legal business brought him $5. It also brought him an unremunerative case where some villains were trying to chouse some negro orphans out of $700. He still has this case. He has waggled it around through various courts and made some booming speeches on it. The negro children have grown up and married off, now, I believe, and their litigated town lot has been dug up and carted off by somebody, but Orion still infests the courts with his documents and makes the <u>welkin</u> <u>ring</u> with his venerable case. The second year he didn't make anything. The third he made $6 and I made Bliss put a case in his hands—about half an hour's work. Orion charged $50 for it. Bliss paid him $15. Thus four or five years of lawing has brought him $26, but this will doubtless be increased when he gets done lecturing and buys that "law library". Meantime his office rent has been $60 a year, and he has stuck to that lair day by day as patiently as a spider.

Then he by and by conceived the idea of lecturing around America as "Mark Twain's Brother"—

that to be on the bills. Subject of proposed lecture, "On the Formation of Character."

I protested, and he got on his warpaint, couched his lance and ran a bold tilt against total abstinence and the Red Ribbon fanatics. It raised a fine row among the virtuous Keokukians. I wrote to encourage him in his good work but I had let a mail intervene, so by the time my letter reached him he was already winning laurels as a Red Ribbon Howler.

Afterward he took a rabid part in a prayer meeting epidemic; dropped that to travesty Jules Verne, dropped that in the middle of the last chapter last March to digest the matter of an infidel book which he proposed to write; and now he comes to the surface to rescue our "noble and beautiful religion" from the sacrilegious talons of Bob Ingersoll.

Now come! Don't fool away this treasure which Providence has laid at your feet, but take it up and use it. One can let his imagination run riot in portraying Orion, for there is nothing so extravagant as to be out of character with him.

Well—goodbye, and a short life and a merry one be yours. Poor old Methusaleh, how did he manage to stand it so long?

Yrs ever,
Mark

Louis Pasteur to His Children

"Joy reigns in the laboratory"

One of the leading bacteriologists of all time, Louis Pasteur's discoveries lay the groundwork for the modern biotech industry. His experiments led to the prevention and cures for the silkworm disease, chicken cholera and rabies. Pasteur discovered the causes of fermentation and developed methods to preserve perishable foods. Despite his achievements, much of Pasteur's career was the subject of ridicule and opposition from disbelieving fellow scientists who questioned his theories.

As described in the following letter, his experiments regarding the cause of, and a cure for, anthrax, a disease that killed millions of cattle and sheep, were treated with the usual skepticism. After months of work, however, Pasteur announced the successful results of his experiments to his children in 1881.

Although Pasteur's primary motivation was to help humanity, the results of his work transformed the food industry and medicine. Today's multibillion-dollar biotechnology industry can be traced directly to Pasteur's experiments.

June 2, 1881

It is only Thursday, and I am already writing to you; it is because a great result is now acquired. A wire from Melun has just announced it. On Tuesday last, May 31, we inoculated all the sheep, vaccinated and nonvaccinated, with very virulent and splenic fever. It is not forty-eight hours ago. Well, the telegram tells me that, when we arrive at two o'clock this afternoon, all the nonvaccinated subjects will be dead; eighteen were already dead this morning, and the others dying. As to the vaccinated ones, they are all well; the telegram ends by the words "stunning success"; it is from the veterinary surgeon, M. Rossignol.

It is too early yet for a final judgment; the vaccinated sheep might yet fall ill. But when I write to you on Sunday, if all goes well, it may be taken for granted that they will henceforth preserve their good health, and that the success will indeed have been startling. On Tuesday, we had a foretaste of the final results. On Saturday and Sunday, two sheep had been abstracted from the lot of twenty-five nonvaccinated ones, and inoculated with a very virulent virus. Now, when on Tuesday all the visitors arrived, amongst whom were M. Tisserand, M. Patinot, the Prefect of Seine et Marne, M. Foucher de Careil, Senator, etc., we found the two unvaccinated sheep dead, and the two others in good health.

I then said to one of the veterinary surgeons who were present, "Did I not read in a newspaper, signed by you, apropos of the virulent organism of saliva, 'There! One more microbe; when there are 100 we shall make a cross'?" "It is true," he immediately answered, honestly. "But I am a converted and repentant sinner." "Well," I answered, "allow me to remind you of the words of the Gospel: joy shall be in heaven over one sinner that repenteth, more than over ninety and nine just persons which need no repentance." Another veterinary surgeon who was present said, "I will bring you another, M. Colin." "You are mistaken," I replied. "M. Colin contradicts for the sake of contradicting, and does not believe because he will not believe. You would have to cure a case of neurosis, and you cannot do that!" Joy reigns in the laboratory and in the house. Rejoice, my dear children.

THOMAS ALVA EDISON TO J. WOOD WRIGHT
"My ambition is to build up a great Industrial Works"

Born in 1847, Thomas Alva Edison transformed American industry and technology. Starting his career manufacturing telegraph equipment, Edison eventually applied his innovative mind to the business of invention. He founded the nation's first research laboratory for the purpose of making inventions in 1876 at Menlo Park, New Jersey. Combining advanced equipment, learned scientists, and clever machinists, the Edison Laboratory cranked out an incredible 400 inventions over the next decade, including the first phonograph (the first recording was "Mary Had a Little Lamb"), incandescent electric lamp, electrically powered locomotive and the two-electrode vacuum bulb. In 1887, Edison built a new laboratory in West Orange, New Jersey, many times larger with more scientists and engineers on staff. The letter below describes the new laboratory to J. Hood Wright, one of many financial backers who helped transform Edison's inventions into manufactured products. By the end of his life in 1931, Edison had more than 1,000 patents credited to him.

Prior to Edison, the typical inventor was a solitary innovator who tinkered in an attic or work shed trying to devise new machines that might save labor. In this way, inventors such as Eli Whitney, Benjamin Franklin and John Deere helped create new machines and tools for a country marked by a shortage of labor and an abundance of natural resources. They were individuals who devised new inventions on pure ingenuity and circumstance. Pooling the skills and talents of many, Edison created an invention factory, hiring people for the specific purposes of making inventions and applying significant financial resources to the endeavor. Henry Ford described Edison's research facilities as the birthplace of modern American technology. After Edison, the purview of invention left the work shed and entered the corporate research laboratory. Bell Systems, Eastman Kodak, General Electric and other major companies created their own centers devoted to research and development.

(1887)

My laboratory will soon be completed. The dimensions are one building 250 ft long 50 wide & 3 stories [high] 4 other bldgs. 25 x 100 ft one story high all of brick. I will have the best equipped and largest Laboratory extant, and the facilities incomparably superior to any other for rapid & cheap development of an invention, & working it up into Commercial shape with models, patterns & special machinery. In fact there is no similar institution in Existence. We do our own casting forgings. Can build anything from a ladys watch to a Locomotive.

The Machine shop is sufficiently large to employ 50 men & 30 men can be worked in other parts of the works. Inventions that formerly took months & cost a large sum can now be done 2 or 3 days with very small expense, as I shall carry a stock of almost every conceivable material of every size and with the latest machinery a man will produce 10 times as much as in a laboratory which has but little material, not of a size, delays of days waiting for castings and machinery not universal or modern. . . .

You are aware from your long acquaintance with me that I do not fly any financial Kites, or speculate, and that the works which I control are well managed. In the early days of the shops it was necessary that I should largely manage them [alone], first because the art had to be created. 2nd. Because I could get no men who were competent in such a new business. But as soon as it was possible I put other persons in charge. I am perfectly well aware of the fact that my place is in the Laboratory; but I think you will admit that I know how a shop should be managed & also know how to select men to manage them.

With this prelude I will come to business.

My ambition is to build up a great Industrial Works in the Orange Valley starting in a small way & gradually working up. The Laboratory supplying the perfected inventions, models, patterns & fitting up necessary special machinery in the factory for each invention.

My plan contemplates to working of only that class of inventions which requires but small investments. . . . Such a work in time could be running on 30 to 40 special things of so diversified nature that the average profit could scarcely be [varied] by competitors. Now Mr. Wright, do you think this is practicable. If so can you help me along with it.

ORVILLE WRIGHT TO HIS FATHER
"Success four flights Thursday morning"

Aviation pioneers Orville and Wilbur Wright made the world's first successful flights in a motorized aircraft near Kitty Hawk, North Carolina. Orville completed the first flight, followed the same day by Wilbur, whose flight lasted 59 seconds and covered 852 feet. Orville sent a telegram to their father later that day to deliver the news. The two brothers stayed involved in the early aviation industry. In 1908, they developed the first plane for the United States Army, which tested successfully the following year.

Kitty Hawk N C Dec 17

Bishop M. Wright

7 Hawthorne St

Success four flights Thursday morning all against twenty one mile wind started from Level with engine power alone average speed through air thirty one miles longest 57 seconds inform Press home ##### Christmas

Orevelle Wright

CLARKE SALES COMPANY TO JAMES JOYCE

"Some placket openings will gap; some eyes will be pulled off"

The zipper, a convenience so ever-present today that it hardly merits consideration, took years and years to become a standard part of modern clothing. It was invented in 1893 as a detachable fastener. After several decades of modification and marketing, it finally acquired its name. The following letter, written by a New York company that had named the device the Plako Fastener, tried to promote the innovative product to a Mr. James Joyce (no relation to the Irish writer).

October 14th, 1908.
Mr. James M. Joyce,
48 Birch St.,
Lewiston, Me.

Dear Sir:

Our article is a necessity nothing else can take the place of. Go out in the street and look at the back of every skirt worn and then count and see if nine out of every ten doesn't need an invisible and secure fastener to close the skirt opening. Ask every woman you know and see if she won't agree with you that all her neighbors' skirts are not fastened neatly.

Some placket openings will gap; some eyes will be pulled off. The majority of placket and waist backs will lack the neat appearance every self-respecting woman requires in the rest of her attire.

Big field for an absolutely secure and invisible method of closing the skirt and in which our PLAKO Fastener has no competitor.

How easy to sell a fastener for the waist which eliminates gaping or opening when on, and wonder of wonders, THE WEARER CAN FASTEN THE BACK OF HER OWN WAIST!

Sell it also to the men: they know what a great need there is for the PLAKO Waist Fastener.

Don't forget that PLAKO is an ideal trouser fastener. This is where the men are interested in their own clothes.

Given this great want of humanity, and an article to satisfy this want, will this not result in a rush of customers and a large profit with so easy a seller?

Every month that your orders equal one gross we will credit you with four dollars on every gross and will send it in check or in goods the following month, as you choose.

Take the PLAKO we are sending you under separate cover, show it to your friends, and get their opinion of it. You will have a number of orders to fill even before you have purchased your set of samples as described in the circular enclosed, "What We Have For You."

Customers?   Everybody.

Selling?   Easy

      None in Stores.

Send your order in quickly and hustle.

Yours very truly,

CLARKE SALES COMPANY.

SALES MGR.

David Sarnoff, on the Future of Radio and Television
"Prospective Radio Business"

A very capable engineer involved in the early experiments with radio, David Sarnoff was a visionary who realized the potential of wireless communications. As early as 1915, he wrote:

"I have in mind a plan of development which would make radio a 'household utility' in the same sense as the piano or phonograph. The idea is to bring music into the house by wireless. . . . The receiver can be designed in the form of a simple 'Radio Music Box' and arranged for several different wavelengths, which should be changeable with the throwing of a single switch or pressing of a single button."

More than any other person, Sarnoff transformed the technology of obscure laboratories into an entire new communications industry. Pulling together financial resources, marketing savvy and organizational capacity he forged the Radio Corporation of America into a multinational corporation, bringing radios, and later televisions, into almost every household in the nation.

The following excerpts of letters and memos by Sarnoff record the evolution of wireless communication in its early years, as well as Sarnoff's extraordinary technological and commercial vision.

Edward J. Nally, President
Radio Corporation of America
January 10, 1920

While dealing with the subject of transmission and reception on shortwaves, *I might record a hunch which I have held for some time and which I have discussed with a number of radio engineers, who I should say in justification of their opinions, definitely disagree with me.* I refer to the possibility of employing shortwaves for long-distance communications and, perhaps eventually, transoceanic communications. The obvious answer to this is that daylight absorption makes impractical the use of shortwaves over long distances, but I doubt whether a careful and exhaustive research has been made on this point. Perhaps extreme amplification, such as is possible with the Armstrong amplifier, or even greater amplification, which should be possible, may detect radio signals from shortwaves where present-day amplification fails to do so. The advantage of employing shortwaves over long distances are, of course, well known to engineers who recognize that greater freedom from static and station interference is possible when employing short waves.

Memorandum to E. W. Rice, Jr., President

General Electric Company

March 3, 1920

The "Radio Music Box" proposition (regarding which I reported to Mr. Nally in 1915 and to Mr. Owen D. Young on January 31, 1920) requires considerable experimentation and development, but having given the matter much thought, I feel confident in expressing the opinion that the problems involved can be met. With reasonable speed in design and development a commercial product can be placed on the market within a year or so.

Should this plan materialize, it would seem reasonable to expect sales of 1 million "Radio Music Boxes" within a period of three years. Roughly estimating the selling price at $75 per set, $75 million can be expected. This may be divided approximately as follows:

1st year	100,000 Radio Music Boxes	$ 7,500,000
2nd year	300,000 Radio Music Boxes	22,500,000
3rd year	600,000 Radio Music Boxes	45,000,000
Total		$75,000,000

January 31, 1922

O. D. Young, Esquire

Chairman, Board of Directors,

Radio Corporation of America

120 Broadway, N. Y. C.

Dear Mr. Young,

BROADCASTING

Now that the idea of radio broadcasting and the sale of devices for use at home in connection therewith, have met with such great enthusiasm and interest, you may wish to review that part of my report to you dated January 31, 1920, or two years ago, on Prospective Radio Business, which dealt with the broadcasting field and from which you will note that the plan was conceived and worked out in commercial detail in 1915, or seven years ago.

I quote from my report to you as follows:

"Sales of 'Radio Music Box' for Entertainment Purposes"

For some years past I have had in mind a plan of development which would make radio a 'household utility' in the same sense as a piano or phonograph. In 1915 I presented the plan in detail to Mr. Nally, but the circumstances attending our business at that time and since then have not been such as to make practicable serious consideration of this subject. However, I feel that the time is now ripe to give renewed consideration to this proposition which is described below:

"The idea is to Bring Music into the House by Wireless"

While this has been tried in the past by wires, it has been a failure because wires do not lend themselves to this scheme. With radio, however, it would seem to be entirely feasible. For example—a radio telephone transmitter having a range of say 20 to 50 miles can be installed at a fixed point where instrumental or vocal music or both are produced. The problem of transmitting music has already been solved in principle and therefore all the receivers attuned to the transmitting wave length should be capable of receiving such music. The receiver can be designed in the form of a simple 'Radio Music Box' and arranged for several different wave lengths, which should be changeable with the throwing of a single switch or pressing of a single button.

"The 'Radio Music Box' can be supplied with amplifying tubes and a loud speaking telephone, all of which can be neatly mounted in one box. The box can be placed on a table in the parlor or living room, the switch set accordingly and the transmitted music received. There should be no difficulty in receiving music perfectly when transmitted within a radius of 25 to 50 miles. Within such a radius there reside hundreds of thousands of families; and as all can simultaneously receive from a single transmitter, there would be no question of obtaining sufficiently loud signals to make the performance enjoyable. The power of the transmitter can be made 5 kw if necessary, to cover even a short radius of 25 to 50 miles; thereby giving extra loud signals in the home if desired. The use of head telephones would be obviated by this method. The development of a small loop antenna to go with each 'Radio Music Box' would likewise solve the antennae problem.

"The same principle can be extended to numerous other fields—as for example—receiving lectures at home which can be made perfectly audible; also events of national importance can be simultaneously announced and received. Baseball scores can be transmitted in the air by the use of one set installed at the Polo Grounds. The same would be true of other cities. This proposition would be especially interesting to farmers and others living in outlying districts removed from the cities. By the purchase of a 'Radio Music Box' they could enjoy concerts, lectures, music, recitals, etc. which may be going on in the nearest city within their radius. While I have indicated a few of the most probable fields of usefulness for such a device, yet, there are numerous other fields to which the principle can be extended.

"In connection with this idea I have had in mind for some time the possibility of connecting up the 'Wireless Age' with the plan, thereby making the Wireless Press a profitable venture. What I have in mind is this:

"Every purchaser of a 'Radio Music Box' would be encouraged to become a subscriber of the 'Wireless Age' which would announce in its columns an advance monthly schedule of all lectures, music recitals, etc. to be given in the various cities of the country. With this arrangement the owner of the 'Radio Music Box' can learn from the columns of the 'Wireless Age' what is going on in the air at any given time and throw the 'Radio Music Box' switch to the point (wave length) corresponding with the music or lectures desired to be heard.

"If this plan is carried out the volume of paid advertising that can be obtained for the 'Wireless Age' on the basis of such proposed increased circulation would in itself be a profitable venture. In other words, the 'Wireless Age' would perform the same mission as is now being performed by the various motion picture magazines which enjoy so wide a circulation.

"The manufacture of the 'Radio Music Box' including antenna, in large quantities, would make possible their sale at a moderate figure of perhaps $75.00 per outfit. The main revenue to be derived will be from the sale of 'Radio Music Boxes' which if manufactured in quantities of one hundred thousand or so could yield a handsome profit when sold at the price mentioned above. Secondary sources of revenue would be from the sale of transmitters and from increased advertising and circulation of the 'Wireless Age'. The Radio Corporation would have to undertake the arrangements, I am sure, for music recitals, lectures, etc. which arrangements can be satisfactorily worked out. It is not possible to estimate the total amount of business obtainable with this plan until it has been developed and actually tried out but there are about 15,000,000 families in the united States alone and if only one million or 7% of the total families thought well of the idea it would, at the figure mentioned, mean a gross business of about $75,000,000, which should yield considerable revenue.

"Aside from the profit to be derived from this proposition the possibilities for advertising for the Radio Corporation are tremendous; for its name would ultimately be brought into the household and wireless would receive national and universal attention."

On March 3rd, 1920, in response to a request from Mr. E. W. Rice, Jr. for an estimate of prospective radio business, I wrote:

"The 'Radio Music Box' proposition requires considerable experimentation and development; but, having given the matter much thought, I feel confident in expressing the opinion that the problems involved can be met. With reasonable speed in design and development, a commercial product can be placed on the market within a year or so.

"Should this plan materialize it would seem reasonable to expect sales of one million (1,000,000) 'Radio Music Boxes' within a period of three years. Roughly estimating, the selling price at $75,000,000 can be expected. This may be divided approximately as follows:

Actual business
done by RCA

1st Year—100,000 Radio Music Boxes	$7,500,000	'22	$11,000,000
2nd Year—300,000 Radio Music Boxes	$22,500,000	'23	$22,500,000
3rd Year—600,000 Radio Music Boxes	$45,000,000	'24	$50,000,000
Total $75,000,000			$83,500,000"

At the time the foregoing reports were made there was in existence neither a practical radio telephone transmitter for sending out such information as is at present being broadcasted, nor suitable device in compact form for reception. The technical developments of the past two years and the exchange of patent rights which resulted in the present "set-up" have made both possible.

The next step is to organize radio broadcasting on the transmitting end as to render real service without confusion or overlapping, thus making possible the dream of bringing entertainment into the home by radio. Efforts are now being directed towards accomplishing this result.

Very truly yours,

David Sarnoff

General Manager

Memorandum to RCA management

April 10, 1922

The radiotelephone, as a receiver of broadcast material, steps out of the role formerly played by a telephone instrument—namely, that of being part of a two-way communicating system, usually for tolls—and enters the new field of being the important element of a one-way communication system.

The usefulness of such devices to the purchaser depends entirely on the character and continuity of the material broadcast by the radiotelephone sending station, or stations, within the range of the receiving instrument. Therefore, the extension of the radiotelephone to the home and the building up and maintenance of a large sales volume will depend on the organization of a broadcast sending service, designed to render a public service of an order which will be acceptable to the average, regarded as valuable by the public, and as such suitably protected by the government as to licenses, interferences, etc.

While it is possible to provide a variety of interesting material for broadcasting purposes, such as lectures, speeches, news, and educational items, yet in order to find popular appeal, the main features of the service will no doubt be musical and entertaining in character. Music, vocal and instrumental, must constitute the foundation of a broadcast service, and the brief experience to date has already demonstrated this fact.

Considering, then, that the radiotelephone, as a broadcast receiver, is (1) a product for the home, (2) primarily a musical instrument, and (3) dependent for its vitality and usefulness on a service which must meet the public taste, principally in music, we at once see the natural relationship between the radio instrument (which for convenience, I shall refer to here as the Radiola) and the phonograph. . . .

In addition to the natural relationship between the Radiola and the phonograph, there are also physical, structural, and economic elements which justify and, indeed, make advisable a happy association of the two instruments, which should live under the same roof. For one thing, they will take up less room in the home if they both stay in the same cabinet. Secondly, they will cost less when purchased as a combination radio and phonograph instrument in one cabinet than if purchased separately with two cabinets. Thirdly, some of the parts—as, for example, the horn or loudspeaker now used with each instrument—need not be duplicated where a combination instrument is used.

Technically, the Radiola and the phonograph are both trying to do the same kind of job, i.e. to reproduce, as faithfully as possible, speech or music. The phonograph employs mechanical means to accomplish this result; the Radiola, the electrical means. The former is old and has about reached the limits of its capabilities. The latter is new, in fact just began, and the future holds for it untold possibilities. Fortunately, the electrical method of sound reproduction is applicable to the phonograph as well as to the Radiola, and any advance or improvement in the radio art of reproduction will be equally beneficial to phonograph-record reproduction, and the same device can be made to serve both purposes.

. . . Rapid and important advances in the art of sound reproduction are bound to follow now that the need for them is apparent and the field promising. Thus, radio may be expected, in the course of developing its own business, to produce inventions and improvements which not only will be applicable to the phonograph industry but may, indeed, technically govern or control the future of the phonograph.

Memorandum
Radio Broadcasting Activities
RCA Board of Directors
April 5, 1923

I believe that television, which is technically the name for seeing instead of hearing by radio, will come to pass in due course. . . . It is not too much to expect that in the near future, when news is telegraphed by radio—say, to the United States—of important events in Europe, South America, or the Orient, a picture of the event will likewise be sent over by radio and both will arrive simultaneously. Thus, it may well be expected that radio development will provide a situation whereby we shall be able actually to see as well as read in New York, within an hour or so, the event taking place in London, Buenos Aires, or Tokyo.

I also believe that transmission and reception of motion pictures by radio will be worked out within the next decade. This would result in important events or interesting dramatic presentations being literally broadcast by radio through the use of appropriate transmitters and, thereafter, received in individual homes or auditoriums, where the original scene will be reenacted on a screen with much the appearance of present-day motion pictures.

Guglielmo Marconi
New York City
September 4, 1930

I am highly interested in information which you gave me about the experiments you are now conducting with ultrashort waves, as I fully believe in the great possibilities which that spectrum offers. As you unlock the secrets of that part of the spectrum, you will bring forward enormous improvements in radio communication and in all radio applications. I am delighted to know that you are working along these lines and wish to reiterate the assurances that I have formerly given you that anything the

Radio Corporation of America can do on its side to facilitate and assist you in your work will be gladly done. . . .

David Sarnoff

STATE FARM MUTUAL AUTO INSURANCE TO POLICYHOLDERS
"Enclosed you will find the emblem for your automobile"

Widespread ownership of automobiles sprung an entire new sector for the insurance industry in the 1920s. State Farm Mutual Auto Insurance of Bloomington, Indiana, was started in 1922 to serve the insurance needs of farmers. It was its automobile business, however, that really flourished. The following 1929 letter to policyholders from its founder and president George J. Mecherle accompanied small plaques to be affixed to automobiles to identify policyholders.

To our Policyholder:

Enclosed you will find the emblem for your automobile, the design of which was selected by the Indiana Farm Bureau Federation for use in the State of Indiana and this design has been made the standard for all States, and we sincerely hope you may always have pride and satisfaction in the organization it represents.

Wherever this emblem is seen it should be a guarantee that the possessor is one who is rightfully entitled to your confidence and respect as a brother member in these organizations, and should you find one in trouble who is carrying this emblem, it is your duty as a fellow member to render him every assistance possible. The fact that each member of these organizations must possess certain qualifications before he can be accepted for membership, is your guarantee that he is worthy of such assistance in time of trouble. These organizations will eventually become what their members make them, and by full cooperation they can be made the greatest of service organizations, so let us each endeavor to make this emblem the insignia of fellowship and neighborly helpfulness.

Should you learn of anyone in possession of this emblem not rightfully entitled to be in such possession, it is your duty as a member of these organizations to notify this office so that proper steps can be taken to correct such a condition.

In attaching the emblem, be sure to attach each end separately to prevent loss should either wire cut through from wear.

Respectfully yours,
State Farm Mutual Auto Ins. Co.
By G. J. Mecherle

MICHAEL J. CULLEN TO PRESIDENT OF KROGER
"Nobody in the world ever did this before"

An energetic manager of a grocery store in the Kroger chain, Michael J. Cullen had an idea on how to improve the merchandising of food. He outlined his idea in a 1930 letter to the president of Kroger, one of the largest grocery store chains in the country. Kroger ignored the letter, so Cullen took his idea and started his own chain stores called "King Kullen"—the first modern supermarket. Cullen introduced the idea of selling certain goods at a loss and heavily promoting the discounted price to lure customers into the store, where they would buy higher marked goods in greater volume.

My grocery equipment would cost two thousand five hundred dollars. My meat equipment would cost about $4,500.00 complete. A total outlay of $7,000.00 for equipment and a $23,000.00 stock of merchandise in each store. In other words, I would have an investment in each store of $30,000.00. My operating expenses would be as follows:

1 Grocery Manager		$50.00 per week
1 Fruit Man		$25.00 per week
1 Assistant Fruit Man		$18.00 per week
1 Assistant Grocery Manager		$25.00 per week
2 Male Clerks	$18.00	$36.00 per week
1 Cashier		$15.00 per week
3 Lady Clerks	$12.00	$36.00 per week
1 Male Clerk		$15.00 per week
12 Extra Saturday Clerks	$2.50	$30.00 per week

Total Salaries	$250.00 per week

I expect to do a grocery business of $8,500 per week per store, a fruit and vegetable business of $1,500 per week, per store. In other words, the kind of stores I have in mind should do a grocery business of $10,000.00 a week and a meat business of $2,500 per week. On the grocery business, including fruit and vegetables, I can operate on a gross profit of 9%. My complete operating expenses on a $10,000.00 a week business would be as follows:

Help	$250.00	2.50%
Rent	58.00	.58

Investment and Money	30.00	.30
Insurance	10.00	.10
Light-heat-water	7.00	.07
Taxes	10.00	.10
Depreciation	10.00	.10
Supervision	20.00	1/5 5 stores .20
Paper, bags, etc.	75.00	.75
Income tax	30.00	.30
Hauling	20.00	.20
Advertising	50.00	.50
Buying	40.00	1/5 5 stores .40
M. J. Cullen	40.00	1/5 5 stores .40
Total		6.50%

Our meat department sales per store would be at least $2,500.00 per week, and we would make a net profit of at least 3% on this meat business. This is the kind of cut-rate Chain of Wholesale selling direct to the public that I want to operate.

I want to sell 300 items at cost.

I want to sell 200 items at 5% above cost.

I want to sell 300 items at 15% above cost.

I want to sell 300 items at 20% above cost.

I want to gross 9% and do a grocery, fruit and vegetable business of $10,000.00 per week, and make a net profit of 2 1/2% on the grocery department, and 3% on the meat department.

You need have no fear regarding the present overhead of the Chain Stores. My buying, advertising and hauling expense of $110.00 per week per store is more than enough to take care of the buying under my supervision; and this could be reduced twenty-five points after I had my fifth store opened.

I would bill all merchandise to the stores at cost, and adopt a cash register check system, that stealing or dishonesty would be impossible. I would inventory these stores every month at cost and their stock gain less all current expenses would be out net profit per month per store.

It would be a little difficult to begin with to buy for my first store, but after my fifth store was opened, I could buy the minimum shipments and ship 80% of same FOB to the store direct, thereby eliminating entirely a warehouse, which is not necessary when these monstrous stores could show a turnover such as I would get.

Can you imagine how the public would respond to a store of this kind? To think of it—a man selling 300 items at cost and another 200 items at 5% above cost—nobody in the world ever did this before. Nobody ever flew the Atlantic either, until Lindbergh did it.

When I come out with a two-page ad and advertise 300 items at cost and 200 items at practically cost, which would probably be all the advertising that I would ever have to do, the public, regardless of their present feeling towards Chain Stores, because in reality I would not be a Chain Store, would break down my front doors to get it. It would be a riot. I would have to call out the police and let the public in so many at a time.

I would lead the public out of the high-priced houses of bondage into the low prices of the house of the promised land.

I would convince the public that I would be able to save them from one to three dollars on their food bills. I would be the "miracle man" of the grocery business. The public would not, and could not believe their eyes. Week days would be Saturdays—rainy days would be sunny days, and then when the great crowd of American people came to buy all those low-priced and 5% items, I would have them surrounded with 15%, 20% and in some cases, 25% items. In other words, I could afford to sell a can of Milk at cost if I could sell a can of Peas and make 2¢, and so on all through the grocery line.

The fruit and vegetable department of a store of this kind would be a gold mine. This department alone may make a net profit of 7% due to the tremendous turnover we would have after selling out daily and not throwing half the profit away, which is done at the present time in 25% of the Chain Stores throughout the land.

Then the big meat department. This would be a beehive. We would have the confidence of the public. They [would know] that every other grocery item they picked up they saved money on same, and our meat department would show us a very handsome profit. It wouldn't surprise me if we could not net 5% in this meat department.

How long are you and your Company going to sit by and kid yourself that in a few weeks this Henderson Radio Stuff and Home Owned Retailed Store propaganda will pass by?

The reason that I know that this proposition can be put over is that I have already put over a similar proposition right here in Southern Illinois. I operated Bracy's Warehouse store in West Frankfort before Bracy bought out Limerick, and did as high as $19,000.00 per week, $9,000.00 on groceries, $3,000.00 on meats and made a net profit of $15,000.00 on this one single store year before last, 1928, and I did this in a mining town of 14,000 people, mines only working half time, with A&P

in the same city and Limerick doing a big business in this same city.

I was never so confident in my life as I am at the present time; and in order to prove to you my sincerity and my good faith, I am willing to invest $15,000.00 of my own money to prove that this will be the biggest money maker you have ever invested yourself in.

A salary expense of 2 1/2%, I know seems ridiculous to you. You perhaps think this is almost impossible. I have had a great many stores under me in the past, and their weekly salary was only 3% with less than $3,000.00 sales. So this 2 1/2% salary basis on a $10,000.00 weekly business is not only reasonable but is practical.

Again you may object to my locating two or three blocks from the business center of a big city. One great asset in being away from the business section is parking space. Another is, you can get generally the kind of store you want and on your own terms. The public will walk an extra block or two if they can save money, and one of our talking points would be, the reason we sell at wholesale prices are that we are out of the high rent district.

My other percent of store expenses I believe you will agree, are not excessive. If anything, I am a few points too high.

Don't let buying worry you in any way whatever. I can handle the buying in fine shape. I could buy goods, ship them direct to my stores, 3% cheaper than you could buy them, store them in a warehouse, and put them all through the red tape that all Kroger items go through before they are sold. If this proposition appeals to you, there is not a question but that Reock and I could work together. It would be an asset, but what I am trying to bring out is, I would put this over without any assistance from Reock.

Before you throw this letter in the wastebasket, read it again and then wire me to come to Cincinnati, so I can tell you more about this plan, and what it will do for you and your company.

The one thought always uppermost in mind—How can I undersell the other fellow? How can I beat the other fellow? How can I make my company more money? The answer is very simple: by keeping my overhead down, and only by keeping this overhead down can I beat the other fellow.

What is your verdict?

JOHN BRAINERD TO HAROLD PENDER
"The possibility of developing and constructing … [a] computer"

The U.S. War Department commissioned the first general-purpose electronic digital computer, called ENIAC, to calculate the trajectories of ballistics. The computer weighed more than 60,000 pounds, used 18,000 vacuum tubes and had a 240-square-foot footprint. John J. Brainerd supervised the construction of ENIAC, known as Project X, at the University of Pennsylvania. He wrote the memo below to Harold Pender, dean of the Moore School at the university, giving an update on the status of the project.

ENIAC ushered in a new era in modern electronics, introducing the computer, which would eventually transform society. On the 50th birthday of ENIAC, University of Pennsylvania students re-created ENIAC's capacity on an eight-by-eight-millimeter chip.

Dean Harold Pender

Dr. J. G. Brainerd

April 26, 1943

Proposed Army Project

As you know, we have had numerous conferences recently with representatives of the Ordnance Department of the Army concerning the possibility of developing and constructing an electronic difference analyzer and computer. These conversations have progressed unexpectedly rapidly, and I therefore want to place before you in writing the situation as it now stands. If the proposed project continues to move as swiftly as it has in the past month, there is a possibility that we might have a letter of intent within another month. We would, consequently, like to have at this time approval for continuing the discussions, the goal of which would be a definite proposal which might be submitted to the Executive Committee.

1. The electronic difference analyzer and computer is a proposed device never previously built, which would perform all the operation of the present differential analyzers and would in addition carry out numerous other processes for which no provision is made on present analyzers. It is called a "difference" analyzer rather than a "differential" analyzer for technical reasons.

2. The proposed project would be sponsored by the Ordnance Department and the difference analyzer, when and if built, would be for the specific use of the Ballistic Research Laboratory of the Army, at the Aberdeen Proving Ground Maryland.

3. The reasons for the Ordnance Department's interest in this device is that its speed of operation would be very considerably greater than that of any present analyzer, and in addition it would carry out many processes not now performed on differential analyzers, but which are required in ballistic computations.

The simplest way of illustrating the desirability of developing the proposed new differences analyzer is probably to point out that the calculations now being performed on the Moore School differential analyzer have fallen far behind the need for them. In the specific case of sidewise firing from airplanes, construction of directors for guns has been held up several months because it has been a physical impossibility to supply to the manufacturers the necessary ballistic data. The proposed electronic difference analyzer would, if successfully developed, not only eliminate such delays but would permit far more extensive ballistic calculations than are now possible with available equipment.

4. The cost of the development of the proposed electronic analyzer is estimated at $150,000. The tenor of the recent conversations with Ordnance Department officers has been that most of this money would be made available to the Moore School if the project were undertaken. It is desirable, however, and we have recommended to the Ordnance department, that one of the numerous units in the proposed new device be developed in the RCA Research Laboratory. This would leave about nine-tenths of the work at the Moore School.

It is not anticipated that a contract of $150,000 would be received immediately. Instead it is probable that money would be supplied for development, and as soon as the various needed units were developed the balance necessary for completion of the difference analyzer would be made available.

5. To provide personnel for the project under discussion we might plan to use the men now working on PL #2 (contract expires June 30) and on PZ #3 and #4 on which work will be completed in the near future. Most of these men are research engineers employed specifically for war research. The two staff members concerned could carry their normal teaching loads.

6. A brief chronological outline of the steps in the development of this project will serve to illustrate how the Moore School has come to be a central factor in it. In August 1942 a group on the staff discussed the possibilities of an electronic difference analyzer and a brief typewritten discussion was circulated. Nothing was done at that time. However, late in March 1943 the Ordnance officer in charge of the Ballistic Research Laboratory's unit now stationed in the Moore School chanced upon the memorandum. He mentioned it at Aberdeen, and we were asked to prepare a report, which was done on April 2. A more complete report was prepared on April 9, when Moore School representatives made a trip to Aberdeen at the Army's request. Shortly thereafter Colonel Simon, in charge of the

Ballistic Research Laboratory, indicated that he was inclined to include $150,000 in his budget for the project. Following this, numerous conferences have been held and it is my understanding that after the conclusion of a conference on April 20, Colonel Gillon of the Office of the Chief of Ordnance stated that the possibilities were so important that the Army should invest the money in the development. It has been pointed out both to Colonel Simon and Colonel Gillon that this is a development project and that there is no certainty that the desired result can be achieved. It is, however, a reasonable chance.

At the present time the situation is that that Colonel Gillon is calling a meeting in Washington some time next week to review details and to discuss procurement and other problems.

J. G. Brainerd

LEVITT AND SONS TO POTENTIAL BUYER
"Enclosed are pictures of all five types of houses"

Owning a house has always been central to the American Dream. The G.I. Bill after World War II helped millions of young men gain the potential to afford a home of their own. Bill Levitt provided a way for them to realize it, simultaneously revolutionizing the construction industry and housing-development patterns across the United States.

Borrowing heavily from Henry Ford's mass-production techniques, Levitt successfully built 2,350 housing units for the Navy during World War II. Armed with this ability, he decided after the war to apply the same practices to creating mass housing divisions at the outskirts of cities. The first one, named Levittown, was built in 1948 on Long Island outside of New York City.

It was a smashing success. Demand, pent up for almost twenty years by the Great Depression and World War II, was overwhelming. Levitt built 17,000 units for the first Levittown at a pace of up to 36 houses a day. Prior to the war, the average contracting company built no more than five houses a year.

Levittown equivalents sprang up across the country. In 1955, 75 percent of the housing starts in the country were for Levittown-like communities. His influence, combined with the rise of the automobiles, lay the groundwork for the dramatic growth of suburbs in the United States.

August 8, 1949

Dear Sir:

The next allocation of houses in Levittown will be held on Monday evening, August 15. Since we expect a large number of people that evening, we ask you to please follow the instructions below carefully so as to make it most convenient for everybody.

1. The houses are for occupancy in late November and December.

2. The allocation will be held at the VILLAGE BATH CLUB IN MANHASSET on August 15. Please be there at 10:00 p.m. Since a different time is assigned to various groups, PLEASE DO NOT ARRIVE BEFORE THE TIME SHOWN. It will merely crowd us and you and will slow up things.

3. Enclosed are pictures of all five types of houses. Make your decision in advance so that you will know when you get there just what house you want. To play safe, bring the pictures with you.

4. At the time shown above, or shortly thereafter, you will be called by name.

5. No further payment is necessary. You have already made your deposit, and after you move in it will be refunded. Please remember that all we are doing on August 15 is allocating houses. NO

OTHER BUSINESS OF ANY KIND CAN BE TRANSACTED THAT EVENING.

6. It is not necessary for both husband and wife to be there.

7. The Village Bath Club is directly in back of the Altman Department Store on Northern Boulevard (Route 25A) in Manhasset. By car, take Grand Central Parkway to Exit 27, Shelter Rock Road. Drive north on Shelter Rock Road to Northern Boulevard. Turn right on Northern Boulevard about a mile and a half to B. Altman Co. (on the right hand side). Turn right about 300 feet to the Village Bath Club. By train, take the Long Island Railroad to Manhasset and a taxi from the station to the Village Bath Club.

Very truly yours,
LEVITT AND SONS, INC.

Hugh Hefner to Newsstand Vendors
"A brand new magazine for men"

Having formerly worked at Esquire *magazine and Publishers' Development Corporation, Hugh Hefner introduced* Playboy *magazine, featuring photographs of partially (and later completely) nude women, in 1953. Among other images, he purchased the rights to a nude calendar photograph of Marilyn Monroe for $500. Hefner wrote the letter below announcing the start of his new magazine (which was then slated to be called* Stag Party) *to newsstand sellers. The magazine was an instant success.*

June 13, 1953

Dear Friend:

We haven't even printed our letterhead yet, but I wanted you to be one of the very first to hear the news. STAG PARTY—a brand new magazine for men—will be out this Fall and it will be one of the best sellers you've ever handled.

It's being put together by a group of people from ESQUIRE who stayed here in Chicago when that magazine moved east—so you can imagine how good it's going to be. And it will include male-pleasing figure studies, making it a sure hit from the very start.

But here's the really BIG news! The first issue of STAG PARTY will include the famous calendar picture of Marilyn Monroe—in full colour! In fact—every issue of STAG PARTY will have a beautiful, full-page, male-pleasing nude study—in full natural colour!

Now you know what I mean when I say this is going to be one of the best sellers you've ever handled.

STAG PARTY will sell for 50c and you'll receive your copies at a profitable 38c. It will be supplied to you on a full returnable basis and, of course, we will pay all shipping costs.

Fill out the postage-paid AIR MAIL reply card enclosed and get it back to me as quickly as possible. With 4 colour printing on the inside pages, we've got to confirm our distribution quantities right away.

It will be nice doing business with you again—especially with a title as good as this one.

Cordially,
Hugh M. Hefner
General Manager.

BILL GATES AND JEFF RAIKES TO
JOHN SCULLEY AND JEAN-LOUIS GASSÉE
"Microsoft is very willing to help Apple implement this strategy"

In what may be one of the most extraordinary memos in the young history of personal computers, Bill Gates—of all people—wrote a letter as CEO of Microsoft urging Apple Computer to license its Macintosh computer to other companies and leverage their investments to benefit Apple.

Gates laid out a strategic business plan for Apple to allow other companies to develop, manufacture, and market computer software and hardware using the Macintosh "architecture." Gates correctly identified that as a single, stand-alone company Apple could not adequately provide all of the software, computer models and hardware options to the personal computer market. He even provided a list of potential corporate partners and contacts for Apple CEOs John Sculley and Jean-Louis Gassée.

Sculley and Gassée ignored the memo. Gates sent a second letter one month later, again urging them to pursue licensing. He never received a response. Subsequently, Microsoft developed its own Macintosh-like architecture with its Windows program and pursued the plan outlined in the following memo on their own. Gates's vision led to the total domination of the Windows operating system in personal computers.

Years later, Gassée acknowledged Apple had made a huge mistake on licensing. "I just did not see how it would make sense," he said. "But my approach was stupid. We were just fat cats living off a business that had no competition."

To: John Sculley, Jean Louis Gassée

From: Bill Gates, Jeff Raikes

Date: June 25, 1985

Re: Apple Licensing of Mac Technology

cc: Jon Shirley

Background:

Apple's stated position in personal computers is innovative technology leader. This position implies that Apple must create a standard on new, advanced technology. They must establish a "revolutionary" architecture, which necessarily implies new development incompatible with existing architectures.

Apple must make Macintosh a standard. But no personal computer company, not even IBM, can create a standard without independent support. Even though Apple realized this, they have not been able to gain the independent support required to be perceived as a standard.

The significant investment (especially independent support) in a "standard personal computer" results in an incredible momentum for its architecture. Specifically, the IBM PC architecture continues to receive huge investment and gains additional momentum. (Though clearly the independent investment in the Apple II, and the resulting momentum, is another great example.) The investment in the IBM architecture includes the development of differentiated compatibles, software and peripherals; user and sales channel education; and most importantly, attitudes and perceptions that are not easily changed.

Any deficiencies in the IBM architecture are quickly eliminated by independent support. Hardware deficiencies are remedied in two ways:
• expansion cards made possible because of access to the bus (e.g. the high resolution hercules graphics card for monochrome monitors)
• manufacture of differentiated compatibles (e.g. the Compaq portable, or the faster DeskPro).

The closed architecture prevents similar independent investment in the Macintosh. The IBM architecture, when compared to the Macintosh, probably has more than 100 times the engineering resources applied to it when investment of compatible manufacturers is included. The ratio becomes even greater when the manufacturers of expansion cards are included.

Conclusion

As the independent investment in a "standard" architecture grows, so does the momentum of the architecture. The industry has reached the point where it is now possible for Apple to create a standard out of their innovative technology without support from, and the resulting credibility of other personal computer manufacturers. Thus, Apple must open the Macintosh architecture to have independent support required to gain momentum and establish a standard.

The Mac has not become a standard

The Macintosh has failed to attain the critical mass necessary for the technology to be considered a long term contender:

a. Since there is no "competition" to Apple from "Mac-compatible" manufacturers, corporations consider it risky to be locked into the Mac for reasons of price AND choice.

b. Apple has reinforced the risky perception of the machine by being slow to come out with software and hardware improvements (e.g. hard disk, file server, bigger screen, better keyboard, larger memory, new ROM, operating software with improved performance). Furthermore, killing the Macintosh XL (Lisa) eliminated the alternative model that many businesses considered necessary.

c. Recent negative publicity about Apple hinders the credibility of Macintosh as a long term contender in the personal computer market.

d. Independent software and hardware manufacturers reinforced the risky perception of the machine by being slow to come out with key software and peripheral products.

e. Apple's small corporate account sales force has prevented it from having the presence, training, support, etc. that large companies would recognize and require.

f. Nationalistic pressures in European countries often force foreign to consumers [sic] choose local manufacturers. Europeans have local suppliers of the IBM architecture, but not Apple. Apple will lose ground in Europe as was recently exhibited in France.

Recommendation

Apple should license Macintosh technology to 3-5 significant manufacturers for the development of "Mac Compatibles":

United States manufacturers and contacts:

Ideal companies—in addition to credibility, they have large account sales forces that can establish the Mac architecture in larger companies:

• AT&T, James Edwards
• Wang, An Wang
• Digital Equipment corporation, Ken Olsen
• Texas Instruments, Jerry Junkins
• Hewlett Packard, John Young

Other companies (but perhaps more realistic candidates):

• Xerox, Elliott James or Bob Adams
• Motorola, Murray A. Goldman
• Harris/Lanier, Wes Cantrell
• NBI, Thomas S. Kavanagh
• Burroughs, W. Michael Blumenthal and Stephen Weisenfeld
• Kodak
• 3M

• CPT

European manufacturers:

• Siemens

• Bull

• Olivetti

• Philips

Apple should license the Macintosh technology to US and European companies in a way that allows them to go to other companies for manufacturing. Sony, Kyocera, and Alps are good candidates for OEM manufacturing of Mac compatibles.

Microsoft is very willing to help Apple implement this strategy. We are familiar with the key manufacturers, their strategies and strengths. We also have a great deal of experience in OEMing system software.

Rationale

1. The companies that license Mac technology would add credibility to the Macintosh architecture.

2. These companies would broaden the available product offerings through their "Mac-compatible" product lines:

• they would each innovate and add features to the basic system: various memory configurations, video display and keyboard alternatives, etc.

• Apple would lever the key partners' abilities to produce a wide variety of peripherals, much faster than Apple could develop the peripherals themselves.

• customers would see competition and would have real price/performance choices.

3. Apple will benefit from the distribution channels of these companies.

The perception of a significantly increased potential installed base will bring the independent hardware, software, and marketing support that the Macintosh needs.

Apple will gain significant, additional marketing support. Every time a Mac compatible manufacturer advertises, it is an advertisement for the Apple architecture.

Licensing Mac compatibles will enhance Apple's image as a technological innovator. Ironically, IBM is viewed as being a technological innovator. This is because compatible manufacturers are afraid to innovate too much and stray from the standard.

eBay to eBay Customers
"Folks, we do apologize"

The risks and opportunities of Internet technology were put on full display in June 1999 when eBay unveiled a new format for its on-line auction service. Hoping to make its Web pages more user-friendly, it launched a new format. EBay's direct access to its customer made it easy to announce the change and explain its advantages.

But when the new technology crashed later in the day, its impact on customer service proved to be immediate. The company's auctions went out of commission for more than two days. But just as the cutting-edge Internet service made eBay vulnerable to technological mishaps, it also provided a vehicle for giving instant updates on the status of repairs.

When the service was finally restored, eBay founder Pierre Mountanos and CEO Meg Whitman wrote a personal apology, placed all of the blame on themselves, gave complete refunds to every affected customer, and pledged to never make the same mistake again.

Date: 06/09/99 time: 07:12:44 PDT
Noticed something different about eBay today? After several months of working on a new way to organize information on eBay—as well as incorporating your helpful feedback—we launched the new eBay site this morning! Many of you helped us by testing our beta (trial) site, which has been accessible to eBay members since April. And others of you even participated in focus groups, one-on-one usability tests, and surveys. . . .

So why did eBay make this change? If it ain't broke, don't fix it, right? Well, we wanted to make eBay easier to use for everyone, including newer eBay members, who may have had difficulty with the old site. The easier we make eBay to use, the more people are likely to bid on items and to create more business for our sellers!

Date: 06/09/99 Time: 18:24:02 PDT We apologize, but we are currently experiencing system problems. Some of you may receive a connection error while this is ongoing. Engineering is working to get everything back to normal as quickly as possible. We thank you for your patience. Regards, eBay

Date: 06/09/99 Time: 18:55:28 PDT **system Update** We are so very sorry, but there have been additional problems with the system and it is not coming back up at this time. Engineering is working diligently to get everything back to normal. Unfortunately this is going to take longer than expected.

We will keep you updated as we work through this. Thank you very much for your patience! Regards, eBay

Date: 06/09/99 Time: 22:03:01 PDT We currently have vendor engineers on site working with our engineers to resolve the problem. We will continue to keep you updated throughout this situation. As stated below, auctions will be extended per our "Automatic Auction Extension Policy." We sincerely apologize for this unfortunate inconvenience and thank you for your patience! Regards, eBay

Date: 06/11/00 Time: 02:00:13 PDT ***** SYSTEM UPDATE ***** Engineering is still working hard to complete the rebuild of the corrupted disk files. We will continue to update you as the recovery progresses. Thank you again for your patience and support during this difficult time. Regards, eBay

Date: 06/11/99 Time: 13:53:28 PDT ***** SYSTEM UPDATE ***** Folks, we do apologize, but it looks like the system won't be up until approximately 16:00-17:00 PDT Engineering found additional corrupted data files. Although no data was lost, they are taking every precaution to ensure 100 percent viability before bringing up the database. Our deepest regrets for this delay, but we want to make sure everything is fully functional before bringing the system back up. Regards, eBay

Date: 06/11/99 Time: 17:37:01 PDT *** Important Letter from Meg and Pierre *** June 11, 1999 To our valued community members: We are sorry. We know that you expect uninterrupted service from eBay. We believe that this is reasonable, and we know we haven't lived up to your expectations. We want to earn back your trust that we'll provide you with this level of service. . . . We want to assure you that our highest priority today—as always—is your trading success. We also understand that keeping the site up and running is crucial to your achievement of this success. We cannot apologize enough for this disruption in our service and in your ability to participate in on-line commerce. . . . We have taken a serious look at our priorities because of this outage. We hope you will give us the chance to show you our commitment to your success and to keeping eBay up and running 24 hours a day, 7 days a week. Our goal: Uninterrupted service. No fancy bells and whistles. We just want to make it work. To help ensure this, we are working diligently on a hot backup system that should automatically limit the length of potential outages to less than an hour or so. We have been working on this system for many months, and it is almost ready. Sadly, if we had this system in place a few days ago, we might have avoided this outage. . . . We are refunding ALL fees for ALL ACTIVE auctions on eBay. We promise to redouble our efforts to make sure that another outage like this one will never happen again. Our sincere apologies, Meg and Pierre

RIGHTS

HOUDINI CLAIMS WATER TORTURE CELL AS HIS OWN
"I will stop anyone infringing on my rights"

Born Ehrich Weiss in Budapest, Hungary, in 1874, Harry Houdini rose from the lowliest of performance venues to the height of international fame. Through hard work, showmanship, physical stamina and shameless self-promotion, Houdini became the world's most famous escape artist.

After pedaling magic tricks in ten-cent vaudeville shows, Houdini changed his act in 1900 to concentrate on escapes. "The King of Handcuffs" became famous for breaking out of jail cells all the while wrapped tight in chains, tire grips and other bindings. In 1913, he introduced his Upside-Down Water Torture Cell, from which he escaped underwater, upside-down and in a straight jacket.

Fiercely competitive, Houdini protected his niche business by throwing doubt on other escape artists and magicians, and patenting his escape-inventions, as this 1913 letter reflects.

Hull.

England.

Feb. 1st 1913.

C. Howard Watson, Esq.

 2 Buckingham St.

Strand

Dear Sir:

Pardon the liberty I am taking in addressing this letter to you, but I wish to warn Managers and the Profession in General that I have invented another sensation viz:—

THE WATER TORTURE CELL

which is the greatest feat I have ever attempted in strenuous career and hereby wish to give notice that I have

SPECIAL LICENSE FROM THE LORD CHAMBERLAIN (Granted May 2nd 1913)

as a Stage Play and I will certainly stop anyone infringing on my rights.

I am notifying the Managers in the United Kingdom by Registered Post explaining the trick, also enclosing colored illustration of the New Mystery and will hold them responsible for any infringement.

Sincerely Yours

Harry Houdini

Important Notice.

DAVID O. SELZNICK TO WILLIAM HAYS

"Frankly, my dear, I don't give a damn"

Responding to a series of controversies during the 1920s, the motion picture industry created a self-imposed code of what was permissible in Hollywood movies. An agency headed by William Hays screened all movies to remove sex, violence, inappropriate language, disrespectful religious references and other potentially offensive material.

In 1939, the producer of the film Gone With the Wind, David O. Selznick, wanted to include the mild epitaph "damn" in a line delivered by Clark Gable near the end of the movie. When Hays rejected the line, Selznick appealed for reconsideration.

October 29, 1939

Hollywood California

Dear Mr. Hays—

As you probably know, the punch line of *Gone With the Wind*, the one bit of dialogue which forever establishes the future relationship between Scarlett and Rhett, is, "Frankly, my dear, I don't give a damn."

Naturally, I am most desirous of keeping this line and, to judge from the reactions of two preview audiences, this line is remembered, loved, and looked forward to by millions who have read this new American classic.

Under the code, Joe Breen is unable to give me permission to use this sentence because it contains the word "damn," a word specifically forbidden by the code.

As you know from my previous work with such pictures as *David Copperfield, Little Lord Fauntleroy, A Tale of Two Cities*, etc., I have always attempted to live up to the spirit as well as the exact letter of the producers' code. Therefore, my asking you to review the case, to look at the strip of film in which this forbidden word is contained, is not motivated by a whim. A great deal of the force and drama of *Gone With the Wind*, a project to which we have given three years of hard work and hard thought, is dependent on that word.

It is my contention that this word as used in the picture is not an oath or a curse. The worst that could be said against it is that it is a vulgarism, and it is so described in the *Oxford English Dictionary*. Nor do I feel that in asking you to make an exception in this case, I am asking for the use of a word which is considered reprehensible by the great majority of American people and institutions. A canvass of the popular magazines shows that even such moral publications as Woman's Home Companion, Saturday Evening Post, Collier's and The Atlantic Monthly, use this word freely. I understand the difference, as outlined in the code, between the written word and the word spoken from the screen, but at the same time I think the attitude of these magazines toward "damn" gives an indication that the word itself is not considered abhorrent or shocking to audiences.

I do not feel that your giving me permission to use "damn" in this one sentence will open up the floodgates and allow every gangster picture to be peppered with "damns" from end to end. I do believe, however, that if you were to permit our using this dramatic word in its rightfully dramatic place, in a line that is known and remembered by millions of readers, it would establish a helpful precedent, a precedent which would give to Joe Breen discretionary powers to allow the use of certain harmless oaths and ejaculations whenever, in his opinion, they are not prejudicial to public morals.

David O. Selznick

GROUCHO MARX TO THE WARNER BROTHERS
"Professionally we were brothers long before you were"

The Warner Brothers legal department wrote a letter to the Marx Brothers in 1946 threatening to sue them if they did not change the name of a movie they were about to release entitled A Night in Casablanca. *The movie studio considered the title too similar to the company's 1942 hit* Casablanca, *starring Humphrey Bogart and Ingrid Bergman.*

Groucho Marx responded to the threat with the letter below. Unimpressed, Warner Brothers demanded to know the plot of the Marx Brothers movie, to which Marx fabricated a ridiculous story, followed by an equally preposterous revision. Warner Brothers did not respond. The Marx Brothers released the movie under the original title, and Warner Brothers never filed a lawsuit.

Dear Warner Brothers:

Apparently there is more than one way of conquering a city and holding it as your own. For example, up to the time that we contemplated making this picture, I had no idea that the city of Casablanca belonged exclusively to Warner Brothers. However, it was only a few days after our announcement appeared that we received your long, ominous legal document warning us not to use the name Casablanca.

It seems that in 1471, Ferdinand Balboa Warner, your great great-grandfather, while looking for a shortcut to the city of Burbank, had stumbled on the shores of Africa and, raising his alpenstock (which he later turned in for a hundred share of the common), named it Casablanca.

I just don't understand your attitude. Even if you plan on re-releasing your picture, I am sure that the average movie fan could learn in time to distinguish between Ingrid Bergman and Harpo. I don't know whether I could, but I certainly would like to try.

You claim you own Casablanca and that no one else can use that name without your permission. What about "Warner Brothers"? Do you own that, too? You probably have the right to use the name Warner, but what about Brothers? Professionally, we were brothers long before you were. We were touring the sticks as The Marx Brothers when Vitaphone was still a gleam in the inventor's eye, and even before us there had been other brothers—the Smith Brothers; the Brothers Karamazov; Dan Brothers, an outfielder with Detroit; "Brother, Can You Spare a Dime?" (this was originally "Brothers, Can you Spare a Dime?" but this was spreading a dime pretty thin, so they threw out one brother gave all the money to the other one and whittled it down to, "Brother, Can You Spare a Dime?")

Now Jack, how about you? Do you maintain that yours is an original name? Well, it's not. It was used long before you were born. Offhand, I can think of two Jacks—there was Jack of "Jack and the Beanstalk," and Jack the Ripper, who cut quite a figure in his day.

As for you, Harry, you probably sign your checks, sure in the belief that you are the first Harry of all time and that all other Harrys are imposters. I can think of two Harrys that preceded you. There was Lighthouse Harry of Revolutionary fame and a Harry Applebaum who lived on the corner of 93rd and Lexington Avenue. Unfortunately, Appelbaum wasn't too well known. The last I heard of him, he was selling neckties at Weber and Heilbroner.

Now about the Burbank studio. I believe this is what you brothers call your place. Old man Burbank is gone. Perhaps you remember him. He was a great man in a garden. His wife often said Luther had ten green thumbs. What a witty woman she must have been! Burbank was the wizard who crossed all those fruits and vegetables until he had the poor plants in such a confused and jittery condition that they could never decide whether to enter the dining room on the meat platter or the dessert dish.

This is pure conjecture, of course, but who knows—perhaps Burbank's survivors aren't too happy with the fact that a plant that grinds out pictures on a quota settled in their town, appropriated by Burbank's name and uses it as a front for their films. It is even possible that the Burbank family is prouder of the potato produced by the old man than they are of the fact that from your studio emerged "Casablanca" or even "gold diggers of 1931."

This all seems to add up to a pretty bitter tirade, but I assure you it's not meant to. I love Warners. Some of my best friends are Warner Brothers. It is even possible that I am doing you an injustice and that you, yourselves, know nothing at all about this dog-in-the-Wanger attitude. It wouldn't surprise me at all to discover that the heads of your legal department are unaware of this absurd dispute, for I am acquainted with many of them and they are fine fellows with curly black hair, double-breasted suits and a love of their fellow man that out-Saroyans Saroyan.

I have a hunch that this attempt to prevent us from using the title is the brainchild of some ferret-faced shyster, serving a brief apprenticeship in your legal department. I know the type well—hot out of law school, hungry for success and too ambitious to follow the natural laws of promotion. This bar sinister probably needled your attorneys, most of whom are fine fellows with curly black hair, double-breasted suits, etc., into attempting to enjoin us. Well, he won't get away with it! We'll fight him to the highest court! No pasty-faced legal adventurer is going to cause bad blood between the Warners and the Marxes. We are all brothers under the skin and we'll remain friends till the last reel of "A Night in

Casablanca" goes tumbling over the spool.

Sincerely,

Groucho Marx

Dear Warners:

There isn't much I can tell you about the story. In it I play a Doctor of Divinity who ministers to the natives and, as a sideline, hawks can openers and pea jackets to the savages along the Gold Coast of Africa.

When I first meet Chico, he is working a saloon, selling sponges to barflies who are unable to carry their liquor. Harpo is an Arabian caddie who lives in a small Grecian urn on the outskirts of the city.

As the picture opens, Porridge, a mealy-mouthed native girl, is sharpening some arrows for the hunt. Paul Hangover, our hero, is constantly lighting two cigarettes simultaneously. He is apparently unaware of the cigarette shortage.

There are many scenes of splendor and fierce antagonisms, and Color, an Abyssinian messenger boy, runs Riot. Riot, in case you have never been there, is a small night club on the edge of town.

There's a lot more I could tell you, but I don't want to spoil it for you. All this has been okayed by the Hays Office, Good Housekeeping and the survivors of the Haymarket Riots; and if the times are ripe, this picture can be the opening gun in a new worldwide disaster.

Cordially,

Groucho Marx

Dear Brothers:

Sine I last wrote you, I regret to say there have been some changes in the plot of our new picture, "A Night in Casablanca." In the new version I play Bordello, the sweetheart of Humphrey Bogart. Harpo and Chico are itinerant rug peddlers who are weary of laying rugs and enter a monastery just for a lark. This is a good joke on them, as there hasn't been a lark in the place for fifteen years.

Across from this monastery, hard b‾Ba jetty, is a waterfront hotel, chockfull of apple-cheeked damsels, most of whom have been barred by the Hays Office for soliciting. In the fifth reel, Gladstone makes a speech that sets the House of Commons in a uproar and the King promptly asks for his resignation. Harpo marries a hotel detective; Chico operates an ostrich farm. Humphrey Bogart's girl, Bordello, spends her last years in a Bacall house.

This, as you can see, is a very skimpy outline. The only thing that can save us from extinction is a continuation of the film shortage.

Fondly,
Groucho Marx

Evelyn Waugh to *Life Magazine*
"I will send a big blue incorruptible policeman to lock you up"

In 1946, the editors of Life Magazine *had an idea to find out from the British comic writer Evelyn Waugh who the models were for some of the characters in his novels and then to publish a series of photographs of them. Waugh, however, objected bitterly to the idea.*

Dear Madam:

I have read your letter of yesterday with curiosity and re-read it with compassion. I am afraid you are unfamiliar with the laws of my country. The situation is not that my co-operation is desirable, but that my permission is necessary, before you can publish a series of photographs illustrating my books. I cannot find any phrase in your letter that can be construed as seeking permission.

You say: "Without consulting you the project will be like blind flying". I assure you it will be far more hazardous. I shall send a big blue incorruptible policeman to lock you up and the only "monumental" work Mr. Scherman is likely to perform is breaking stones at Dartmoor (our Zing Zing).

Yours faithfully,
Evelyn Waugh

BILL GATES TO COMPUTER HOBBYISTS
"Most of you steal your software"

One of the wealthiest men in history, Bill Gates started his career as a young computer programmer complaining that there was no money in developing computer software. A Harvard dropout, Gates and high-school friend Paul Allen teamed up to develop a version of the computer language BASIC to run the first personal computer, the Altair, in 1975.

The two young men founded Micro-Soft, a software developer of operating systems and computer applications. They invested time and money into the venture, but at first gained little return. Much to their frustration, computer hobbyists simply copied or took their software programs without paying royalties. Gates vents his frustration in this "OPEN LETTER TO HOBBYISTS."

Gates, of course, learned how to leverage his operating systems into massive profits for Microsoft, eventually making himself the richest man in the world. His strong-arm tactics, however, led to a federal anti-trust lawsuit, claiming that Gates used unfair business practices, derived in part to overcome the problem outlined 25 years earlier.

AN OPEN LETTER TO HOBBYISTS

To me, the most critical thing in the hobby market right now is the lack of good software courses, books, and software itself. Without good software and an owner who understands programming, a hobby computer is wasted. Will quality software be written for the hobby market?

Almost a year ago, Paul Allen and myself, expecting the hobby market to expand, hired Monte Davidoff and developed Altair BASIC. Though the initial work took only two months, the three of us have spent most of the last year documenting, improving, and adding features to BASIC. Now we have 4K, 8K, EXTENDED, ROM and DISK BASIC. The value of computer times we have used exceeds $40,000.

The feedback we have gotten from hundreds of people who say they are using BASIC has all been positive. Two surprising things are apparent, however: 1) Most of these "users" never bought BASIC (less than 10% of all Altair owners have bought BASIC), and 2) The amount of royalties we have received from sales to hobbyists makes the time spent on Altair BASIC worth less than $2 an hour.

Why is this? As the majority of hobbyists must be aware, most of you steal your software. Hardware must be paid for, but software is something to share. Who cares if the people who worked on it get paid?

Is this fair? One thing you don't do by stealing software is get back at MITS for some problem you may have had. MITS doesn't make money selling software. The royalty paid to us, the manual, the tape, and the overhead make it a break-even operation. One thing you do is prevent good software from being written. Who can afford to do professional work for nothing? What hobbyists can put 3-man years into programming, finding all bugs, documenting his product and distribute it free? The fact is, no one besides us has invested a lot of money in hobby software. We have written 6800 BASIC, and are writing 8080 APL and 6800 APL, but there is very little incentive to make this software available to hobbyists.

Most directly, the thing you do is theft.

What about the guys who resell Altair BASIC, aren't they making money on hobby software? Yes, but those who have been reported to us may lose in the end. They are the ones who give hobbyists a bad name and should be kicked out of any club meeting they show up at.

I would appreciate letters from any who wants to pay up, or has a suggestion or comment. Nothing would please me more than being able to hire ten programmers and deluge the hobby market with good software.

Bill Gates
General Partner
Micro-Soft
1180 Avarado SE, #114
Albuquerque, NM 87108

CARL SAGAN TO *MacWEEK*
"My endorsement is not for sale"

In 1993 Apple Computer began developing a series of new computers, one of which went by the code name Carl Sagan, in honor of the famed astronomer. When Sagan learned of it in an article in Apple's magazine, MacWEEK, *he fired off the following letter incensed at the unauthorized use of his name.*

Apple changed the code name to BHA. Sagan's temper cooled only temporarily. When he learned that the letters supposedly stood for "Butt-Head Astronomer," he forced Apple to change the code name again and filed a lawsuit for defamation of character. Sagan lost the case at the district court level, appealed, and then settled the case for an undisclosed amount.

January 10, 1994

I have been approached many times over the past two decades by individuals and corporations seeking to use my name and/or likeness for commercial purposes. I have always declined, no matter how lucrative the offer or how important the corporation. My endorsement is not for sale.

For this reason, I was profoundly distressed to see your lead front-page story "Trio of Power PC Macs spring toward March release date" proclaiming Apple's announcement of a new Mac bearing my name. That this was done without my authorization or knowledge is especially disturbing. Through my attorneys, I have repeatedly requested Apple to make a public clarification that I knew nothing of its intention to capitalize on my reputation in introducing this product, that I derived no benefit, financial or otherwise, from its doing so. Apple has refused. I would appreciate it if you so apprise your readership.

Carl Sagan
Director, Laboratory for Planetary Studies
Center for Radiophysics and Space Research
Cornell University
Ithaca, NY

Jim Clark to Chancellor Michael Aiken
"I have always viewed NCSA as part of a public university"

The sometimes blurred distinction between information acquired from academic research and commercially patented technology came to a head in 1995 when the small upstart company Netscape burst on to the scene.

Hotshot computer programmers trained at the University of Illinois National Center for Supercomputer Application (NCSA) developed a new Internet browser system using NSCA's "mosaic" technology. When they formed Netscape with Silicon Valley entrepreneur Jim Clark, the university claimed the company was infringing on its technology.

Clark wrote this letter to the university's chancellor explaining his company's position and seeking to settle, which the two ultimately did.

November 7, 1995

Dear Chancellor Aiken,

This is a final attempt to establish a dialog between you and me as heads of our respective organizations. The behavior of the University and its agents, by threatening litigation with Mosaic Communications and impugning our integrity to our customers, has interfered with the lawful business activities of our company. Please set aside some time to read this letter yourself, as your response is required to avoid what will imminently become a legal dispute that will develop into a media circus that neither of us can control.

As Chairman and Founder of Silicon Graphics, I was personally responsible for supporting your institution and NCSA with in excess of a million dollars of donated equipment. I have no desire to do anything other than express support and respect for your organization, but the business objectives of NCSA articulated by your attorneys at our meeting last Tuesday create a serious conflict of interest for the University. . . .

Within five days of the original idea, our company was founded. We recruited programmers from the University of Illinois, the University of Kansas, the University of California at Berkeley, General Magic, Lucid, Oracle, Sun Microsystems, and Silicon Graphics. Around the beginning of June, the team began the design and implementation of a client-server system. It always has been and always will be an independently developed system. We issued strict rules about not referring to NCSA Mosaic source code on the Net, and told former NCSA people to destroy any copies of NCSA Mosaic they had in their possession on leaving the University. Along the way we hired three other alumni of the University of Illinois—all former NCSA workers who had moved to California before we formed the company. Later, Rob McCool's brother, Mike McCool, also asked for a job at the company and was hired. All these people have significant ownership stakes in the company. . . .

According to Ms. Marcia Rotunda of the University in our November 1 meeting, NCSA is a "business" entity of the University, and NCSA views that Marc and I were aiming to disable the business objectives of NCSA by targeting its employees for recruitment. This was the first time a University representative has said anything like this. I have never considered NCSA to be a business, and I believe the University has an inherent conflict if it intends to operate NCSA as a business. If I had known NCSA was a business, I would never have donated Silicon Graphics equipment. I have always viewed NCSA as part of a public university supported with the public funds from the National Science Foundation and other government agencies.

The University has claimed rights to the creations of these students and staff members and has chosen to commercialize these creations. These students have not disputed the University's claim, nor have they yet asked that the University share the royalties it derives from their creations.

We have been informed by your outside attorney that the University considers these former students, staff member, and our company to "inherently be in violation of the University's intellectual property rights." But we have honored the intellectual property rights of the University and all third parties. Moreover, our claims are easy to verify by examination, as we have offered to the University many times. At one point you recommended pursuing a third-party examination of our source code to verify our claims.

The University alumni who formed this company are angry that the university where they were educated is now trying to prevent them from working in areas directly related to their education unless they are willing to pay a "tax." This is the very word used by the University's designated business agent, Mr. Colbeth of Spyglass, in referring to the way our company should view a license to NCSA Mosaic.

I realize the University's relationship with Spyglass is constraining, but if you establish that we are not in violation of the University's intellectual property, the University can be free of this dispute even if Spyglass chooses to continue it. The University has the power to establish this by proceeding with a third-party comparison of the programs in dispute.

Your response to my letter of October 3 in which you agreed to proceed with an external examination conveyed the attitude I would expect from such a respectable institution as the University of Illinois. But I am baffled by the trend of our relationship since that letter. The alumni of your institution who founded our company are indebted for the education they have received, but they are confident in their rights to do what they are doing, and I am equally confident in backing them in these rights.

A university is a center of reason, and I am a reasonable man. You and I have the responsibility and authority to resolve this. Doing so can yield a fruitful relationship that we can all enjoy. Not doing so will yield nothing. I respectfully request that the two of us meet immediately and resolve this dispute without further resort to the legal system.

Sincerely,

James H. Clark

Chairman and CEO

Mosaic Communications

WORK AND BUSINESS ETHICS

JOHN ADAMS TO ABIGAIL ADAMS
"Keep the Hands attentive to their Business"

John Adams was a successful Boston lawyer with a wife and four children when he was elected to the First Continental Congress in June 1774. Uncertain about his political experience and fearful that his legal practice might suffer, he worried about his financial future. These fears were exacerbated by misgivings about indiscreet expenses on a boat, books, and a Boston home.

Adams shared some of his concerns in this letter to his wife, Abigail, vowing that no matter what it took, he would find a way to make ends meet, if by no other means than sheer perseverance.

July 1, 1774

Abigail,

I am determined to be cool, if I can; I have suffered such Torments to my Mind, heretofore, as have almost overpowered my Constitution, without any Advantage: and now I will laugh and be easy if I can, let the Conflict of parties, terminate as it will—let my own Estate and interest suffer what it will. Nay whether I stand high or low in the Estimation of the World, so long as keep a Conscience void of Offence towards God and Man. And thus I am determined by the Will of God, to do, let what will become of me or mine, my Country, or the World.

I shall arouse myself ere long I believe, and exert an Industry, a Frugality, a hard labour, that will serve my family, if I can't serve my Country. I will not lie down and die in Despair. If I cannot serve my Children by the Law, I will serve them by Agriculture, by Trade, by some Way, or other. I thank God I have a Head, an Heart and Hands which if once fully exerted alltogether, will succeed in the World as well as those of the mean spirited, low minded, fawning obsequious scoundrels who have long hoped, that my Integrity would be an Obstacle in my Way, and enable them to out stripe me in the face.

But what I want in Comparison of them, of Villany and Servility, I will make up in Industry and Capacity. If I don't they shall laugh and triumph.

I will not willingly see Blockheads, whom I have a Right to despise, elevated above me, and insolently triumphing over me. Nor shall Knavery, through any Negligence of mine, get the better of Honesty, nor Ignorance of Knowledge, nor Folly of Wisdom, nor Vice of Virtue.

I must intreat you, my dear partner in all the Joys and Sorrows, Prosperity and Adversity of my Life, to take a Part with me in the struggle. I pray God for your Health—intreat you to rouse your whole Attention to the Family, the stock, the farm, the Dairy. Let every Article of Expence which can possibly be spared be retrench'd. Keep the Hands attentive to their Business, and [let] the most prudent Measures of every kind be adopted and pursued with Alacrity and Spirit.

I am &c.,
John Adams

LEOPOLD MOZART TO WOLFGANG AMADEUS MOZART
"When there is no money, friends are no longer to be found"

A well-known professional musician himself, Johann George Leopold Mozart gave up his career as a conductor and composer to promote the extraordinary talents of his son, Wolfgang Amadeus Mozart. In 1763, by the time he was seven years old, Mozart had performed before royalty in Germany, France and England. The father tirelessly promoted and managed his young son's career.

But as the boy turned into a man, Mozart did not pursue his career with the same devotion as his father. To his father's great dismay, the young Mozart had a light heart and enjoyed social diversions. The following two letters were written from father to son while the younger Mozart toured the royal courts of Europe, where he was easily distracted, falling into a romantic relationship with a younger singer, and failed to earn an income.

[Salzburg,] November 24, 1777

Mon très cher Fils!

Your long and quite unnecessary sojourn has ruined all your prospects. . . . So far you have just had a holiday and have spent the time in enjoyment and amusement. . . . You must adopt quite a different manner of living and an entirely different outlook. There must be attention and daily concentration on earning some money. . . . When there is no money, friends are no longer to be found, and that too even if you give a hundred lessons for nothing, compose sonatas and . . . play the fool every evening from ten o'clock until midnight. . . . For in the long run everything recoils on your poor old father.

Salzburg, Feb. 11th, 12th, 1778

My Dear Son!

I have read your letter of the 4th with amazement and horror. I am beginning to answer it today, the 11th, for the whole night long I was unable to sleep and am so exhausted that I can only write quite slowly, word by word, and so gradually finish what I have to say by tomorrow.

Up to the present, thank God! I have been in good health; but this letter, in which I only recognize my son by that failing of his which makes him believe everyone at the first word spoken, open his kind heart to every plausible flatterer and let others sway him as they like, so that he is led by whimsical ideas and ill-considered and unpractical projects to sacrifice his own name and interests, and even the interests and claims of his aged and honorable parents to those of strangers. This letter, I say, depressed me exceedingly, the more so as I was cherishing the reasonable hope that certain circumstances which you had to face already, as well as my own reminders, both spoken and written, could not have failed to convince you that not only for the sake of your happiness but in order that you may be able to gain a livelihood and attain at length the desired goal in a world of men in varying degrees good and bad, fortunate and unfortunate, it was imperative for you to guard your warm heart by the strictest reserve, undertake nothing without full consideration and never let yourself be carried away by enthusiastic notions and blind fancies.

My dear Son, I implore you to read this letter carefully—and take time to reflect upon it. Merciful God! Those happy moments are gone when, as child and boy, you never went to bed without standing on a chair and singing to me *Oragna Figata Fa*, and ending by kissing me again and again on the tip of my nose and telling me that when I grew old you would put me in a glass case and protect me from every breath of air, so that you might always have me with you and honor me.

Listen to me, therefore, in patience. You are fully acquainted with my difficulties in Salzburg—you know my wretched income, why I kept my promise to let you go away, and all my various troubles. The purpose of your journey was two-fold—either to get a good permanent appointment or, if this should fail, to go off to some big city where large sums of money could be earned. Both plans were designed to assist your parents and to help on your dear sister, but above all to build up your own name and reputation in the world. The latter was partly accomplished in your childhood and boyhood; and it now depends on you alone to raise yourself gradually to a position of eminence such as no musician has ever attained.

You owe that to the extraordinary talents which you have received from a beneficent God; and now it depends solely on your good sense whether you die as an ordinary musician, utterly forgotten by the world, or as a famous *Kapellmeister*, of whom posterity will read—whether, captured by some woman, you die bedded on straw in an attic full of starving children, or whether, after a Christian life spent in contentment, honors and renown, you leave this world with your family well provided for and your name respected by all. . . .

You think all your ill-considered fancies as reasonable and practicable as if they were bound to be accomplished in the normal course of nature. You are thinking of taking her to Italy as a prima donna. Tell me, do you know of any prima donna who, without having first appeared many times in Germany, has walked on to the stage in Italy as a prima donna? . . . What impresario would not laugh, were one to recommend to him a girl of sixteen or seventeen, who has never yet appeared on a stage! . . . How can you allow yourself to be bewitched even for an hour by such a horrible idea, which must have been suggested by someone or other! Your letter reads like a romance. . . . Quite apart from your reputation—what of your old parents and your dear sister?

My son, you should regard me rather as your most sincere friend than as a severe father. Consider whether I have not always treated you kindly, served you as a servant his master, even provided you with all possible entertainment and helped you enjoy all honorable and seemly pleasures. . . . Hurt me now if you can be so cruel.

Write to me by the next post without fail. We kiss you both a million times and I remain your old honest father and husband.

Sir Walter Scott to Charles Scott
"Solitude and ennui you must endure"

Concerned about the future work prospects of his son, the poet and novelist Sir Walter Scott wrote the following letter to his fourth child urging him to study his books over a Christmas holiday at Oxford rather than go on a trip to Wales. Scott's warning that he could not assure his son future security was well founded. A few years after writing this letter, his investments turned sour and he went into debt for the rest of his life. Charles stayed at Oxford for the Christmas holiday.

Edin. 1st Dec. 1824

My Dear Charles,—

I write briefly at present to say that with every wish to yield to whatever suits your comfort I do not think it advisable that you should leave Oxford in the short Christmas vacation as you propose in a letter to Sophia. Nothing suffers so much by interruption as a course of study—it is in fact just stopping the stone while it is running down hill and giving yourself all the trouble of putting it again in motion after it has lost the impulse which it had acquired. I am aware that you propose to *read* in Wales but as the only object of your leaving college would be to find amusement I rather fear that to that amusement study is in much danger of being postponed. . . .

You will meet with many men and these by no means such as can be termed either indolent or dissipated who will conceive their business at College well enough done if they can go creditably through the ordinary studies. This may do very well for men of independent fortune or who have a direct entrée into some profitable branch of business or are assured from family connection of preferment in some profession. But *you* my dear Charles must be *distinguished*, it will not do to be moderate. I could have got you a good appointment in India where you might have plenty of field sports and made money in due time. But on your affording me proofs when under Mr. Williams that you were both willing and able to acquire knowledge I was readily induced to change your destination. God knows if I have chosen for the best but this I am certain; that you like every youth of sufficiently quick talent have the matter much in your own power. Solitude and ennui you must endure as others before you, and there is the advantage in both that they make study a resource instead of a duty. The greatest scholars have always been formed in situations where there was least temptation to dissipation. I do not mean that which is mischievous and criminal but the mere amusement, in themselves indifferent and even laudable, which withdraw the mind from serious study.

I beg you therefore to remain *inter silvas academi* although they are at the present season both lonely and leafless. We shall think of you with regret at Christmas but we will be comforted with thinking that you are collecting in your solitary chambers the means of making yourself an honour to us all and are paying an apprentice fee to knowledge and distinction.

ANDREW CARNEGIE TO HIMSELF
"Spend the surplus each year for benevolent purposes"

In 1868, the future steel magnate and philanthropist Andrew Carnegie wrote a letter to himself vowing to not become a prisoner of the money he made. Employing hard-nosed tactics and keen business acumen, Carnegie came to dominate the steel industry over the next thirty years. Having amassed an incredible fortune, he later gave most of it away to charitable causes.

Beyond this [$50,000] never earn—make no effort to increase fortune, but spend the surplus each year for benevolent purposes… Man must have an idol—the amassing of wealth is one of the worst species of idolatry—no idol more debasing than the worship of money…. To continue much longer … with most of my thoughts wholly upon the way to make more money in the shortest possible time, must degrade me beyond hopes of permanent recovery.

CHARLES DICKENS TO HIS YOUNGEST CHILD
"Never take a mean advantage of any one"

Shortly before Charles Dickens' youngest son embarked for a journey to Australia, Dickens wrote a letter urging him to embrace good morals in his new career.

September, 1868

I write this note to-day because your going away is much upon my mind, and because I want you to have a few parting words from me, to think of now and then at quiet times. I need not tell you that I love you dearly, and am very, very sorry in my heart to part with you. But this life is half made up of partings, and these pains must be borne. It is my comfort and my sincere conviction that you are going to try the life for which you are best fitted. I think its freedom and wildness more suited to you than any experiment in a study or office would have been: and without that training, you could have followed no other suitable occupation. What you have always wanted until now, has been a set, steady, constant purpose. I therefore exhort you to persevere in a thorough determination to do whatever you have to do, as well as you can do it. I was not so old as you are now, when I first had to win my food, and to do it out of this determination; and I have never slackened in it since. Never take a mean advantage of any one in any transaction, and never be hard upon people who are in your power. Try to do to others as you would have them do to you, and do not be discouraged if they fail sometimes. It is much better for you that they should fail in obeying the greatest rule laid down by Our Saviour than that you should. I put a New Testament among your books for the very same reasons, and with the very same hopes, that made me write an easy account of it for you, when you were a little child. Because it is the best book that ever was, or will be, known in the world; and because it teaches you the best lessons by which any human creature, who tries to be truthful and faithful to duty, can possibly be guided. As your brothers have gone away, one by one, I have written to each such words as I am now writing to you, and have entreated them all to guide themselves by this Book, putting aside the interpretations and inventions of man. You will remember that you have never at home been harassed about religious observances, or mere formalities. I have always been anxious not to weary my children with such things, before they are old enough to form opinions respecting them. You will therefore understand the better that I now most solemnly impress upon you the truth and beauty of the Christian Religion, as it came from Christ Himself, and the impossibility of your going far wrong if you humbly but heartily respect it. Only one thing more on this head. The more we are earnest as to feeling it, the less we are disposed to hold forth about it. Never abandon the wholesome practice of saying your own private prayers, night and morning. I have never abandoned it myself, and I know the comfort of it. I hope you will always be able to say in after life, that you had a kind father. You cannot show your affection for him so well, or make him so happy, as by doing your duty.

LOUISA MAY ALCOTT TO AN UNIDENTIFIED FRIEND
"Work is my salvation"

The author of Little Women, *Louisa May Alcott describes some of the challenges of balancing work with child-rearing.*

November 1872

Work is my salvation. H. W. Beecher sent one of the editors of the "Christian Union" to ask for a serial story. They have asked before, and offered $2,000, which I refused; now they offered $3,000, and I accepted.

Got out the old manuscript of "Success," and called it "Work." Fired up the engine and plunged into a vortex, with many doubts about getting out. Can't work slowly; the thing possesses me, and I must obey till it's done. One thousand dollars was sent as a seal on the bargain, so I was bound, and sat at the oar like a galley-slave.

F. wanted eight little tales, and offered $35 apiece; used to pay $10. Such is fame! At odd minutes I wrote the short ones, and so paid my own expenses. "Shawl Straps," Scrap-Bag, No. 2 came out, and went well.

Great Boston fire; up all night. Very splendid and terrible sight.

December—Busy with "Work." Write three pages at once on impression paper, as Beecher, Roberts, and Low of London all want copy at once.

(This was the cause of the paralysis of my thumb, which disabled me.)

Roberts Brothers paid me $2,022 for books. S. E. S. invested most of it, with the $1,000 F. sent. Gave C. M. $100—a thank-offering for my success. I like to help the class of "silent poor" to which we belonged for so many years—needy, but respectable, and forgotten because too proud to beg. Work difficult to find for such people, and life made very hard for want of a little money to ease the necessary needs.

—Anna very ill with pneumonia; home to nurse her. Father telegraphed to come home, as we thought her dying. She gave me her boys; but the dear saint got well, and kept the lads for herself. Thank God!

Back to my work with what wits nursing left me.

Had Johnny for a week, to keep all quiet at home. Enjoyed the sweet little soul very much, and sent him back much better.

Finished "Work,"—twenty chapters. Not what it should be—too many interruptions. Should like to do one book in peace, and see if it wouldn't be good.

The job being done I went home to take Mary's place. Gave her $1,000, and sent her to London for a year of study. She sailed on the 26th, brave and happy and hopeful. I felt she needed it, and was glad to be able to help her.

I spent seven months in Boston; wrote a book and ten tales; earned $3,250 by my pen, and am satisfied with my winter's work.

A Reader to a *Jewish Daily Forward* Editor

"My former partner is a very decent man"

For sixty years the Jewish Daily Forward *served as the central newspaper for the Jewish community in New York City's Lower East Side. One of its most popular features was an advice column. Readers wrote the newspaper with questions, complaints and concerns. Many letters were published in the column with a response from the editor. The letter below concerned a partnership between two very generous businessmen.*

[1907]

Worthy Mr. Editor,

I am a working man, and two years ago I entered into a partnership with another worker. We took in several other people, whom we paid well, and we all earned good wages.

During the two years we worked together, I was sick for three weeks, but my partner, who worked with the whole "set" of workers, gave me the usual half of the profits. I didn't want to take it, since I hadn't worked, but my partner, an honorable man, brought me the entire half.

Some time ago my partner got sick, and the first two weeks, I, too, gave him half of what we earned. But when I wanted to give him his share after the third week, he didn't want to take it. He explained to me then that the partnership would have to be dissolved because his doctor had told him to stop working. I had to agree to it.

Now my former partner has a small business, but he is not doing well. I, on the contrary, have worked a full season with the whole "set" and earned a good deal.

My question now is whether I have an obligation to my former partner, because since he became sick and left me I am earning more than usual. I want to remark that I am a family man with young children, but I don't want to take what belongs to another. If you, Mr. Editor, will tell me I have a duty to him, I will fulfill it.

My former partner is a very decent man, and when I go into his house and see his need, my heart aches. I imagine that he would deal better with me in such a situation. I even loaned him three hundred dollars for his business, which he'll surely repay, but that's a separate matter.

I thank you in advance for your good advice.

Respectfully,

A Reader

Answer:

It is comforting to see that there is still compassion in the world. According to the official rule of "mine" and "thine," the writer of the letter, after the partnership was dissolved, owes his partner nothing at all. But according to the rule of human kindness, he should give any and all help with an open hand to his faithful and honorable friend.

JOHN D. ROCKEFELLER, JR. TO JOHN D. ROCKEFELLER, SR.

"Philanthropy on so colossal a scale"

John D. Rockefeller, Sr. amassed an enormous fortune as founder of Standard Oil Company, accumulating wealth equal to two percent of the gross domestic product of the entire United States. Belying his reputation for cold-hearted ruthlessness, Rockefeller gave away huge chunks of his fortune.

The following letters between Rockefeller and his son reflect the methodical approach the family took to philanthropy and the breadth of their generosity. Although some critics accused Rockefeller of resorting to philanthropy as a public relations gimmick, Rockefeller had been donating money to an assortment of causes from the very start of his business career.

The Rockefellers' charitable endeavors helped set a new standard for professional philanthropy and directly resulted in dramatic improvements in severeal fields. Rockefeller money helped lead to extraordinary gains in public health, education for minorities and the poor, the historic preservation of Colonial Williamsburg, the success of significant cultural and environmental protection enterprises and hundreds of other enterprises.

26 Broadway

New York

December 31, 1906

Dear Father:

Not long since you spoke to me of your thought to found a large trust to which you might turn over considerable sums of money to be devoted to philanthropy, education, science and religion. At the time I raised the question as to whether it would be possible to get together a single group of men who could be expected to have knowledge and interest along so many different lines. I desire to make herewith an alternative suggestions, which is the result of frequent conferences with Mr. Gates and Mr. Murphy.

It is, that you establish several trusts, incorporating under existing state or Federal Laws, or securing special charters from the State or the Federal Government if desirable.

Let the Board of Trustees of these various foundations for the present consist in each instance of Mr. Gates, Mr. Murphy and myself as a nucleus, with two added members, and let the incorporation be made with a Board of five. This would make possible early incorporation and the transfer by you to these various trusts of whatever sums you might desire in the immediate future.

Let the question of working out a permanent organization of these Boards be taken up at our leisure, with a view to the selection of the very best men available in each instance. This can not be done in a hurry, but may require several years of thought and study.

In the letter of gift from yourself to each of the respective trusts, let it be stated that during your life you will retain a veto power. This power could be extended to the life of your son if thought wise, although my present feeling is that such a request would tend to lessen the interest of the Trustees and free them from responsibility. In the remote future you must of necessity trust to the character and integrity of the men who come after you. It is not reasonable to suppose that those whom you or your family may select will doubtless be quite as trustworthy as those selected in the appointed ways hereafter?

This method of organization has the following advantages:

1. It can be quickly effected, enabling you at an early date to make such gifts to the various trusts as you may desire.

2. It does not require the elaborate working out in advance of the detail of organization and the selection of the Board.

3. The veto power being in your hands makes the situation practically the same as though the funds were being dispersed through your own office as at present, only that their permanent abiding place will have been selected and arranged by yourself.

We suggest the foundation along the lines above outlined of the following trusts, and I will state them in order of their importance as we see it:

ESTABLISHMENT OF A FUND FOR THE PROMOTION OF CHRISTIAN CIVILIZATION;

Through this agency you would contribute the amounts which you are contributing annually through the American Baptist Missionary Society, to the foreign work of the Young Men's Christian Association, and such special gifts as you have made of late years to the Congregational Board of Foreign Missions, the United Presbyterian Board of Foreign Missions, and to Young Men's Christian Association buildings in the foreign field. $500,000 of annual income would probably not more than cover these items. In addition there would lie open not only the foreign missionary fields of all denominations, reached through their respective Boards, but the Y.M.C.A, the educational field, and generally any philanthropic or social work in the foreign field which might be regarded as worthy of assistance. The purpose of this foundation is necessarily so broad that so long as the world stands funds could wisely and usefully be dispensed in accordance therewith.

In addition to the three gentlemen of your office we would suggest for Trustees of this fund, Mr. John R. Mott, of the International Young Men's Christian Association, who has perhaps a broader knowledge of missions and Christian work throughout the world than any other living man, and he might some day become the secretary of the Board, giving his entire time to the work; Mr. Robert E. Speer, secretary of the Presbyterian Board of Foreign Missions, a man second only to Mr. Mott in ability, education, breadth of view, and sympathy. It would be desirable to select the other members with the greatest care and without any sense of haste.

We feel that a contribution of $25,000,000 could be made to this Board at the outset. As I have already pointed out the income of half that amount would be required to meet the contributions which you are already making.

ESTABLISHMENT OF A FUND FOR THE PROMOTION OF CHRISTIAN CIVILIZATION IN THE UNITED STATES.

This would be similar to the Fund for the Foreign Fields. The income from this fund could meet the contributions to the Home Mission Society which you are now making, those to the City Mission Society, and those to the various State Conventions; also all Contributions to churches might be met from this fund; contributions to Y.M.C.A.s in this country, as well as gifts for other forms of social and philanthropic work. The income from a gift of $5,000,000 to this trust would probably not much more than meet the contributions which you are now making to the objects above referred to, and $10,000,000 might perhaps be safely given.

As to the Trustees of this foundation we are not at present prepared to make any suggestion beyond the three gentlemen in the office.

A TRUST TO HOLD FUNDS WHICH WILL EVENTUALLY BE REQUIRED FOR THE UNIVERSITY OF CHICAGO, THE GENERAL EDUCATION BOARD AND THE ROCKEFELLER INSTITUTE FOR MEDICAL RESEARCH.

The University will require as much as $10,000,000 more, the General Education Board an equal amount, and the Rockefeller Institute probably not less than $5,000,000. We therefore suggest that this foundation be one of $25,000,000.

Unlike the other foundations this would not require to be a permanent foundation, but in the letter of gift it could be stated that within a period of say twenty-five years not only the income but the principal of the fund should be distributed in the ratio above suggested to the three institutions for whom it would be founded.

As Trustees of this fund, in addition to the three gentlemen in the office, I have thought of Harold and Parmalee, or perhaps instead of Parmalee, Mr. Ryerson of Chicago. Mr. Ryerson would be a splendid man for the position, the only question being whether his relationship to the University of Chicago would incapacitate him. We feel that no one of these institutions in whose interest this fund is to be created should know of its establishment, hence the desirability of keeping the Board small in a sense in the family.

This, then, gives you the lines along which we are thinking. If to any extent whatever these thoughts meet with your approval we will be glad to give them further study with a view to maturing something definite and tangible.

Affectionately

John

26 Broadway

New York

April 9, 1926

Dear Father:

Our talk at Ormond recently in regard to the motives and circumstances which led to the establishment of your various philanthropic boards and foundations has moved me to make this resume of the salient facts in the situation, thinking it may some time be of value.

The Rockefeller Institute for Medical Research, conceived by Mr. Gates and started with a pledge from you dated May 25th, 1901, of up to $20,000 a year for ten years, was the first of the eleemosynary enterprises which you organized. Its charter was obtained from New York State on May 28th, 1901. The total contributions for principal which you have made to the Institute to December 31st, 1925, amount to $39,904,602.76....

The General Education Board, established under a Federal charter granted on January 12th, 1903, with an initial gift of $1,000,000, for current needs, was the second philanthropic institution organized. Your interest in negro education and the contributions which you had been making to many negro schools for a number of years through the American Baptist Education Society, led to the serious consideration of the formation of a trust fund of two or three million dollars, to be devoted to that particular object. It also caused me to accept Mr. Robert C. Ogden's invitation to join one of his trips to the South for the purpose of visiting various negro educational institutions. On that trip I met and had the opportunity for full conference with many of the leaders in that educational field. The result was the establishment of the General Education Board, with a charter broad enough to cover all fields of education throughout the United States, irrespective of race, creed or color.

Your initial give to the General Education Board for principal was made on October 3rd, 1905, in the amount of $10,000,000. Subsequent gifts in 1906, 1907 and 1909 total $20,916,063.80.

In 1919, 1920, and 1921 you made three gifts for Medical Education, aggregating 45,579,082. In 1919 a gift for the increase of teacher's salary of 50,125,949. Your total gifts for the principal amount therefore, to $126,623,094.80....

Although the promotion of negro education was the original interest of the Board, it shortly concerned itself with education in a broader sense. While it has continued its interest in and support of negro education, by far the largest part of its funds, roughly nine-tenths, has gone into the endowment of universities and colleges for whites throughout the land, and into the promotion of medical education on a sound and scientific basis.

This broadening of the Board's field in the United States suggested the opportunity for service to education in foreign lands, which resulted in my establishing on January 16th, 1923, the International Education Board, with a Virginia charter, enabling it to deal with any educational problems throughout the world and gifts toward current needs of more than $1,000,000.

To the International Educational Board I have contributed for principal $20,050,947.50. The Board has made appropriations from principal to December 31, 1925, of 186,125 leaving a balance of principal unappropriated December 31, 1925 of $19,864,822.50....

With the establishment of the General Education Board, the field of education in the United States began forthwith to receive full attention so far as our obligations therein were concerned. In the meantime, your own miscellaneous benevolences had been growing and ramifying so that the desirability of the establishment of a fund with worldwide freedom in the eleemosynary field became increasingly evident. Whereupon, on March 14th, 1913, the Rockefeller Foundation was brought into being, with a New York State charter and an initial gift from you of $100,000,000. With a view to having this new foundation provide adequately for these personal gifts which you had been making up to that time, you stipulated that $2,000,000 of the annual income of the fund should be available for such purposes as you might designate, leaving the balance free for such general uses as the Trustees might see fit. This provision, after being in force for several years, was revoked by you, the entire income of the fund falling under the control of the Trustees.

In addition to the initial gift for principal of $100,000,000 made to the Foundation, further gifts for principal were made as follows:

February 28, 1917	25,765,856
December 19, 1919	50,438,768.50....

At the same time, there were certain intimate personal enterprises, chiefly denominational and religious, in which you and Mother continued to have a special interest. Thus it came about after Mother's death that you established the Laura Spelman Rockefeller Memorial, in 1918, with a New York State charter, that there might be a continuing provision for such enterprises as these. Your initial gift to the Memorial for the principal was October 8, 1918 $3,857,287.12. It has been followed by further gifts for principal, totaling 70,018,287. Making a total now on hand of $73,875,457.37.

At the outset the Memorial operated largely in this intimate field, and still does to some extent. However, as its resources greatly increased and as a result of its various studies of the fields of human need, the Trustees have been led increasingly to concentrate their efforts along the line of the social sciences. At the same time, they have continued to have in mind an interest once expressed by you and highly appropriate in view of the memorial character of the fund, in the needs of women and children....

A summary of the above shows our gifts of principal to these various philanthropic corporations as of December 31st, 1925, to be as follows:

Rockefeller Institute	39,904.602.76
General Education Board	126,623,094.80
International Education Board	20,050,947.50
Rockefeller Foundation	176,204,624.50
Laura Spelman Rockefeller Memorial	73,875,457.37
	$436,658,726.93

Less principal appropriated:		
General Education Board	$55,418,302.46	
International Educational Board	186,125.00	
Rockefeller Foundation	11,000,000.00	66,604,427.46
Leaving total available principal resources,		
Aside from the several unimportant		
Omissions noted, heretofore, of		$370,054,299.47

The reasons which led to the formation of each of these boards stand out clearly and sharply. In the pursuance of a lifelong policy, you were feeling your way along in a new and untried field, taking only such steps from day to day as seemed clearly wise and deferring the taking of further steps until they became equally clear and wise. To have brought all these activities into being at one time and through a single organization would not have been possible, at the onset, for the following reasons:

1. Because the wisdom of setting aside substantial sums of money in this way had not been proved.

2. Because you would not have been ready to give such unprecedented sums at any single moment.

3. Because public opinion had not been educated up to the point of understanding and approving philanthropy on so colossal a scale.

4. Because you were not ready to enter a world field then.

5. Because it would have been well nigh impossible at that time to find men big enough, wise enough, experienced enough to deal with so mighty a problem.

At the same time, as you said to me at Ormond, if you were proposing today to set aside for the well-being of mankind throughout the world the total sum of money which has been put into these foundations, you would undoubtedly combine all the activities, with the exception of the Rockefeller Institute—which ought properly to be an independent entity—in the hands of a single board with a charter as broad as the charter of the Rockefeller Foundation. With the soundness of that conclusion I am in complete accord. In the light of the experience of the last thirty years, I am convinced that one representative board with competent officers and staff and with departmental committees of the board to deal with the various fields, instead of the separate boards that now exist, could cover the whole field with ease and economy. Such a plan of organization would result in much saving and the prevention of many overlappings in fields, in which, with the best intention of everyone's part, duplications at least to some extent have been almost inevitable under the present set-up.

Trusting that you may find this resume as interesting to read as I have found it to write, I am,

Affectionately

Your son

John D. Rockefeller, Jr.

Golf House

Lakewood, N.J.

May 4th, 1926

Dear Son:

I have read with much interest your letter of April 9th, summarizing certain matters which we have talked over on the occasion of your visit to Ormond, during the winter.

As I again review our philanthropic gifts during the past thirty years, I feel we did well to proceed slowly and cautiously as we did. If the whole thing were to be done today, you have rightly understood me as feeling it should be done, and doubtless could be done, through a single organization, with many economies and the avoidance of such overlapping as you point out. It may and very likely will be wise, if not in the immediate future, a little later on, to bring some or all of these boards themselves, certainly various of their departments, into closer cooperation and affiliation. As rapidly and as fully as such steps become wise and desirable, their being taken would seem to me eminently appropriate and advisable. While the management of these funds is wholly in the hands of the several boards of trustees, because I regard this matter as so important for the best accomplishment of the purposes for which the funds were established, I would like to have you send to the trustees of each board a copy of your letter to me and of this letter to you, so that it may be clear to them and their successors that no act of mine in establishing these separate boards should ever be construed as indicative of my wish that they should always remain separate, or as a reason why the fullest and most complete cooperation or affiliation or absorption should not ultimately take place, if and when in the judgment of those responsible such steps are deemed to be wise.

Affectionately

Your Father

John D. Rockefeller

THOMAS EDISON TO WILLIAM FEATHER
"There seems to be no actual reason why we should sleep"

Thomas Edison was one of the fiercest proponents and practitioners of good old-fashioned hard work. Quotations attributed to him include:

"Genius is one percent inspiration and ninety-nine percent perspiration."

"I never did anything worth doing by accident, nor did any of my inventions come by accident; they came by work."

And "Everything comes to him who hustles while he waits."

As this letter to business writer William Feather makes clear, Edison applied his extraordinary work ethic to the business of inventions and demanded that his workers do the same.

From the Laboratory of Thomas A. Edison
Orange, N. J.
September 16, 1919

Dear Mr. Feather:

I received your letter of September 10 in regard to sleep. Until the last six years, and over a period of 40 years, I and my experimental assistants worked on an average 18 hours daily. New men found it very difficult to get used to 4 or 5 hours sleep, but in a short time they became accustomed to it and I have never heard of any one of them being injured.

I find that men who once worked with me for a number of years and then left, kept up the habit of working long hours. I think any person can get used to it. One remarkable thing that they all agree on is that it stops dreaming. This is perhaps due to a deeper sleep.

If the world had been differently arranged and the sun had shone continuously, I do not think that anybody would require or take sleep. There seems to be no actual reason why we should sleep, from a scientific standpoint.

I noticed in automobiling through Switzerland that the towns which had electric lights had many new buildings and the people were active and on the streets at 12:00 o'clock, midnight, whereas in towns without electric lights, everybody was in bed about 8:30 and the town was a dead one.

Thomas A. Edison

GEORGE BERNARD SHAW TO
BIOGRAPHER ARCHIBALD HENDERSON

"Anybody can get my skill for the same price"

In this excerpt from a letter to his biographer Archibald Henderson, George Bernard Shaw makes it clear that the lesson to be learned from his experience is that success does not come from any special genius, but the drudgery of hard work.

[Archibald Henderson]

. . . I advise you in anything you write to insist on this training of mine, as otherwise you will greatly exaggerate my natural capacity. It has enabled me to produce an impression of being an extraordinarily clever, original & brilliant writer, deficient only in feeling, whereas the truth is that though I am in a way a man of genius—otherwise I suppose I would not have sought out & enjoyed my experience, and been simply bored by holidays, luxury & money—yet I am not in the least naturally "brilliant" and not at all ready or clever. If literary men generally were put through the mill I went through & kept out of their stuffy little coteries, where works of art breed in and in until the intellectual and spiritual product becomes hopelessly degenerate, I should have a thousand rivals more brilliant than myself. There is nothing more mischievous than the notion that my works are the mere play of a delightfully clever & whimsical hero of the salons: they are the result of perfectly straightforward drudgery, beginning in the ineptest novel writing juvenility, and persevered in every day for 25 years. Anybody can get my skill for the same price; and a good many people could probably get it cheaper. Man & Superman no doubt sounds as if it came from the most exquisite atmosphere of art. As a matter of fact, the mornings I gave to it were followed by afternoons & evenings spent in the committee rooms of a London Borough Council, fighting questions of drainage, paving, lighting, rates, clerk's salaries &c, &c, &c, &c; and that is exactly why it is so different from the books that are conceived at musical at homes. My latest book, *The Common Sense of Municipal Trading*, is in its way one of the best and most important I have ever written. I beg you, if you write about my "extraordinary career", to make it clear to all young aspirants, that its extraordinariness lies in its ordinariness—that, like a greengrocer & unlike a minor poet, I have lived instead of dreaming and feeding myself with artistic confectionery. With a little more courage & a little more energy I could have done much more; and I lacked these because in my boyhood I lived on my imagination instead of on my work.

[George Bernard Shaw]

H. L. MENCKEN TO WILL DURANT

"There is in every living creature an obscure but powerful impulse to active functioning"

Newspaper columnist H. L. Mencken wrote the following letter in 1933 to Will Durant, author of
The Story of Philosophy, in response to a question about the meaning of life. Mencken found satisfaction
in his life through hard work.

You ask me, in brief, what satisfaction I get out of life, and why I go on working. I go on working for the same reason that a hen goes on laying eggs. There is in every living creature an obscure but powerful impulse to active functioning. Life demands to be lived. Inaction, save as a measure of recuperation between bursts of activity, is painful and dangerous to the healthy organism—in fact, it is almost impossible. Only the dying can be really idle.

The precise form of an individual's activity is determined, of course, by the equipment with which he came into the world. In other words, it is determined by heredity. I do not lay eggs, as a hen does, because I was born without any equipment for it. For the same reason I do not get myself elected to Congress, or play the violoncello, or teach metaphysics in a college, or work in a steel mill. What I do is simply what lies easiest to my hand. It happens that I was born with an intense and insatiable interest in ideas, and thus like to play with them. It happens also that I was born with rather more than the average facility for putting them into words. In consequence, I am a writer and editor, which is to say, a dealer in them and concoctor of them.

There is very little conscious volition in all this. What I do was ordained by the inscrutable facts, not chosen by me. In my boyhood, yielding to a powerful but still subordinate interest in exact facts, I wanted to be a chemist, and at the same time my poor father tried to make me a business man. At other times, like any other relatively poor man, I have longed to make a lot of money by some easy swindle. But I became a writer all the same, and shall remain one until the end of the chapter, just as a cow goes on giving milk all her life, even though what appears to be her self-interest urges her to give gin.

I am far luckier than most men, for I have been able since boyhood to make a good living doing precisely what I have wanted to do—what I would have done for nothing, and very gladly, if there had been no reward for it. Not many men, I believe, are so fortunate. Millions of them have to make their livings at tasks which really do not interest them. As for me, I have had an extraordinarily pleasant life, despite the fact that I have had the usual share of woes. For in the midst of those woes I still enjoyed the immense satisfaction which goes with free activity. I have done, in the main, exactly what I wanted to do. Its possible effects upon other people have interested me very little. I have not written and published to please other people, but to satisfy myself, just as a cow gives milk, not to profit the dairyman, but to satisfy herself. I like to think that most of my ideas have been sound ones, but I really don't care. The world may take them or leave them. I have had my fun hatching them.

Next to agreeable work as a means of attaining happiness I put what Huxley called the domestic affections—the day to day intercourse with family and friends. My home has seen bitter sorrow, but it has never seen any serious disputes, and it has never seen poverty. I was completely happy with my mother and sister, and I am completely happy with my wife. Most of the men I commonly associate with are friends of very old standing. I have known some of them for more than thirty years. I seldom see anyone, intimately, whom I have known for less than ten years. These friends delight me. I turn to them when work is done with unfailing eagerness. We have the same general tastes, and see the world much alike. Most of them are interested in music, as I am. It has given me more pleasure in this life than any other external thing. I love it more every year. ...

H. L. Mencken

JOHN STEINBECK TO ELIZABETH OTIS
"I simply can't make money on these people"

Overcome by the suffering of destitute farmers wiped out by the great Dust Bowl of the 1930s, John Steinbeck refused to accept money for articles he wrote describing their plight. Steinbeck attributed their situation to selfish business interests. His experience with the migrants led to his novel The Grapes of Wrath, *for which he won a Pulitzer prize and the National Book Award.*

Los Gatos

March 7, 1938

Dear Elizabeth:

Just got back from another week in the field. The floods have aggravated the starvation and sickness. I went down for *Life* this time. *Fortune* wanted me to do an article for them but I won't. I don't like the audience. Then *Life* sent me down with a photographer from its staff and we took a lot of pictures of the people. They guarantee not to use it if they change it and will send me the proofs. They paid my expenses and will put up money for the help of some of these people.

I'm sorry but I simply can't make money on these people. That applies to your query about an article for a national magazine. The suffering is too great for me to cash in on it. I hope this doesn't sound either quixotic or martyrish to you. A short trip into the fields where the water is a foot deep in the tents and the children are up on the beds and there is no food and no fire, and the county has taken off all the nurses because "the problem is so great that we can't do anything about it." So they do nothing. And we found a boy in jail for a felony because he stole two old radiators because his mother was starving to death and in stealing them he broke a little padlock on a shed. We'll either spring him or the district attorney will do the rest of his life explaining.

But you see what I mean. It is the most heartbreaking thing in the world. If *Life* does use the stuff there will be lots of pictures and swell ones. It will give you an idea of the kind of people they are and the kind of faces. I break myself every time I go out because the argument that one person's effort can't really do anything doesn't seem to apply when you come on a bunch of starving children and you have a little money. I can't rationalize it for myself anyway. So don't get me a job for a slick. I want to put a tag of shame on the greedy bastards who are responsible for this but I can best do it through newspapers.

I'm going to see the Secretary of Agriculture in a little while and try to find out for my own satisfaction anyway just how much of the government's attitude is political and how much humanitarian. Then I'll know what course to take.

I'm in a mess trying to catch up with things that have piled up in the week I was gone. And of course I was in the mud for three days and nights and I have a nice cold to beat, but I haven't time right now for a cold so I won't get a very bad one.

Sorry for the hectic quality of this letter. I am hectic and angry.

Thank you for everything.

Bye,

John

MRS. JOHN D. ROCKEFELLER TO HER SONS
"An appeal to your sense of fair play"

Generosity for later Rockefeller generations was not just about money. Abby Aldrich Rockefeller, the wife of John D. Rockefeller Jr., wrote her three sons while they were attending college on the importance of treating all people with respect. Responding to the civil rights movement of the 1950s, she described prejudice as "one of the greatest causes of evil in the world," strongly encouraging her sons to assist the repressed in all of their endeavors.

Dear John, Nelson and Laurence,

For a long time I had very much on my mind, and heart, a certain subject. I meant to bring it up at prayers, and then later have it for a question be discussed at a family council. But the right time, because of your father's illness, never seemed to come.

Out of my experience and observations, has grown the earnest conviction that one of the greatest causes of evil in the world is race hatred and race prejudice. In other words, the feeling of dislike that a person or nation has against another person or nation, without just cause, an unreasoning aversion is another way to express it.

The two peoples or races who suffer most from this treatment are the Jews and the Negroes. But some people "hate" the Italians, who in turn hate the Yugoslavs, who hate the Austrians, who hate the Czechoslovaks, and so it goes endlessly.

You boys are still young. No group of people has ever done you a personal injury. You have no inherent dislikes. I want to make an appeal to your sense of fair play, and to beseech you to begin your lives as young men by giving the other fellow ... a fair chance and a square deal.....

Put yourselves in the place of an honest, poor man who happens to belong to one of the so-called "despised" races. Think of having no friendly hand held out to you. No kindly look. No pleasant, encouraging word spoken to you. What I would like you always to do is what I try humbly to do myself. That is, never to say or do anything that would wound the feelings or the self respect of any human being. And to give special consideration to all who are in any way repressed.

That is what your father does naturally, from the firmness of his nature, and the kindness of his heart. I long to have our family stand firmly for what is best and highest in life. It isn't always easy. But it is worthwhile.

Your Mother

NORMAN ROCKWELL TO HARRY W. BROOKS

"A little talent, a lot of ambition, some self-confidence
and a pile of hard work"

A consummate workaholic, illustrator Norman Rockwell placed more credit for his success on his industry than his talent. This letter was written in response to a query about his "secret."

March 8, 1965
Mr. Harry W. Brooks
President
Plasti-Line Inc.
Knoxville, Tennessee

Daer Mr. Brooks:

In reply to your letter of February 8th, I feel a little presumptive to give a formula for success, but here goes:

"A little talent, a lot of ambition, some self-confidence and a pile of hard work."

Sincerely yours,
Norman Rockwell

DAVID OGILVY TO RAY CALT
"If all else fails, I drink half a bottle of rum"

Advertising man David Ogilvy wrote this description of his work habits in response to a letter from Ray Calt, an executive at another advertising agency. Despite—or perhaps because of—Ogilvy's application of hard work and an unorthodox approach, he developed a reputation as one of the finest copywriters in the advertising business.

April 19, 1955

Dear Mr. Calt:

On March 22nd you wrote to me asking for some notes on my work habits as a copywriter. They are appalling, as you are about to see:

1. I have never written an advertisement in the office. Too many interruptions. I do all my writing at home.

2. I spend a long time studying the precedents. I look at every advertisement which has appeared for competing products during the past 20 years.

3. I am helpless without research material—and the more "motivational" the better.

4. I write out a definition of the problem and a statement of the purpose which I wish the campaign to achieve. Then I go no further until the statement and its principles have been accepted by the client.

5. Before actually writing the copy, I write down every conceivable fact and selling idea. Then I get them organized and relate them to research and the copy platform.

6. Then I write the headline. As a matter of fact I try to write 20 alternative headlines for every advertisement. And I never select the final headline without asking the opinion of other people in the agency. In some cases I seek the help of the research department and get them to do a split-run on a battery of headlines.

7. At this point I can no longer postpone doing the actual copy. So I go home and sit down at my desk. I find myself entirely without ideas.

I get bad-tempered. If my wife comes into the room I growl at her. (This has gotten worse since I gave up smoking.)

8. I am terrified of producing a lousy advertisement. This causes me to throw away the first 20 attempts.

9. If all else fails, I drink half a bottle of rum and play a Handel oratorio on the gramophone. This

generally produces an uncontrollable gush of copy.

10. Next morning I get up early and edit the gush.

11. Then I take the train to New York and my secretary types a draft. (I cannot type, which is very inconvenient.)

12. I am a lousy copywriter, but I am a good editor. So I go to work editing my own draft. After four or five editings, it looks good enough to show to the client. If the client changes the copy, I get angry—because I took a lot of trouble writing it, and what I wrote I wrote on purpose.

Altogether it is a slow and laborious business. I understand that some copywriters have much greater facility.

Yours sincerely,

D. O.

BEN & JERRY'S ICE CREAM VALUE-BASED BUSINESS VIEWS
"Politics and business don't mix"

Ben Cohen and Jerry Greenfield, the founders of Ben & Jerry's Ice Cream, aggressively promoted a "value-based" business ethic in the way they ran their company. Ranging from advocating for progressive causes to buying materials for their ice cream in environmentally conscious ways, Ben & Jerry's was one of the leading companies in a new wave of progressive business practices in the 1980s and 1990s.

Other activities have included allowing non-profit organizations to place messages on their ice cream boxes, sending employees on humanitarian trips, and buying nuts from growers who protect the rain forests, even if it costs more. On the package for their Rainforest Crunch, for example, Cohen and Greenfield wrote a brief letter stating:

"This flavor combines our super creamy Vanilla ice cream with chunks of Rainforest Crunch, a cashew & Brazil nut buttercrunch made for us by our friends at Community Products in Montpelier, Vermont. The cashews & Brazil nuts in this ice cream are harvested in a sustainable way from tropical rainforests and represent an economically viable long-term alternative to cutting these trees down. Enjoy! Ben & Jerry"

Although Ben & Jerry's value-based business practices earned it many fans and customers, it has also cost the company the business of many who disagreed with the founder's liberal politics, as the letters below reflect. Others have criticized the company's policies as being ineffective, or pointed out that the company struggled financially because of Ben and Jerry's progressive business practices.

Dear Ben, Jerry, et al:

Thank you for what I perceive as your corporate consciousness. I saw a television report about your "Peace Pop" and admire your overall efforts at helping/promoting worthy causes. You're a refreshing change in the "Me" age. Rest assured you'll continue to receive my support and my ice cream dollar(s). In fact, if you ever want a free actress for a commercial, let me know. I'm a writer/actress and I can't imagine a better way to express my support and use my abilities.

Sincerely,
Tara M.
Springfield, Ill.

Dear Ben and Jerry:

I am basically a cheapskate and never buy anything unless it's 50% off, *but* because of your efforts to save the rainforests I am now buying *your* ice cream. Keep up the good works! The planet needs more like you!

Martha S.
Montclair, NJ

Dear Sirs,

Politics and business don't mix. Sometimes, even though you love something, you have to give it up for a more important cause. This is the conclusion that I have regretfully arrived at, after delighting on your absolutely fabulous English Toffee Crunch "Peace Pop" and then reading the lies being spread about guns by your package wrapper, and by the "Children's Defense Fund" in their "Cease Fire! Campaign."

The same Constitutional right that permits you to spout anti-self-defense/anti-gun propoganda on your packages and in the media gives me the right to vote with my wallet. As much as I love your products, and I truly do, I choose to no longer enjoy or recommend your products.

Sincerely,
Richard B.
New York, NY

Permissions Acknowledgments

Branson, Richard: From *Losing My Virginity* by Richard Branson, copyright © 1998 by Richard Branson. Used by permission of Times Business, a division of Random House, Inc.

Brews, Margery: One letter from A Medieval Family by Joseph Gies and Frances Gies. Copyright © 1988 by Joseph Gies and Frances Gies. Reprinted by permission of HarperCollins Publishers, Inc.

Buffett, Warren: Three letters reprinted with permission from Warren Buffett.

Cohen, Ben and Greenfield, Jerry: Reprinted with permission of Simon & Schuster from *Ben And Jerry's Doubledip* by Ben Cohen and Jerry Greenfield. Copyright © 1997 by Ben Cohen and Jerry Greenfield.

Cullen, Michael J.: Reprinted with permission of King Kullen Grocery.

Enrico, Roger: Letter to PepsiCo employees reprinted with permission of PepsiCo, Inc.

Gates, Bill: "An Open Letter to Hobbyists" reprinted with permission from Microsoft Corporation.

Hanff, Helene: From 84, *Charing Cross Road* by Helene Hanff, copyright © 1970 by Helene Hanff. Used by permission of Viking Penguin, a division of Penguin Putnam, Inc.

Hefner, Hugh: Letter reproduced by Special Permission of *Playboy* magazine. Copyright © 1953, 1998 by Playboy. All rights reserved.

Hirschfeld, Al: From *The Paper's Papers: A Reporter's Journey through the Archives of The New York Times*, by Richard F. Shepard, copyright © 1996 by Richard F. Shepard. Used by permission of Crown Publishing Group, a division of Random House, Inc.

Iacocca, Lee: From *Iacocca: An Autobiography* by Lee Iacocca with William Novak, copyright © 1984 by Lee Iacocca. Used by permission of Bantam Books, a division of Random House, Inc.

Selznick, David: Reprinted by permission of the Harry Ransom Humanities Research Center at The University of Texas at Austin.

Sloan, Alfred P.: © Alfred P. Sloan. Reprinted by permission of the Harold Matson Co., Inc.

Steinbeck, John: "3/7/38 letter to Elizabeth Otis" by John Steinbeck, from *Steinbeck: A Life In Letters* by Elaine A. Steinbeck and Robert Wallsten, editors, copyright 1952 by John Steinbeck, © 1969 by The Estate of John Steinbeck, © 1975 by Elaine A. Steinbeck and Robert Wallsten. Used by permission of Viking Penguin, a division of Penguin Putnam Inc.

Watson, J. Thomas, Jr.: From *Father, Son & Co.* by Thomas J. Watson, Jr. and Peter Petre, copyright © 1990 by Thomas J. Watson, Jr. Used by permission of Bantam Books, a division of Random House, Inc.

Welch, Jack: Reprinted with permission of General Electric.

White, E.B.: "North Brooklin" and "To The Editor of the Ellsworth (Maine) American" from *Letters Of E.B. White*, collected and edited by Dorothy Lobrano Guth. Copyright © 1976 by E.B. White. Reprinted by permission of HarperCollins Publishers, Inc.

Wright, Frank Lloyd: The letters of Frank Lloyd Wright are Copyright © 1986, 2001 The Frank Lloyd Wright Foundation, Scottsdale, AZ.

INDEX